THE

Telewo

HANDB

You bought the book . . . now join the club

Included in the price of this book is a six-month online subscription to the Telework Association, including the e-zine which keeps you up to date with teleworking developments and provides information on teleworking job vacancies. Check out **http://www.telework.org.uk** to get further information about the Telework Association.

THE
Teleworking
HANDBOOK

4th edition

Written on behalf of the **Telework Association**
by Alan Denbigh

A & C Black • London

4th edition 2003
A & C Black Publishers Limited
37 Soho Square, London W1D 3QZ
www.acblack.com

ISBN 0-7136-6511-4

Originally published 1996 by The Telework Association

Second edition 1998
Third edition 2000

A CIP catalogue record for this book is available from the British Library.

A & C Black uses paper produced with elemental chlorine-free pulp, harvested from
managed sustainable forests.

Cartoons by Colin Wheeler

Typeset in New Baskerville

Printed and bound in Great Britain by
Bath Press, Bath

For further information on activities undertaken by the Telework Association, contact:
The Telework Association
Freepost CV2312
WREN Telecottage
Kenilworth
Warwickshire CV8 2RR
Tel: +44 24 7669 6986 or 0800 616008
Fax: +44 24 7669 6538
Email: info@telework.org.uk
http://www.telework.org.uk

Contents

Foreword vi

How to use this book vii

Acknowledgements viii

Chapter 1: Overview 1

Chapter 2: For researchers 23

Chapter 3: International perspective 55

Chapter 4: Alternative workplaces 93

Chapter 5: For teleworkers and wannabees. 133

Chapter 6: Implementation in organisations 155

Chapter 7: Self-employment and start-ups. 207

Chapter 8: Technology and techniques 255

Chapter 9: Staying safe and legal 295

Chapter 10: Disability and teleworking 333

Chapter 11: Training for teleworkers 349

References and contacts 367

A word from our sponsors 383

Index 385

DISCLAIMER

While every effort is taken to ensure the accuracy of the information given in this book, no liability can be accepted by the author or publishers for any loss, damage or injury caused by errors in, or omissions from, the information given. Readers are expected to check all essential information and to seek professional or expert advice as appropriate to specific circumstances.

The provision of contact details for products and services does not imply any endorsement of those products or services by the authors or publishers.

Web references were checked in October 2002 but the authors and publishers can take no responsibility for the accuracy, content or obsolescence of websites referred to in this publication.

Foreword

As the availability and take-up of versatile computing and high-speed communications becomes a reality for companies and citizens, the capability and opportunities for achieving more flexible ways of working are greater than they have ever been. Telework is one such opportunity which employers, employees and the self-employed can now grasp with confidence as a normal way of working.

However, working apart only succeeds where there is a management style of trust and a respect for the diverse needs of all of us who have a job of work to do. Telework offers a way of working that not only helps balance the demands of work and home, but can also create space for reflection and lead to more productive ways of carrying out tasks.

There are many practical issues associated with telework, ranging from the technical through to employer-employee relationships. This new edition of the Handbook updates its guidance on these and other subjects. It is an extremely valuable resource not only for those contemplating teleworking, but also for the rapidly increasing numbers who have already chosen this way of working.

Stephen Timms,
Minister for E-commerce

How to use this book

This book is aimed at several different audiences, and was not intended to be read from cover to cover. These guidelines, and the contents list and index, may help you to find the information you need quickly.

Companies

Start with Chapter 1, *Overview*. Then read Chapter 6, *Implementation in organisations*, and Chapter 9, *Staying safe and legal*. It would probably also be useful to read Chapter 4, *Alternative workplaces*, Chapter 10, *Disability and teleworking* and Chapter 11, *Training for teleworkers*. You may want to get IT staff to read the section in Chapter 6 on IT issues, as well as Chapter 8, *Technology and techniques*.

Employees who want to be teleworkers

Start with Chapter 5, *For teleworkers and wannabees*, followed by Chapter 4, *Alternative workplaces*. If you want to put a cost benefit case to your employer, you may also find it useful to read Chapter 1, *Overview*, Chapter 6, *Implementation in organisations* and Chapter 8, *Technology and techniques*. You may also find Chapter 9, *Staying safe and legal*, Chapter 10, *Disability and teleworking* and Chapter 11, *Training for teleworkers* to be worthwhile.

Self-employed (or those who want to be)

Start with Chapter 5, *For teleworkers and wannabees*, followed by Chapter 1, *Overview* and Chapter 7, *Self-employment and start-ups*. Other useful chapters will be Chapter 4, *Alternative workplaces*, Chapter 8, *Technology and techniques* and Chapter 9, *Staying safe and legal*.

Researchers and students

Start with Chapter 1, *Overview*, followed by Chapter 2, *For researchers* and Chapter 3, *International perspective*. Depending on your field of study, almost any of the other chapters may also be useful.

Planners and policy-makers

Read Chapter 1, *Overview*, Chapter 2, *For researchers*, and Chapter 9, *Staying safe and legal* – plus any other chapters which fit your area of interest. Information on development issues is in Chapter 3, *International perspective*.

Disability issues

Read Chapter 5, *For teleworkers and wannabees*, and then Chapter 10, *Disability and teleworking*. Other chapters which may be relevant include Chapter 4, *Alternative workplaces*, Chapter 9, *Staying safe and legal* and Chapter 11, *Training for teleworkers*.

Telecottages and telecentres

This information is in the *Importing work to rural areas* section on page 79, and in the *Telecottages (and IT training centres)* section on page 121.

Acknowledgements

The preparation of this unique book involves extensive and specialist research. We are grateful to the support of sponsors in helping to offset these costs:

▦TISCALI

Tiscali have introduced a new product perfect for teleworkers, SmartTalk DayTime Extra – an innovative low cost telephone service that allows you to make significant savings on your phone bill – with extra savings on UK calls during working hours! It costs nothing to set up, works with your existing phone number, and has no minimum contract period or monthly subscription fee. Call rates are amongst the lowest in the industry. *See* **www.tiscali.co.uk/smarttalk** or call 0800 954 2223 quoting DM121 – or *see* page 383 for more details.

ON LINE WITH
consorte

Consorte provide flexible, location independent, virtual call centre solutions that deliver the benefits of lower line charges, and elimination of call forwarding costs. *See* **www.consorte.co.uk** or *see* page 384 for more details.

Information and assistance in preparing this book has been received from many different sources, and in many cases from information available over the Internet. The Telework Association wishes to thank all those who have contributed their time and knowledge, in particular:

Andrew Bibby, journalist; Kitty de Bruin, Netherlands Telework Association; Stephen Cawley, Editor, *PC Live*, Dublin; Patrick Cotter, Waterstones Bookshop, Cork; Mark Dyer, accountant; Michael Clark, Cheltenham and Gloucester College of Further Education; Denise Cox, email marketing consultant; Brian Goggin, Wordwrights; Gil Gordon, Gil Gordon Associates; Paul Healy, Small Planet, Dublin; Brian Higton, Cygnet Solutions; Chris Hudson, Communications Workers' Union of Ireland; Ursula Huws, Analytica; Malcolm Lake, Effective Quality Management; Deborah Lowe, co-editor of *Teleworker Magazine*; Sheila McCaffrey, KITE; Steve McPherson, BT Workstyles; Bill and Cathy Murray, Small World Connections; Patrizio di Nicola, Italian Telework Association; Brian O'Kane, Oaktree Press; Barnaby Page, former co-editor of *Teleworker Magazine*; Joanne Pratt; Stephen Simmons, Cornix; Peter Skyte, Amicus/MSF section; Peter Thomson and Chris Ridgewell, VIP Consultants; Nicole Turbe-Suetens, French Telework Association; Colin Wheeler, cartoonist; the staff of the WREN Telecottage; Louis Wustemann, former editor, *Flexible Working* magazine

The data security section was partly contributed by Graham Welsh of RSA Security Services (**http://www.rsasecurity.com**) and Teddy Theanne of Annixter Distribution. Stephen Pritchard helped us to keep up to date with technology issues in this edition. Steve Donnelly provided expert advice on disability benefits.

Overview

WHAT IS TELEWORKING?

Teleworking is working at a distance from the people who pay you, using information and communication technologies (ICT) to keep in touch with employers, colleagues or customers. You can work at home, on the move, at a customer premises or in a centre providing ICT facilities – in fact, anywhere you want to outside the 'normal' office.

The jargon surrounding teleworking can be confusing. Various terms are used, including teleworking (the catch-all term), telecommuting (often used in the US to describe working for one employer but spending some time working from home), distance working, flexible working, flexiplace working, mobile working, remote working and e-working (that last one is favoured by the European Commission).

There are many misconceptions about teleworking. Teleworkers don't just work at home – they work from many different locations. The majority of teleworkers are not women carrying out clerical tasks and combining work with family responsibilities, but middle-aged men with high levels of education, usually in managerial or professional positions. Most employed teleworkers only telework for part of the working week – in fact the average figure is about 1.5 days. And nearly half of the teleworkers in Britain are self-employed. It's quite unusual to find companies where everyone is teleworking. In most companies where teleworking is available, it's an option taken up by less than 10% of the workforce (although this may be because it is only on offer to a small number of employees).

Teleworking is part of a range of flexible work practices which are becoming widespread. Other new forms of work include flexitime, part-time working, jobsharing and career breaks. The umbrella term for many of these work practices is 'work-life balance'. Teleworking is one of a number of ways for companies and self-employed people to manage the stressful changes in traffic congestion, property costs, skills shortages, and family duties affecting working life.

In Britain the government has set up a website to look at work-life balance issues (**http://www.dti.gov.uk/work-lifebalance**), and has distributed a £16.3m Challenge Fund to help over 500 employers explore work-life balance policies aimed at promoting a healthy balance between an individual's work and their life outside work. A national standard for work-life balance is also being introduced, administered by the Work Life Balance Company Ltd. (**http://www.worklifebalancestandard.co.uk**).

WHAT DO EMPLOYERS OFFER?

Workplace flexibilities and facilities offered	% of establishments offering
Bereavement leave	91.0%
Part-time working	76.1%
(About 80% of part-timers are female)	
Care leave	55.9%
Paternity leave	44.5%
Varying hours	38.3%
Compassionate leave	38.0%
Career breaks	27.0%
Workplace counselling or stress management	26.0%
Study leave	22.5%
Working from home	22.5%
Territorial Army leave	13.9%
Information on local provision of childcare	11.9%
Flexitime	11.5%
Term-time working	6.6%
Jobsharing	5.6%
Reduced hours	4.5%
Compressed week	2.5%
(At the time of writing over 500 employees at Lloyds Bank use this technique)	
Annualised hours	1.9%
Creche	1.7%
Subsidised nursery places outside work	1.1%

Thirty percent of non-homeworkers would like to work at home some of the time, but 87% believed that their employer would not let them.

Source: Hogarth T, Hasluck C, Pierre G, Vivian D, Work-Life Balance 2000: Results from the Baseline, Department for Education and Employment, Research Report RR249, 2001

Where are we now?

Academics can argue (*see* Chapters 2 and 3), but teleworking has been around for the best part of 30 years now, and we are able to answer many of the important questions about this form of work. We don't know all the answers, though, and some of the remaining issues will be resolved by new technology developments that we can't foresee.

The most important unresolved issue is that, despite the promotion of teleworking as a tool for work-life balance, there are concerns that it is used to extend working hours, perhaps to the detriment of occupational health.

Argument won	Jury still out
Teleworkers are more productive	Teleworking often leads to longer working hours
Teleworking is growing	Teleworking causes serious data-security problems for corporate IT departments
Teleworkers are more satisfied with their working lives	Teleworking negatively affects career prospects
Teleworking can provide work opportunities that would not otherwise exist for some people with disabilities	Teleworking significantly reduces pollution caused by car traffic and energy usage
Teleworking can provide work opportunities that would not otherwise exist for some people in rural areas	Teleworking leads to urban sprawl because people can commute longer distances
Teleworking is generally supported by trade unions and labour organisations	Teleworking is a perk offered to high-status employees, mainly men, and adds to the disparity in working conditions between men and women
Teleworking can reduce individual commuting journeys	Teleworkers have reduced stress levels
Teleworking can help to lower rates of staff turnover	Teleworking results in a financial return on investment in teleworking equipment and running costs by employers
Teleworking does not create new occupational health and safety problems (where suitable procedures are in place)	Teleworking is only really effective where high-speed (broadband) Internet connections are available

REASONS FOR IMPLEMENTING TELEWORK

There are five main reasons for adopting teleworking:

- **Reduced office costs:** companies can keep down costs and increase productivity. Where a large number of staff telework, there can be substantial savings on office property costs. Some smaller but fast-growing companies use teleworking to expand staff numbers while remaining in their original premises.
- **Better work-life balance:** more flexibility, less commuting stress, and better balance between home and work lives, especially for those with caring responsibilities or disabilities. This leads to less absenteeism, improved recruitment and better staff retention.

- **Environmental considerations:** reduced commuting can mean less pollution, less energy usage, better use of office space and less traffic congestion.
- **Improved, cheaper technologies:** rapid developments in the use of broadband, the Internet and the development of touchdown spaces for mobile workers are increasingly making teleworking a practical alternative.
- **Business resilience:** various events such as strikes, severe weather, natural disasters and terrorist attacks can threaten business continuity. Teleworkers can often carry on working when this is not possible for office-based colleagues.

BT: 4500 TELEWORKERS AND 47,000 REMOTE-ACCESS USERS

In 1993 BT began an ambitious project called Workstyle 2000, later revised and renamed Options 2000, to get 7500 of its 119,000 staff working from home by March 2000. The project was introduced to staff in a series of roadshows. BT also offered a one-off grant of £650 to staff taking part, to cover extra furniture and equipment. Office costs were halved between March 1993 and March 2001, saving £230 million.

Senior executives believe that as well as saving money on premises costs, Options 2000 makes workers more productive, and helps the environment by cutting down on car journeys. The initiative followed a six-month trial involving 36 workers at BT Cellnet. The results showed that 91% of staff were satisfied with teleworking and 77% felt it had increased their productivity. Car usage dropped by a total of 86,000 miles.

It will be at least 2005 before the impact of the larger Options 2000 project can be fully assessed. The scheme is voluntary, aimed at administrative staff and there is a guarantee that teleworkers will be treated equally with office-based staff. The company has said that the change reflects a move from supporting buildings to supporting people, pointing to developments like an online intranet system to order company cars as further evidence of this shift in emphasis.

An independent survey of the project by Bradford University showed that most employees have responded positively, but a small minority feel pressured. Drawbacks have included technical problems, isolation, longer hours and 'not warming to the change in home-work balance'. The survey included a transport analysis showing that car users saved an average of 235 miles per week while train users saved 195 miles per week. The researchers commented that the Options 2000 scheme increases the premium on interpersonal skills, requiring a managerial 'sixth sense'.

A recent update to the Bradford research for the 5000 people now registered with BT's renamed Workabout scheme has been carried out by the Sustel project – results will be available at **http://www.sustel.org**

COMMUTING IS TOP CAUSE OF STRESS

A survey by pollsters MORI for telecommunications company Mitel in 2001 found that commuting and office politics are the most stressful aspects of office life. MORI surveyed 364 office workers and found that in order to be able to work from home, two in five would seriously consider moving jobs, and over a quarter would take a cut in salary.

Some 41% of workers rate travel as the most annoying aspect of their job, followed by office politics (37%) and constant interruptions (33%). A quarter of office workers spend between one and two hours per day travelling.

Calculations by Nicholas Corder[1] indicate that if a worker who earns £20,000 for a 37.5-hour week actually includes their real hours (around 44 hours on average in the UK) and then includes travelling time, work-related social time, cleaning bills, lunches and takeaways when you don't have time to cook, then in fact instead of receiving their apparent hourly pay rate of £11 they are receiving £4.46 – just above the national minimum wage of £4.10.

WHAT KIND OF JOBS CAN BE TELEWORKED?

As a general guide, any job that does not involve physical production, extensive face-to-face customer or team contacts or expensive specialist equipment, can be teleworked. Often a job which may not seem to have potential for teleworking can contain a number of sub-tasks that can be clumped together and carried out through teleworking, even though other tasks must be carried out at the conventional office.

Other tasks suitable for teleworkers include those where the work can be easily measured, those that involve mental rather than physical effort, and those that do not require extensive hands-on management.

Typical teleworker categories include:

- **Professionals and managers:** architects, accountants, management, marketing, public relations, human resources, project managers, account managers, finance, financial analysts and brokers.
- **Support workers:** bookkeepers, translators, quality managers, trainers, proofreaders, indexers, researchers, administrators, web designers.
- **Mobile or field workers:** company representatives, surveyors, quantity surveyors, engineers, inspectors, estate agents, auditors, journalists, insurance brokers, landscapers.
- **Information technology specialists:** systems analysts, software programmers, technical support, software localisation engineers and some hardware engineers.
- **Clerical workers:** data-entry staff, secretaries, call-centre agents.

TELEWORKERS HELP AA AND PRUDENTIAL PROVIDE FLEXIBLE RESPONSE

The AA takes calls from motorists requiring assistance. Details of the calls and motorists' locations are then entered into computers by call-centre workers. Since 1997, some of this work has been done from people's homes. Staff working at home have ISDN lines and PC workstations provided by the AA, connected to the central call distribution system which routes incoming calls to teleworkers. All standard call-centre functions are available, including the facility for supervisors to listen in on calls and check performance.

Pauline Hardwicke works from home for the AA

The AA's interest in teleworking began with a recruitment problem. Its Leeds call centre was suffering competition from neighbouring centres for a limited number of workers in the 'call centre capital' of Europe. They also wanted to make their shift times more flexible because most calls happen in two peaks – from 7.30 a.m. to 11.00 a.m. and from 4.30 p.m. to 8.30 p.m. – corresponding to the rush hours. Split shifts are a lot easier to manage for staff who don't have to travel to work. The teleworkers can also provide backup staff temporarily available to manage peaks in demand.

A pilot of nine people, which included four registered disabled teleworkers, was so successful that the AA decided to close its Leeds call centre and move the staff entirely to teleworking. There are now 50 teleworkers in the Leeds area, and another 100 based near the AA's remaining call centres at Newcastle and Cheadle. About half of the Leeds teleworkers are employed by British Gas, now also owned by the AA's parent company Centrica. The AA's media relations officer Denise Raven explains: 'Since they were owned by Centrica as well and also had a call centre in Leeds, it seemed a good idea to open teleworking to them.'

There have been some changes since the initial pilot. The AA no longer recruits people directly into teleworking because they were not absorbing the AA's corporate culture. Denise says: 'When we recruit we say that the job has the potential for teleworking, and when a teleworking opportunity comes up, they can go for it.' The team-leaders, formerly based at the call centres, are now also home-based, and teleworkers are no longer restricted to split-shift work.

The remarkable productivity of the AA teleworkers, which was measured at between 37% and 45% higher than normal, has settled down to a more than creditable 30% increase. Turnover among the home-based staff is also very low (around 5%) in comparison to industry standard turnovers of 25%. However, because of the high set-up costs for each teleworker of about £5000 a year, there are no plans for further expansion at the moment. In fact, according to Ian Hunter, brought in by the AA in 2001 as the telework programme manager, home-based staff need to be at least 50% more efficient if the company is to be able to justify the extra equipment and running costs involved.

All teleworkers are now expected to meet a target of 12.6 calls per hour. The seven homeworking teams are pitted against each other in performance league tables using figures from the AA's Rockwell ACD switch, which also measures total time signed in for work, time spent on breaks and time spent on call administration (wrap-up time). Ian has instituted bi-monthly team meetings where each team-member receives a detailed breakdown of their performance. This move was not well received initially but call rates shot up in response. Ian also focuses on what he calls 'leopards with spots' – those agents who were poor performers when they worked in the call centre, and who have not improved now they are working from home. He confronted one female teleworker whom he claims was trying to combine call handling with childcare, and has invoked disciplinary measures against others deemed to have unacceptable sickness records.

The monitoring system also involves each team-leader managing about 20 agents, and aiming to have two one-to-one sessions with their homeworkers at their homes each month, resulting in a lot of time spent driving around the region. The AA has brought in a messaging system to post memos and briefing notes directly to teleworkers' monitors, as well as sending information by fax, but the teleworkers do not have email facilities. Ian is also trying to improve the development and motivation of his teams by getting experienced teleworkers to mentor others, and providing a deputy post for team-leaders who handle things when the team-leader is away.

At the Prudential insurance company, an initial trial of five distributed call-centre agents showed substantial productivity increases of around 20%. Call-centre communications manager Shaun Martin said that the increase was immediately visible: 'Agents are not disturbed because they are away from the main call centre.' The trial involved direct sales of PEPs and pension products. Technology, provided by Special Telephone Systems, includes either ISDN or Kilostream connections for all agents utilising a satellite working feature on its Supercall 2000 ACD device.

The Pru has found the flexibility to summon up extra capacity using teleworkers particularly valuable. Over Christmas they were able to get an extra teleworker online in a few minutes, instead of the more normal four-hour delay during which customers would have otherwise heard a recorded announcement. Shaun Martin believes that his project is unusual because it is set up as an external extension of the office rather than a remote operation. Another tactic the Pru has recently employed is outsourcing some call-centre work to lower-cost Indian locations.

The success of the initial trial was combined with a 1999 initiative to reduce accommodation costs which involved various methods of flexible working. A telework case study in the Life and Pensions division allowed 30 people to test the suitability of the concept. This study used ADSL technology but suffered from technical problems with reliability and usage costs. Despite the problems, a larger rollout was again proposed resulting from the trial. Agents visit the office regularly to keep in close touch with colleagues.
http://www.theaa.co.uk and http://www.prudential.co.uk

THE ADVANTAGES

Benefits for employers

Greater productivity

As quoted in published research, productivity gains due to teleworking range from 10% to 60%. The improvements can be attributed to three factors.

- **Reduced distractions:** teleworkers can avoid distractions such as office gossip, interruptions by colleagues, noise in open-plan offices or call centres, etc.
- **Reduced commuting problems:** staff can be available for work at a given time irrespective of traffic conditions, strikes, breakdowns, etc. Some use the extra time released by avoiding commuting to work longer hours.
- **Better coverage during emergencies:** teleworkers can provide a service when their office-based colleagues are unable to come to the office due to severe weather, strikes or other disruptions.

Reduced sickness and absenteeism

A number of studies have shown that teleworkers tend to have lower absenteeism rates. Research for the Telework America Association in 1999[2] suggests that when teleworkers have to take time off for family or personal obligations (health, banking, legal, car repairs, family events or emergencies), most go back to work once the event has been dealt with (which typically takes two to four hours), whereas office workers tend to take an entire day off.

Also, fewer people to mingle with means fewer bugs to spread, and no central office means no 'sick building' syndrome.

Increased staff flexibility

Staff working from home tend to show greater flexibility. Financial services companies using call-centre agents working at home have found that they tend to volunteer for extra shifts during times of high workload. Teleworking can also assist companies in providing out-of-hours services by removing the need for travel at unsociable or even dangerous times.

Increased staff retention

Retaining staff avoids high costs for recruitment and training of new employees. Where staff need to relocate to fit in with a partner's career, teleworking may provide a retention solution. Teleworking can also provide easy access to the skills of former staff members, increasing the available skill pool and helping maintain 'corporate memory'. A survey of 1953 technology professionals at the website **http://home.techies.com** in 2001 indicated that 96% wanted to work from home for at least a few hours every week – 39% said they'd take a pay-cut to be able to do so. However, only 48% were currently

BIG BLUE TAKES TIME TO SAVE PROPERTY COSTS

In a paper for IBM Global Services written in 2002, three senior IBM staff advise fellow HR managers on the issues relating to 'mobilising your workforce'. IBM reports that approximately 100,000 of its total workforce of 325,000 work remotely.

On premises, the authors report that in 1991 IBM allocated 241 square feet of office space per employee. By 2001, the target was 150 square feet, and IBM UK had actually achieved 120 square feet, mainly through 'mobile work practices'. IBM estimates that the cost of office space for a homeworker is less than half that for a conventional worker. Despite these figures the authors warn that 'reducing real-estate costs takes time and a short-term investment is likely to be required to achieve it'.[3]

allowed to work from home. Closer to home, East Riding Council (*see* p. 205) managed to reduce staff turnover in its housing benefits section by 60%.

Reduced property costs

Companies with a high proportion of staff who are often away from the office may introduce desksharing (also called hotdesking). Staff do not have dedicated desks but are provided with access to meeting space, office supplies, 'touchdown' space and other facilities when they are in the office. This can save up to 50% of the space required in traditional offices but requires a high level of IT competence on the part of staff. Companies like AT&T and Cisco have found that widescale rollout of teleworking can allow them to trim their property portfolio by 20–30%.

Reduced unnecessary trips for mobile workers

Providing mobile workers with facilities, such as laptops and mobile phones, to work from home or when on client premises can cut out many unnecessary trips to central offices. It can also increase productivity, employee satisfaction and customer satisfaction. Teleworking can be an effective way of managing a regionally based service without a network of offices.

Using labour in a different locality or time zone

Many call centres and shared services centres which carry out customer service and administrative tasks use time differences to provide faster turnaround. For example, US companies often use locations such as Ireland or Eastern Europe to provide a service which is 'overnight' in relation to the North American time zones. The Indian software industry provides US and European companies with access to IT skills in short supply, largely through teleworking, at highly competitive prices.

Accessing a wider skills pool, or skills only needed on occasion
Companies requiring specialist skills can use teleworking to recruit over a wider geographical area. A Europe-wide survey of 7000 employers showed that 11% of employers also use teleworking to access the skills of teleworking freelancers ('e-lancers' – *see* **http://www.emergence.nu**).

Facilitating relocation or disaster recovery
On 24 September 2001, the *Wall Street Journal* reported that the ability to work remotely proved invaluable for law firms, consultants and others including news reporters located in Lower Manhattan after 11 September. Empire HealthChoice was one of the companies which found itself without an office due to the tragedy. Since that time the company has decided on a less centralised setup and is planning to use two locations in New York City with about 10% less space than it had before. Some employees will work from neighbourhood offices, and some from their homes. The company is quoted as saying: 'We're finding we can do things that we would have been sceptical of in the past. Hundreds of people are dialling in from home right now. We have had high levels of productivity from people that are working remotely, and I think we'll take what we've learned from this experience and turn it into improving quality of life.'

Benefits for employees

Job satisfaction
Teleworkers are more satisfied with their work than non-teleworkers. Clear evidence of this is available from the staff turnover results for call centres which have allowed their agents to work from home. ARO Call Centre based in Kansas City brought down its turnover rate from 60% a year to 4% after installing technology which allowed 85 of its 100 employees to work from home.

A 1993 European research study[4] suggested that teleworkers can in fact suffer more stress than office-based workers, but they are happier with their lot, and the stress symptoms decline the longer a person has been teleworking. The PATRA report also noted that teleworkers suffer fewer problems, such as repetitive strain injury, probably due to their freedom to take breaks and move around when they wish. Teleworking can also satisfy the desire for autonomy and escape from office politics that a number of workers express.

Freeing up commuting time and expense related to office work
According to figures issued by the Department of Environment, Transport and the Regions in April 2000, commuters take an average of 23 minutes to complete their journey to work (in London this rises to 34 minutes). The average weekly journey time therefore accounts for around five hours per week

– over half a working day simply to get to work and back. The time and the cost is usually borne by the employee.

A promotional leaflet jointly published by the Telework Association and the RAC in 2002 estimated the true costs of commuting as follows, for a manager living in Didcot and working in London.

Salary	£26,000
After tax and NI	£20,353
Cost of rail travel	£3910
Annual car costs in order to travel to station	£2395
Car parking	£336
Total income after tax and travel	£13,711
Travel hours per week	17.5
Working hours	48.0
Total hours per week	65.5
Income/hours based on 48 working weeks per year	£4.36/hour

An earlier 1998 report by NERA for the RAC Foundation, *Motors or Modems?*, predicted that one in ten car journeys could be replaced by 'virtual travel'. The Foundation believes that 40% of the people who want to work from home will do so by 2007; that up to 6% of shopping and banking trips will be replaced by services delivered over the Internet; and that the use of video conferencing will expand to replace 25% of business travel by 2007.

Aside from transport costs for cars or public-transport season tickets, there are a number of costs which, taken together, mount up for the employee. These include business clothing and laundry/dry cleaning costs, and the cost of lunch and drinks. Those who commute often do not realise that for perhaps a 13-hour day out of the house, they are being paid for little more than half of their hours.

Improving personal productivity

In August 2001, a survey of 1953 technology professionals at the website **http://home.techies.com** found that control over the work schedule was the second most popular reason for working from home. 'The greatest bonus is the fact that I can work when I am productive, whether that's early in the morning or late at night,' said one web developer. A programmer said: 'Since junior high school I've known I'm more productive late at night than during the day. If I didn't have flex hours and the ability to telecommute I'd continue to suffer from being a "night person".'

A TELEWORKING ALTERNATIVE TO RETIREMENT?

Pauline Knight has worked for IBM Ireland in Dublin for over 20 years and is currently involved with the company's community relations programme with schools. 'I had been thinking about retiring because my husband, who is already retired, had been complaining that he never saw me – but I didn't feel ready to quit, despite the stresses of the job such as having to be on the road by 6.30 a.m. to be sure of getting a parking space in central Dublin. My boss suggested I try working from home and, although my first reaction was one of panic, I've spent two or three days at home since last summer. You certainly need to be self-disciplined but I do a lot of work with teams in the US and the flexibility is very useful to take account of the time difference.'

Retaining work after relocation

If your partner needs to relocate for work, what happens to you? One possible option if you want to keep your existing job is to ask your employer to consider a teleworking arrangement. This was the motive behind moves at the US Department of Defense to get up to 25% of eligible employees teleworking – it is an attempt to mitigate the disruption to partners caused by the standard military practice of employees moving location every few years.

Balancing work and caring for families

Used wisely, teleworking can help parents combine work with child-rearing, and allow fathers greater involvement with their children. While most jobs require the teleworker's presence during a core of hours in order to communicate with colleagues, many tasks may not require this core presence, giving the teleworker the opportunity to work at times convenient to them – which can sometimes be early in the morning or late at night to fit in with the needs of other family members.

Providing jobs in remote or rural areas

Nearly every European country can provide some examples of work opportunities made available in rural areas through teleworking. However, the problems should not be underestimated as good telecommunications infrastructure is required and most teleworking jobs require high levels of skill. *See* **http://www.work-global.com** for an example.

Providing jobs for people with disabilities

Teleworking can provide access to work for people who find the conventional office a difficult environment, particularly those with disabilities and chronic illnesses. It can be particularly useful for those whose disability restricts their working time to a series of short periods. However, because of the high levels of skill that are usually required, it tends to be an option for those who have acquired their disability, or already have a track record in conventional work, rather than for those who have always coped with their disability. It is also important to ensure that teleworking is not used as an excuse for not providing accessible premises at the office, and that people with disabilities do not find they become marginalised or isolated through teleworking.

THE CONCERNS

Worries for employers

Management resistance to the change
Many surveys indicate that the attitude of the management is the main barrier to teleworking. The Small World Connections/*Flexible Working* magazine 1997 corporate teleworking survey indicated that the attitude of senior managers was considered a negative factor in 60% of teleworking schemes. When BT

TELECOMMUTING MYTHS

The state of Arizona in the US has run a large-scale telecommuting programme which was evaluated by a team from Arizona State University. The evaluation team came up with a list of common 'myths' brought up by people in focus groups as initial barriers – barriers which were not borne out by the actual experience of telecommuting:

- *I won't know they're working at home.*
- *I won't get promoted if I telecommute.*
- *Telecommuters must work at home five days a week.*
- *Telecommuters are not available when you need them.*
- *Telecommuting isn't for everyone so it's not fair.*
- *Everyone will want to telecommute.*
- *Equipment will be expensive.*
- *Telecommuters cause more work for supervisors.*
- *Telecommuters cause more work for co-workers.*
- *Our type of jobs aren't compatible with telecommuting.*
- *The public would not support state employees working from home.*
- *Our employees deal with confidential information so they can't telecommute.*

The actual experience refuting these issues can be found at
http://www.teleworkarizona.com/telework_files/myths.htm

experimented with its teleworking directory-enquiries operators in Inverness, as far back as 1994, it found that middle-management resistance to change was a far greater obstacle than the technical issues which had to be overcome.

Trust and monitoring issues

The Nextra survey published in spring 2002 of about 200 HR managers in companies with over 100 employees found that nearly a quarter (23%) of senior managers don't trust staff to work flexibly – representing a considerable barrier to teleworking, and often resulting in requests to monitor teleworker productivity.[5]

The Gee Publishing/Small World Connections 1999 survey found a split between the attitude to teleworking for managers and for administrative and clerical employees. The two main groups of people within organisations who were teleworking on an ad hoc basis were managers and professional/technical staff who were perceived to be in a position of trust – their superiors were confident that they would not slack when working at home. But over 80% of respondents did not offer teleworking even on an occasional basis to administrative or clerical staff, who were viewed as needing support from colleagues and as being essential to the effective running of the main office. These figures are borne out by the UK Labour Force Survey which shows that in 2002, a mere 8% of teleworkers were administrative or secretarial staff.

Some work-tasks, such as answering directory-enquiries calls, are very easily measured and unlikely to create much of an issue. Others, where work measurement is less easy, need to be piloted on a longer-term basis until comparative statistics reveal whether value for money is being achieved.

In all approaches a degree of trust is involved, and managers need to bear in mind that even in the existing office-based situation, where they can 'see' if someone is working, there is actually no guarantee that the work is being done, or being done efficiently. Conversely, not being able to see the employee does not alter this reality. A change from 'eyeball' management to management by results is required to see whether the work done represents good value to the employer, is completed to the correct quality and is delivered on time.

Loss of motivation

Contrary to expectations, most research shows that motivation is not a major issue; problems with teleworkers overworking are more likely to be encountered. However, the survey results need to be treated with some caution because many teleworking pilot studies have involved volunteers, anxious to make the system work, who may well have regarded working from home as a privilege that they were keen to retain. The results of the US Population Census questions on homeworking for 2001 support the anecdotal experience that loss of motivation is not a problem.

Main reason for working at home as listed by US Population Census 2001[6]

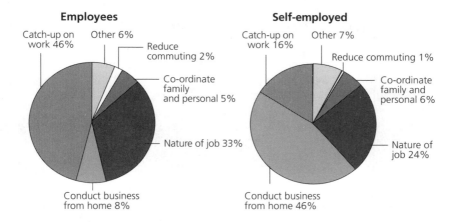

Employees

Catch-up on work 46%
Other 6%
Reduce commuting 2%
Co-ordinate family and personal 5%
Nature of job 33%
Conduct business from home 8%

Self-employed

Catch-up on work 16%
Other 7%
Reduce commuting 1%
Co-ordinate family and personal 6%
Nature of job 24%
Conduct business from home 46%

Isolation leading to loss of management control and corporate culture
The BT directory-enquiries project in 1994 found that, although they had designed voluntary opportunities for teleworking team-members to socialise, some preferred to use the time for their own hobbies or home activities.

The Small World Connections/*Flexible Working* magazine 1997 corporate teleworking survey indicated that nearly two-thirds of companies (60%) were worried about loss of feedback, just over half of companies (53%) were worried about isolation, and just under half about loss of control (47%). However, there was a split between non-teleworking companies, 56% of whom were worried about isolation, as compared to 35% of those already using teleworkers. The authors queried: 'Have the attitudes of managers changed in the light of their experience of teleworking, or have organisations with favourable managers implemented teleworking earlier [than others]?'

Some of the distractions that make up 'normal' office life also provide important informal communications systems and training opportunities which are not available to teleworkers. However, where teleworkers are linked by the corporate email system, it is often used for social contact and informal communication as well as to send and deliver work.

Security and confidentiality worries
Risks to corporate security and information systems posed by teleworking include confidential information being overlooked or overheard; theft of

NORTEL NETWORKS: 25% OF WORLDWIDE WORKFORCE TELEWORK

Canadian telecoms company Nortel Networks has been running a telecommuting programme for several years and offers the teleworking option to 90% of its staff. By 2000 the company had 10,000 teleworking employees. By 2002 nearly 20,000 employees had attended one-day training sessions to prepare themselves for teleworking, and it is expected that the number of teleworkers will increase to 15,000 by the end of the year. About 40% of the teleworkers are in Canada, mainly around Ottawa. The rest are in the US, but there are nearly 1400 Nortel teleworkers in Europe.

In Britain and Ireland, around 600 staff telework. Nortel says that 'telecommuters have reported 11% higher employee satisfaction ratings and 24% higher productivity than the general Nortel Networks population'. Overall, telecommuters register 35% higher on Nortel's measures of employee effectiveness, and staff turnover has reduced by 24% (though it should not be forgotten that the telecoms industry is currently in a period of employment contraction which also reduces staff turnover). Property savings as a result of teleworking are quoted in the region of $65 million. Nortel is an international company with employees in 56 countries, so the convenience of participating in audio conferences across time zones from home, rather than having to drive to the office at an ungodly hour, is considered a major bonus by employees.

Nortel supports its teleworkers through a multidisciplined project team in the Information Services division, known as Teleworking and Mobility Services. Once an employee has the agreement of their manager for teleworking, a form on the company intranet is completed which automatically notifies all relevant departments, and orders the required ISDN line and home-office equipment. Teleworkers are usually up and running in 15–20 days. The company also has a policy of gathering its teleworkers together on a regular basis to share experiences and problems and to build regional communities of teleworkers who can support each other. The groups feed information back to Nortel, ranging from suggested techniques for managing workflow to better methods of data backup.

The company also sells its 'HOMEbase' home-office solution which it uses for its own staff, consisting of an ISDN router securely connecting phone, fax and PC. Companies with Nortel Meridian telephone switches can take advantage of a range of 'Remote Office' and 'Home Office' products to support their teleworkers – all tested extensively by Nortel's own teleworking staff.
http://www.nortelnetworks.com/network/telecommuting.html

laptops or data disks; infection by computer viruses; failure to back up important files; and problems with keeping information up to date due to different versions of the same information being held centrally and by the teleworker. New concerns are currently being raised in relation to the 'always-on' GPRS wireless devices that are becoming available, about the security of wireless networks within corporate buildings, and in relation to the increased risk of hacker attacks on broadband Internet connections.

A top news story in 2000 was the successful attack by a hacker on the Microsoft network. The intruder used a hacker tool known as the QAZ Trojan which allegedly emailed stolen network passwords from an employee's home machine to a drop point in Russia.

However, security is often perceived as a teleworking risk because it is assumed that the existing arrangement is automatically more secure than a distributed working method. The process of trialling telework allows risks to be identified, and appropriate measures to be taken depending on the value and sensitivity of the information concerned (*see* p. 268). Many companies believe that trust and confidentiality are key issues in maintaining security: therefore, teleworking trials often involve existing company employees of long standing, rather than new recruits.

Companies with strong security cultures such as Motorola, Microsoft, Sun and IBM have set up secure systems to allow their staff to log in from locations around the world, and are continually increasing their numbers of mobile workers and teleworkers. It is therefore clear that security technology is not an insurmountable obstacle.

Cost of equipment and support

Starting up a teleworking option usually involves employers in the purchase, installation and support of additional IT equipment, as well as running costs for telephone calls and Internet access. However, recent surveys of larger employers have shown that cost is no longer perceived as a major barrier to teleworking schemes, probably as a result of the reduction in prices for IT equipment, and increased awareness of the productivity increases related to teleworking. A survey of 200 HR managers in 2002 indicated that only 15% felt the cost of implementing and supporting flexible working to be prohibitive.[7]

Some small-scale studies have indicated that it can be hard for companies to justify the cost of an extra set of IT equipment for a home office if the employee concerned only works part-time, and if their skill level and charge-out value to the company is low.

Requirement to draft new company policies

Preparing company policies can be a time-consuming function for HR staff. In smaller companies without a separate HR function, it may well be a responsibility that falls between a number of managers and which does not

merit high priority. Mitel's 1998 survey carried out by MORI interviewed 465 'knowledge workers', of whom 65% said that teleworking was held back by a lack of company policy. In the US, the results of the 2001 Population Census show that only 17% of the 13 million-plus employees who work from home at least once a week are involved in any kind of formal arrangement for homeworking with their employer. A consensus seems to have emerged among UK employers that changes to employment contracts are required only where the teleworker is expected to work at home for more than 40% of the time, at which point the contract is amended or supplemented to state that home is the permanent workplace.

Technology

Close analysis reveals that 'technology' worries usually relate to provision of a high-speed connection to the Internet. Senior HR staff at IBM sum up the problem: 'There is often a significant difference between what can in theory be achieved by the latest technology, what is required for the job in hand and what is available in practice to the majority of remote workers ... [a 56k modem] is a lot slower than most workers will have been used to when working in the office, and some tasks that were possible in the office become impractical when working remotely.'

There is some evidence from the US that broadband is fundamental to effective teleworking. Recent studies by Booz Allen Hamilton and AT&T

indicate that teleworkers can perform more of their work at home with fewer problems relating to speed and reliability when they have broadband (*see* Chapter 3). However, many experienced telework practitioners would consider that some technology issues can be dealt with through training and experience – such as planning work-tasks to suit location. While situations differ, for many teleworkers perhaps as much as four-fifths of work-tasks can be carried out offline and then delivered over the Internet.

Lack of bandwidth is often the number one challenge faced by teleworkers, but other technology problems can include non-standard configurations of hardware and software which are not well supported by the IT department, and inadequate training or staffing of helpdesks leading to ineffective support of teleworkers.

However, basic aspects of IT provision also cause dissatisfaction. A Gartner Dataquest survey in 2002 of 316 IT managers and 200 teleworkers found that the IT specialists thought 45% of all teleworkers were mobile. In fact, 68% only connect from their homes, leading to some incorrect decisions on support. Teleworkers were reasonably happy with the IT support they received, but not with the equipment or data connections provided. Nearly one-fifth have to provide their own equipment. Their expectations of IT support were also low and some 71% relied on colleagues for help. Up to 8% have to sort out their own IT problems or buy new machines when they fail. Nearly half (42%) have to take their machines back to the office if repairs are needed.

Worries for employees and the self-employed

Keeping 'office' and family separate

Teleworkers who work at home need to be able to 'switch off' from work. Conversely, clear understanding is needed between the teleworker and their family to minimise interruptions during working hours. Children can find it difficult to understand that a parent is physically present at home but not available to them. Partners may find irregular working hours in the evening and weekends difficult to cope with. Additionally, neighbours, friends and pets may not initially take the working arrangement seriously.

Despite the rosy picture, working from home can cause family stress, particularly if the teleworker does not have a separate room or office for work. Often training schemes are in place for the employee and their manager, but no-one remembers that the family will also need informal training. Typical strategies include ensuring there is a separate 'home office', use of voicemail on the work telephone line to buffer after-hours calls, and clear understandings about work duties with the family.

Isolation

The disadvantage most frequently reported by teleworkers is isolation from the companionship of the workplace. A 2001 survey of 1593 IT professionals at the website **http://home.techies.com** found that 76% thought telecommuters should visit the office at least once a week. Of those who were already telecommuting full-time, half agreed that once-weekly visits were needed. In fact, on a scale of 1–5, loss of interaction with colleagues was rated equal first, at 3.6, as the greatest negative impact.

Solutions include ensuring regular managerial contact, supplemented with face-to-face meetings for the work-team on a regular basis, and involving the teleworkers in decisions and development. The use of suitable technologies such as audio conferencing, Microsoft Netmeeting, Lotus Notes, instant messaging and video conferencing can also assist.

Reduced career prospects

'Out of sight, out of mind' is a real fear for many teleworkers, who feel that they will not get the same opportunities for promotion, or that the work they will be offered will be more routine and less challenging than that given to in-office colleagues. Some managers interpret a desire to work from home as a lack of commitment to corporate culture.

Teleworkers may feel that they have continually to remind their employer that they are there, what work they are performing, that they are serious about their career and that teleworking is not a soft option. In addition, many teleworkers

---

BT TELEWORKERS GIVE MIXED RESPONSE

Researchers from the University of Bradford studying staff in BT's Options 2000 flexible working scheme (see also p. 4) found that personal responses to the scheme varied widely. Most were happy, but negative responses included social isolation, lack of contact with colleagues, difficulties with working from home, problems with information systems and a tendency to work long hours. Comments included:

'It is important to ensure that one's manager is fully comfortable with the arrangement. Unfortunately, there are a number of people who believe that homeworking equates to skiving.'

'While being out of contact can in some respects be seen as a downside, the lack of interruptions means greater productivity. As work tends to be completed on time, this reduces pressure.'

'I spend a lot of time in London, so productivity will improve dramatically if I work from home on the days when I'm not travelling instead of travelling.'

'Not only am I isolated from my team, I am seated in an extremely unsuitable position. No view of the outside world, no restaurant, too far from the local shops, no immediate colleagues.'
http://www.wfh.co.uk

feel they are prevented from taking on opportunities to manage others. The techies.com survey found that 29% of telecommuters felt the most negative impact of their work-style to be the lack of opportunity to manage others.

However, there is evidence that teleworking need not affect career prospects, from technology-based companies that have implemented teleworking on a large scale. At AT&T, nearly one-fifth of those who cease teleworking do so because they have received a promotion, which ties in with the other AT&T survey results showing higher performance appraisal for teleworkers. The survey also indicates that 60% of teleworkers think telework has no effect on their career, while 32% think it has a positive effect. Only 6% believe there to be negative consequences.

Access to training
Teleworkers need to ensure that their skills are kept up to date and that they are not left out of training opportunities, both formal and informal. This is a particular issue for self-employed teleworkers, who have to find, fund, prioritise and make time for training themselves in the face of competing pressures from clients.

Personal security
Mobile teleworkers (such as salesmen operating from car and home) can be vulnerable to attack, burglary and car crime due to the high value of the IT equipment and samples that they may carry with them.

Moving to self-employment
Sometimes a move to teleworking is accompanied by a move to self-employment, involving the usual risks of self-employment, such as the need to earn adequate income, insure against sickness and incapacity, contribute to a pension fund, and buy new equipment periodically. Potential self-employed teleworkers should seriously consider the risks involved in giving up a conventional job, such as reduced social welfare benefits, as well as examining the many opportunities that self-employment can offer.

A teleworking 'veneer' will not prop up a business idea that is fundamentally unsound. Those moving to self-employment should use market research to satisfy themselves of the viability of their service.

SO WHAT'S THE CONCLUSION?

Current changes in patterns of employment seem likely to lead to more teleworking, with trends towards increased employment in managerial and professional jobs suitable for teleworking, more part-time workers, more service and IT-based jobs, and more women at work who require flexible employment patterns.

Teleworking has not spread at the speed originally predicted, and there appears to be a slow-down in its growth in the more developed countries such as the US and UK, with some incomplete evidence of a trend towards a final level of about 16–17% of the workforce in first-world countries.

This is hardly surprising considering the cultural and technological barriers to its adoption – it is a form of work which requires a generational change in management techniques, and where suitable technological tools have only recently become available. Despite the rumours, teleworking certainly isn't dead or even showing signs of sickness. Most companies that use it plan to expand their usage further. AT&T's annual teleworking report states: 'If telework did not increase organisational and personal efficiency and effectiveness, if it did not add value to the economic system, it would not have survived the Darwinian struggle that all new technologies must face. Businesses could just as easily absolutely forbid telework as openly permit it.'

While there are many gaps in the data and research available on teleworking, enough progress has been made for three things to be certain:

- Teleworking continues to spread as a trend, driven by improvements in technology, the cost of office property, a desire for work-life balance and productivity and commuting pressures.
- Most people who telework, like it.
- Almost all pieces of research into telework should be treated with suspicion unless you have access to details of the questions asked and survey samples used.

Much of the research to date has been funded, designed or driven by companies which sell teleworking technology or have a vested interest in presenting teleworking in a positive light. Base your actions on your own research, trials and experiences – it's your life, your family and your money.

2   For researchers

A LITTLE HISTORY

The terms 'telecommuting' and 'teleworking' are attributed to US academic and consultant Jack Nilles, who in 1973 worked on the first documented pilot telecommuting project with an insurance company. In the 1970s – the era of oil crises – the concept of moving the work instead of the gas-guzzling commuter made sense. But the idea took time to catch on because a number of factors had to be in place for it to work: a good reason to do it, cheap and reliable data communications, and organisations that were willing to change the way they worked.

The recessions of the late 1980s and early 1990s dampened economic activity and removed one of the main drivers for teleworking – the need to expand organisations without incurring crippling increases in overheads. In 1994 the European Union placed the adoption of telework at the top of the Bangemann Report list of actions to make Europe more competitive. The EU set a target of 10 million teleworkers in Europe by the year 2000.

In the UK and the US, unrealised predictions were made for the potential of telework. There was a surge of interest in the topic in the late 1990s, due to pressures caused by economic growth and skills shortages. Inevitably, the recession which began in 2001 will affect the growth of formal teleworking schemes due to bugetary restraints within companies.

HOW MANY TELEWORKERS ARE THERE?

The problem with counting teleworkers is that there has been little general agreement on what constitutes a teleworker, or on how to measure teleworking – whether teleworkers are employed, self-employed, part-time or full-time, what sort of ICT equipment they use or where they are located.

National statistical offices have only recently started to look at how to provide reliable information on the growth of teleworking. Telework research has mainly involved small, unrandomised sample surveys which are often funded by organisations that wish to promote equipment or service sales and may seem open to bias. However, even these estimates can be useful in sketching out trends and giving some guidance on how differing legal and social conditions affect teleworker numbers.

The UK LFS figures

Britain is currently the only country in Europe to regularly collect large-sample figures on teleworking through the Labour Force Survey (LFS). This is carried out by the Office for National Statistics (ONS) in the spring quarter of each year and covers some 68,000 households. The US carries out a number of occasional large-scale surveys including a detailed analysis every four years through its equivalent of the LFS, the US Population Census. There are moves afoot by Eurostat to introduce some basic questions on teleworking into the European Community Labour Force Survey on an annual basis (*see* Chapter 3, *International perspective* for a more detailed analysis of figures and trends in other countries).

The UK LFS survey identifies people who spent one day working at or from home in the reference week of the survey question (occasional teleworkers). It then checks whether these people use both a computer and a telephone to do their work. Those who do are identified as teleworkers.

Teleworker homeworkers are those who in their main job work mostly in their own home and use a computer and a telephone to complete their work-tasks. Teleworkers using home as a base work in a number of different locations, as well as on the move. Occasional teleworkers are those who do not usually fall into the other two categories, but who happened to spend at least one day doing so in the reference week when the survey was taken.

Finally, the ONS asks a filter question to determine whether the computer and telephone are essential for the 'teleworker' to complete their work – this smaller group are called 'TC teleworkers' in the ONS analyses. The results are interesting and differ from the media stereotype of a teleworker as a female clerical worker with children who is working from home full-time.

In spring 2002 the total number of broad-definition teleworkers was 2.272 million. Of these, 1.892 million are 'TC teleworkers' who could not perform their job without using a telephone and a computer.[8] The figures for 'Other' teleworkers have not grown significantly since 1997 (*see* figure opposite).

The table below shows that numbers of TC teleworkers have almost doubled from 1.014 million in 1997 to 1.892 million in 2002, and that the number of teleworkers working at home has increased by 19% between 2001 and 2002. There does appear to be some evidence of a tail-off in the rate of increase over the past two years, but whether this is a trend or an anomaly is not yet clear.

Employees and self-employed whose work from home required both a telephone and a computer (TC teleworkers) (000s)

Year	1997	1998	1999	2000	2001	2002
Work at home	225	256	255	312	347	412
Work from home	504	589	693	805	887	882
Occasional	285	301	357	477	549	598
Total	1,014	1,146	1,325	1,593	1,783	1,892
Percentage increase		13	16	20	12	6

Source: ONS – Labour Force Survey

Teleworkers, all types, spring quarter, not seasonally adjusted

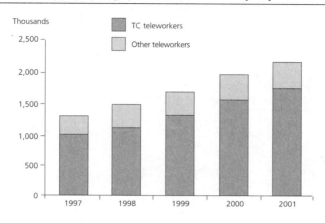

Source: Hotopp U, Teleworking in the UK, Labour Market Trends, June 2002. Note that the 2002 figures are not included because the LFS data were regrossed in April 2002 so they are not directly comparable

Teleworkers by occupational group, spring 2001, not seasonally adjusted

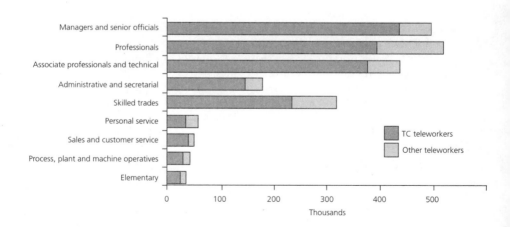

Source: Hotopp U, Teleworking in the UK, Labour Market Trends, June 2002

For the year 2001, TC teleworkers represented a figure of about 6% of all those in employment. Using the broad definition of telework (including those who use but do not require a computer and a telephone when working at home, also referred to as 'Other' teleworkers) the figure rose to about 7.4% of those in employment.

Employees and self-employed whose work from home required both a telephone and a computer (TC teleworkers), spring 2002

	Work at home	Work from home	Occasional	All
Men	47%	79%	66%	68%
Women	53%	21%	34%	32%
Employees	41%	46%	84%	57%
Self-employed	59%	54%	16%	43%
Full-time	56%	84%	90%	80%
Part-time	44%	17%	10%	20%
Managerial, professional, technical	66%	65%	89%	73%
Administrative and secretarial	24%	3%	4%	8%
Craft trades	3%	22%	4%	12%
Sales and customer service	–	3%	–	–
Other occupations	4%	6%	3%	5%

Source: ONS – Labour Force Survey

Some 74% of all teleworkers are found in the private sector as opposed to the public sector – similar to the split in the overall workforce. Those who need to use both a telephone and a computer (TC teleworkers) are more likely to be private-sector workers (88%). Nearly one-quarter of all teleworkers work in the real estate, renting and business-activities sector.

The proportion of teleworkers who are self-employed has been reducing as a proportion of all teleworkers. The growth rate for employed teleworkers between 1997 and 2001 was 88% for TC teleworkers, compared to 52% for self-employed TC teleworkers.

OTHER UK SURVEYS

A survey of 200 HR managers in companies with over 100 employees was carried out in spring 2002 by Citigate Technologies.[9] The sample was not randomised, but turned up some interesting views. Some 11% reported providing staff with modems and laptops, though only 8% provided remote access to corporate email and files. Only 4% of companies felt that the IT department was the most active in promoting flexible working.

Teleworkers by industry, spring 2001, not seasonally adjusted

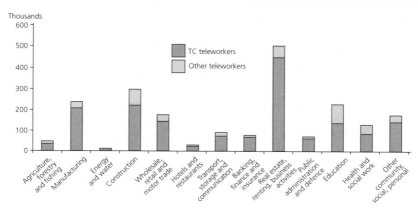

Source: Hotopp U, Teleworking in the UK, Labour Market Trends, June 2002

Perhaps related to this, the hardest part of implementing flexible working was felt to be supplying and supporting the resources needed (35%), closely followed by the issue of senior management not trusting staff to work flexibly (23%). Only 14% found cost a barrier. Nearly half (43%) have no guidelines on flexible working. The most desired form of flexibility was not teleworking equipment but better childcare support.

The Oftel Business Use of the Internet surveys are carried out on a quarterly basis. The May 2002 survey of 810 companies with less than 250 employees found that 13% of SMEs pay for (at least some) home Internet usage for employees working from home, a figure which is roughly in agreement with the Citigate survey. The figure rises to 27% for companies with 51–250 employees. Overall, the survey found that 63% of all Small and Medium Enterprises (SMEs) have Internet access.[10]

Occasional or ad hoc teleworking is much more common than planned schemes. The 1999 Small World Connections/Gee Publishing survey of 122 organisations found that up to 85% of British financial-sector companies use ad hoc teleworking, ranging down through 60% of IT and professional services companies and 45% of government-sector organisations to a mere 29% of manufacturing companies. As with formal schemes, there is a general trend that the larger the organisation, the more likely they are to have ad hoc teleworking. Four main reasons are given for using ad hoc teleworking:

■ To work on a particular project/deadline (98%).
■ To deal with a domestic crisis (78%).

- Because of disruption due to severe weather, strikes, etc. (75%).
- Because of illness (52%).

In early 1998, BT surveyed 500 large organisations employing over 50 people in Britain, and found that three-quarters of those with over 1000 employees had some sort of flexible working arrangements in place, including work from home, on the move or based at various locations. Overall, 16% had employees teleworking on a regular basis. The Small World Connections/Gee Publishing survey found that 61% of organisations offered flexitime but only 14% offered home-based teleworking, although 25% expected to be offering or expanding teleworking options within three years.

Teleworking still remains a minority work-practice in most companies. A survey for Ireland's Information Society Commission of 830 companies by MRBI found that although 39% reported providing remote access to their computer networks, less than 5% of companies have more than 10% of their workforce carrying out any teleworking at all.

Ireland

Ireland does not yet collect regular telework figures through its Quarterly National Household survey (the equivalent of the UK LFS). However, questions derived from a simplified version of the UK LFS questions were asked in autumn 2002, with results available from the Central Statistics Office in spring 2003 (**http://www.cso.ie**). Figures from the EMERGENCE project based on employer interviews indicate that only about 5% of small companies in Ireland (those with less than 50 employees) use any kind of teleworker, with similar figures for mobile teleworkers (**http://www.emergence.nu**). Figures from a survey by MRBI in 2001 which included larger companies suggested a higher figure of 12% of companies using teleworkers (**http://www.ework.ie**).

AGE, CLASS AND GENDER

Despite media stereotypes, European and US surveys show that most teleworkers are middle-aged men with good levels of education in managerial or professional positions. While some of the gender differences appear to be occupational (there are more men in telework-suitable jobs), it is important to see whether these figures represent sexual discrimination. Some early studies into gender differences in teleworking compared high-level professional male teleworkers against low-level clerical female workers, leading to the predictable conclusion that women fare worse than men when they telework. To examine whether this problem was widespread, in the mid-1990s the Social Affairs directorate of the EU commissioned Ursula Huws of Analytica to carry out a survey using a properly controlled sample across Europe.[11]

Female teleworkers have tended to be concentrated in areas such as data entry, telesales or routine computer programming, whereas male teleworkers have tended to be professionals or executives involved in systems design, sales management or engineering. To avoid this distortion Huws selected her sample of 188 freelancers through a translation agency with workers in all European countries, and discovered that gender differences in conditions, problems experienced and other factors were much smaller than had been previously reported.

In fact, although women teleworkers had previously been reported to have greater difficulty with interruptions from family, Huws found that they tended to opt for clearer boundaries and working hours than their male counterparts, suggesting that they prefer and instigate a more rigid work structure. Huws also found that quite a few of the male teleworkers were 'new men' who had chosen to telework in order to be with their children or partners, and to adopt a less stressful, rural lifestyle. Men who made these choices were 'feminised' in labour-market terms, often adopting less secure and lower-paid work in exchange for their lifestyle choice.

Overall, both men and women suffered from high levels of stress and insecurity. Twenty per cent worked more than 50 hours a week; 12% worked over 60 hours and 9% over 70. Huws comments: 'Although the most common reason given for preferring to work from home was the desire for autonomy or "to be my own boss", these self-employed teleworkers had little or no control over the flow of work. Periods without work could not be enjoyed as "leisure" but were times of hardship and anxiety about where the next job might come from.'

The Mitel 1998 Teleworking Britain survey indicated a significant gender split, with fewer female respondents (30%) inclined to telework compared to male counterparts (40%) – though other surveys have indicated that women have a more favourable attitude to teleworking than men.

In 2002, the ONS published an article by Ulrike Hotopp of the Department of Trade and Industry, analysing the teleworker figures.[12] About 67% of teleworkers are men, compared to 53% men employed overall (not just teleworkers). Nearly all teleworkers in the skilled trades are men (95%). For the managers and senior officials group, three in four teleworkers are men. Yet in the administrative and secretarial grouping just one in five are men, while in the personal services group the figure is one man for every seven teleworkers. It appears that there are simply more men in the occupations where teleworking is most likely to be found.

Some 43% of TC teleworkers were self-employed, compared to about 11% of all those in employment. Hotopp concludes that it is this relatively high number of self-employed teleworkers which is responsible for the apparent gender imbalance in teleworking (some 72% of all self-employed people are men). Women teleworkers are more likely to work part-time, but then four-fifths of all part-time workers are female.

The Institute of Employment Studies has gleaned further interesting information from the 1999 UK LFS figures[13] on teleworkers' family relationships and disabilities: 'Given the fact that teleworkers are more likely to be married and in their 30s and 40s than non-teleworkers, the differences are slight and it would be difficult to use these statistics to support an argument that teleworking results from a lifestyle choice to put family before work.'

In relation to age, unpublished analysis of the 2001 UK LFS figures by Ulrike Hotopp indicates that there are very few teleworkers aged under 25 (3% compared to 15% of all employees). The over-55 and 25–34 age-groups show similar percentages of teleworkers to those for all employees. However, teleworkers are over-represented by about 5% in the 35–54 age-group. Analysis of the 1998 US Current Population Survey by Vincenzo Spezia of the ILO also showed that teleworkers tended to be older than the onsite workforce, with the highest concentration in the 36–45 age group.[14]

There can be little doubt that at present, teleworking is a work-life balance option that is more likely to be available to people with high levels of education and income who have occupations in which they are trusted to manage themselves – in other words, middle-aged, middle-class men.

SELF-EMPLOYMENT

According to the UK LFS figures, about 43% of the teleworkers in Britain are self-employed compared to around 11% of the labour force as a whole. By comparison, the self-employment figures for Europe are around 13% of the labour force (much of the difference is made up of small farmers in southern Europe), and for the US, up to 16%. The figure of 43% in the UK represents a reduction in the proportion of teleworkers who are self-employed compared to previous years, when they amounted to nearly half of all teleworkers.

This change may in part reflect that to some extent, the LFS has measured existing small, home-based businesses going online, rather than any change in workplace. As a large number of these are now online, the growth in this part of the teleworker numbers is not increasing, compared to the increases in employed teleworkers. There is considerable discussion about how to distinguish the 'e-enabled self-employed' from those who use ICTs as a core function in carrying out their businesses. Currently this is mainly done by looking at the occupation and sector of the self-employed person alongside their work location (e.g. someone who is involved in construction and works from home is more likely to be 'e-enabled self-employed' than someone involved in translation who works at home and uses ICTs as a core part of their work).

In its predictions on growth, the EMERGENCE project has tried to separate out these 'e-enabled self-employed' from those who use ICTs as a core function in carrying out their businesses. Based on the LFS figures for the year 2000, EMERGENCE estimated that there were about 3.08 million e-enabled self-

SELF-EMPLOYED SILVER SURFERS

Self-employed people over the age of 50 are more likely (63%) to use a computer in the course of their business than those under 50 (47%). In fact, the over-50s are creating 50% more enterprises than ten years ago according to a survey by Barclays Bank carried out in 2001. The average turnover of 'silver surfer' businesses is £70,000 compared to £104,000 for the under-50s, but most (51%) use the business to supplement a pension, with just 27% reporting the business as their sole source of income. Nearly 35% started their business as a consequence of retirement, redundancy or dissatisfaction with their previous job.

See http://www.barclays.co.uk/economicreports/pdfs/over_50.pdf

employed compared to 1.45 million 'e-lancers' or self-employed teleworking freelancers.

In the US, a move towards self-employed teleworking for professionals has been charted by journalist Dan Pink as the move to a 'free-agent nation'. Pink says that skilled staff look at the collapse of the old equation, where they gave their loyalty to a company in exchange for job security, and vote with their feet for autonomy, believing that having five or six clients is more secure than having one employer. His articles can be found at
http://www.fastcompany.com

GLOBALISATION AND E-OUTSOURCING

A major business advantage of teleworking is that, because it consists of ICT-based tasks, work can be quickly and cheaply sent around the world to wherever the skills are available and cost-effective. Outsourcing has been a fact of life in the software and call-centre sectors for a number of years. Some countries have proved better at using these techniques than others, but there is still a general tendency to use outsourced services that are 'local' rather than far away or in another country.

EMERGENCE interviewed 800 UK companies and found that some 11.3% were outsourcing work to a call centre over a telecommunications link. Some 17% of UK companies were supplying services over ICTs, and London was the third most popular destination for ICT-based work (due in no small part to the financial-services sector in the city of London).

WORKING HOURS

An evaluation of the BT Workabout flexible working scheme by Bradford University (http://www.sustel.org) showed that 68.5% worked longer hours. Figures from the US CPS[15] (the equivalent government survey to the European labour force surveys) for 2001 show that the main motivation for 46% of the 19.1 million employed workers who work at home at least one day a week is to catch up on work. On average, those who do not have a formal arrangement to work at home, and are not paid for their work at home, spent seven hours each week working at home. The CPS figures look at all who work from home, not just teleworkers, but around 80% of US homeworkers used a computer, while 63% use the Internet or email.

The 1999 survey by US association Telework America suggests that American teleworkers typically work nine days each month at home, but of that time only three hours per week is during normal business hours – the remainder is work outside conventional hours. The survey also found that 42% of teleworkers work long hours – between 50 and 75 hours per week. An analysis by Vicenzo Spezia of the ILO[16] based on the US Current Population Survey 1998 figures found that for those who work at home and have a computer, and use email or the Internet, 32.3% work over 45 hours a week compared to 17.9% of onsite workers. The figures were particularly clear in relation to men – 43.3% worked over 45 hours compared to 25.6% of onsite workers.

A December 1999 survey by Stanford Institute for the Quantitative Study of Society in California looked at 4113 adults and found that over a quarter of workers who use the Internet for more than five hours a week said that it increased the amount of time spent working at home without cutting back at the office (**http://www.stanford.edu/group/siqss**).

However, there is another view of this issue, supported by the 1999 Statistics Canada workplace and employee survey – that teleworkers happen to be in occupations where hours are longer. The Statistics Canada analysis shows that university graduates in knowledge-based industries work longer hours than those with lower levels of education or workers in other sectors.

A group of Dutch researchers[17] looked at whether occupations where teleworking is allowed might be those where increased output was rewarded. They wondered whether, if there is a relationship between long hours and teleworking, it might be to do with the way in which those likely to telework are rewarded, in that long hours are taken as a measure of commitment to work and high performance. They used two data-sets taken from a large self-completion website survey on wage indicators, but weighted according to data from the Dutch labour force survey to make it representative of the general working population. They found a significant relationship between longer working hours and teleworking (46.1 hours compared to 39.5 hours). However, if the figures for those with access to the teleworking option but who have not yet chosen to telework are compared with those of actual teleworkers, then the difference in working hours is not significant. The other factors which were positively associated with long hours were wage rate, having a company car, expense allowances and commuting allowances. These factors were also positively associated with teleworking.

WHY AREN'T THERE MORE TELEWORKERS?

Is the potential there?

As part of the EMERGENCE project (**http://www.emergence.nu**), researchers from the Institute of Employment Studies attempted to assess future trends in teleworking based on the number of workers in appropriate occupations for teleworking such as managers, computer professionals, writers, creative performing artists and administrative associate professionals in 1998.[18] The estimates for the UK were that 21.4% of men and 24.0% of women, representing an overall percentage of 22.6 of those employed, were 'potential' teleworkers. Ulrike Hotopp comments that this is likely to be an overestimate, since not all employees whose occupations are suitable for teleworking will take up the opportunity, but nevertheless for the UK it indicates that 'currently less than one-third of the telework potential is being taken up'.[19] The most recent LFS figures show that there may be some tail-off in the overall rate of growth.

Some commentators have taken a very different view of the LFS figures. The TUC document *Telework – the new industrial revolution*, published in 2001, claims: 'Most telework is old wine in new bottles: the self-employed running businesses or working freelance from home, and managers and professionals taking work home – employed teleworkers who usually work at home rather than in the office account for less than one in ten of all teleworkers and only 0.5% of employees.' (**http://www.tuc.org.uk/work_life/tuc-3664-f0.cfm**)

The TUC document suggests that the only new form of working is employee homeworking, although mobile workers whose lives have altered dramatically due to the introduction of ICTs might disagree, as might those who have been enabled to start up their own businesses by the possibility of a low-cost home-based arrangement. It has been clear for some years that full-time telehomeworking for employees is not widely popular (although there are some successful public-sector and call-centre schemes), so the low level of take-up of such an arrangement noted by the TUC might not seem so surprising. The EMERGENCE results indicate that employed telehomeworking is the least popular arrangement, reported by just 1.4% of employers.

The TUC report draws on US figures and work on the 1996 UK census by Felstead, Jewson et al[20], as well as recent work-life balance surveys to imply that the vast majority of teleworkers are taking home unpaid work. It also points out that the percentage of overall employment represented by jobs most commonly associated with teleworking (managerial, professional and associated) is growing, which is likely to lead to further telework growth regardless of other factors.

One piece of the jigsaw in trying to piece together the potential for teleworking growth is the importance of clear approval of teleworking arrangements by the social partners (government, unions and employers). The conclusion of a framework agreement at European level in 2002 (*see* Chapter 3) is likely to lead to national agreements in a number of countries including the UK. There is already a committee in place tasked to create a UK code of practice on teleworking; this will probably define how the European agreement will be implemented in Britain. The committee is hosted by the Department of Trade and Industry and has representation from the CBI, the TUC, the Employers' Organisation for Local Government, ACAS, the Health and Safety Executive and the Telework Association.

It is clear is that teleworking is continuing to grow, particularly people working at home, but there are barriers to its spread which have prevented the very high growth rates predicted some years ago.

A wider problem

Some of the barriers to teleworking are specific technology issues – such as rollout of broadband. The digital divide is likely to affect equality of access to teleworking. A report for the Housing Corporation and the Joseph Rowntree Foundation[21] indicates that social-housing tenants and their children are at an increasing disadvantage compared to those in owner-occupied housing because they do not have a room from which they can work or study. Many social landlords' tenancy schemes discourage or forbid use of the home for business. Initiatives to wire-up deprived communities rarely attempt to support home-based employment.

Robert Taylor, in a short article for the ESRC on the future of work-life balance initiatives, makes an often-ignored point: 'For non-skilled and semi-skilled workers earning relatively low wages, the costs involved at present in reconciling paid work and childcare can often be prohibitive. Too many of the lobby groups on this issue concentrate on the concerns of professional women who have children – we need to refocus this discussion to cover the millions of working mothers and fathers who lack the financial means at present to lessen the difficulties of bringing up children and working at the same time.'

Other barriers to teleworking are problems related to organisational change, which are apparent in the large gap between those who state that they wish to take up flexible working practices, and those who actually do, despite the clear pressures of long hours, workload and commuting times which could be relieved by flexible working.

Teleworking is often introduced as one of a number of work-life balance policies by companies – often in conjunction with flexitime working. Work-life balance describes the need for the balance between an individual's work and their life outside work to be healthy – or at least, not unhealthy. The incentive for companies to consider work-life balance issues is the general consensus that 'satisfaction outside work may enhance employees' contributions to work'.[22] The term 'work-life balance' is generally preferred to 'family friendly' now, because not all employees have families, so work-life balance is felt to be more inclusive of the whole workforce.

LANDMARK EMPLOYMENT TRIBUNAL TELEWORK CASES

Most employers know that a blanket refusal to allow a woman returning to work after having children to work part-time is likely to be unlawful on the grounds of indirect sex discrimination. A recent Employment Appeal Tribunal ruling judged that a request to work from home was conceptually similar to a request to work part-time at the employer's workplace (Lockwood v Crawley Warren Group Ltd 2000).

Mrs Lockwood had resumed work as an accountant at the end of her maternity leave. Her childcare arrangements involved her mother, who unfortunately became ill and could not go on looking after the baby. The woman was unable to find alternative childcare arrangements at short notice and put forward two alternatives to her employer – that she would work full-time from home, or that she would take six months' unpaid leave to sort out the situation.

Mrs Lockwood's employer offered two weeks' leave on condition that she return to work full-time at the office after two weeks. She resigned.

The case extends the potential scope of indirect sex discrimination to cover proposals by a female employee for alternative working arrangements. The Employment Appeal Tribunal ruling in favour of the woman was based on the employer failing to put forward reasoned, objective arguments for requiring the woman to work full-time at the employer's workplace.

Sue Nickson, head of employment law at Hammon Suddards Edge, says: 'While the Lockwood case does not establish a right to work from home, it does emphasise the need for employers to give careful consideration to any proposals for alternative working arrangements by a woman with childcare responsibilities.'

A 1998 Employment Appeal Tribunal decision (London Borough of Hillingdon v Morgan) established that an employer does have an obligation to consider temporary teleworking to assist an employee with a physical problem. Ms Morgan, who suffered from ME, asked if she could work from home temporarily. Hillingdon council refused and attempted to redeploy her instead. The tribunal found that a large employer should have been able to facilitate a staged return to work.

Although parents in the UK do not have an automatic right to demand work-life balance options from employers, they do have a right to request to work flexible hours when returning to work after the birth of a baby (Employment Act 2002). Under legislation introduced in April 2003, men and women with children under the age of six and parents with disabled children up to 18 will be able to request forms of flexible working from their employer, including being employed in a part-time capacity. Companies are not compelled by the law to grant such a request, but could be taken to an employment tribunal to challenge any refusal on the grounds of business needs.

Researchers from the Institute of Employment Studies carried out qualitative interviews and focus-group research in six British companies with over 500 employees that had well-developed work-life balance and flexible working practices. The companies reported that although they had made significant efforts to introduce flexible working practices, take-up was relatively low, although latent demand appears to be quite high.[23]

The interviewees reported a number of barriers:

- Perceived impact on career prospects.
- Incompatible organisational cultures (e.g. entrenched long-hours culture; unsupportive attitudes and behaviours of managers and colleagues).
- Heavy workloads.
- Lack of knowledge of available options, especially where the employer relies on the employee to identify possiblities.
- Lack of infrastructure and technology (e.g. IT facilities for working from home).
- Impact on earnings, as some flexible working practices such as part-time work or career breaks are not affordable for employees, particularly those on lower wages.
- Managers felt that they did not have sufficient support in deciding who should have access to which options. They felt that it was difficult to be fair to everyone, particularly support staff such as IT or administrators, whose access to work-life balance practices tends to be more restricted.
- Managers were also worried about how to deliver their workloads with reduced or differently organised resources.

The IES researchers comment: 'A key point from our data is that there appears to be a significant amount of latent demand. While a small number of people had requested a different working pattern and been turned down, many more had not felt able to ask. Line managers in particular were often concerned about how their business needs could be met with flexible workers. Employees often sensed, or were made explicitly aware of, these views, and did not bother to ask.' Yet when the researchers asked specific questions about the organisation and the line manager, it was clear that organisational attitudes rather than those of the line manager were the barrier, since around 68% agreed or strongly agreed that their line manager was sympathetic to their need for work-life balance.

Two very specific behaviours of managers caused particular problems to those who had taken work-life balance options. One was the tendency of directors and senior managers to call meetings at no notice, starting at 5.30 p.m. The other was to request very late in the day, immediate action for reporting next day, which meant that only colleagues working conventional long hours were able to take up the request.

DISTRIBUTING THE DAY TO KEEP TIME FOR CIARA

Deirdre Cashion is a 30-year-old sales distribution manager with network infrastructure company 3Com in Dublin – and she has a three-year-old daughter, Ciara. Deirdre has taken up a teleworking option offered to some staff since 2000. 'I suppose it's really about not having to stick to set hours,' she says. 'My husband Pat is a self-employed central heating engineer. Because we both work it can be a real struggle balancing work and home.'

Deirdre lives in Ashbourne, in theory only 40 minutes away from the 3Com office in Blanchardstown. In reality, the journey is severely affected by Dublin's traffic congestion problems. Deirdre's job involves visiting clients but she was having to travel backwards and forwards to the office to get paperwork completed – processing orders, chasing stock and dealing with enquiries. It often meant working late and last-minute phone calls to Pat asking him to collect Ciara from the creche.

'Now that I'm teleworking, I can structure my day to take in all the things I need to do. I can pick up Ciara and catch up on the paperwork anytime I want. I don't have to drive into work at the beginning of each day – I can go straight to appointments I've lined up the day before. It really is a new freedom.'

Deirdre is pleased that she has not had to give up large parts of the house to work. 'I have a desk in the corner in the bedroom with a PC and laptop. The only extra equipment is a LAN modem about the size of a video cassette. This has two phone ports for the phone and fax, and four LAN ports which allow me to hook up my laptop and desktop PCs. It's easy to install, easy to use and easy to maintain.'

Balance is the key for Deirdre, who says that so far it is working very well: 'I'm happier, my husband's happier, and of course Ciara is happier. The real beauty of teleworking for me is that I can choose when I work. I can start earlier in the morning and do a bit in the evenings if I need to. When Ciara has gone to bed and the washing-up's done, then, typically, the laptop will come out and I'll have a chance to get the urgent things done and prepare for the next day.'

'It is easy to get sucked into working all hours of the day and night, which means increased productivity for the company, but it can be a danger from the family perspective. With the equipment sitting in your home there's always the temptation to do more and more. I think I probably do work harder for that reason, but at the same time I don't mind because I know I can take an hour or two off in the middle of the day. You do have to draw a line and say, "Right, that's it, I'm finished for tonight and I'm going down to watch TV."'

Another interesting result of this qualitative research was that none of the organisations appeared to be collecting data they would need if they were to systematically monitor take-up of work-life balance options, and evaluate the costs and benefits of these initiatives.

An annual survey by *Management Today* found in 2001 that 57% of 1274 UK managers surveyed were convinced that government initiatives to tackle work-life balance issues would fail. Yet the demand for flexible working was high, with 68% of managers looking for new ways of working. Only 36% reported that their organisation offers flexible working options. The same number considered flexible working to be career-limiting (and among women, 43% of respondents felt that flexible working was career-limiting).

A survey of 670 Chartered Accountants carried out by Work Life Research Centre in 2001 found that 99% work longer than their contracted hours – on average about ten hours a week longer. Over half (57%) often or always work in the evenings, and over half often or always come home from work too tired to do other things, while over a third (37%) often or always work at weekends and nearly a third (27%) do not take up their annual leave entitlements.

The survey found that for respondents with young children, teleworking was the most frequently used tactic to mitigate these long working hours. Respondents reported that 30% of those with young children used portable technology to work at home through formal schemes. Working from home was used informally by 40%, while this group also reported that the policy they most wanted (46%) but which was not offered to them was technical and financial support to set up a home office.

However, others reported that they were deterred from taking advantage of flexible working policies by the perceived negative effect on their careers. They reported that they would be encouraged to use flexible working if such practices were not seen as a lack of commitment with an attached stigma that could damage their careers.[24] Similar barriers were found in a study on attitudes to work-life balance covering four European countries, but showed clear differences between countries based on social attitudes to the importance of non-work activities, and on national differences in management culture (*see* p. 67).

US teleworking consultant Gil Gordon has on many occasions stated that in his opinion, the main barrier to teleworking is managers of his own generation (early 50s), who tend to have more old-fashioned views on corporate culture and commitment, as well as lower levels of IT skills, and who generally prefer managing by observation to managing by results. Gordon believes that until this generation of managers retires, growth in teleworking will be restricted.

TECHNOLOGY SHIFTS

The wireless revolution

Those who remember WAP will say, 'what wireless revolution?' – but be assured, it is on its way. Handsets for the faster, always-on GPRS networks (also called 2.5G) are becoming widely available, and GPRS gadgets such as the Siemens XDA and the Blackberry email device, not to mention the Sidekick – a gadget the size of a bar of soap which does email, voice, PDA functions and a digital camera all in one – are already beginning to infiltrate companies. Watch out for the appearance of Bluetooth voice-activated cordless headsets attached to the ears of the technologically trendy.

Airports and railway stations, not to mention Starbucks cafés and touchdown centres in company offices, are starting to provide 'WiFi hotspots' – public areas supplied with 802.11 wireless Internet connectivity that can be used by gadgets with WiFi cards such as laptops. Card costs are low and BT already offers a commercial WiFi service in some locations.

It's not all plain sailing – WiFi carries heavy processing overheads that drain battery life in mobile devices, and there are some concerns about its security. The much-hyped Bluetooth technology is also finally beginning to become available, offering fast wireless connections between peripheral devices such as printers, mobile phones and laptops over short distances.

The picture is certainly confusing. Will it all mean more or less laptop use? Some Goldman Sachs employees in the US were given the Blackberry devices, which look like complex pagers with a keyboard. Their use of their laptops fell by 45% and one-fifth of the Blackberry users abandoned their laptops altogether – using a Blackberry, you can catch up on your email in a taxi. But the cost is substantial (currently estimated at around $900 per user per year according to figures from Boston Consulting Group), so the increased productivity may only be economical for highly paid mobile staff until prices reduce.

It seems clear that handhelds such as PDAs are considerably more popular than laptops among field staff. Salespeople find laptops cumbersome, and dislike the delay and distraction of booting-up a laptop in front of a customer. Alcatel, the telecoms equipment-maker, found that there was a fivefold increase in the amount of survey information sent back from the field by sales staff after they introduced handhelds. The vision of the future put forward by the technology gurus sees instant conferences between three or four people, no matter where they are. A customer might ring a call centre, and the agent could patch together a technician and a sales rep to solve the problem immediately, referring to knowledgebases, stock levels and appointment diaries in the process. In this context it's interesting to note that sales of PDAs appeared to drop in 2002. The next big thing, or a gadget craze that won't last?

Equally uncertain is the future of the 'next generation' 3G mobile technology. Large sums were paid by telephone operators for 3G licences, but some are now seeking to renegotiate the deadlines and coverage specifications for rolling out the technology, even in sophisticated Scandinavian markets. In some countries, hard-won licences have been handed back to telecoms regulators.

PCs get more mobile

While all IT shipments have been affected by the recent economic slowdown, it is still clear that the market for portable PCs is increasing at the expense of desktop models, as shown in the table below:

IT hardware shipments, UK

Year	1999	2000	2001	2002 (est.)	2003 (est.)
Portable PCs	923,437	1,290,661	1,343,525	1,542,729	1,787,047
Desktop PCs	4,338,201	4,662,374	4,150,355	4,013,830	3,980,245

Source: European Information Technology Observatory, 2002

EITO estimates that there are now a respectable 84 business PCs for every 100 white-collar workers in the UK, but a mere 33 PCs per 100 population overall (compared to 50 per 100 in Denmark). The Eurobarometer 53.0 survey carried out in spring 2000 and covering 15,700 EU citizens indicated that around 36% of UK households have desktop PCs, while 8% have laptops and 6% have palmtops or handhelds. These figures are all slightly above EU averages except for palmtops, where the UK rates third highest, after the Netherlands and Sweden. (For more detailed European comparisons, *see* p. 59.)

Breaking the speed barrier – is it worth the cost?

Definitions differ, but 'broadband' usually refers to data connections that are faster than the standard ISDN speeds of 128 kbs, say 0.5 Mbs upwards. Broadband services may be the key to more effective and widespread teleworking. A study by Booz Allen Hamilton in the US indicates that more teleworkers with high-speed connections (43%) can perform all of their work at home compared to those who have dial-up connections (31%). Twice as many high-speed users (44%) said they suffered no problems with speed or reliability compared to dial-up users (22%).[25] Conversely, broadband-providers are becoming increasing convinced that teleworking is the key application that will provide demand for broadband connections. A study carried out by Boston Consulting Group in 2001 quoted by DSL equipment suppliers Alcatel determined that homeworkers who have a DSL connection reduce their unproductive time by a factor of nine.

The Positively Broadband alliance of equipment manufacturers and telcos in the US also carried out a survey of 1000 registered voters on teleworking in April 2002. The survey found that of those who commute (just over two-thirds of the sample), about one-third would prefer the option of telecommuting over a higher salary. Of those who were not telecommuting but were working, some 46% said that it was either the nature of their job or the culture of their organisation that prevented them from doing so. Nobody responded that they had tried telecommuting but that it had failed.

In addition to providing high-speed Internet connections with better security, DSL broadband connections can offer a voice service, known as voice-over DSL or VoDSL, on the same line as the data connection. According to Alcatel, VoDSL can save 75% of the startup costs and 10% of the recurring costs of a separate voice line. It can also provide instant access to a corporate telephone directory, screen pop-up of names of corporate callers, as well as standard PBX-type features such as call transfer, call forwarding-on-busy, etc., all of which allow the corporate teleworker to work from home almost exactly as they would in the office.

Alcatel also gives some suggested prices that network operators could use for different teleworker service offerings. Interestingly, what appears to be exactly the same suggested service description is given for two offerings, Residential Deluxe and Basic Teleworker. However, at the time of writing, Residential is priced at $10/month/teleworker less than 'Basic' – so, just by defining a service as business-related, a premium can be charged. Corporate buyer, beware![26]

Britain is slowly following in the steps of the US and moving towards broadband communications. ISDN (which is a narrowband technology providing speeds of 128 kbs) is already available and widely used by teleworkers, while new technologies such as cable modems and ADSL are available in urban and suburban areas. The number of residential broadband connections in the UK reached 1 million in October 2002. The Oftel quarterly survey of business usage of the Internet interviewed 810 UK businesses with fewer than 250 employees in May 2002. The survey found that 63% of businesses have Internet connections. Of these, 55% use standard dial-up lines, while 36% have ISDN, 3% leased lines, 9% broadband and 1% other. The broadband connection figures are unchanged compared to February 2002, while the ISDN figure has shot up from 29%.[27]

As with ISDN, ADSL is available only within about 4 km of the nearest ADSL-capable exchange, so a re-run of the recent sagas which teleworkers have encountered in obtaining ISDN service in rural areas seems inevitable. The cost of converting exchanges, and the lack of serious competition or clear demand in a time of economic downturn, means that only exchanges with a large number of high-value business subscribers, such as city centres, are currently offering ADSL – at a price.

Virtual call centres

Call-centre employment is continuing to grow rapidly in the UK (there are now thought to be well over 5000 UK call centres), but this sector continues to cause controversy due to its high levels of staff turnover of 25–30%, anecdotal evidence of poor working conditions and high stress-levels for agents. For some years now technology has been available to allow call-centre agents to work from home, with calls diverted from the call centre through its ACD switch.

A survey by the Telework Association and the Institute of Employment Studies sponsored by Mitel and published in 1999 found that only 4% of call centres employed homeworkers, but that 42% expected to do so in future and 44% were cautiously positive about the idea, believing that it is a good idea to use homeworkers in some cases. Most major financial services operations in Britain were believed to be considering offering this option to staff. However, this type of 'virtual' call-centre employment does not appear to be taking off yet.

The call-centre managers surveyed saw barriers to homeworking due to the strong hands-on management tradition in the sector, worries about data security and fraud and about how to deliver training and team-building exercises to teleworkers. Informal training and consultation with other staff on unusual calls were also seen as being restricted for homeworkers.

In addition to the problems listed above, there is the cost of setting up equipment at agents' homes, and of redirecting calls. The AA's telework manager, who looks after around 150 home-based agents, reports that although their home-based agents are more productive, they need to be around 50% more productive to make up for the additional equipment and running costs. The AA has also instituted a policy of offering teleworking only to existing staff who are already working in their call centres, and not to new recruits.

The financial services trade union UNIFI points out that there are some

THE WILLOW 'VIRTUAL AGENT' NETWORK

Willow CSN, based in Florida, provides contract call-centre work to self-employed 'virtual agents' working from home for inbound call centres. Traditional call centres use the home-based agents both on a scheduled and an on-call basis to cover peaks in demand. Willow works with the Dade County School Board to train the agents, who must purchase their own PC costing about $3500. Special software and circuit boards are installed on the PCs.

Prospective agents first have to pass a basic computer literacy test using Windows. Then they have to complete a telephone-based HR questionnaire. Next, they have to complete a communications assessment involving live script-reading to test for pronunciation, voice tone, ability to use standard English and so on. Finally, a background check for criminal records is made. About 30–35% of applicants are successful and move on to the next stage, where they receive 40 hours of classroom training followed by up to two weeks of applied training (theoretical and simulated call handling) for particular tasks. The classroom training includes a module where each agent prepares a business plan containing details on how they plan to recoup their investment.

Willow maintains a call centre with about 70 agents in Fort Lauderdale, but the rest of its 1600 agents are home-based. A data centre in Atlanta hosts network facilities, routers and switches. Agents use a corporate intranet to log their PCs on, and also separately log into the telephone switch using touch-tone access codes. Although it's possible for agents to use a standard modem, Willow reports that up to 90% have high-speed Internet connections.

The agents themselves decide what hours they will work, and when, but Willow's scheduling system rewards those who volunteer more hours, and volunteer for unpopular shifts or clients. The company's clients post their scheduling needs (how many agents and what hours) and agents bid to be included. Currently Willow's clients include GE, Gap, the American Automobile Association and the Home Shopping Network. Call centres are charged for each call connection followed by an extra amount for each minute of agent time thereafter. Willow guarantees that:

- *its agents will rank in the top 20% of the call centre's agents or Willow will replace them and pay $500;*

- *clients' network costs for switching calls to the cyberagents will be 10% less than in-house costs or Willow pays the difference;*

- *clients' lost or abandoned calls and on-hold call time will be reduced by at least 50% or Willow will reduce the clients' network access cost by 10%;*

- *the rate of loss for cyberagents will be 50% less than the in-house rate.*

Adapted from information in Call Centre Management Review at **http://www.incoming.com** and **http://www.callcentermagazine.com** as well as from the Willow website **http:// www.willowcsn.com**

AGENTS AT HOME TAKE TIME TO SELL

Alliance and Leicester are among a number of companies trialling call-centre work carried out by teleworkers. In spring 2000, 12 experienced agents who work on loan applications began a teleworking trial. Support manager Andy Powell explains: 'We were simply running out of people in Leicester, and using teleworkers can allow us to cope with fluctuations in demand'. The scheme is already helping with workflow – some staff are now on standby for an additional two hours per day, up to a maximum of six hours a week.

Andy Powell also reports: 'We've had a couple of people ring in on a quiet Saturday afternoon with nothing to do who have actually asked to work, when it would have been too much of an effort to come into the office.' Productivity appears to have improved – the underwriters are producing more decisions and the agents are spending less time wrapping-up the administrative work after each call.

The technology used involves ISDN lines to allow for the security and monitoring facilities required for call-centre work. The teleworkers have to log out of their terminals if they take a break, and the terminals also lock up during periods of inactivity. 'Someone breaking in would have to know the system – you would have to know a whole raft of procedures taking up five or six screens, and creating a virtual security tunnel,' comments Andy. 'Also, we can see them logging on and logging off from the system, and we check that the addresses being searched match the addresses of applicants.'

Alliance and Leicester provided training on the different phone systems used with the teleworking equipment, as well as on the use of email. High-specification workstations are provided, including work cabinets from Kinnarps, non-slip mats, electrical surge protectors, fire extinguishers and additional lighting. Supervisors were also trained in the specific health and safety risks of homeworking.

Staff are working on their existing employment contracts with an addendum to cover the homeworking contract. They can be fully reinstated to office-based working if the trial doesn't work out.

Like other employers, Alliance and Leicester were surprised to find that interruption from pets and family members was not a problem for the homeworkers. In fact, other employers with agents at home such as BT, the AA and Northern Vending Services have found that although calls may take slightly longer, results are better (sales are up, for example). This is put down to the lack of distracting background noise from call-centre colleagues.

http://www.alliance-leicester.co.uk

disadvantages to homeworking that can affect call-centre agents, in particular the possible loss of premium payments for night and weekend working, and the loss of social interaction in the call centre that can make monotonous work more bearable.

The European Commission-funded research project TOSCA surveyed over 500 call centres around Europe and found only marginal experimentation with teleworking. One media sector organisation was using teleworkers in France. In Ireland an emergency service for the Electricity Supply Board was experimenting with teleworkers, as were two market research organisations. Ten Italian centres were using teleworkers. In contrast, an online global survey of call-centre managers taken at callcenterworld.com in May 2001 indicated that 21% of respondents were using 'agents/reps who work from home'.

The future for virtual call centres is unclear, but there is some speculation that the introduction of broadband connections to call centres will allow employers to provide exactly the same technology for agents at home where required, and may increase the usage of 'agents-at-home' in the medium term. (*See* **http://www-it.fmi.uni-sofia.bg/TOSCA/** for detailed results of the survey.)

ASK THE EXPERTS

Given the wide variety of factors that will affect the growth and type of teleworking in the next five years, what do the experts see when they consult their crystal balls? The Telework Association has expert contacts in a number of organisations and countries, some of whom contributed to this section.

Contributors

Michael Clark, data analyst and research fellow, Countryside and Community Research Unit, University of Gloucester **http://www.glos.ac.uk/ccru**
Kitty de Bruin, founder of the Dutch telework association and partner in many EU research projects on telework mailto:kitty.de.bruin@teleworkforum.nl
Gil Gordon, well-known US consultant and author of the world's most useful teleworking site at **http://www.gilgordon.com**
Ursula Huws, internationally famous researcher on teleworking-related issues since the 1980s, motivating force behind the UK LFS teleworking analyses and director of the EMERGENCE EU project on e-work and
e-outsourcing **http://dialspace.dial.pipex.com/town/parade/hg54**
Steve McPherson, BT Workstyle Consultancy Group **http://www.wfh.co.uk**
Joanne Pratt, US researcher who has published several papers analysing teleworker numbers mailto:joannepr@swbell.net
Stephen Simmons, Cornix Researcher and founder of the former National Association for Telework **http://www.cornix.co.uk**
Peter Skyte, Amicus/MSF section and former chair of the MSF Information Technology Professionals Association **http://www.amicus-m.org**
Louis Wustemann, formerly editor of *Flexible Working* magazine mailto:lw@sivill.demon.co.uk and contributor to *Teleworker Magazine*

Is the growth tailing off?

Teleworking appears to have reached about 20 million in the US, 9 million in the EU overall and 2 million in the UK under broad definitions, but there seems to be a tail-off in growth in the US. Where do you think it will stop? What percentage of the labour force will be teleworking in five years' time?

SS: It will stop at about twice the current US level.

SM: Growth will continue, quickly for the self-employed and gradually for organisations with the strong resistance to change culture exhibited by many decision-makers.

JP: I foresee a more fluid mixing of work and personal or family tasks for most workers. The growth won't be easy to measure because technology makes the new work-patterns seamless.

UH: The introduction of any new technology tends to follow a classic S-curve, with a slow start, followed by an accelerated uptake which then slows down again as saturation point is reached. We expect that by 2010 around 17 million Europeans will be working wholly or partly away from their offices using ICTs to connect to employers or clients. If employment continues to grow generally there will continue to be some growth in teleworking. The exception is the category that we call 'e-enabled self-employed'. These are people who do work which is not directly information-related (e.g. craftspeople) but who use ICTs to run their home-based businesses. The evidence is that the overall numbers of people who do this sort of work are not growing in Europe.

LW: I think the numbers will push up as the technology becomes cheaper and younger workers become older and assert work-life preferences. We might hit 3–4 million in the UK at the most.

GG: The more figures I see, the more I suspect them. In addition to definitional problems, we now have to cope with the blending of various forms of telework into a broader umbrella category of mobility. It will become harder and more meaningless to count 'pure' telework. The trends that create interest in and need for mobility – improved technology, personal lifestyle choices and corporate operating pressures – will only grow in strength.

MC: Linking telework to growth in the service sector, particularly the growth in self-employment in these sectors, points to continued growth. Employment in the banking, finance and insurance sector increased by 39% in the ten years to spring 2002. Self-employment in this sector grew by 25% over the same period. It can be suggested that the current housing-market boom has also led to an increased movement of actual/potential teleworkers to more rural locations due to lower rural house prices.

KB: More and more work is knowledge work done with the help of computers. In the Netherlands we are aiming for 15% of the labour force teleworking but it depends partly on the percentage of knowledge workers.

What does broadband do for teleworkers that they can't do already?

SS: Keep data online rather than in shoe-boxes (after all, the search engines for shoe-boxes are poor).

SM: It's about helping to do some things at a more acceptable rate, such as online processing of data – for example, processing of scanned customer correspondence.

PS: Ability to transfer graphics, video, etc., more efficiently.

JP: Having a fast, always-on connection vastly enhances teleworking. Keyword searching means less frustration and time lost on simple questions like 'What time is it in Hong Kong?' and 'Where's that article I read last week?'.

LW: Talk happily over video (if anyone ever decides that they want to).

GG: There's the convenience factor of being able to do what you can already do on analogue even faster. And there are things that are only possible with broadband like large file transfers, better use of real-time conferencing and faster responses for transaction-based applications like call-centre work. The compelling need is where you need to carry out tasks in the second category.

MC: I don't think broadband will have much impact on how teleworkers operate or communicate with existing employers or clients. But given that many contracts won depend on informal networks of communications, video conferencing will greatly improve the ability of the teleworker to tap into these networks and improve communication.

KB: Have meetings online, see more results and information about projects through better collaboration tools. I see lots of opportunities for online consulting, searching for work, feedback sessions and so on.

Is teleworking causing a new form of sexual discrimination?

Why do there appear to be more male multilocational teleworkers than female, but more female full-time, home-based teleworkers? Do the figures represent some form of sexual discrimination, and if so, how can this be tackled?

SM: In my organisation this isn't the case. I think where there's an informed debate this doesn't usually apply, so raising people's awareness through improved communication should help.

UH: The figures represent the occupational segregation which exists already in the workforce. Men are more likely than women to be on the middle-to-senior level grades and in the technical, professional and managerial occupations which are involved in this type of work (involving a varied range of duties, interfacing with clients, etc.). Women are more likely to be on lower grades and in single-skill occupations involving doing the same thing from the same spot such as word-processing, editing, proofreading, virtual call-centre work, etc. The reasons for this are complex. There are both push and pull factors. Women with children often choose work that fits in with being available at short notice for their families, and fit in with the short working days dictated by school timetables. Employers adapt jobs to be attractive to this workforce, from whom they can expect reasonably low wage demands and a long-term commitment – a process of mutual adaptation takes place. 'Male' jobs are designed to attract ambitious people seeking variety and scope for development and prepared to put in long hours.

PS: There is both sexual discrimination and job segregation. More men than women are at the top of organisational hierarchies. The higher up the organisation, the more control you have over working life and pattern. I also think there is a skills and pay differentiation between full-time home-based teleworkers and male multilocational teleworkers.

JP: The US data shows that there are more male teleworkers because there are more male workers. In fact, equivalent percentages of male and female employees telework. But women with children under six years are a marked exception. Some 66% work at home, compared to 39% of male parents of young children. I think this shows that women who are their own boss can adjust their schedules to take care of a young child and work-tasks. As the child enters its teens, the gender differences narrow. Apparently, the dads don't mind supervising a self-sufficient child.

LW: The majority of multilocational jobs are made up of male-dominated jobs such as sales reps and service engineers. This sort of thing will only be solved by a gradual loosening of stereotypes and gender assumptions.

GG: I wasn't aware of this, but assuming that it's correct, it may reflect something about the gender mix in the job categories. But if you are talking about men and women doing the same type of jobs, then it suggests some sort of self-imposed limitation based on traditional divisions of household duties.

KB: Of course it represents discrimination but this has been so for years and years – it is harder for women to get top posts. Now, more and more women are highly educated – but even so it will take maybe another ten years before we have equality. It depends also on each country's culture.

How can rural areas compete with cities and suburbs for telework?

Will the satellite solution for non-broadband areas work for rural teleworkers?

SS: The jury's still out.

SM: Yes – why not?

PS: I suspect that the difference is not just about technology, but more about the nature of organisations which are based in cities – they tend to have a higher degree of centralised location.

JP: Broadband, in whatever form it can be supplied, will narrow the gap between geographical areas.

LW: I think government will have to step in to make sure that broadband or an equivalent gets to most places.

GG: Well, we've learned that they can't compete for long by lower labour-costs alone, because there will always be a third-world country with lower labour-costs. I think the key is to find ways for rural labour to create value – not just to do the same work, but to do it cheaper. Some rural areas seem to be getting broadband access faster than cities by bypassing wired infrastructure.

MC: The growth in telework in rural areas is probably driven more by lifestyle choice and housing markets than by technology. Broadband will facilitate telework but not create it.

KB: It depends on the speed and the price of the broadband solutions for rural areas.

Does teleworking reduce traffic congestion?

SS: No. Increasing congestion causes increasing telework.

SM: We have some independent figures that suggest it does for BT. The concept of choosing not to travel in the rush hour when you don't always have to is a no-brainer.

UH: There's no evidence to support this. But neither is there much evidence of the opposite. There is a desperate need for some rigorous and well-designed research in this area. The most plausible hypothesis is that there will be a reduction in rush-hour peaks with traffic spread more evenly over different times of the day and different routes.

PS: Not as yet. Perhaps the development of congestion-charging in some cities (Durham, London) might begin to enforce a change.

JP: Not as much as was originally hoped. There is some time-shifting of trips as more work is carried out in homes and locations distant from the employer.

LW: Not that I have seen.

GG: Not that I have seen, at least not in a sustainable way. The problem is so bad in most cities that the reduction caused by telework won't even be noticed. There's always one more car waiting to get into the congestion to replace the one that leaves. Since the end of World War II, we have glorified the value of single-occupant vehicles and created infrastructure and land-use patterns to support them. We are in a mess of over-reliance and telework can't undo this.

MC: There is no empirical evidence of this but one can speculate that it has altered transport-use patterns – fewer short-hop car commutes but more long-distance train and plane trips to visit clients.

KB: A study by the City of Amsterdam calculated that 100,000 teleworkers would reduce the traffic by 300 million kilometres a year and reduce CO_2 emissions from private cars by 2.6% per year.

Work-life balance: why the gap between demand and reality?

SS: The transaction and opportunity costs are high. Social evolution will occur, involving new vernaculars for work.

SM: Many organisations still seem to operate on a traditional basis, even though they may have procedures and policies in place which they do not utilise. This is not so prevalent in companies with recruitment and retention issues that can be addressed by work-life balance policies.

UH: Most decent-paying jobs bring with them an expectation of putting in long hours and being available at short notice. 'Commitment' is seen as putting job requirements above family ones. Most of the time, part-time or other family-friendly options imply a degree of interchangeability between workers, thus making the jobs unsuitable for high-flying or leadership-potential positions. It's assumed that you need to have heroes at the top on standby to deal with any crisis that arises.

PS: I am not completely convinced that teleworking as practised by larger employers always improves work-life balance. It can liberate but it can also imprison.

JP: Wait for the kids to grow up. Eighty-six percent of US college students are online. They use instant messaging and jump around the Internet. They didn't have to learn this technology. They were born with a cellphone in their mouths, not a silver spoon.

GG: I hate to pick on them again, but it's the middle-aged, middle-level managers who are the obstacle. They cling to old assumptions about the value and nature of supervision and continue to stand in the way. It is not because they are particularly mean or untrusting. They have maybe 30 years of experience and reinforcement that equates close supervision with good supervision. This will only change when those managers in my age-range (early to mid-50s and older) retire, die or are downsized in large numbers. Alternatively if those managers encounter enough corporate pain for which telework is one possible solution things may change. I have seen many obstinate managers turn into telework accepters (if not supporters) when they are squeezed by enough pain. And it's not as if the whole lot is bad − I know plenty of managers in this age-group who are strong telework supporters.

LW: Fear and ignorance. The right to request is a start, and perhaps as Gil says, it will happen as the older managers retire. Better design of new housing might make a difference but would only affect a minority.

MC: Is there any empirical evidence for this? If so, I think it is more to do with personal priorities and work culture. While many like the idea of flexible working, the work culture in Britain would not see such activities as enhancing one's ability to scale the career ladder. I think telework is best suited to people with an established reputation or career, or those with alternative lifestyle aspirations. It's an issue of management as well as of employee culture.

KB: Is there such a gap in the UK? In Holland telework is often part of work-life balance programmes. Awareness programmes by some ministries might help.

Will we ever see a change to management by results?

What needs to be done to make this happen? Are there really any trade secrets to successfully managing dispersed teams, or is it just common sense?

SS: No, and nothing needs to be done. It's a good technique in some circumstances. For trade secrets, you'll have to read my book.

SM: Well, it's definitely not common sense, because it's not commonly found. I think it's rather a question of applying best management expertise.

UH: I'm writing a book about this – watch this space!

PS: Too many employers still monitor work performance by input (time spent, etc.) rather than output. There is also too much use of command and control of workers.

JP: While common sense goes a long way to facilitating virtual teams, skilled management helps a lot.

LW: That depends on where management fashion goes. Management by results may be necessary for teleworking but it is not straightforward common sense. There is just as good an argument to be made for management by inputs, which militates against remote management. Managing remote teams seems to be about listening very carefully to what people say so that you hear about problems before they build up.

GG: I've long maintained that management at a distance is essentially the same as management up close – only a few things need to be done differently, a brand-new approach is not required. The problem is that generations of managers have become lazy and sloppy about the basics of good management and have allowed close proximity to substitute for good practice. This is a latent problem in the office that really shows up at a distance. But I'm thinking that managing a dispersed team is quickly becoming a must-have skill – almost every organisation has these situations even where there is no telework, such as dealing with multinational subsidiaries, or experienced staffers who refuse to relocate. It's becoming increasingly rare to see any manager have his or her full team in the same office, especially if we are talking about professional-level staff.

KB: A lot of American companies have always worked in this way, and more and more companies are changing to profit/loss responsibilities allocated per department, which will influence things a lot. Competition will drive the change automatically. And you do need the right ICT tools to make it happen.

Does teleworking lead to longer working hours and more time pressure?

SS: It makes work more bursty – not more problems, but different problems.

SM: It can do, and this is a real issue for many. However, many people already work very long hours in the office and then have to journey home afterwards.

PS: It varies widely but in many cases, teleworking can lead to longer working hours as work-pressures intensify.

JP: This is my big concern. It's not so much that people don't have access to

technology − time will take care of that − but that we haven't evolved guidelines for using our tools and are still treating them as toys. I'm expecting a backlash as employees resent the expectation that they'll be available 24 x 7. It will be interesting to see if the backlash takes the form of new legislation, or whether the reaction to stressful overwork is solved in ways we can't anticipate.

LW: It does if you are disorganised like me.

MC: For those who are self-employed, yes.

GG: Possibly, but it's not a direct result. When work and life are under the same roof, the boundaries that used to exist between the two become permeable and sometimes disappear. The technology that enables so much telework also allows people to become leashed to their work. I believe the bigger problem exists for employers who have become blinded to the value of creating cross-training and management-succession plans because they think that their key people will always be available anytime, anywhere. This is a huge risk.

KB: In the beginning, yes. Most teleworkers are volunteers and want to prove everything is working well. Generally people who choose teleworking are independent, self-motivating types. Most of the people I interviewed for my book said that telework reduces stress. The fact that they work late is still seen as 'overtime' even though they are choosing their work-schedule themselves. The timesheets of teleworkers seem to show a shift in working time involving an early start, less work between 16:00 hours and 20:00 hours followed by a peak on the network again between 20:00 and midnight.

Are IT departments the real barrier to increased teleworking?

SM: Not all are against change, but they are under pressure to deliver with limited resources to a fixed pattern (named places and hours). When we suggest they need to support people whenever and wherever, not surprisingly, they don't often jump with joy at the prospect.

UH: In some cases IT departments have accumulated too much power in the decision-making process, and the technology has become the master instead of the servant it should be. IT staff often see installation and maintenance in people's homes as a hassle which they resist. I'm not convinced this is a very widespread problem. Control-freak line managers who want to have their staff under their eye are a much bigger problem.

PS: I think the real barriers are organisational and managerial, not technical.

JP: They are part of the problem. Their first reaction is 'I don't have enough staff now' and 'I don't have budget for home-office equipment'. The reflex response is to assume they'll have to service PCs in teleworkers' homes.

GG: I don't think so. IT departments may be unintentional barriers because of the increased pressure put on them to ensure network security, but otherwise I have found that most IT groups are fairly willing telework supporters, and may even be strong telework users. The company function that has much more potential to roadblock is human resources.

KB: Not if the board has decided on telework and provided the right budget. Security is their main concern, but this is not really a major barrier. In Holland even the tax department and the police telework.

Is there any future for public telecentres?

(Not cybercafés or touchdown/hotdesking facilities that are owned and used by one company.)

SS: No. The successful examples are cases of the 'spotlight effect' where an excessively good resource is applied – the same resources would produce equally good results wherever it was applied.

SM: BT has no evidence with which to make a response.

UH: Possibly in areas where the market isn't big enough to support commercial cybercafés. I travel a lot and have noticed that the poorer the country, the easier it is to find public access to the Internet. The place I had most difficulty finding somewhere to check email was California – in the end I found one in a Latino ghetto where migrant workers were emailing their families in Mexico. They've become a bit like laundromats – something which is only necessary to provide publicly for people who can't afford to own the technology itself.

JP: No! What may work are business centres like Kinko's which rent cubicles or offices by the hour, week or month and carry the cost of the real estate, equipment and admin staff.

LW: They seem like a very good idea but they perhaps belong to a different age, unless someone can find a solid profit-model on which to base them.

MC: My research indicates that there is no evidence such centres can facilitate the support of teleworking activities. I do think there is a role for geographically based teleworker networks, particularly for the self-employed, who can share ideas and work and find out about the opportunities around them.

GG: They are a piece of the puzzle, but not a big one. The technology that might raise their value is WiFi – wireless networks. That might make them another choice of drop-in location. Where all they offer is access-by-the-minute and *latte*, I don't think they are sustainable.

KB: Only if they provide facilities not available at home. They have failed in Holland to date. I do see a possibility for neighbourhood centres that provide meeting space, lunch, cultural activities, and perhaps computer repair and backup services.

Will there be an anti-teleworking backlash?

Or is the genie out of the bottle – people see how much sense there is in working this way and there's no going back?

SS: Teleworking is just another form of work now, like office work or shop work. It's not rocket science.

SM: Where it's done well it succeeds. Most large organisations seem to have a significant but unidentified population of tacit teleworkers who persist in trying to work flexibly despite a lack of support from the organisation.

UH: Success should be measured by a growth in the numbers of people doing this at a particular time (and the LFS results suggest there is a background steady growth). Teleworking is about increasing choice, which includes the choice to drop something when it stops working for you.

LW: Several good schemes have been overtaken by organisational restructuring. Don't forget the old saw – how do you make God laugh? Tell him your plans.

MC: The key thing people forget is the importance of the work being locationally independent of the client. Translators were locationally independent long before the advent of the PC. They used paper, pen and fax.

GG: This isn't an either-or question. Cases of true telework failure are fewer and fewer, and most are due to bad implementation, not a bad concept. It is no more likely that organisations will decide to herd everyone back into the office five days a week than it is that we will all give up laptops and PCs and return to dumb terminals. We are moving along a path to continued, broadened use of mobility. Telework will fade away in that the smarter organisations will realise that the key issue is work. Tell people what is expected of them, give them the resources, spell out the deliverables and then let them deliver. The where, when and how is increasingly less important.

International perspective

COMPARATIVE RESEARCH

United States

Current Population Survey

The US Current Population Survey (CPS) is the equivalent of the UK LFS and is based on a similar size of sample of about 60,000 people. Its questions about homeworking are not asked in the same way, which makes direct comparison problematic – it only asks about work at home, while the UK LFS attempts to capture some mobile teleworkers who work 'from home, using home as a base', as well.

The last time that the homeworking questions were asked, in 2001, it was found that 25 million people were working at home in the US for at least one day a week (the total US working population during this period was approximately 132 million). Of these, 19.8 million or around 80% used a PC, and 63% email or the Internet. Using the PC usage figures, about 11% of those in employment could be considered teleworkers. Using the email/Internet figures (probably more closely comparable with the UK LFS definition of 'requiring a computer and telephone to complete their work'), about 9% of those in employment could be considered teleworkers, compared to about 6% in Britain. (**http://www.bls.gov/news.release/homey.nr0.htm**)

- About half of those who usually worked at home were employees taking work home on an unpaid basis, and these people usually put in about seven hours a week at home.
- A further 17% had a formal arrangement to be paid by their employer for work at home – these people worked about 18 hours a week at home on average.
- The remaining homeworkers (about 30%) were self-employed – a considerably lower figure than the 43% of UK teleworkers who are reported to be self-employed.
- Nearly four-fifths of those regularly working at home were employed in managerial, professional and sales jobs – similar proportions to those found in the UK.
- The US Department of Labor reported that 'women and men were about equally likely to do some job-related work at home', but that the 'work-at-home rate for parents was slightly higher than for persons without children'.

Analysis by Joanne Pratt of previous CPS figures has shown that there is one sector where women with young children are over-represented – those who are self-employed and work at home. For this class, the participation rates in 1991 were 5.9% of men, and 25.5% of women. Further, women without children represented 19.1% participation while those with children under six years showed 43.6% participation. Joanne Pratt believes that women with small children are choosing home-based self-employment as the only feasible way of combining work and childcare – but there is no evidence to date as to whether they choose this option because former employers would not allow them to telework.

The ITAC surveys
The American telework association, which has had several names and incarnations (International Telework Association and Council (ITAC), Telecommute America), and is now known as Telework America, has undertaken a number of small-scale surveys on teleworking.

In 2000, the survey results indicated some 28 million people working away from the office in the US – an increase of 20.6% over the previous year. Of this 28 million, 24% worked on the road, 22% worked from home, 8% worked in telework centres and 4% worked in satellite offices. Nearly half (43%) worked in more than one of these locations. Only nine million were working at home at least one full day per week. The incomes of teleworkers tended to be higher (in the lower $50,000 range) than those of non-teleworkers (in the lower $30,000 range). Teleworkers also tended to have larger homes than non-teleworkers (the average size difference was 500 square feet). Teleworkers' commuting times were longer (63 minutes) on average than those of non-teleworkers (45 minutes). Some 77% were more satisfied with their career now than before they began teleworking. On average teleworkers worked remotely for about 20 hours per week.

In 2001 the survey showed that two-thirds of teleworkers expressed increased job satisfaction. Four-fifths (80%) felt a greater commitment to their employer. This survey was carried out by the Social Science Research Centre of Old Dominion University by the method of random-digit dial telephone interviews, followed by purging out business numbers and selecting interviews to create a sample of 1170 interviews geographically representative of US households – a method intended to ensure that small-sample surveys are comparable to results produced by the CPS.

AT&T's telework surveys
The telework programme at AT&T has been in existence for a decade. The latest results for their annual employee survey[28] (2001–2002) indicate that frequent teleworkers are working from home more often (up by 7%), but occasional teleworkers are spending more time in the office than in the past (working from home for these teleworkers was down by 7%).

Looking at managers who work from home at least one day a week, AT&T reports that they are more likely to be female, aged 35–44, and work in the R&D, IT, marketing or sales divisions. They usually have company-paid equipment and are more likely to have company-paid broadband access to the AT&T intranet.

The biggest benefit for the company by far is increased productivity. AT&T teleworkers report that they gain about one hour of productive time each day at home – estimated to be worth about $65m a year to the company. The company also found that intensive teleworkers (known in AT&T as 'full-time virtual office managers') receive higher managerial appraisals than their office-bound peers. The teleworkers report that nearly two-thirds of the time they save by not commuting is spent on work, but there is also increased productivity per unit hour in addition to the commuting benefit.

Overall, comparing satisfaction figures between those whose teleworking equipment is paid for by the company and those whose do not receive financial assistance, the authors conclude that 'paying or reimbursing telework setup costs is an excellent example of an employee benefit that quantitatively increases personal and job satisfaction'.

Retention is another key aspect of the telework scheme for AT&T. More than half (56%) of the teleworkers who had received competing job offers factored the ability to work at home into the decision to stay with the company. In addition, teleworkers say if they were told they could no longer work from home, one in three (33%) would look for another job within the company or quit.

Interestingly, although the report was written before the 11 September tragedy, the authors highlight in their conclusion the positive effects of a distributed workforce on business continuity in the face of adverse events as an underestimated benefit of teleworking.

Of course in a company the size of AT&T, there are some employees who cease teleworking. The reasons for stopping are interesting. Over a third (36%) find that, due to lack of technology, they are less productive at home (about half the AT&T teleworkers have broadband connections – the rest rely on dial-up). Another third report that they have changed job or manager. Over a quarter report that they experience a lack of face-to-face communication. However, nearly one-fifth do so because they have received a promotion, which ties in with the results showing higher performance appraisal for teleworkers. The survey also indicates that 60% of teleworkers think telework has no effect on their career, while 32% think it has a positive effect. Only 6% believe there are negative consequences.

The authors claim that when they look further into the data, five of the six reasons given by non-teleworkers for not teleworking relate to access speed (broadband). At this point it should be mentioned that AT&T does sell broadband, so they would say that, wouldn't they?

Public-sector teleworking

A number of measures have been approved by the government to promote teleworking, particularly in the public sector. According to figures reported by the US General Accounting Office in 2001, about 16.5 million employees telecommute at least once a month, with 9.3 million employees telecommuting at least once a week.[29]

IDC reports drop in home offices
Research by IDC in 2001 indicated that the number of US households with an income-generating home office declined for the first time. A detailed examination of the figures shows that the number of households with full-time home-based businesses continued to grow, but that part-time home businesses dropped significantly as households found it more difficult to support casual, part-time businesses – they were moving to full-time operation or ceasing activity.

According to Raymond Boggs, spokesperson for IDC, 'more corporate homeworkers are returning to traditional work practices, even as colleagues are starting to work from home for the first time'. IDC found that roughly one-third of US households had a home office. However the growth rate had been only about 0.6%, the same as for households in general. Of these home offices, 78.9% had a PC, a figure that agrees closely with the US CPS results for people who work at home and use a PC. Nearly the same proportion had printers, and about half of the PC-equipped offices also had scanners, but only around 10% of home offices had networked PCs.

Figure 3.1: Teleworking prevalence in the EU

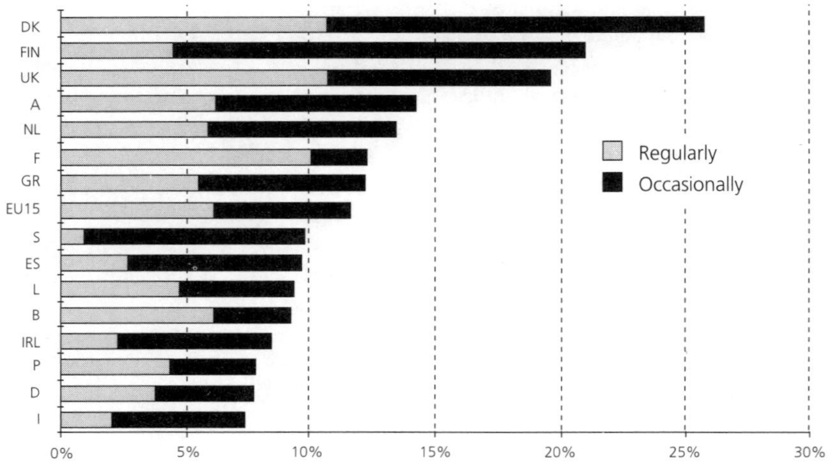

Source: Eurobarometer 54.0, 2000. Base 3730 respondents

Europe

Eurobarometer

The European Commission carries out regular, widescale polls around Europe on a variety of issues through its Eurobarometer surveys, which have a sample size of around 15,700 in the 15 member states. In the year 2000 the survey found that around 6.1% of respondents were teleworking regularly, with a further 6.6% teleworking occasionally.

European Working Conditions Survey

The European Foundation for the Improvement of Living and Working Conditions sponsored a spring 2000 survey of 21,703 Europeans about whether they teleworked at home. About 1% reported that they teleworked all the time, while 5% said they spent at least a quarter of their time teleworking from home. The UK figures were significantly higher.

Figure 3.2: Teleworking from home in the EU

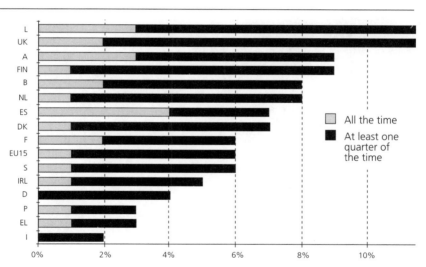

Source: Third European Survey on Working Conditions, 2000

ECATT

The European Commission's Information Society Technologies directorate sponsored the EcATT survey, which interviewed 7500 people in the EU member states and 4000 businesses in early 1999.

Figure 3.3: Types of regular telework as a percentage of labour force

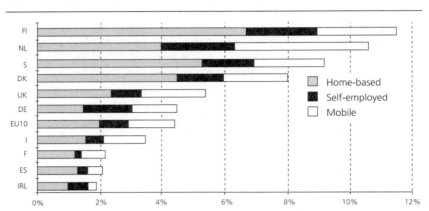

Source: Telework data report (population survey) ten countries in comparison, EcATT project, Bonn, 2000

- One-third of EcATT teleworkers are described as 'occasional', working from home less than one day a week.
- Of the regular teleworkers, over half spend hours equivalent to just one day a week teleworking. Less than 7% work at home full-time.
- 81% of regular (more than one day a week) teleworkers are men.
- 68% of teleworkers are in the 30–49 age-group.
- Most teleworkers have high levels of education or are qualified professionals (60%) – twice the figure for the labour force as a whole (30%).
- The larger the company, the more likely it is to have teleworkers. More than half of all European teleworkers are employed in companies with over 250 employees.
- Teleworking is most prevalent in the financial/business services sector (8.5%) and the distribution, transport and communications sector (5.5%).
- The differences between teleworking and non-teleworking households are small, indicating that the media stereotype of women teleworking to combine family and work duties is inaccurate.

According to EcATT, there are considerable differences in the prevalence of teleworking in different European countries ranging from 2.8% in Spain to 16.8% in Finland. The project estimated the total European figure at 9 million in autumn 1999 based on its small-scale surveys of employers and the general population (**http://www.ecatt.com**).

THE EUROPEAN COMMISSION'S TELEWORK TRIAL

Two directorates of the European Commission – Employment and Social Affairs, and Information Society – jointly carried out a teleworking trial in 1999. According to John Sherwin, who designed and monitored the trial for the Commission, the teleworkers – who all spent part of their time in the normal office – carried out four main activities when they were teleworking:

- *preparing for meetings and visits to member states;*
- *drafting reports;*
- *reading background materials;*
- *dealing with emails.*

John found that of the 169 teleworkers, 87% reported that their personal productivity improved as a result of teleworking – only 2% reported a deterioration. The main advantages were found to be fewer interruptions, and the ability to work at more convenient times of the day. Advantages affecting fewer than 50% of the teleworkers were reductions in stress, improvements in working environment, and improved work-life balance.

There was some disparity between the views of the teleworkers and those of their managers. For example, most of teleworkers considered that they were getting more work done, but only a minority of their managers agreed. Most thought there was no change. However, most managers considered the quality and timeliness of work improved. The managers were also less satisfied with communication arrangements for the teleworker, and for their team members, than the teleworkers. Over two-thirds of the teleworkers' colleagues found that there was no impact on them due to teleworking, and a substantial minority reported that they preferred it when their colleague was teleworking.

SIBIS

The SIBIS project carried out by the EcATT team in 2002 came up with a figure of 2.4% of the labour force teleworking regularly for part of the week in the UK, compared to 2.1% in the EU (sample size 11,382, of which 1000 were in the UK). The SIBIS results are very much at odds with the LFS (sample size 69,000), with SIBIS reporting a stagnation of homeworking and a boom in occasional, mobile and self-employed teleworking (**http://www.sibis-eu.org**).

FAMILIES

The FAMILIES project carried out 107 case studies of various types of atypical working, including some teleworkers, in different types of family structures in Ireland, Italy, Germany and Denmark. The researchers suggest that women are more likely to adopt home-based teleworking for family reasons, while men are more likely to do it for work or personal reasons. Over 75% of those interviewed reported increased job satisfaction.

Stress levels appeared to be similar to the wider European workforce, except for couples with no children, where they were higher, often due to a change to self-employment or to long working hours. Also, men were more likely to report that they felt their partners or family were more frequently fed up with the pressure of their job than the general male workforce. Where there was a change in domestic responsibilities, there was sometimes an improvement in the share-out of chores where a man began e-working, but when women began e-working there tended to be a deterioration.

Over two-thirds were happy with their working arrangements, and these tended to be people with more than six months' experience of the new working arrangement, who had overcome 'teething problems'. Single parents were least likely to expect to continue e-working indefinitely, reflecting an aspiration to return to more conventional arrangements.[30]

e-living project

The e-living project is a 'longitudinal panel survey' where each subject is studied several times over a period of time. The e-living sample consists of 1750 households in Britain, Bulgaria, Germany, Italy, Israel and Norway. Of the different categories studied, one is similar to teleworking – the e-living 'Net homeworkers' who use a PC and Internet connection. The factors strongly associated with Net homeworking include living in Britain or Germany, having a degree and high-level PC skills, being self-employed, being able to control your own working hours, having an above-average pay rate and longer than average working hours. Commuting time is not associated with teleworking.[31]

International

EMERGENCE project

The first attempt to look at e-working on a global scale, including issues of outsourcing, is the EMERGENCE project, funded under the European Commission's Information Society Technologies Programme. During 2000 this project surveyed 7000 establishments with more than 50 employees in the 15 EU member states plus Hungary, Poland and the Czech Republic. A series of extensions to the project has since been researching e-working in smaller companies in some countries, and has extended the surveys to Australia and some Asian countries.

Project director Ursula Huws of the Institute of Employment Studies summarises: 'This study looks at employers' use of e-working, and not at the total number of teleworkers in the way that the Labour Force Survey does in Britain. It also gives some indications of the market areas for e-working.' EMERGENCE found that nearly half of all European employers now use e-work (27 million out of 55 million). Around 11% are using e-lancers (e-working freelancers) while around 10% use multilocational e-working employees. Both of these forms of e-work seem to be emerging as mainstream business activities. EMERGENCE takes a rather broader approach than narrow questions about use of ICTs when working at home. The project defines 'e-work' as 'activities involving processing of information and its delivery via a telecommunications link carried out away from the main premises of an organisation'. There are four main categories as shown in the figure below.

		Contractual	
		Internal/employees	*Outsourced*
Type of workplace	*Individualised (away from 'office' premises)*	Employed telehomeworkers Mobile employees	Freelance teleworkers or mobile workers
	On shared 'office' premises	Remote back offices /call centres Employees working in telecottages or other third-party premises	Specialist business service supply establishments Outsourced call centres

Source: Huws U, O'Regan S, eWork in Europe, Institute for Employment Studies report 380

The EMERGENCE researchers found that the stereotype of teleworking – full-time home-based work by employees – is one of the least popular forms of e-work, used by 1.4% of employers. In addition to looking at the type of e-work practised, the EMERGENCE project studies shifts in the location of employment within and between European regions, and globally. The surveys looked at both who is using e-work and who is supplying it. The survey results show about 42% of British employers using e-work, just under the European average of 49%. About 18% of British employers report that they supply e-work (eServices) – again below the European average of 21%.

The types of work outsourced (and so the markets for e-working) are interesting in that they relate quite closely to the types of e-working tasks advertised for freelancers on websites such as smarterwork.com or even the Telework Association's own online e-zine. The apparently low level of sales may well be due to call centres which carry out telesales tending to merge their activities into general customer services.

Work arrangemenn	% of employers using
E-working within organisations	
Any e-employees at all	11.8
Multilocational teleworking	9.9
Employees in remote back-offices	6.8
Home-based teleworking employees	1.4
Remote call centre outside own region	1.4
Employees in telecentres/telecottages/offices owned by third parties	0.9
Call-centre employees in telecottage/telecentre	0.3
Outsourced e-working	
Any e-outsourcing	43
E-outsourcing within own region	34.5
E-outsourcing to another region (usually within own country)	18.3
Outsourced call centre	15
E-lancers	11.4
Outsourced call centre with telecoms link	11.1
E-outsourcing to companies in other countries	5.3

Source: Huws U, O'Regan S, eWork in Europe, Institute for Employment Studies report 380

Figure 3.4 E-working used by function

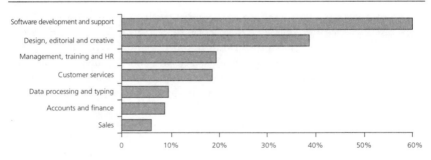

EMERGENCE has also attempted to estimate future trends in e-working.[32]

Type of e-worker	2000	2010
Telehomeworkers (person equivalent)	810,000	3,170,000
Multilocational e-workers (person equivalent)	3,700,000	14,332,000
E-lancers	1,450,000	3,040,000
E-enabled self-employed	3,080,000	6,580,000
Totals	**9,040,000**	**27,122,000**

Source: **http://www.emergence.nu**

The ILO analysis

The UN's labour body, the ILO, published a detailed analysis of teleworking in 2001.[33] In the main, the document compiles results from existing research worldwide and comments on labour-related and social issues. It contains information on countries outside the EU and North America which is often hard to obtain.

The Australian Bureau of Statistics counts two types of teleworkers – those who can access their employers' computer from home through a modem (6.4% of those in employment in November 1999) and those who have a telework agreement with their employer to work from home (4.8% of those in employment). These figures are almost triple those recorded for February 1998.

Statistics Canada used its workplace and employee survey in 2000 to look at work at home in conjunction with motivation, remuneration, reimbursement of work-at-home costs and ICT equipment usage. Unfortunately the results have not yet been published.

In Singapore, where PC and Internet use is among the highest in the world, a 1999 IT Household survey found that half of all households have PCs, 42% have Internet connections, and 19.9% of home PCs get work-related use.

TRENDS AND ACTIONS

Europe

The EU Framework Agreement

At European level, a framework agreement between employers and trade unions on teleworking was concluded in 2002 (**http://europa.eu.int/ comm/employment_social/news/2002/jul/145_en.html** or **http://www.ueapme.com/docs/various/2002/teleworkfinal.pdf**).The main points of the agreement can be summarised as follows:

- Telework is voluntary for the work or the employer concerned.
- Teleworking may be required as part of a worker's initial job description or it may be engaged in as a voluntary arrangement subsequently. Unless telework is part of the initial job description, the decision to telework is reversible which might imply a return to the employer's premises at either the worker's or the employer's request.
- Teleworking does not affect employment status.
- Teleworking should not affect employment conditions.
- The employer is responsible for taking appropriate measures to ensure that data protection laws are complied with. The teleworker is responsible for complying with data protection rules.
- The employer respects the privacy of the teleworker.

- Any monitoring system must be proportionate to the objective and comply with Directive 90/270 covering VDUs.

- As a general rule, the employer is responsible for providing, installing and maintaining the equipment necessary for regular telework unless the teleworker uses their own equipment. The employer is responsible for loss or damage to equipment and data used by the teleworker.

- If telework is performed on a regular basis, the employer compensates or covers the costs directly caused by the work, in particular communication costs.

- The teleworker must take good care of equipment provided and must not collect or distribute illegal material via the Internet.

- The employer is responsible for the protection of the occupational health and safety of the teleworker and must inform the teleworker of the relevant company policies. The teleworker is responsible for applying these policies correctly. To verify this, the employer, workers' representatives and relevant authorities have access to the telework place within the limits of national legislation and agreements. Where the teleworker is working at home, there must be prior notice and agreement.

- The teleworker's workload and performance standards are the same as those of comparable employees at the employer's premises.

- The employer takes measures to prevent the teleworker from becoming isolated from the working community in the company, e.g. by providing opportunities to meet with colleagues on a regular basis.

- Teleworkers should have the same access to training and career-development opportunities as comparable workers at the employer's premises and be subject to the same appraisal policies.

- Teleworkers should receive appropriate training for the technical equipment at their disposal and at the characteristics of this form of work organisation. Teleworkers' supervisors and colleagues may also require training.

- Teleworkers have the same collective rights as other workers and no obstacles can be put in their way in relation to communicating with workers' representatives.

The reaction from trade unions has been fairly positive to date, except for the lack of connection of the right to return to the employment contract. The detail of the agreement makes it clear that whether teleworking is required is specified in the job description, a document which can be changed by employers easily, rather than in the employment contract. It is not yet clear how the agreement will be implemented in the UK and Ireland but a route encompassing a new legal status for codes of practice may be required. Otherwise the agreement will be enforceable in the other member states but voluntary in the UK and Ireland. Implementation is likely to occur through a code of practice agreed by the social partners in a process co-ordinated by the DTI, with input from the Telework Association.

EU teleworking tax and employment laws

A number of European countries have also made individual rulings mainly relating to the income-tax consequences of teleworking.

- In Denmark, computers supplied by employers for private (not business) use are no longer subjected to tax as long as they are also available to be used for work.
- In Belgium, a contract on homeworking must be signed. If it is not, then the teleworker is entitled to claim 10% of the gross salary as teleworking expenses.
- In Holland, companies can give a small allowance to teleworkers. There must be a written teleworking contract specifying at least one day a week working from home. The company can also supply a computer without incurring tax. However there are problems about the definition of one day (as opposed to 20% of work-time) especially for people who work 'from home' rather than 'at home'.
- In Germany, if someone works for more than 50% of their time at home they can get some tax deductions. The authorities are strict on requiring proof that at least half of the time is spent at home, requiring letters from employers.
- In Ireland, the Revenue Commissioners have issued a statement of practice on e-working available at **http://www.e-work.ie/uploads/eWorking_and_Tax_IT_69.pdf** which makes it clear that benefit-in-kind charges will not be incurred where provision of items is primarily for business use. The leaflet also states that employers are entitled to make small payments for heating and electricity costs. Finally, where part of a private home is used for e-working by employees, there is no restriction of the principal private residence exemption from capital gains tax.

National attitudes to work-life balance

A study of 400 parental couples in France, Italy, Denmark and Ireland[34] throws further light on the the gap between apparent demand for work-life balance measures including teleworking and their actual take-up.

The results showed that Irish fathers worked the longest hours, an average of 45 hours each week compared to 41 hours in the other three countries, and 33 hours for mothers. They also had the longest commuting times – an average of 42 minutes. Irish families had to work more hours to support themselves than families in the other countries (77.5 hours each week compared to 74.5 hours in Italy and Denmark).

Pressure of time rather than the availability of and expense of childcare was felt to be the biggest problem for the Irish couples interviewed – an interesting result given that childcare costs consume a higher proportion of working parents' earnings in Ireland than in any other member state (reported in *The Irish Times* 17 May 2001).

Despite these results, the Irish couples interviewed agreed more strongly that 'men in work-family programmes are less serious about their career' than those of other nationalities. The same was true for women participating in work-family programmes, but the strength of agreement was not as strong. Interviewees with higher social economic status were more likely to agree with the statement. In addition, the Irish couples agreed that 'to be viewed favourably, employees must put jobs ahead of families', a statement that the Italian and Danish couples disagreed with, but the French couples agreed with even more strongly than than the Irish couples.

It is interesting to contrast the Danish results from the survey. Danish men worked the shortest hours in comparison to the other three countries, while women worked slightly longer hours (although in all cases women worked fewer hours on average than men from the same country). The time taken to get to work was significantly shorter than in Ireland. Danes also disagreed slightly that men who took part in work-family programmes were less serious about their careers. In relation to women, they disagreed on this point strongly; nor did they feel that employees had to put their jobs ahead of their families.

One of the report authors, Professor Liz Højgaard, points out that Denmark already had the highest female labour participation in the EU, at around 73.5%, at the end of the 1980s, alongside the highest rate of public childcare facilities (around 80% coverage of the age-group 3–9 years). Although other European countries are now catching up, she feels the fact that it is a comparatively older development in Denmark may account for some of the national differences found in the study.

United States

Since 2001, legislators have been extremely active in the United States, putting forward a number of bills. Long-time telework commentator Gil Gordon is a little sceptical on whether they have any practical effect: 'The good news is that telework is showing up on the radar screens of some friendly legislators, thanks in part to the diligent efforts of members and staff of Telework America. The very fact that legislators are willing to attach their names to these kinds of initiatives is nothing to sneeze at. The only concern I have about some of these efforts is they may be nothing more than symbolism – important symbolism to be sure – but not likely to create much behaviour change.'

The Telework Tax Incentive Act plans to provide a $500 tax credit for telework-related expenses such as software, home-office furniture, fax machines, etc. The tax credit would go to whichever party, employer or employee pays for the work-at-home site. In order to qualify, employees must telecommute at least 75 days per year.

The National Telework and Air Quality Pilot Project is a government initiative aimed at reducing automobile emissions and energy consumption in five cities. Companies in those cities will be allowed to accumulate government credits for implementing telework schemes. The project is based on research indicating that if an individual teleworks for 1.8 days a week instead of driving their average commuting distance, the miles saved represent about 48 pounds of emissions a year. However, the agency responsible for monitoring the scheme, NEPI, has itself suffered financial problems and its future is unclear.

The Small Business Telecommuting Act aims to raise awareness about teleworking and encourage telecommuting options to be offered. The legislation directs the Small Business Administration to create a programme in a maximum of five SBA regions at a cost of up to $5m over two years. Actions can include developing educational materials, conducting outreach to small business and acquiring equipment for demonstration purposes. The bill directs the SBA to undertake special efforts to assist individuals with disabilities who are small-business owners or employees.

11 September 2001

The US Government Services Agency (GSA) issued guidelines to federal employees after the 11 September tragedy on using telework as a recovery tool. Due to increased security precautions and road closures, traffic congestion became particularly severe in the Washington DC Metropolitan and New York City areas. Telework and alternative work schedules were suggested to assist in reducing commuting time.

Telework was also recommended for some employees who have experienced trauma in the workplace, including those involved in the 11 September tragedy. The guidance states: 'Teleworking can be helpful for the employee recovering from trauma if it shortens a long, stressful commute and gives more time with loved ones. On the other hand, if not correctly designed, the telework arrangement has the potential for making it even more difficult for an employee to recover from trauma. If the needs of the employee are addressed in a respectful, sensitive way, an arrangement can be developed to meet the employee's and the agency's needs. A telework schedule such as Tuesday and Thursday, for example, would give an employee two respites from commuting, while at the same time allowing the healing experiences of being around the fearful place and being with co-workers who are similarly affected. An employee who feels uncomfortable at home alone might work well in a telework centre.' The GSA also offered a 60-day free trial use of telework centres in the Washington DC Metropolitan area from March to June 2002.

MILITARY ORDERS 25% TELEWORKING

The US Department of Defense has developed a telework policy which calls for 25% of eligible employees to telecommute by the end of 2001, with 25% increases in the numbers for three subsequent years. Department of Defense managers are now required to identify which of their employees are eligible for telework, based on some broad criteria given in the policy.

The plan is for telecommuting to take place at least one day in every two weeks. Employees and their supervisors have to sign a telework agreement covering work schedule, security and equipment issues, which also records the anticipated reduction in commuting times for the employee.

One motive behind the new policy is that, due to the usual practice of military employees moving location at regular intervals, it is hard for spouses to have continued employment. Teleworking spouses are more likely to be able to retain their employment creating greater 'portability in occupation'.

For information on various US government teleworking schemes *see* **http://www.telework.gov**

American Express asked 30 staff who provide expense management services for New York clients to work from their homes after the attacks so that their offices could be used by other employees who had lost their offices close to the World Trade Centre. American Express already had a telecommuting scheme and was familiar with what was required, but suffered logistical problems such as shipping computers to employees at home, or trying to get extra broadband lines installed by telecoms companies swamped with emergency repairs. They also had to round up around 200 IT staff to install communications software onto each person's PC, and train some employees in their use via telephone support.[35,36]

Sun lost about 190 flexible seats accommodating 290 employees in the disaster, but found that as a consequence of the resilience that its existing teleworkers provided, senior management support for the company's iWork programme actually increased. Sun is now opening a larger 220-seat flexible facility in Manhattan.

Nearly half of 1609 companies interviewed by the Masie Centre after the attacks said that they had increased their use of digital collaboration tools such as audio-, video- and web-based conferencing. Video-conferencing equipment-maker Tankberg Inc. said enquiries about its products went up by 30%, while Qwest Communications reports a 30% increase in usage of its web-based and audio-conferencing products.

However, use of video conferencing also jumped after the 1988 Pan Am

Flight 103 air disaster, and again after the Gulf War, but then fell again once business travel returned to normal levels. After the 1994 Los Angeles earthquake, there was a 25% increase in teleworking which subsided back to pre-earthquake levels within a year. Of 5000 American Express employees displaced from company headquarters, only around 800 are still telecommuting, and some of these were on existing telecommuting schemes. A survey of 164 companies polled by Gartner Dataquest at the end of September 2001, found that around 25% said they would now significantly expand or encourage telecommuting.

Teleworking commentator Gil Gordon reported receiving far fewer enquiries after the 11 September disaster than after previous events such as the Los Angeles earthquakes. Gil sees this as a positive sign that people are implementing telework on a steady basis, and are much more aware of the options open to them than they have been in previous years.

RURAL DEVELOPMENT

A global perspective on telecottages

Bill Murray of Small World Connections collated material for *Telecentre Models around the World*, funded by the International Telecommunications Union, a UN body. He looked at different stages of development with the help of international authors. What follows is a summary of some of the material and does not necessarily represent Bill's view or those of the ITU.

The first development stage is using telecentres to provide access to basic ICT facilities. Currently telekiosks, providing just telephony and possibly fax services, are growing in number in Africa, while Hungary is seeing explosive growth of telecentres, with over 500 planned to open.

In the second stage, once access to ICTs becomes reasonably cheap and widespread, telecentres must reinvent themselves through offering training or commercial services; otherwise they die. This pattern can be seen in Sweden, Newfoundland, Brazil, Finland, Germany, Holland, the UK, Ireland and parts of Australia and usually sees a considerable reduction in telecentre numbers.

In the third stage, rurally based telecentres must work out what to do once they have trained the people in their area. They often face competition from existing training providers such as local colleges which also want to provide IT and open-learning offerings. Solutions involving state funding have included becoming open-learning support centres, or broadening activities to become general centres for community development. Where income is partly or entirely commercial, the solution has often been based around call-centre services, as these services do not require workers with as high a level of IT skills as professional or niche teleworking businesses.

Murray concludes that telecentres are stepping stones which allow less-developed regions to catch up and that successful models must be adapted to local conditions.

Some commentators think telecentres are not a good use of public funding. In his 1998 paper *Telecentres in Germany and abroad – top or flop?*, Werner Korte of German consultancy Empirica argues that common problems have been seen in all countries:

- Lack of commercial focus (e.g. projects with several aims, some non-commercial).
- Lack of access to state funding from a single source, necessitating excessive negotiations with a range of grant-giving bodies.
- Offering services which did not add any significant value to what was already available on the market (e.g. secretarial services).
- Locating in a remote area with access only to low skill levels and basic IT training, resulting in service offerings suitable only to local sale (not high-level enough to attract distant customers) – yet there is no local market due to the remoteness of the area.

Korte also noted common success factors including:

- An income anchor such as a regular large customer.
- An entrepreneurial spirit, usually through a single person, the 'local champion'.
- Good business ideas aiming at market niches; or alternatively, broadly based, attractive service ranges.

Korte concluded: 'For the not too distant future I do not expect [telecentres] to become a "hot growth industry". Rather we should identify how they could further be developed to serve specific functions for society and industry that we want them to fulfil and leave new business creations to the market.'

Donnie Morrison, the force behind the Lasair and Western Isles teleworking project in Scotland, is also pessimistic about centres. 'The bottom line is that telecottages as originally envisaged have now moved on. They were absolutely the right thing to do at the time but could never be economically viable as they were. Now we have commercial companies setting up in rural areas and the better availability of good telecommunications. That means the centres are not an essential part of the equation. For a telecottage to survive it needs to have a commercially focused manager with appropriate skills. These are the very people who are now setting up commercial operations and the old telecottage is left to struggle.'

In 1996 Michael Clark of the Countryside and Community Research unit at Cheltenham and Gloucester College carried out research based on telecottages in the Dyfed and Powys areas of Wales, and on teleworkers in South-East

Britain. In the subsequent book, Clark says that 'there was only a small amount of evidence to suggest that telecottages were creating new teleworking opportunities directly'. Just under half indicated that they were outsourcing work to teleworkers; the number involved was small and the work tended to be low-skilled and part-time. Clark concludes: 'the most important attributes for successful teleworking appear to be expertise, reputations and networks of client contacts developed within former employment, usually within large, mainly urban-based, organisations.'[37]

But don't be put off if you are determined! According to Bill Murray there are over 700 telecentres in the western world, plus rest-of-world figures collected over the Internet by Paddy Moindrot that tot up to 847 cybercafés, 112 multipurpose community telecentres and 557 organisations that 'don't quite fit' the usual telecentre description.

ICT access centres

The UKOnline centres demonstrate the latest flavour in ICT access centres with a development focus. These are community-based centres for people who have limited or no access to new technologies such as the Internet and email. Most also provide opportunities to use the new technologies to learn new skills and update existing skills, in conjunction with the LearnDirect scheme. LearnDirect is a scheme aimed at all adults, regardless of employment status or age, providing access to training either through LearnDirect centres, or online.

Many centres are based around existing schools and colleges, but there are also centres which are in libraries or in high street Internet cafés. One example is the Next Life chain of Internet centres in London and Bristol (**http://www.nextlife.co.uk**). UKOnline centres do not directly receive money for their status, but get branding support and benefit from a national marketing campaign. They also get online support in the form of advice and guidance in marketing the scheme and identifying content and materials to assist clients who wish to learn about ICTs. *See* **http://www.dfes.gov.uk/ ukonlinecentres/** to find your nearest centre.

It could be contended that the telecottage concept is living on in the DirectSupport programme. Part of the UKOnline initiative, this scheme has distributed about £2m funding to 98 centres run by voluntary and community organisations. The project was intended to provide access for these organisations to the UKOnline funding, given that they tend not to have the skills, contacts and IT knowledge to access funding on their own.

The DirectSupport project included awareness-raising, bid-support and mentoring for the organisations involved, which have included community centres and village halls as well as specialist voluntary support groups. DirectSupport is a consortium of agencies that includes Action with Communities in Rural England (ACRE), Community Action Network (CAN),

Community Development Foundation, Partnerships Online and the National Rural Environment Centre (Ruralnet).

Mike Gadsby of the Headway charity, which helps people with head injuries, said: 'It was a breath of fresh air – I've never before come across a government funding source where so much help was available. DirectSupport really understand the difficulties that we have in bidding, and our mentor was marvellous.' Mike is spending his £20,000 grant on a computer network with adaptive softwware and hardware for the disabled and a broadband Internet link via BT Learning. Revenue to sustain the centre will come from the LearnDirect scheme.

Charities find that teleworking fits the bill

Charities are always looking for innovative ways to carry out their intensive workloads within budget. Teleworking can help in two ways: by providing alternative and inexpensive ways of holding meetings, and by providing staff who can work 'as needed' on specific campaigns.

The environmental charity World Wide Fund for Nature (WWF) used teleworking, email and video conferences to save airfares while preparing its submission to CITES, the convention on endangered species.

WWF activist Stuart White explains that the organisation has 15 regional organisers covering four or five countries each. 'Part of the job is providing PR, managing volunteers and creating a local profile. All the regional offices are home-based teleworkers and have been for at least 10–12 years,' says Stuart, who also reports that the organisation has an 'email culture'.

'Being an environmental organisation we use telephone conferencing a lot, and have video-conferencing facilities which are mainly used to link to our other offices. I even interviewed someone for a job over the video link – they were in Switzerland, so they came into the Swiss WWF office and used the link.' (**http://www.wwf.org**)

Joanna Lockwood at the Royal National Institute for the Blind (RNIB) has used the work listings in the *Teleworker* magazines to recruit telephone canvassers. Joanna is one of six area managers responsible for fund-raising. The canvassers, equipped with just a telephone and a desk, spend between 10 and 20 hours a week calling RNIB contacts to ask them to sell raffle tickets. They work on permanent part-time contracts, and the RNIB looks after the health and safety aspects of employing someone to work in their own home. 'It's very exciting,' says Joanna. 'The listings have been great, with 15 people coming forward. We are always looking for good, professional, committed teleworkers.' (**http://www.rnib.org.uk**)

The rural urban divide

In rural areas, teleworking has been promoted as a way to support job creation without sacrificing greenfield sites to manufacturing industry. Geographically

isolated areas which suffer disadvantages through increased transport costs can also benefit from teleworking jobs. There have been many case studies of individuals, usually with specialist skills, relocating to remote rural areas and continuing to offer services over the Internet. However, the Internet and e-commerce may also prove a threat to rural economies – for example where city vans deliver books ordered from Amazon.com while local bookshops close down through lack of trade. Rural dwellers find it harder to select, buy, maintain and get support for computers because they have fewer computer shops and are less likely to have contact with people who have good IT skills and can act as mentors for new computer users.

Although telework undoubtedly offers opportunities to rural dwellers, it is city and suburban dwellers who are currently benefiting because of the greater availability of skills and the higher levels of telecoms infrastructure and physical communications that are available in urban areas.

The Rural Development Commission's study on Teleworking and Rural Development (1996 – the RDC has now restructured as the Countryside Agency) found that existing statistics were unreliable, but that, in the main, professional teleworking was concentrated in London and south-east England, while home-based work for a single employer tended to be carried out by low-paid women in peripheral areas. The report was also pessimistic about back-office functions such as call centres being relocated to rural areas,

ALSTON MOOR CONNECTS TO THE FUTURE

A successful bid to provide online access for the remote rural area of Alston Moor in Cumbria was made by Telework Association member Daniel Heery, working for Voluntary Action Cumbria.

Local employment is mainly in primary industries such as quarrying, mining and agriculture, but the remoteness of the area means that many people do not register when they are unemployed because it involves a 50-mile round trip to the local employment office on a bus that leaves at 7.00 a.m. and returns at 6.00 p.m. There is some seasonal work, but the continued crisis in agriculture is continuing to put employment at risk.

The project, supported under the Capital Modernisation Fund, will wire up 1200 of the 1300 homes in the area, which is located on the eastern edge of Cumbria, 20 miles east of Penrith and 25 miles south-west of Hexham. It will use a range of technologies, including PCs, satellite, digital whiteboards, ADSL, video conferencing and laptops. Minister for Learning and Technology Michael Wills commented: 'We know that only one in five members of the poorer D and E social groups have used the Internet compared with over two-thirds of professionals. This is a digital divide which must be overcome.'
http://www.cybermoor.org

suggesting that these tend to locate in industrial urban areas with large labour pools.

The RDC study did identify some areas of opportunity for rural areas including Internet marketing of specialist rural products, tourism teleworking, information services and services aimed at rural communities.

In a literature review on the effects of ICTs in rural areas carried out for the EU AsPIRE project in 2002, Seamus Grimes picks out a number of elements that disadvantage rural areas: 'New technologies must be seen as a two-edged sword for rural areas, which increasingly become exposed to more intense competition from beyond the boundaries of local market areas.'[38]

Grimes points to the problems rural SMEs have in obtaining technical support, and to the way in which ICTs are tending to remove intermediary services like banks from rural locations. In addition, costs for Internet access are generally much higher in rural locations (e.g. in rural Australia, where they are around three times what urban dwellers pay). Technologies like DSL are also a problem – in the US over 56% of cities with populations of about 100,000 have DSL, while less than 5% of cities with less than 10,000 population have DSL.

He also reviews literature which indicates that rural businesses tend to be pressured by customers and suppliers into using ICTs – this is the key factor affecting adoption once the ICTs are available. There is also a massive gap between being connected to the Internet and actually using it to make payments, even in 'high-tech' countries such as Sweden, where less than 4% of businesses were offering e-payment facilities in 2000.

It is interesting to note the contrasting results of a study commissioned by the Countryside Agency in the UK, who asked pollsters MORI to reanalyse their Technology Tracker survey looking for differences between rural and urban areas. MORI found a gradual but consistently rising overall trend in personal Internet usage at home, at work and elsewhere but overall little difference in the trend based on geography. During the period analysed, August 2000 to January 2002, rural usage rose from 29% to 44% while urban usage rose from 33% to 44%. Mixed rural/urban area usage rose from 32% to 46% (**http://www.countryside.gov.uk/stateofthecountryside/default.htm**).

Affording broadband

How, in an environment where telecoms companies are struggling, can broadband high-speed connectivity be provided to homes and businesses outside economically attractive city centres? Patricia Hewitt, when minister for e-commerce in 2001, said that rural areas in the UK would have to justify their need for higher capacity broadband telecoms before any government help would be available: 'What we don't want to do is invest enormous amounts of money in what the market would do anyway, nor do we want to commit enormous amounts of money to something that consumers are not going to do.' She pointed to the downside of the often-quoted example of Singapore, which invested $300 million to provide 98% coverage of the population with broadband – it is only used by 2% of the population.

Hewitt's successor Stephen Timms, an acknowledged expert in the telecoms field, said in June 2002 that he did not favour tax breaks to support the rollout of broadband infrastructure, but reiterated that schemes to bring together public-sector customers to provide broadband nodes outside the main rollout areas did merit attention. This view was supported by the results of a scheme to provide ADSL access in Wales which met with limited takeup.

The purely commercial approach can also bellyflop, as discovered by subscribers in the US during 2001 when a number of cable and DSL suppliers went bust, blanking out nearly a million connections around the country. It is also important to remember that not every home needs broadband. The US consulting company Parks Associates carries out annual surveys on ICT usage. In 2001, Parks Associates noted that 75% of its sample of 1000 online homes are happy with their speed of connection to the Internet.

However, there is a £30m scheme to promote broadband use which is being implemented through the UK's regional development agencies. A typical example is the £3m scheme which will be delivered by the East of England Development Agency. This includes a 'connecting communities' competition, with prizes of financial support towards broadband connections, publicity for

DIGITAL PENINSULA NETWORK – SUPPORTING CORNISH TELEWORKERS

Digital Peninsula is a membership organisation with paying subscribers which offers information services to support teleworkers, freelancers and small businesses using digital technology. It was initially funded by a European Commission grant, with matching funding from BT, local authorities, rural development organisations and training and enterprise councils.

Members pay a subscription of about £3 to £10 to join. Project co-ordinator Steve Miller says that start-up businesses value the network for high-quality advice on how to get online. The bigger vision of the project is to market Cornwall as a place to locate e-business – a bit of a problem due to infrastructure issues (ADSL is not scheduled to reach Cornwall until 2005).

The project website markets the skills of members and provides information on grants, as well as technical and business advice.
http://www.digitalpeninsula.com

specific applications to assist businesses through roadshows, and a broadband brokerage to identify areas with threshold broadband demand where local partnerships can be put in place to speed up rollout.

BT, the main supplier of broadband in the UK through its ADSL offerings, is currently running a web-based registration system where customers express interest and the rollout of ADSL to exchanges outside city centres is prioritised according to the number of interested customers. It appears likely that only about 80% of BT's exchanges will be upgraded to ADSL in the medium term (*see* **http://broadband1.bt.com**). There is some disagreement among industry commentators about BT's threshold levels for converting exchanges (200–500 subscribers), with the campaign group **http://www.broadband4britain.com** stating that the true figure should be closer to 50 subscribers.

In response to this situation, the Countryside Agency is auditing 100 market towns of 2000 to 20,000 people which service their surrounding areas on their broadband availability and requirements. The data collected will be passed on to the relevant regional development agency to work up a town plan for broadband connection.

In Cornwall the ACT NOW scheme is a partnership between BT and key public-sector organisations. Its plans are in two parts – funding for the upgrade of 13 local exchanges, and actions to encourage small businesses to use the new technologies that broadband can provide.

The British 'no government cash' approach is not mirrored elsewhere in the world. France committed £150m to finance broadband in areas where it was not economically viable in 2001. Sweden is spending £700m on achieving 98%

broadband coverage. The US government has earmarked $750m to assist with deploying rural broadband to about six million homes.

According to research group NetValue, in July 2002 only 6.1% of Internet-connected households in the UK were using broadband. In contrast Denmark tops the European league with 24.5% penetration, followed by Germany, France, Spain and Norway. Italy trails in behind the UK. However, the introduction of cheaper ADSL services by BT did lead to a doubling of ADSL connections between December and May 2002.

While there are alternatives to ADSL or cable broadband for rural dwellers, currently they have their limitations. Satellite technology is still expensive, and not useful for applications which require large amounts of data to be uploaded as well as downloaded (*see* p. 281). Higher speed GPRS wireless networks are still largely restricted to high population areas. It is possible that 3G wireless services, when they are eventually rolled out, may provide a solution. But of course, as any rural dweller can tell you, there are many areas which geographically, let alone economically, cannot receive current GSM mobile signals, so the broadband divide for rural dwellers appears to be here to stay.

A 2002 report from the Local Futures group calling for a London-wide joined-up policy on ICTs (E-London and the London Plan at **http://www.localfutures.com**) points out that even in the capital, broadband is generally only available in the 'watchstrap' area between Heathrow and the city of London. The report points out that there are two digital divides – a basic IT literacy required to operate email, and a second more advanced set of skills required to take advantage of new opportunities such as e-commerce. Although good progress has been made on the first digital divide, the authors are concerned that in reality 92% of London businesses generate less than 10% of their turnover from the Internet – they are on the wrong side of that second digital divide.

Importing work to rural areas

There is clear evidence from case studies that teleworking can provide high-quality work in rural areas; the big question is why it has not been more successful as a tool for economic development. In the main the problem seems to be that most projects are set up on a 'supply side' basis (i.e. we have the teleworkers, all we have to do is wait for someone to start using them), rather than an approach which begins by looking at market demand.

Apart from small back offices like 3Com in Spiddal, and individual professionals, projects trying to use teleworking to develop rural areas tend to fall into three main groups: telecentres, skills registers (or job brokerage services) and call centres.

3COM SPEAKS IRISH IN SPIDDAL

Networking infrastructure company 3Com set up a satellite office for its research and development team in 1998. Nothing unusual about that – except that the office is located in a small village in the Gaeltacht Irish-speaking region near Galway city, once a by-word for poor employment prospects.

Tadgh Creedon, director of the research centre, says that 3Com, which manufactures network interface cards, hubs, switches and the well-known Palm Pilot organisers, had been having problems recruiting design engineers in Dublin due to the 'Celtic Tiger' boom.

However, they identified a rich seam of talent on the west coast of Ireland close to the area where Digital had formerly had its Irish operation. 'We couldn't get the right people to come to Dublin, so we went to the right people instead – we call it distributed development.'

Tadgh explains that the Spiddal team works closely with teams in Silicon Valley and other global locations. Spiddal has access to high-bandwidth telecoms, and much of the work involves maintaining and supporting the computers and software needed for silicon design, a process which can take place remotely.

Telecottages and telecentres

While there are a small number of successful examples of telecottage or telecentre projects bringing work into rural areas (*see* East Clare Telecottage, p. 125), in general these projects have not been sustainable. There is now enough experience from projects in different countries and regions for some lessons to be drawn, although there is little published research available on the topic.

The client base of most telecentres does not match the profile that we know represents teleworkers, based on quantitative surveys such as the UK LFS and EcATT. Teleworkers tend to be male, middle-aged and to have third-level education. Telecentre and telecottage clients tend to be female, either young with small children (20–35) or women returning to work after a long absence (45-plus), and to have second-level education. There is anecdotal evidence to suggest that marketing of telecentres has not been well directed and that problems have arisen from offering a diverse range of low added-value services.

GLOBAL WORK OPPORTUNITIES IN THE WESTERN ISLES

Western Isles Council and Western Isles Enterprise have taken an integrated approach to the problem of replacing traditional employment. Led by the charismatic Donnie Morrison, the islands have actively marketed the skills of their highly educated residents and their availability for teleworking contracts through a skills register of some 600 inhabitants and other measures which make up the 'Work Global' initiative. So far, so standard – an approach which has sunk without trace in many rural areas.

Donnie Morrison was formerly the sales and marketing director of a computer company, and began his jobs crusade by setting up the Highlands and Islands Enterprise Board's skills register, an action of the Western Isles ICT advisory service. 'At first we made the mistake of restricting the register to IT skills – it is now just a skills database. We look, for example, for people with language skills and then give them the IT skills,' says Morrison.

Morrison followed up by starting Lasair (which means 'red hot' or 'flame' in Gaelic), a limited liability company providing editing services. The first client was an American company indexing and abstracting business journals. Other Lasair clients include the Metropolitan Police Forensic Laboratory and the legal journal *Scots Law Times*, as well as various scientific publishers. The Lasair teleworkers got grants of up to 70% for their equipment, are self-employed and have to 'bid' for any available contracts.

Currently Lasair has about 14 people, mainly women, carrying out telework, and manager Seonag McVicar reports that she regularly uses about 25 teleworkers out of a total pool on the skills register of 80. However, commercial margins are tightening for the editing and abstracting work with competition from low labour cost locations, and there is also the threat of 'smart software' that could make some of the work obsolete.

Seonag reports that web services such as design and hosting of sites are now more in demand than the editing and abstracting services, but that Lasair has not been affected by the global economic downturn.

The Work Global initiative has also lobbied to provide the islands with broadband infrastructure and improved GSM infrastructure, and recently achieved funding of £1.5m for a broadband wireless network. Donnie reports that over £5m has been spent in locating ICT centres in villages throughout the Western Isles – but these are not telecottages. 'These are highly specified offices designed from the outset as buildings which could meet the demands of any high-tech company. They are typically located in the more populated village areas and are designed to accommodate between 35 and 50 people, have raised floors with structured cabling systems, backup power generation and a UPS system.'

The project continues to pursue teleworking opportunities as well as mainstream ICT business setups. Donnie reports that a recent addition to the stable is growing rapidly – a company which provides legal secretarial services, where barristers and solicitors dictate into digital recording systems and then transfer sound files over a secure VPN network to teleworkers according to particular document templates. For the clients the advantage is a very fast turnaround, and higher throughput of work. For the secretaries, the pay rates are higher than for local firms plus they can work from home and have flexible hours. However, payment is on 'throughput' rather than hourly rates – otherwise known as piecework.

Work Global has also persuaded an emergency services call centre, Criticall to locate in the area. Work Global's unique selling point is that the region has the highest number of graduates per capita in the UK.

The intiative is claimed to have created or retained over 175 jobs (not all simultaneous) and to have ensured that at least 50 people have been employed through teleworking (both home- and office-based) at any one time since its inception.

Lasair Tel: 01870 602757 Email: seonag@btinternet.com
http://www.lasair.co.uk
Work Global Email: donnie@work-global.com **http://www.work-global.com**

There seems to be a general consensus among those who have been involved in 'work-brokerage' projects for teleworkers that only about 10% of candidates who present themselves as 'wannabee' teleworkers are truly committed, suitably skilled, and able to deliver work. Only a few projects have attempted to deal with this reality by involving candidates in trying to identify realistic goals for themselves and adapting training to fit those goals.

Telecentres also need to understand that a proportion of their successful candidates are likely to move into conventional employment elsewhere. So not only is the rate of failure high, but those who are successful may well not stay with the project. This is not necessarily a failure from the individual's viewpoint, but it is a problem for sustaining the project.

In order to assist in marketing services, and to achieve a sufficient level of quality control, it is important that projects identify and aim towards niche markets where they can show expertise. Almost all telework job-seeking projects have started off with a wide offering of different services, later refined to a narrow range of niche products for practical and economic reasons.

Those who make the decisions on outsourcing telework are often urban dwellers who can be prejudiced against rural dwellers, assuming that they will provide a sub-standard service. Additionally, when outsourcing decisions are made, employers will often restrict applicants to particular geographical boundaries – a trend evident from the Telework Association's own teleworking job opportunities e-zine, Telework Online (*see* **http://www.telework.org.uk**).

TELETASK PROJECT PLAGUED BY PROBLEMS

In 1998 Andrew Hunter, a former telecentre manager and president of Australia's rural telecentre association, achieved funding of approximately £200,000 from the Australian Federal Government to fund Teletask, a project that aimed to provide quality-controlled, professional-standard services using rural teleworkers. Andrew had previous practical experience in getting work and managing telecentres but still found that a number of practical issues beset the project.

The first problem was a resistant market – a survey of Australian managers in 1999 showed that 26% would outsource work abroad, but only 16% were prepared to outsource to rural/regional locations.

Trade unions were active in blocking projects to outsource work from the public sector, and Teletask received no government contract work whatsoever.

Teletask registered some 750 people in its teleworker database. Despite this, the organisation frequently struggled to find 10 available to staff contracts received. Andrew reports that most could not or did not complete work to standard or within the time allocated. He found that approximately 10% of the candidates were competent teleworkers, and that of these, about 40% left to take on permanent employment, based on the training and work experience they achieved through Teletask.

Andrew's colleague Graham Mackay is trained in Myers Briggs MTBI Personality Profiling. The two collaborated to design and implement an online profiling system aimed at predicting the successful teleworkers, but found the process time-consuming and ineffective. Andrew describes it as 'more of an operational problem than anything else – only the wannabees did it while the hot prospects said "when you've got the work, I 'll do it". The problem was, when the work came in, the lead time rarely allowed for such niceties.'

Teletask also found that other telecentre co-ordinators were not capable of managing their teleworkers, requiring considerable extra supervisory work which was in excess of that which would have been required if the teleworkers were managed individually rather than through the telecentres.

Rural telecommunications infrastructure was poor (especially broadband) and costs were high, amounting to a significant competitive barrier.

Despite these difficulties, Teletask has identified and developed a successful niche service (Internet transcription) and established clients in Australia, Japan and the US. During 2001, it was responsible for directly or indirectly generating about 100 jobs. Andrew feels the slimmed-down Teletask, now an independent entity that must survive without funding, will ride out the current problems in the ICT sector.
http://www.teletask.com.au

A project champion (or two) who can market the skills of the telecentre and solve workflow or technical support problems is vital. Without such a person, the project will fail. Unfortunately, anyone with suitable skills living in a rural area is likely to be in demand for various tasks, not just running a telecentre.

The above points do not in any way take away from the importance of telecentres (and cybercafés and school access centres and libraries, etc.) in providing access to IT facilities and training for rural dwellers. They are relevant for those considering how to make a telecentre, particularly one in a rural area, viable in the long term. The following examples illustrate the use of teleworking to import work to rural areas.

Skills registers for regional marketing
The boxes on pages 81–3 give two contrasting views.

Call centres
The RDC 1996 report indicates that back-office operations tend not to locate in rural areas because they need large labour pools. This was confirmed by the results of the TOSCA project in 2001, which found that 79% of 513 call centres surveyed were in capital cities or large, economically attractive cities – the survey found few reports of call centres located on rural greenfield sites at all. Additionally, industry estimates of high staff turnover rates support the idea that call centres need continual sources of new recruits .

One interesting example of work being imported to a rural area is the West Cork Technology Park located one mile outside the market town of Clonakilty in West Cork. The Park managed to get a broadband link despite its rural location, and is located close to third-level colleges in Cork city as well as to Cork airport. Enterprise agencies have focused on attracting a cluster of distance-independent ICT businesses including a call centre, a contact centre and a software development company. The local area is able to offer an excellent living standard and cheaper property costs than competing urban locations. *See* **http://westcorktechnologypark.com**

ENVIRONMENTAL IMPACTS

Teleworking is theoretically good for the environment because it reduces traffic pollution, uses less energy than conventional office work and encourages rural development.

Transport substitution

Figures from the Department of Transport, Environment and the Regions published in 2001 give an average journey-to-work time in Britain of 25 minutes, rising to 42 minutes in London – which amounts to about five hours per week. For those who use rail or tube the figures rise to about ten hours a week spent travelling to and from work. Over 70% of those in work use a car to commute. The average distance to work is 8.1 miles.

Business travel journeys were considerably longer than any other kind of trip at just over 20 miles, while commuting journeys at about 8 miles were similar in length to all types of leisure trips (**http://www.transtat.dft.gov.uk/facts/ntsfacts/travwork/travwork.htm**).

Flexible working consultants HOP (*see* **http://www.flexibility.co.uk**) in their report Telecommuting 2000[39] say that the average UK worker commutes 2906 miles each year and travels a further 1622 miles on business. The costs of commuting, borne by the employee, are about £500 a year on average. For staff with high mileage, the financial cost is huge. Mileage of 20,000 a year incurs costs of around £10,000, while indirect congestion-related costs can amount to a further £5000. HOP list four ways in which ICT can be used to reduce the need for travel, and thus reduce travel-related pollution of the environment:

- Teleworking from home, on the road between visits, or from different company sites.
- Collaborative working such as netmeetings or audio conferences that replace physical travel to meetings.
- E-commerce delivering services and products to customers electronically.
- Development of remote monitoring and diagnostic techniques using ICTs.

Andy Lake of HOP believes that the direct traffic substitution effect of teleworking is fairly well established – where someone remains at home for the day working instead of travelling into work, there is a clear saving of travel miles. Andy also points out that in the UK only about half of all trips by car are work-related, and that in his estimate the maximum amount of work which can be carried out flexibly is about 30–40% since most people who telecommute only do so for 1–2 days per week.

An evaluation of traffic reduction effects at Surrey County Council's Epsom telecentre concludes: 'The average length of each car journey from home to work falls by approximately 19% to 13 miles... the average duration of each car journey from home to work falls by approximately 36% to 30 minutes ... based on current usage there is a travel distance saving of 30,000 vehicle miles per year.' Teleworking by Hertfordshire County Council trading standards was also shown to reduce business travel: 'In-work travel time has reduced by a healthy 10%... in-work miles reduced by 9000 representing a 5–8% reduction.'

The RAC Foundation[40], working from research by NERA, Heriott Watt University and Critical Research, predicted that, by 2007:

- Teleworking would cut commuter traffic by 18%.
- Video conferencing would cut business travel by 20%.

BT'S FLEXI-WORKERS MAY SAVE 170 MILES A WEEK

A study undertaken by researchers at the University of Bradford looked at the working habits of some BT staff taking part in its Options 2000 scheme (see also page 4).

Applying the average reduction in work trips to all the Options 2000 scheme gives figures of 424,000 miles of car travel saved and 190,000 miles of rail travel saved each week. However, the researchers caution against using these figures without making allowance for additional domestic trips (e.g. to collect children from school) which may not have been made before staff joined the Options 2000 scheme. They reported that the following activities were taking place during existing trips to and from work (the sample was 73% male):

Shopping	14%
Take children to school	12%
Collect children from school	7%
Leisure activities	8%
Drop off or collect partner	7%

http://www.wfh.co.uk

- IT effects, e.g. on load planning, would cut lorry journeys by 20%.
- Teleshopping would reduce shopping trips by 6%.

However, these estimates appear to be quite optimistic, particularly as they do not take account of substitution trips. Work by Patricia Mohktarian and colleagues in the US[41] indicates that the teleworker at home may take on additional trips, such as responsibility for the school run, or shopping, and these are not accounted for in most studies. A recent technical paper published by the California Energy Commission[42] based on 1998 data suggests that the total reduction in vehicle miles travelled due to telecommuting is 0-2%.

Figures relating the length of commute to the likelihood of telecommuting are also instructive – you need to have quite a long journey before this figures as a motivation for teleworking, despite the media stereotype of commuters desperate to avoid taking the (s)train ... A non-random survey of 1953 technology professionals carried out by the website **http://home.techies.com** found that distance from work had little to do with the extent of tele-commuting until workers' homes were over 50 miles from the office. Survey respondents living over 49 miles from work were about twice as likely to work from home for half the business week. There were also seven times as many full-time telecommuters in this group.

A study in Dublin carried out in 1998[43] suggested that there would probably only be a 1% substitution effect caused by teleworking, rising to a mere 1.5% by

2016. Amárach interviewed 503 Dubliners and found that 7.6% occasionally worked from home using a computer, though more than half of these spent less than a day a week at home. The report used benchmarking and data from the Dublin Transportation Office (DTO) to estimate the transport substitution effect of teleworking on the morning peak traffic and found it to be small using the DTO's 'most likely' scenario: if 17% of employed people telecommuted in 2016, the peak reduction would be 5.3%. However, to put these figures in context, in the shorter term (next five years) the reduction in total trip numbers predicted from telecommuting is only slightly less than that of the Luas adapted-tram system planned for Dublin.

A study in Cambridge based around a trial of flexible working by the city council suggested that if all employers adopted teleworking for suitable tasks, the traffic reduction effects would amount to 4–8% across the day, with larger reductions during the morning and evening peaks. Andy Lake points out that such a reduction is completely wiped out by the government's projected increases in traffic growth rates, and that in Cambridge, where 25% of commuters cycle, some of those adopting teleworking are already using environmentally friendly forms of transport.

In the US, clean-air legislation has led a number of large companies to introduce telecommuting programmes in order to reduce environmental damage caused by their employees commuting to work, particularly in California.

In Holland, action by the transport ministry, concerned at the negative effect of congestion on the economy, has led to over a third of companies adopting traffic-demand management plans, including telework options such as staying at home and using email to avoid the morning peak. However, an early study in Holland[44] also found that teleworking nearly always replaced trips by bicycle or public transport – it did not reduce car travel, and in fact led to a slightly higher proportion of all trips happening by car.

Gil Gordon points out in his July 1999 edition of *Telecommuting Review* (**http://www.gilgordon.com**) that transportation trends remain stubbornly static in California, despite heavy state incentives towards telecommuting and public transport. Between 1990 and 1998, the proportion of people driving to work alone dropped by a marginal amount from 78.2% to 77.3%. Gordon quotes a presentation by Anthony Downs of the Brooking Institution who believes that traffic congestion will continue to increase because it is a result of our pursuit of objectives such as flexibility and speed which we don't want to give up. John Adams, a University College London geography professor, agrees and has predicted that the new technologies will encourage us to move more rather than less, leading to a polarised, car-dependent Britain suffering urban sprawl, increased crime, and less time spent in local communities or with neighbours and friends due to increased time spent interacting with colleagues on the Internet.

One step which appears unpopular with transport operators, but which might encourage more teleworking, would be a revision of existing season-ticket arrangements for public transport. Currently you buy a ticket allowing a particular trip for a period of time – say a year – and the cost depends on the distance. When you telework you are 'wasting' a day of the transport you have already paid for. On many transport systems in Europe, the *carnet* system is used instead, where you buy a number of prepaid tickets which you use up as you wish – much more telework-friendly. Chiltern Railways offer a *carnet* system providing a saving on 10% of tickets, but other UK rail operators seem to be resisting the idea. A press officer for Great Western Trains said: 'The public already criticise us for having too many ticket options.'

Energy savings

There is very little research which attempts to separate out energy savings due to reduced commuting from specific energy savings due to work outside the traditional office. The EU SAVE project, operated by EA Technology in Sheffield (**http://www.eatechnology.com**), estimated that working at home consumes up to 80% less energy than working in an office. Similar reductions in carbon dioxide emissions are also achieved. The project surveyed 106 Sheffield office workers and 22 homeworkers. Andrew Wright of EA Technology commented: 'The average energy consumption for offices is much greater than for domestic use because it's a lot less controlled – corridors need heating, lights are left on for cleaners, PCs are left on in the evening and so on. A shift to teleworking would also create a much flatter electricity load profile – currently domestic and office supplies impose peaks on the system in their different areas, requiring additional system capacity and the starting-up of less efficient generators at peak times.' Home offices are also occupied full-time, in contrast to wasted office space. Cornell University estimated that over 40% of all desks are unoccupied on any given work day, the equivalent of three million empty desks in the UK.

Dr Brad Allenby of AT&T, giving evidence to a US government committee, estimated that energy used for lighting and computers was the same between the traditional office and the home, but that energy consumed for telephone calls was actually slightly higher at home – at about 5.25 kwH/day – than that in the traditional office – about 1.3 kwH/day, because each call would be likely to travel through an average of four separate telephone switches.

Planning and urban sprawl

Tight planning regulation in Britain has prevented urban sprawl problems from developing to the extent visible in Ireland and the US, although population growth is increasing the development pressure in south-east England. There has been an unresolved debate over whether teleworking relieves or alternatively increases urban sprawl by making work feasible at

SERVICE 12 – JOB SATISFACTION THROUGH TELEWORKING

Service 12 is the Italian name for directory enquiries. Italian sociology professor Patrizio di Nicola carried out a survey of 100 volunteers for a Service 12 teleworking scheme in 1999, which involved interviewing the teleworkers before they changed their work practices, and again after eight or nine months. Patrizio also interviewed line managers based in the Service 12 call centres, and some senior managers.

Patrizio reports: 'Telecom Italia provided workstations which could be totally closed, and which almost disappear when not in use, so it was very easy for the teleworkers to locate in any part of the house. We found that 41% had a room that was used as their office. Some 18% used a hobby room, while 20% worked from part of what they described as a library or study. In addition 13% worked in a bedroom and 1% worked in a corridor or in the entrance hall of their home. We found that the least satisfied teleworkers were those who used the bedroom, because they could never get away from their work.

'This is a job with very poor career prospects and a rigid working time, so immediately, one of the main benefits of teleworking – flexibility – is not present. Although the workers' location changes, their rigid shifts do not. Despite this, we found that in the first survey some 14.5% said that their work satisfaction was low. This reduced to 5.4% after eight or nine months – some 10% of people passed from being very unsatisfied with their work to being satisfied. The percentage of people who were highly satisfied also increased, from 15% to 21%.

'Despite the high unemployment rates in Italy, and despite the monotonous nature of the job, before the trial some 40% of the teleworkers told us they would not consider leaving Telecom Italia. Afterwards, this percentage rose by about 5% – i.e. people felt themselves to be close to the firm because of teleworking. In addition, the teleworkers proved to be more productive. Their answering time was 21 seconds compared to 25 seconds for the non-teleworkers.

'The advantages included 17.6% who found that commuting time was reduced, 18.7% who found that commuting costs were reduced, and 55.6% of those with families who found that they had more time for their families. The disadvantages included 49% who complained of lack of information, and 22% who experienced isolation.

'Concerning the colleagues of the teleworkers, at the beginning of the trial, 47% were against teleworking and felt that it reduced job security. After the trial the percentage against teleworking had dropped to 27%. We also asked the teleworkers what they would do if Telecom Italia opened a call centre close to their homes. 76% said they would remain at home, 10% said perhaps telework, 10% said perhaps the call centre, and 4% only definitely said they would use the call centre.'

After the results of the survey were published, the telework scheme was extended to a further 100 operators. All teleworkers' equipment was upgraded to allow them to link to the company intranet and email systems. (mailto:patrizio@dinicola.it) longer commuting distances from the office. There is some evidence from the US ITAC surveys that when teleworkers move house, they don't show any tendency to move further from the office (in the 2001 results, of those who moved, 52% moved closer to their employer, 29% moved away and 19% moved to a new house the same distance from their employer). However, the ITAC survey for 1999 also shows that for teleworkers who work at home, their average distance from the office, at 19.7 miles, is longer than that for non-teleworkers at 13.3 miles – or 63 minutes for teleworkers compared to 45 minutes for non-teleworkers (**http://www.telecommute.org**).

This is supported by the information on main motivation for teleworking from the US current population survey, which indicates that reducing commuting time is relevant only for between 1% and 2% of those who work at home.

LABOUR RIGHTS AND WORKING CONDITIONS

A comprehensive European framework agreement between employers and unions was signed in summer 2002, covering many aspects of teleworking including provision of equipment and the right to return to the office (*see* p. 65). This agreement is the first on working conditions achieved through dialogue between the social partners rather than by directive from the European Commission.

There has been a general European consensus that those who work from home need protection from what Bill Walsh of Amicus-MSF union describes as the 'long and discreditable history of exploitation of home workers'. In 1996, the International Labour Organisation issued an international convention on homeworking, providing minimum levels of protection. The convention covers employees and the 'pseudo self-employed', but not the genuinely self-employed, whom the convention describes as those with 'the degree of autonomy and of economic independence to be considered an independent worker under national laws, regulations or court decisions'. The convention specifies the following rights:

- the homeworkers' right to establish or join organisations of their own choosing and to participate in the activities of such organisations;
- protection against discrimination in employment and occupation;
- protection in the field of occupational safety and health;
- remuneration;
- statutory social-security protection;
- access to training;
- maternity protection.

The ILO convention has been adopted in Ireland and Finland, and moves are afoot for ratification in a number of other countries. *See* **http://www.wiego.org/main/membershome.shtml** for updates.

Up to half of the teleworkers in the UK are self-employed, and face problems which are related to their employment status, such as longer working hours. Other difficulties faced by self-employed teleworkers include getting training to maintain their skills, and anomalies of social-welfare systems that disadvantage those who become ill or otherwise unemployed, when compared to traditional, office-based PAYE employees. In general, welfare systems have not moved with the changes in work patterns. In the UK and Ireland, if you have been self-employed for more than a year, you are only entitled to minimal, means-tested welfare benefits (unemployment assistance) should you become unemployed or suffer disability or illness. Although self-employed people in Britain pay national insurance, their contributions only cover the National Health Service and Old Age Pension, not the wider range of benefits available to PAYE employees.

While a few trade unions have opposed the introduction of teleworking and flexible work on the grounds that it leads to casualisation, low pay and loss of employment rights, most have seen it as an employee-led movement, and a few have seen it as an opportunity to increase their membership and provide services to the new breed of workers. The CWU in Ireland and the HK Union in Denmark, have made attempts to organise teleworkers, including the self-employed, with mixed results.

In an interesting recent turnaround, a public-sector telework programme in the US was recently stopped by the employer in circumstances where the union was effectively demanding the right to telework for employees. Around 300 senior patent examiners in the US Patent and Trademark Office were taking part in a telework trial where most were working from home one day a week. When the pilot concluded in May 2002, their union, the Patent Office Professional Association, wanted to roll-over the existing arrangements and continue teleworking. Their employer refused, and a war of words between the two sides took place via press, radio and websites.

The union president said that an 11th-hour list of changes was presented by the employers which could not be responded to in time, and that the list of grades allowed to telework proposed by the employers meant that the Patent Office would not be able to meet the terms of the 'Wolf' bill which requires a certain percentage of US government-agency workers to be be allowed to telework.

Unlike most European programmes, the Patent Office employees had mainly bought their own hardware, software and home-office furniture. The employer wanted to limit teleworking in future to include only those who run machines with Windows XP or Windows 2000. According to the union president, the employer had also claimed that they saw no financial benefit from the programme – in fact it cost the agency money – but the union says the calculations did not include valuations of indirect effects on employee morale, traffic congestion, air pollution, enegy consumption, and commuting time and costs for employees.

HOME OFFICES

Detailed information on teleworker equipment and home-office safety and legal issues is given in Chapter 8, Technology and techniques and Chapter 9, *Staying safe and legal*.

The basics

As a general guide, employers should treat the home-office work area and equipment used as though they were part of their main office site. It is common practice that equipment should be supplied by, and remain the property of, the employer, largely for reasons of support, data security and health and safety. In fact, the recent European framework agreement on teleworking specifies that employers should normally supply teleworking equipment. In some situations it may be appropriate for employees to use their own equipment, but if this occurs, the equipment must be assessed from a health and safety viewpoint as well as for its suitability.

Veteran teleworkers favour a separate building for the home office to provide a work environment away from the potential distraction of the home, to assist with 'switching off' at the end of the day and to prevent work material from becoming distributed around the house. Failing a separate office, the space for the home office should be carefully chosen to take it out of the main family thoroughfare – and ideally it should be lockable.

Check that you have enough power and telephone sockets (you may also want to allow for future expansion when running cables); that ventilation, file storage and lighting will be adequate; and that you can lock storage, and even the home-office room itself, if necessary. Get surge-suppressed sockets for your PC and other IT equipment which should prevent damage due to voltage spikes such as may occur during thunderstorms. Make sure you have a smoke detector and a fire extinguisher, and that there is an adequate escape route from the home office in case of fire. Get a first-aid kit. All cables need to be tidied away so that you cannot trip over them.

If you have more than one PC, invest in a home network – it will save you considerable time shuttling data from one machine to another on disks and allow you to share facilities such as backup devices, Internet connections and printers more effectively. A four-port network hub and cables can cost less than £80. A wireless network like Buffalo or Netgear that avoids spaghetti junctions of cable costs around £300 for a kit including two network cards and a personal firewall (and of course, also saves you the cost of the cabling).

Furniture should be adjustable to provide correct working heights – a good-quality, comfortable, adjustable chair is especially important. Ian Fletcher-Price of ergonomic office furniture supplier Posturite UK Ltd comments: 'Invest some time in getting the ergonomics right. Reducing stress is the reason many of us choose to work from home in the first place. If you only make one ergonomic investment, buy a good-quality office chair. The position of the computer on the desk is also vital – make sure you are sitting directly face-on to the computer screen. Position your screen at the right height so the top of the visible screen is at eye-level.'

Saving space

Home offices are often characterised by lack of space, so good use needs to be made of available room. Both office- and home-furniture manufacturers produce special ranges such as lock-away desks and cabinets where computers can be kept, space-saving furniture (e.g. wall beds, high-level shelving) and home-friendly office furniture. *See* **http://www.homeworkingsolutions.co.uk/** for some examples.

If you can afford it, get a thin LCD screen, or an all-in-one PC where there is no separate CPU unit.

Think about an ergonomic extending arm for your screen to sit on so you can push it out of the way when you don't need it, and so you can ensure that the monitor is in the ideal position when you do need it (**http://www.ergotron.com**).

Buy a combination printer/fax/scanner – HP have some good ones at **http://www.hp.com**

If you are one of those techies who has to have five PCs operating at once, think about the KVM Smart2 switch which allows you to operate two PCs off one screen and keyboard (**http://www.minicom.com/smart2ports1.htm**).

Shelving – obvious but vital. Make sure it's in an accessible place so you don't overbalance or strain your back lifting down files and reference works.

Sometimes teleworkers simply collect office supplies when in the office, but there are also many online stationery stores that will deliver around the country such as **http://www.viking.co.uk**

Garden offices

The rise in teleworking numbers has seen a vast increase in the number and and variety of 'garden offices' – workspace that can often be put up in the grounds of a house without planning permission as long as it does not exceed a certain size, and which has the advantage of separation from the house, providing fewer domestic interruptions. In addition, garden offices allow homeworkers to compartmentalise their lives more successfully between home and work – you can close the door and walk away from it without being tempted to overwork late into the night. Some suppliers are now reporting that they are getting enquiries from companies who want to assist staff in acquiring a garden office, usually through some form of soft loan.

What to think about

Design – does it fit with your house?

Size – will you need it made to measure, or is there a range of modular sizes?

Quality – are you paying enough for a long-term solution?

Portability – if you move, can you take it with you?

Insurance – check it out with your insurance provider.

Reference sites – can you see one that's been in position for a while to check how it has weathered?

Insulation – vital or you'll freeze in winter and boil in summer.

Groundworks – most will require something put in place, although not necessarily full concrete foundations.

Power – don't forget that computers multiply.

Telephone – one trick is to put down plastic water pipe with 24-core cable pulled through (flush through a cork attached to a fishing line first, then tie on the cable). This can be attached to a telephone point in the house.

Glazing – laminated double-glazing helps with insurance and security.

Paths – you need one to keep down the mud in the winter.

Orientation – consider the views and the effect of the sun. Overhanging roofs can keep out excessive light and heat.

Security – a proper lock and double-glazing. You may also want to try a security device on the PC, such as as cable locks or armoured casing.

Here is a brief flavour of some of the current offerings, which range from the utilitarian to the luxurious.

The Work Yurt

A circular building based on building design from Asia Minor, with a clear roof and clear upper walls, supplied in kit form with overhead lighting and mains sockets. Its inventor Robin Towsey says that the circular design makes maximum use of the available space, with a large desk area and plenty of space for IT equipment and files. Towsey says the Work Yurt eliminates the cost and hassle of an extension, the social intrusion of a conservatory, and the crudity of having to work in a garden shed. Tel: 01420 472117.

The Home/Office Studio

This is a small rectangular office with windows that features a modular construction – it breaks down into pieces which can fit through a standard 760 mm x 1980 mm doorway. Tel: 01604 870325 or 0797 4861229.

The Home Office

A secure, fully wired and insulated unit at prices starting from £9910 that can be installed in two days. More spacious than some. Temple Co Ten, Tel: 01283 712710 or **http://www.tc10.com**

The Henley garden office

Forest Garden timber buildings

These are ornate timber buildings in a range of designs which may fit in better if your garden is also ornate. Tel: 01886 811030 or
http://www.forestgarden.co.uk

The Ardis

A flat-packed futuristic-looking garden shed that probably won't need planning permission. The Ardis is delivered including materials for foundations. Prices start from £7000 – more information from **http://www.ardisdesign.co.uk**

The Henley

The Henley sees itself as the new company car, according to Managing Director Charles Dalton, who reports that companies are now assisting with garden-office purchases by setting up leasing deals which can be offset against tax. The Henley has five external skins, double-glazing, electrics and telephone points, and can be delivered and installed ready-to-work in just one day. On planning permission the manufacurers say that if in doubt, you should asked your local planning department: 'Planning permission will be required if you live in a conservation area, if it's within five metres of your home, or if it's between you and the highway.' The manufacturers advise informing your neighbours too. The Henley occupies just six square metres of floorspace and if you move, its modular construction means it can be taken with you or sold on to another user. Costs £4999. **http://www.henley-offices.com**

The online park bench

We kid you not. MSN (Microsoft Network) persuaded Bury St Edmunds council to install laptop power and communications sockets in a park bench at Abbey Gardens in 2001. MSN paid the phone bills for the first three months of the trial. Of course, being a park, vandalism was to be expected. Two teenagers took a handset to the park, managed to get a free international line and attempted to phone the bench's sponsor, a Mr Bill Gates. As a result, mobile, national and international calls are now banned. The Gardens are patrolled by park keepers who keep an eye on the bench, which also has weatherproof flaps to protect the sockets.

Scandia Hus

Garden lodge, Scandinavian style – bespoke timber frames. Tel: 01291 437050.

Southern Sheds

'Quality garden buildings.' Tel: 01634 200694.

Communications: it's good to talk

This section focuses on the communications aspects of teleworking equipment – more technical details and information abour PCs and the Internet are dealt with in Chapter 8, *Technology and techniques.*

Teleworkers have to make maximum use of all the communications tools available to keep in touch with the people who pay them. Because you are not physically in the same office, it is vital to respond quickly and effectively so that your client or employer feels secure that you are on top of your work for them and they can rely on you to complete the task. It's good to talk, as the advert goes, but for teleworkers the secret of success is to pick the right communications tool for the job.

Teleworkers don't have the luxury (or nuisance, depending on your view) of constant face-to-face meetings, with all the nuances of body language and time for discussion, or informal chats in the corridor. It is very easy to pick up the wrong end of the stick and make an expensive mistake, or develop a grudge or irritation with a colleague which would never happen in the conventional office environment. Learning to be a teleworker requires good attention to communications tools and skills. On the other hand, face-to-face meetings for teleworkers often take on new and more interesting roles – they may become about team-building, training, developing relationships and discussing possibilities rather than about imparting routine information.

Telephone

A separate line is vital to separate personal and work calls. This is desirable for both professional and psychological reasons. Phone costs should be paid for directly by the employer so that there is no perceived tax benefit. Whether you

go for ISDN or not (*see* below), you will probably want a separate telephone line so that you can easily distinguish business and personal calls and monitor business costs. Business lines are more expensive than residential, but usually guarantee a faster fault-repair service and entitle you to a free text-only Yellow Pages entry.

If there are problems supplying an extra line, a service from BT called Call Sign allows two numbers to be handled from one phone, with each line distinguished by a separate ring (e.g. home and office calls or voice and fax calls). The choice of service providers is growing too fast for detailed coverage in a book. Comparisons between different operators' costs and offerings can be found at **http://www.tariffcentre.com** The regulator Oftel also has guidelines for comparison services at **http://www.oftel.gov.uk/consumer/price_compare/ index.htm**

If your job involves a lot of telephone work, the best solution is a cordless handset which connects to a good-quality headset. Don't throw out your old conventional handset though − if you have a power-cut the chances are that your snazzy cordless phone will stop working even though the phone-line itself is not affected. In order to keep answering your calls during a power failure you will need to plug the old analogue handset directly into the phone socket. These are available for about £100 − one supplier is **http://www.headsetco.co.uk** General advice on telecoms services is available at **http://www.telecomsadvice.org.uk** which is subsidised by various telcos.

You can improve the flexibility of your telephone with some low-cost enhancements. Different phone companies offer slightly different services under slightly different names, but offerings are similar. Call Waiting alerts you when a caller is trying to get through while you're using the phone; you can switch between calls. Call Diversion redirects incoming calls to any other number, so you can receive them at someone else's premises or on your mobile – and it's quite a sophisticated function. For most handsets code 21 diverts all calls, code 61 just diverts calls not answered while code 67 diverts calls which come in to a busy line. Three Way Calling lets you talk to two other numbers simultaneously for small 'audio meetings' or audio conferences. Caller Line Identification allows you to see on a display who is calling your number. Call Minder sets up a personal voice mailbox that works like an answering machine, recording messages when you're out or engaged, and playing them back to you through the phone. None of these services requires any extra equipment other than a standard touchtone telephone handset. Some are even free – all you have to do is ask for them.

Keep a duplicate message book by the phone for writing brief notes of telephone calls. This gives you a record of information from the telephone call, and also provides a method for other people in the house to take messages and leave them for you in an agreed format and place.

Mobile phones are hugely convenient but unless you have a flawless memory, you still need a way of recording the salient details of the message while pulled over at the side of the road, or walking along a railway platform. Most phones now have a message-taking utility. You can record the details of the mobile call straight away, and play back the recording for action when you return to the office. You can also use your mobile phone to dial your home or office voicemail and leave details of the message or idea for collection and action later.

Corporate voicemail systems can often be used to take messages for teleworkers, though some can be hard to programme remotely when you are at home. Make sure your voicemail message is dated, states when you will be next available, and whether an alternative number can be called. The voicemail service also answers if a second caller rings when you are busy with another call. You need to know how to call forward using the company's PABX (switchboard) to ensure that your calls will follow you home on a day when you are teleworking. Forgetting to set call forward the night before is a common, practical teleworking problem and teleworkers should assign an 'office buddy' who knows how to redirect their extension to overcome this difficulty.

Some systems offer remote call diversion – a useful facility to redirect your calls from any phone. You dial your number and when you get the voicemail greeting, enter a PIN code followed by the new number to divert to – this way you can ensure that your calls follow you when out of the office. Increasingly, transferable personal numbers are also being used. A permanent or personal number is assigned by the company which can be linked to various different locations – mobile, home, office – as appropriate by the teleworker.

Featureline is a BT system which can turn a collection of separate lines at various premises into a switchboard using facilities on the local digital exchange. It is used by many 'virtual companies' where most people work from home. Phones at locations up to 30 miles apart can be used as switchboard extensions, with facilities such as call diversion, call transfer between extensions, ring back when free, ring back when next used, call barring, five-way call waiting and three-way calling. Call answering can be set up in cyclical hunting to ensure even distribution of calls between a set of lines at different locations. At the time of writing, Featureline costs £99 for a new line, or £15 to upgrade an existing line, plus rental charges of £50.58 per quarter.

There are also some service companies that offer message-taking services by using call diversion from the teleworker's home, in conjunction with caller line identification tools to create a customised, human response which can be important in certain occupations.

CTI technology (computer telephony integration) is now widely available through packages such as Goldmine (**http://www.goldminesw.com**) which can use features such as caller line identification to allow your PC to produce relevant information from your database about a caller, and to record and make calls without physically having to dial. This is useful for people involved in sales and support.

For directory services you can search online at **http://www.bt.com/directory-enquiries/** or at **http://www.yell.com** You can also get the entire UK business subscriber phone catalogue in database format on CD-ROM for a mere £99.95 plus VAT from Thomson Directories (**http://www.infospace.com/uk.thomw/**) – this has more search possibilities and can also be used for printing out mailing information at a cost of about 11p per address.

Internet telephony

Many large companies are also now beginning to integrate their data networks to provide voice services as well as data over an IP connection – when high-bandwidth Internet connections are used, the quality of the voice connections is unaffected. The basic idea behind VOIP in the company setting is that voice calls are treated like data and sent down the same wires. Your telephone number becomes a specific IP address. If you move around the country, call redirection becomes simple because every time you attach your PC or phone, the VOIP software can redirect your calls to you, making supporting mobile teleworkers much easier.

Some companies, such as Nortel and Cisco, install a router and high-speed Internet connection for their teleworkers as standard. This allows phone and data services to be accessed as if the homeworker were in the office (e.g. speed dial and corporate phone directories) without increasing data security risks. VOIP calls are cheaper to make for international calls than standard PSTN calls. Many recent PBXs already have the facility to allow connections via VOIP to remote workers. Otherwise, companies that are upgrading their communications systems can convert from a conventional PBX to a 'voice server' which attaches to the company LAN rather than to the telephone system.

ISDN (Integrated Services Digital Network) lines

Where teleworkers need access to company databases, or require larger amounts of data transfer, but VOIP is not available, an ISDN line may be suitable. This allows faster transfer of data, high-quality voice communication and basic video conferencing. A number of devices (up to six) can share the same ISDN line, so only one is likely to be required per teleworker. However, only two devices can be used at any one time on standard 'basic rate' ISDN.

ISDN is not available on some older exchanges although BT says that over 90% of the population is now covered (which does not equate to 90% of the country), so enquiries will need to be made with your telephone supplier for specific locations, especially in rural areas. ISDN will not normally work if you are more than 4 km from the local exchange although in some circumstances distances of nearly 8 km have been found to work. Don't accept a bland 'everyone can get ISDN' answer. Ask them to check specifically whether your exchange does ISDN and if you are within the distance limit from the exchange for it to work reliably. Bear in mind that ISDN is essentially a 1990s technology rapidly being replaced by newer broadband technologies such as DSL – although if DSL is not available on your exchange, ISDN will provide better facilities than a standard dial-up line.

BT's HomeHighway ISDN offering costs about £75 for conversion of an existing line with rental of about £25 a month (**http://www.bt.com/ homehighway**). Check the details of the scheme on the informative website.

For information on broadband services and video conferencing *see* Chapter 8, *Technology and techniques*.

Audio conferencing

A telephone communication method which is often overlooked as being 'low technology' is the audio or telephone conference. Audio conferences for up to three people can be arranged through the basic call services available on your phone on request from most telephone companies.

Telephone companies and specialist teleconferencing firms will set up calls for more than three people on a one-off basis – the technological bells and whistles are at their end, and participants can use any normal phone. There are two flavours of audio conference – dial-in and dial-out. For dial-in conferencing, the conference participants dial a special telephone number and are greeted by a receptionist who checks their identity before linking them to the conference.

Theoretically up to 20 people can join in an audio conference, but from the point of view of running an effective meeting, audio conferences work best with

CONFERENCING TECHNIQUES

● *Appoint an effective chairperson.*

● *An agenda and any other supporting documentation which participants need to have available should be sent round in advance of the audio conference.*

● *The smaller the group, the more effective the audio conference will probably be at reaching decisions or deciding on a plan of action.*

● *The chairperson should begin the conference (unless everyone knows each other and is used to the technique) with brief introductions and a summary of any rules (such as identifying yourself when you speak and not assuming that everyone else will recognise your voice).*

● *Participants should ensure that they are in a quiet space with few interruptions. Try to avoid rustling papers, chewing and slurping if you are on a speakerphone.*

● *Because you can't use glances and gestures, remember to address by name the person you want a response from.*

● *Wait your turn and try to avoid interruption – not just for politeness, but also because some conference 'bridge' software with speakerphones will allow only one person to be heard at a time. If you jump in, you cut them off.*

● *Avoid very open statements such as 'any comments', especially with a large group. Instead use a round-robin technique to gather points or else specify which people you want to comment.*

● *Where decisions are crucial or have major financial or legal implications, consider taping the call and getting it transcribed if necessary.*

up to ten people. Audio conferences are extremely cost-effective for a group of people who need to discuss a topic but don't want the time and expense of a face-to-face meeting. If some only need to listen in without talking, you can have an audience of hundreds on a single call – this is sometimes done when companies give briefings on their financial results to stockmarket analysts.

BT offers a conferencing service aimed at the residential sector, called Buzz-in. Up to 20 people can call in to any number you specify from 6.00 p.m. to 6.00 a.m. weekdays and all weekend with some international access. There are no registration charges but each caller pays 10p per minute (*see* **http://buzz-in.bt.com**). Community Network offers a service for non-profit organisations at **http://www.community-network.org**

Another form of audio conferencing allows a remote participant to join in a face-to-face meeting by means of a speakerphone. Ideally, the speakerphone should have 'full duplex capability', which means that those present in the room and the remote participant can all speak at once without cutting each other off. Phones which do not have this capability require participants to be very careful about not talking over one another. For more than one remote participant, you'll need an 'audio bridge', a piece of hardware which attaches to the switchboard or PBX. If you want to remind those in the face-to-face meeting to include the audio-conferencing members of the group, try sticking a sign on the speakerphone with the person's name in large letters.

Fax

Where fax facilities are required more than occasionally, an additional line rather than a line shared between telephone and fax is recommended to avoid annoying busy lines. If significant online work is being performed, a separate line for the Internet should also be installed, otherwise your faxes won't be able to come in because you are online. If the online usage is low then sharing Internet access with the fax line should be adequate. It may be worthwhile to consider installing one ISDN line which can be used for different purposes simultaneously (such as fax and voice calls – *see* above). Telephone companies also offer 'faxminding' services where faxes are stored by the company and can be retrieved by dialling a special number from any fax or a PC-based fax. More information on mobile and 'virtual' fax services is given in the mobile messaging section below.

Many people now use computer-based faxes, saving the cost of a separate fax machine. Using this route, unless you have a scanner, you will not be able to send graphical pages such as sketches or diagrams, except where they have been created on the computer. As the computer fax modem is usually also used for email, if you handle a lot of messages on the same modem and telephone line you may find the fax is occupying the line when you want to send email and vice versa. You will need to leave your computer on all the time so that faxes can be received on a 24-hour basis. If your computer crashes it will prevent further faxes from being received until it is reset.

For those who need more than a computer-based fax system, but have limited home-office space or don't wish to leave their PC on all the time, a combined printer/fax/scanner/copier device may be the answer.

Email

There are three keys to the successful use of email:

- Use a mail reader which allows the filing of messages into different folders, and which will allow you to sort or search messages by sender, subject and date. This allows easy retrieval of information or instructions relating to a project.
- Use a mail reader with an easy-to-use address-book function, which allows you to quickly 'lift' an email address from an incoming message.

■ Keep a pad by the computer when you are reading your email to write down information such as instructions received which you need to act on. Of course you can print out the whole message, but usually it's only a couple of words that you actually need. Either way, do something to put the information on your action list, or you may forget the contents immediately after reading the email.

Post and couriers

In many situations, work still needs to be sent by post – even if it's on disk! Unless you have access to ISDN file transfer, the practical limit in cost and time terms for moving files around by email is about 2–3 megabytes. In fact, many ISPs block emails which exceed this size. The postal service (or courier where extra speed is required) provides a largely reliable and fast door-to-door service. If you are working for a company, you must ensure that company mail is regularly delivered to you – for example, pigeonholes can be allocated and regularly swept by the internal system before being redirected, or you may have an office buddy who checks your mail for anything urgent on days when you are teleworking.

It may also be necessary to make arrangements for urgent deliveries via courier on occasion. Be clear on issues such as the last posting time at your local postbox or office, the time at which your post arrives (in some rural areas this can be as late as 3.00 p.m., causing problems for teleworkers who need to turn work round fast) and the different services available, such as Swiftair, registered post and Mailsort. Courier companies will have 'last pickup' deadlines for your area, and different delivery times for areas of the world. You don't know when you'll need them, so make sure you have up-to-date pricelists and contact numbers for all your delivery services.

Log all incoming and outgoing post so that if anything goes missing, you can show when and how it left you. Where disks arrive by post, check immediately that they are readable, even if you don't plan to work on that project for a few days. That way, if there is a problem, you can request a replacement disk without disturbing your schedule, and the client won't know that you 'sat on it' for a few days – it can be difficult to explain why you are phoning up to request a new disk the day before the deadline...

Security

Physical security, data security and insurance issues are covered in detail in Chapter 9, *Staying safe and legal*. Many commercial insurers have developed specific home-office policies to reflect the move to teleworking. Domestic insurance policies will not normally cover home-office equipment including PCs, so teleworkers must notify their home-contents insurers of their intention to work from home.

Security surveys show that the most likely causes of home-office problems are not viruses or hacking, but more basic issues such as power cuts, hard-disk crashes or fire damage. For more information on data security *see* Chapter 8, *Technology and techniques*. Make sure you know the procedures for backing up data (usually you will be required to store some backups away from the home office), and any specific instructions concerning the storage of important or sensitive papers such as locked storage space.

ON THE MOVE

Tools and equipment

Mobile phones

First things first: chances are you need a phone that can handle data. GSM phones are really too slow to be useful in sending and receiving email or accessing the web, although it is possible. Most network operators now offer slightly faster HSCSD service (a flavour of GSM), and many are rapidly rolling out GPRS services.

All mobile workers can benefit from spending a bit of time with their phone manual and their mobile service provider's website to work out how to do some of the following (available on most current models):

- Use playback/voicemail functions – your mailbox number is usually one digit different from your normal mobile number.
- Switch on EFR (Enhanced Full Rate) technology which improves call quality on many phones.
- Automatically divert calls to a message minder or alternative number when your phone is out of signal coverage or battery life, to avoid your clients finding that your mobile number rings out.
- Use call waiting and call hold to answer a second call coming in when you are already talking.
- Restrict the phone's dial-out usage to a small range of numbers (useful if your mobile is ever likely to be used by other members of the family). You can also bar international calls from being made or received.
- Use your phone to programme-in numbers and names so that the identity of frequent callers appears on the phone before you answer (e.g. you tell the phone that number 123 456789 is your important client Sam, and Sam's name will then pop up on the phone's screen whenever he calls so you can answer 'Hi Sam – how can I help you?').
- Send SMS text messages to other mobile users from your phone or through your service provider's website.
- Send and receive fax calls (if you have a mobile which can do this) or divert faxes to a suitable number as appropriate (many providers offer a fax mailbox service which can store messages until you have a fax number available for redirection).

MOBILE PHONE USE IN CARS TO BE BANNED?

The British government, having dragged its feet for years on this topic, is now warning drivers against using mobile phones except where they have pulled over. Although so far no specific offence has been legislated, companies may wish to ensure that their employees are given instructions on safe use of mobiles.

Research from the Transport Research Laboratory in 1998 showed that drivers using mobile phones show the same lack of control as motorists who have drunk the legal maximum – and the risk is the same for hands-free phones. An experiment by insurance company Direct Line in 2002 using driving simulators compared the effect of talking on a mobile phone to that of a blood alcohol level above the legal limit using 20 subjects. The results showed that reaction times were approximately 30% slower when talking on a mobile phone than when legally drunk – and about 50% slower than would be expected under normal driving conditions.

John Howard of RoSPA commented: 'A passenger will shut up if you get into a difficult situation or understand why the driver has broken off the conversation. But if you are talking to head office or to a client, there is a natural inclination to continue the conversation. There is research to show that people try to drive through much narrower gaps when they are on the telephone than they would normally.' RoSPA believes that mobile phones have been implicated in at least 16 road deaths, and has called for a ban on the use of mobile phones in cars.

Present legislation can fine drivers up to £2500 plus endorsements for careless driving, and in extreme cases could impose two years' imprisonment, unlimited fines and disqualification. In the US some states have brought in legislation which bans the use of hand-held phones but allows the use of hands-free car kits. In Ireland, similar legislation under which drivers using hand-held mobiles could be fined up to 345 euros or banned from driving for six months is currently mired by issues raised by the Gardai (police) on how the ban is to be enforced in practice.

■ Use your phone with a laptop computer to send and receive email or to access the Internet.

■ Some phone retailers now offer a service where you can have all the numbers you have laboriously programmed into your phone stored so that if your phone is stolen or damaged, the numbers can be loaded onto a new phone quickly. Also some newer, higher-end models now come with software that allows you to back your phone up to your PC or laptop using a cable or infrared connection.

■ If you are usually at one base but occasionally use a mobile, consider keeping your mobile number private and just diverting your office phone when out of the office. This allows you to give out just one number, and avoids problems with messages on mobile voicemail sometimes going unheard for days because you're in the office and the mobile is switched off.

PDAs

Before buying or ordering a laptop, check out PDAs (personal digital assistants). These devices are considerably lighter than a laptop and use less power (the Handspring Visor will run on one set of AAA batteries for about a month), and are currently developing very fast. You can get PDAs which will allow you to collect email, act as a mobile handset and run some basic applications such as word processors. *See* p. 259.

A number of new devices which are hybrids between PDAs and GPRS phones (sometimes known as 'combos') are appearing on the market, such as the Blackberry, so you should consider whether or not these could carry out some of your data and phone functions, releasing you from the need to lug a laptop everywhere. A good source of practical information on PDAs is the website **http://www.youcanworkfromanywhere.com** which is maintained by 'Phil Montero, the mobile man'. Think through carefully the relative merits and capabilities of PDAs in relation to the functions you personally require when on the move before making a decision.

Laptops

If you have a say, make sure your laptop is an ultra-slim, portable model and not a weighty desktop replacement. They are more expensive but your back will be eternally grateful. Wireless hardware (WiFi or 802.11 standard) is now widely available as an add-on for laptops and can make connecting to the office network a doddle.

The downside of choosing an ultra-slim notebook-type machine is that of course, there is less room for add-ons. They also tend to be less robust. Typically it will cost extra to include a CD-ROM drive, which often has to double up with other functions either through units which slot in and out of the computer, or via a docking unit. Often some ports (such as PS1, parallel or serial) are missing from notebook machines and can only be added through a docking unit.

Make sure you have an extra battery to increase your working time when away from a power source – and also because the battery will probably die before the laptop, at which point you will find it is not possible to get a new battery as they are now obsolete. Also spend time optimising settings on your laptop for minimum power use – typically you can control how quickly the laptop blanks its screen and powers down its hard disk if there is no activity, and you can cut down the number of autosaves carried out by programmes such as Word.

Some laptops allow you to dim your screen or work in black and white mode to save power. There are also chargers which will recharge two batteries at once, though they come at a price. A device from APC can allow your laptop to

LETTING THE TRAIN TAKE THE STRAIN FOR MOBILE WORKERS

A summer 1998 survey by BT showed that of 500 business train-travellers, over two-thirds worked on the train. About half of those who worked 40 hours a week did so, plus over 80% of those working more than 55 hours a week.

Companies came in for some stick with 14% of 'journeyworkers' frustrated that they did not have the right technology. Nearly one in five believed they could reduce their working hours and improve efficiency if they had the right equipment.

Almost half wanted carriages dedicated to executives who want to work, and 40% wanted power supplies for laptop computers installed on trains. Only 12% said that they would like to see trains with mobile meeting rooms, and would be prepared to pay for these.

recharge from your car's cigarette lighter, or from aeroplane in-flight seat connectors (*see* **http://www.apc.com/gb**). If you travel outside your own car, a lock for your laptop bag can be a very useful extra.

A poll by MORI sponsored by laptop-makers Toshiba in 2000 found that laptop-users work longer hours than the average worker, and believe that they are more productive. The survey found that 44% of working laptop-users are on duty for 45 hours or more a week. Their average working week is 5.6 hours a week longer than the national average working week of 37.91.

Nearly two-thirds of users (64%) believe their laptop has made them more productive, but almost three in ten (2%) admit they have worked longer hours since getting the technology. Interestingly, nearly four in ten (39%) of laptop-users who work say they never work from home, while one in four (26%) say they are prevented by employers from working from home more regularly.

Just over half of laptop-users (54%) access the Internet through the device while 57% use it for email. Three out of five (62%) admit to not using all the functions on their laptop that could be of use to them.

More than two-thirds (70%) agree that developments in mobile technology will offer them more freedom in their working lives. Only one in five (20%) said that they found it more difficult to separate home and work life since getting their laptop, while just one in ten (10%) felt they were 'too dependent' on their laptop.

Two good sources of practical tips on laptop use are **http://www.roadnews.com** and **http://www.youcanworkfromanywhere.com**

Until now, one haven of escape for the hard-pressed mobile worker has been air travel. But the last refuge from the 24-hour workplace is about to disappear. United Airlines, Delta and American Airlines are to install the Boeing broadband Connexion service, offering Internet connections to every seat on 1500 aircraft for a cost of about £15 an hour. Fortunately this development is not likely to spread to Europe for some time yet.

Remote access to your desktop PC

Need to download that vital presentation file you left behind as you rushed to catch your plane? Many company networks provide facilities for forwarding mail to web mailboxes, and some permit direct web-mail access to their mail servers – although some do not for security reasons.

There are various products which can help you to get access to email and files when you are on the move. Some have been around for a while, like PC Anywhere, and provide 'remote control' of your desktop computer. You can install PC Anywhere on your office PC and your home PC or laptop. The office PC can act as the 'host' and be set to answer an incoming call from the remote, at which point it will allow the remote PC to control it. Other similar packages are Carbon Copy and Timbuktu. Many companies do not allow these connections for data security reasons.

There is also a new generation of products that can provide access from any other Internet-connected device, including PCs in cybercafés, or a PDA that you carry around with you. Examples include 'I'm in touch' (*see* **http://www.01com.com**) or the subscription service GoToMyPC (**http://www.gotomypc.com**). Both products include encryption security using 128 bit SSL encryption (often used for Internet-based banking services) so that installing this software does not open up your desktop PC to hacking.

However, these products only work if your desktop PC has an 'always on' Internet connection with its own dynamic or static IP address, such as that provided via a DSL connection. An advantage of this approach is that there is no need to synchronise data when you return to the office – you simply access the PC remotely, read, reply to and if necessary delete emails. Additionally, I'm in Touch allows you to view email attachments such as PDF files remotely, even if the device you are using while on the move does not have suitable browser software. This product can also notify your mobile device of the arrival of emails, and notify or forward fax or voicemail messages to a remote location.

Printers

Many mobile workers can get away with just using printers in the office, or at home, or at a touchdown centre or cybercafé. Another option is to fax the document from your laptop to a local fax in order to produce a printout.

But if you have to actually lug a printer with you to do your job (e.g. for producing written quotes onsite for customers), get a compact printer. There are three basic types: thermal, thermal transfer (like a till-roll or an old-fashioned fax without plain paper), or inkjet. Thermal and thermal-transfer printers can be very small and light, but inkjet output is generally of higher quality. Most black-and-white portable printers can manage a maximum speed of about four pages a minute. If you do need to print multiple pages, pay attention to sheet-feeder facilities and battery life. NiCad batteries can usually manage about 90 pages and be recharged in the printer; NiMH batteries can usually do about 250 pages but take longer to recharge. Operating costs (cartridges, etc.) tend to be higher for portable printers because all the supplies have to be smaller and lighter. Examples include the Pentax Pocketjet which weighs less than half a kilo including the rechargable battery, and various HP models.

Motorway touchdown centres
Both the hotel and food group Whitbread and motorway services provider Moto (formerly Granada) have dipped a toe into providing roadside touchdown facilities for teleworkers. The public response hasn't been as expected, and the BT joint venture with Moto entitled Workspace has been put on the back burner in favour of a cheaper network of bookable meeting rooms located in 40 Travelodges around the UK.

Initially Workspace opened three 6000 square foot BT-branded lounges at service stations along the M4, offering hotdesks, secure data connections, video-conferencing facilities, secretarial support and meeting rooms, as well as showers, food and drink. They were planned for an average two-hour stay by customers, with capacity for around 80 people each. The project involved over £1m of venture capital funding.

These three centres are to remain open, but instead of expanding to a network of 100, the focus is now on smaller and more basic centres offering meeting rooms with flipcharts and video equipment. There are no plans to offer solo drop-in facilities at the new sites. An editorial in *Teleworker Magazine* commented: 'Touchdown desks are having to compete hard with a free seat right next door in the Little Chef or burger bar. With only a handful of centres in place, which were not supported by a significant marketing campaign, and not highlighted on service-station entrance signs, maybe they weren't given the best chance.' **http://www.workspace.travelodge.co.uk**

Getting deliveries
For mobile teleworkers who work from home as a base, one frustrating problem is receiving deliveries. Whether it's a courier with your replacement laptop, or the postman with a box of office supplies, if it won't fit through your letter box it can involve waiting in, or games of tag where those annoying little cards saying 'we tried to deliver' pop through your letterbox. There are several possible solutions to this problem.

The Hippo is a lockable, strong metal box which can be securely fastened in a suitable place outside your house. You leave the Hippo unlocked, and well signposted from your front door. The delivery company opens the Hippo, leaving the package (and if necessary receiving a signed permission slip to deliver from you, if there is a problem about the need for a signature). The

THE INDISPENSABLE POST OFFICE

Royal Mail is finally catching up with ideas pioneered some six years ago by Roger Purkiss, postmaster of Keswick Post Office in the Lake District.

Royal Mail is proposing that post offices should become places to collect purchases made over the Internet, and host computers providing customers and staff with Internet access. Roger trialled the Telework Association's remote shopping initiative with Great Universal way back in 1994. And he has had do-it-yourself computer access available for eight years. He also makes and sells PCs.

In 2000 he opened a first-floor extension to the post office with five workstations, known as U-compute: 'We originally thought people would hire computers to do their own work but that only worked to some degree. They were far happier to bring us work and for us to do it for them. We also found all the little guest houses had their own machines and wanted all those supplies like ink cartridges – from there we moved on to making and selling our own PCs.'

Purkiss is impressed by the EasyEverything cybercafé operation (see page 117) but realises that most people just need to pick up their email quickly, so his pricing is currently set at £2 for 20 minutes. He also plans to provide a babysitting service: 'If we can open later than our current 8.00 p.m., parents can leave their children here occupied on the computers whilst they go out for a peaceful dinner!'

Of course Keswick, as a major tourist centre, is slightly unusual in having a large summer population of visitors needing computer access; but Royal Mail should keep an eye on Roger's next moves as he's clearly ahead of the game.

delivery company closes the Hippo, locking it until you get home and can use your personal key to retrieve the package (**http://www.giraffemarketing.co.uk**).

If you are based in a city you can use a serviced office to receive packages, or the Mail Boxes, etc. service run from EasyEverything cybercafés (**http://www.easyeverything.co.uk**). And of course don't forget your local post office. Many, especially in rural areas, are happy to sign for and look after packages but not all offer this service. Try out Royal Mail's Decide and Deliver service next time you are web shopping (**http://www.royalmail.com**).

International travellers

A set of international power and phone connectors is vital if you are going to be travelling abroad (*see* **http://www.teleadapt.com** or **http://www.laptoptravel.com**). You may also need to set your dial-up connection so that it does not check for a dialtone, since the dialtone at your destination may not be one the computer can recognise. This is normally done by going into the Windows control panel and checking your modem settings. Find the call preferences section and make sure that anything labelled 'wait for dial tone before dialling' is unchecked.

Print a hard copy of your contacts database and take it with you – otherwise, if your laptop goes down, the contacts list will be useless.

Switch to online banking if you haven't already.

Keep a printed list of helpline numbers for your vital equipment and software. Store a printout of your passwords separately in a secure place, especially any user IDs and passwords for accessing email services.

Steve Kropla's website **http://kropla.com** is well worth investigating. It includes a worldwide phone guide explaining how to get online from different locations around the world. There is also a country-by-country catalogue of power supplies and plug types around the world, as well as information on dialling codes and telephone connectors.

Some luxury hotels specialising in business travellers are beginning to take on board the need for better connectivity. Ritz-Carlton hotels have introduced 'technology butlers' who can help guests access the web, receive faxes and email on their own laptops and even help with software configuration. The Hilton chain is also planning to provide wireless net access for guests. Business travellers will receive an Ethernet card at check-in which can be inserted into a laptop, providing a data link to the hotel's LAN at speeds ten times faster than a dial-up modem.

Mobile messaging

Faxing on the move

There are many digitally based fax services available. Most will offer free incoming faxes that are delivered via email (usually as Acrobat .pdf files), and low-cost outgoing faxes billed monthly. These types of services are particularly useful when you are working abroad as you do not incur international call charges.

Try **http://www.e-fax.com** or **http://www.j2.com** or **http://www.eFax.com** This is a rapidly changing area and it is worth checking out **http://www.northcoast.com/savetz/fax-faq.html** for a list of current service offerings around the world. An example of a not-for-profit email to fax service with widespread coverage can be found at **http://www.tpc.int**

Picking a suitable ISP

Not all Internet service providers are set up for remote use outside their local area. If you are going to be working abroad and you have any say in the choice of ISP, try to use one which has local access nodes in a number of countries, such as AOL. If you are going to be located in one country for a while, a subscription with a locally based ISP may be the best answer (if there are no language difficulties). Hotmail is another possibility (**http://www.hotmail.com**) but its use is not allowed for security reasons in some companies.

Cybercafés and web kiosks

The simplest and cheapest way to pick up your email on the move is to use public Internet access points. Most of these simply provide access to a web browser, so to get your email you must either subscribe to Microsoft's Hotmail free email service (*see* above) or use one of the other webmail services such as **http://www.web2mail.com** Unfortunately, the web kiosks often found in hotels and tourist venues in Europe are often restricted to a certain number of local websites and may not allow webmail access.

Some companies provide their own version of webmail systems to allow secure access to email by employees using a simple web browser. If you do not have this type of access, another solution – sometimes not particularly beloved of the IT department – is to redirect your mail either to a personal email account which you can access through a web browser, or to a service such as Hotmail.

Security

Mobile workers need to take particular care to avoid physical security risks such as mugging and theft. Don't leave computer equipment visible when you park your car. If you are approached by a mugger, give up the laptop immediately (of course you had stored your data backup disks separately from the laptop, hadn't you?).

Some local authorities whose teleworkers have to meet with clients outside office premises arrange for staff to ring a designated contact before and after their meeting.

Surveys indicate that up to 10% of laptops are stolen each year. Take extra care of laptop bags in public places such as airports and railway stations. If you are supplied with a lockdown cable (like a bicycle cable padlock, which attaches securely to the laptop casing), use it when in hotels or other public places to lock the laptop to an immovable bit of furniture if you are leaving it unattended. Always take the bag to the toilet with you in public places unless someone you trust is available to look after it in your absence.

Think about investing in one of the new generation of laptop bags that don't look like laptop bags – instead they come in the form of saddlebags or rucksacks, so that they don't advertise 'expensive computer in here', but are adapted with extra padding and strengthened, comfortable straps, to carry a laptop. Alternatively you could use a traditional briefcase.

Don't forget that when you use a laptop in a public place, such as on a train, there is always a risk that other people could overlook sensitive company information.

SHARED FACILITIES

Prospective teleworkers are often concerned about isolation problems if they work exclusively alone. There are many forms of telework which involve working alongside other people, including telecentres, telecottages, cybercafés, neighbourhood offices, bureau services such as the US chain Kinko's, and serviced or 'virtual' offices like those provided by the Regus chain.

Some companies with a high proportion of teleworkers or mobile workers create special group spaces with facilities such as meeting rooms and touchdown spaces to facilitate their teleworkers. They may combine the provision of these facilities with schemes for desksharing (or losing office desks altogether) to save on premises costs.

Telecentres and neighbourhood offices

'Telecentre' is a term that often overlaps with telecottage, but is sometimes used to refer to small call centres or 'back office' operations where work is carried out away from the employer's main location. They are usually commercially run operations servicing one company. A related idea is the 'neighbourhood office', a telecentre run for company staff to use as a base away from the main office. A number of councils in Britain now have neighbourhood offices/telecentres to reduce time spent travelling by their staff. In the US, government departments are the main supporters of neighbourhood offices. The Washington Metropolitan area runs a number of telework centres to help government employees avoid commuting at a cost of about $50 a week, recoverable from a grant scheme.

Many of the telecommuters seem to value the equipment and peace in the centres as much as the commuting time saved: 'I enjoy coming to the Manassas Telework Centre because not only is it peaceful, but it has better office equipment than my official duty station. The computers are faster, the printers print cleaner documents, and there is never a line for running copies.' 'Being in an office with seven other people, I find unnecessary interrruptions and noise a constant problem. I find that by going to the Manassas centre, I am relieved of unnecessary interruptions and can concentrate on my job.'[45] However, a General Accounting Office report in 2000 reported that the centres were underused.

Cybercafés and serviced offices

Most cities now have a variety of places where you can pay to get Internet access when you are on the move. *Internet* magazine keeps a list of British cybercafés at **http://www.internet-magazine.com/resource/cybercafes/ index.htm**

Teleworkers often need other facilities which they cannot obtain in their home office, such as meeting space, high-volume photocopiers or expensive software used only occasionally. Some printshops provide access to such services, but US chain Kinko's, which now has over 900 branches in eight countries,

HORSES FOR COURSES

The Easyoffices website is a useful place to start reviewing the possibilities for different types of office space. It offers assistance in finding a number of different types of office, including:

- **Flexible office** – short-term lets that can include facilities management.

- **Serviced offices** – ready-made offices often fully equipped with furniture, telephone lines, Internet access, reception and kitchen facilities. Personnel are usually on hand to provide building and infrastructure support.

- **Virtual offices** – various services ranging from a basic mail-box facility to a complete mailing address, telephone answering, email hosting and short-term hotdesking service.

http://www.easyoffices.com

including four outlets in London, is considered the expert in supporting what is known in the US as the 'free agent' movement – self-employed people including teleworkers. Kinko's opens around the clock and provides opportunities for 'self service' access to computers and the Internet as well as expert staff who can carry out tasks such as desktop publishing or digital copying as required.

There are Macs (set up as 'design stations' with software like Quark and Photoshop ready installed) as well as PCs, and helpful staff, who are known as 'co-workers'. US commentator Dan Pink describes Kinko's as 'the Cheers bar for the Free Agent Nation – a place full of quirky and compelling characters' and Kinko's staff as 'the yeomen of the Information Age. People trust them with their ideas. They do more than make copies. They manufacture dreams'. UK press officer Michael Taylor says the next move will probably be expansion to a chain of stores in Manchester or Leeds (**http://www.kinkos.com**).

A more 'corporate' version of this idea is the European chain Regus, offering meeting rooms with presentation facilities, answering, secretarial and reception services, offices, video conferencing and 'touchdown' space in major cities around the world. In August 2002 Regus advertised that it had 420 locations in 240 cities covering 51 countries. The company says that you can 'walk in, sit down, start work' and avoid meetings in crowded lobbies and bars. Space can be booked by the hour or day by phone or online, and all the centres have a variety of room sizes. Regus promotes video conferencing as a way of saving up to 75% of the costs of business travel to meetings, and says that business people are increasingly concerned with confidentiality issues of meeting in public places.

Regus also operates serviced business centres and business space for companies with longer-term space requirements such as temporary office expansion or special projects. The advantage is an all-inclusive price covering security, maintenance and IT facilities which avoids the need for capital investment in property. Additional features such as catering or reception services are also available as required. Reception services include dedicated lines, mail and fax forwarding services, and the use of prestigious business addresses for mail (**http://www.regus.com**).

SPACES FOR TEAMS AND TOUCHDOWN AREAS

Electronic workspace

If you are working as part of a distributed team, you may find it useful to consider a private space on the web where your team can 'congregate' – any team-member who has web access and the relevant passwords can log in and check on things, no matter where they happen to be.

Most services offer space to upload and share documents (a 'library'), calendar functions with email notification of meetings, group email (where an email to one address reaches everyone in the group), the ability to 'vote' or set up questionnaires on issues, discussion forums and functions to allow document revisions to be tracked. Some services offer facilities for databases of information to be shared online.

The workspace can usually be set up very quickly and access is restricted to your team-members. Payment is usually on a monthly subscription model based on the number of team-members you want to connect and the selection of features you chose to use. *See* **http://www.btquickplace.com** or **www.intranets.com** or **http://www.projectplace.com** (or the free services **www.smartgroups.com** and **http://www.visto.com**). Bear in mind that free can mean slow and advert-ridden, or just free at the moment – until the charges start in six months' time.

For a higher-level, 'professional services automation' approach that is used by many large consulting, technology and accounting companies, *see* **http://www.portera.com**. Portera's products include additional functions like tracking timesheets and payroll for distributed teams, hosting information such as company policies, and providing employee communications such as personalised newsletters. There are also sophisticated project-management tools. Other offerings reviewed by *Fast Company Magazine* (**http://www.fastcompany.com**) include: **http://www.eroom.net** (does not support audio or video conferencing), **http://www.done.com** (very quick to get up and running), **http://www.hotoffice.com** (needs an always-on Internet connection) or **http://www.magicaldesk.com** (has some Mac compatibility).

Physical workspace

The first change to office workspace that companies make usually involves desksharing. This tends to happen when staff in the same department work out

CYBERCAFÉS GO EASY IN THE HIGH STREET

Stelios Haji Ioannou, the founder of affordable airline easyJet, turned his attention to making the Internet cheap and accessible for all in 1999 with startling results – there are now 21 stores in eight countries including the world's largest cybercafé with 800 PCs in Times Square, New York.

There are six easyEverything centres in central-London locations such as Oxford Street and Trafalgar Square, providing a total of 2200 terminals. Other European locations include Barcelona, Brussels, Berlin, Rome and Amsterdam.

James Rothnie, easyEverything's PR director, explained that previous cybercafés had been on a small scale: 'Cybercafés tended to be one-off, owner-managed establishments without the capital or business skills to set up a bigger operation. Most of them charged more than £5 per hour. On the other hand people don't really want to spend £1000 updating their hardware at home every year. We've broken the mould by appealing to all age-groups and avoiding the bohemian, techie style of cybercafés.' Stelios himself described the competition as 'small, often dirty, with a techie atmosphere', and pointed out that with a network of reliable cybercafés in place in major cities, businesspeople can leave their laptops at home knowing they will be able to receive their email, as can tourists and young people with no home PC access.

The easyEverything centres have PCs with 15-inch flat-screen monitors and 2-megabite connections to the Internet. Most are open 24 hours a day, seven days a week. The price of access fluctuates depending on how busy the centre is – a screen at the front counter details how much access you can get for £1.

In a typically entrepreneurial move, Stelios is now offering easyEverything franchises for cities around the world. Franchisees pay an initial startup cost plus a percentage of revenue, but can keep all the revenue from add-on services such as catering, advertising, copying, printing and currency exchange.

http://www.easyeverything.co.uk

of the office for such a high proportion of their time that it is no longer felt they need to maintain an individual desk that is nearly always empty.

Many companies moving along the road to flexible working have started to provide shared, internal short-stay offices, commonly called 'touchdown space', for mobile staff or those who telework for a significant proportion of their time. These staff may no longer have their own desks and need somewhere to get office supplies or have a meeting, or to use facilities they can't access when they are out of the office − such as photocopiers or binding equipment for reports (*see* page 203). Other terms which are used for these shared workspaces are 'hotdesking facilities', or in the US, 'hotelling'. Typical features of touchdown space include:

PROJECTPLACE KEEPS BEEP BEEPING

Jeremy Millard works for the Danish Technological Institute as a project manager of international teams, mainly for research projects funded by the European Commission. He regularly uses Projectplace to help teams communicate. 'What I like about it is that it is relatively cheap, paid on a monthly subscription, easy to use and it works,' he explains.

'There are lots of functions I don't use that much, such as the messaging forums; but there's a very useful document store and you just drag and drop files from your PC into the store as you need. Also you don't need to look at Projectplace every day because it automatically sends you email alerts when anything changes — for example if someone has requested a meeting, or updated a document – and the email contains a hyperlink to the changed item. The project address-books are compatible with Outlook, and the functions for requesting and arranging meetings are very simple to use.'

One of Jeremy's current projects, BEEP, includes a database of case studies, some of which are teleworkers.

See http://www.beep-eu.org

- Suitable ergonomic furniture where staff can sit comfortably and work on documents and computers.
- Data connections to the company network.
- Power connections for recharging laptops.
- Telephone connections (these are usually cordless DECT phones with a PIN system where the touchdown worker enters an identifying code which routes all their calls to the local extension).
- Cradles for recharging the cordless phones.
- Meeting rooms.
- Informal shared working areas.
- Booking systems for reserving workspace.

BT Cellnet has introduced a mobile working scheme called WorkOut which includes touchdown space as well as bookable desks and café-style meeting areas. The touchdown desks consist of basic desks without IT equipment but with power and data connections. The bookable desks have IT equipment and fixed telephones. The meeting areas are intended to encourage shorter meetings and breaking away from a 'meeting room' culture. BT Cellnet also provides personal lockers for secure storage and a shared stationery cupboard to replenish supplies for the 'workouters'. Although finding space for these areas has been a challenge, the result has been that formerly 'dead' space such as entrances and atria can now be used more productively (**http://www.wfh.co.uk**).

The first problem faced by companies travelling this route is to estimate how much touchdown space will be needed, and how many desks can be 'saved' through sharing. The best method is some kind of monitoring of existing desk occupancy – such as logging how many desks are in use at different times of the day for a given period of time.

Some companies have made quite drastic changes in the direction of distributing their workforce and moving towards touchdown space, but then found that this way of working only suited a small number of their staff. A famous case in point was the Chiat Day advertising agency in Los Angeles, which took out personal space for some 300 staff members as long ago as 1995. When staff were working in the office, they would contact the receptionist to get a phone, a laptop and a reserved desk space. Unfortunately, more people preferred to remain in the office than had been expected, which meant there often wasn't enough space (or enough laptops) for anyone who came into the office after 9.00 a.m.

Chiat Day also found that some staff began hoarding equipment and did not adapt well to the new arrangement, reporting that some creativity was lost due to the lack of collaboration and proximity between team-members. After three years of the experiment the company went back to a larger traditional office with personal space even for some staff whose jobs were largely mobile. The company has retained its cordless phone system which allows staff to tell the switch where they are and receive calls anywhere in the office, or to have calls diverted to mobiles or other locations.

Some early moves towards alternative workplaces were clearly made without sufficient planning on how to replace team interactions. In 1998 it was reported that over a quarter (27%) of alternative workplace projects which removed dedicated workspaces from employees led to decreased morale.[46]

Many companies who took a more measured approach to the change, and to tackling employee resistance through training and benefits 'trade-offs', have reported greater success for their touchdown space. Hertfordshire County Council managed to make major space-savings after asking support teams at social services to evaluate their own working practices and decide between themselves who needed permanent desks and who could hotdesk and/or telework from home.

However, problems common to all shared space, from school playgrounds to canteens to motels, are apparent with most schemes. Because touchdown workspace does not 'belong' to staff personally, some people do not treat it with respect. US telework consultant Gil Gordon has an essay on his website (**http://www.gilgordon.com**) entitled 'Telephone rings, onion rings and other annoying things: getting along in shared cubicles and offices without tearing out your hair'.

Planned approaches to counteract problems with desksharing and touchdown space include increased consultation with employees; phased introduction; longer training sessions; requiring attendance in the office for

SHELL UK: CULTURE CHANGE A STEP TOO FAR

After just three years, Shell has closed three of the four telecentres it set up for workers around London. Over 18 months from 1998, Shell's retail arm swapped a prime Central London office for a mixture of homeworking and sharing space at satellite offices located near the company's filling stations around the M25. More than 100 staff from Shell Mex House moved into surplus Shell buildings around the M25 refurbished as telecentres, including a former distribution depot and a former car showroom. About 50 staff were also equipped with home offices.

Property costs were reported to be cut by 45%, and at the same time, the company reorganised into a flatter management structure based around products rather than regional operations. The idea was also intended to bring retail support staff closer to the Shell Select shops in petrol stations.

Each satellite office had the same layout. By reception there was a break-out zone for ad-hoc meetings and drop-in working with data points built in to the furniture. Next there was a services hub with stationery storage, printing, scanning and fax facilities. Further back from the reception bustle were meeting spaces of varying sizes and a larger area of workstations with PCs. At the back of the space lay quiet enclosed spaces for concentrated work. The centres were open 24 hours and staffed by receptionists from 9.00 a.m. to 5.00 p.m. Outside that time, staff gained access with a swipe card. All instructions for facilities and equipment were set out both on labels attached to the machines and in a handbook issued to all staff.

Now, around 100 staff have been brought together in a new base-office in Staines, while about 40 with home offices will continue to telework. According to Peter Sherman, Shell Retail's UK Property Manager, the decision to recentralise was not a result of poor usage – or of logistical problems. Managers decided to pull the plug because they felt that employees were not in sufficiently close contact with the organisation on a day-to-day basis. Sherman comments: 'In a business with very narrow margins you have to move quickly. It is difficult to get the spark you need if people are remote and cannot be contacted easily.'

Just one centre, in Golders Green, has been kept as a drop-in facility for staff working in North London. However, homeworking is seen to have been a success for the field staff who work most closely with the Shell Select shops. Sherman said: 'We want to keep the best bits of what we had before.' Staff who opted for home offices have been given a laptop with docking station and combined fax/printer/scanner plus a budget of £600 to buy homeworking furniture. Full training and instructional handbooks formed a vital part of the project.

team meetings at least once a week; developing informal social 'cybercafé' spaces at the office with free snacks and newspapers; and greater use of electronic workspace tools. Some large technology companies such as BT have also introduced webzines and intranet newsgroups aimed at teleworkers. Generally, touchdown-space strategies work best for employees who are already nomads, such as sales staff, technicians and consultants.

Another development in physical workspace used mainly by technology and consulting companies is the use of team rooms, or team workspace. Here, everyone working on a particular project is given a space where they can decide themselves how to use or personalise the space, depending on team needs, work patterns (including teleworking) and personalities. When the project finishes, the team room is reallocated to another project.

TELECOTTAGES (AND IT TRAINING CENTRES)

A telecottage provides its local community with low-cost access to computer and telecommunications equipment, which in turn can provide access to information services, training courses and work. Most rely on provision of IT training for their main income and tend to be community-oriented rather than business-oriented. Telecottages often support local teleworkers and small businesses.

The first centre to claim the title telecottage in the UK – the Moorlands Telecottage – was set up in 1989, but like many good ideas, it appears that telecottages were being independently 'invented' in a number of places. A Telework Association survey turned up examples which predate the first Swedish telecottages in 1985, such as Daily Information in Oxford, which operated for 22 years up to 2001 and thus probably still holds the 'longest serving' telecottage title. Numbers of telecottages peaked at 165 in 1998. The Telework Association now requires all telecottages shown on its map to be members (published in *Teleworker Magazine* and on the website **http://www.telework.org.uk**) and currently lists just over 80 organisations.

Many different forms of telecottage have been set up. Some are community-oriented and offer training and use of resources for community groups. Others are highly equipped commercial enterprises.

Whatever the flavour, centres need to adopt a commercial attitude if they are to survive beyond an initial grant-funded start-up. A key to success is the creation of a core business, usually software training, around which other complementary services are offered. Because rural areas are often short of resources, telecottages can also become a focus of community and commercial activity where teleworkers can network, using each other's services to provide backup on larger contracts.

TYPICAL TELECOTTAGE SERVICES

- **Computer use** – *PCs and Macs charged per hour, with up-to-date software for Internet access, word processing, spreadsheets, desktop publishing, webpage authoring.*

- **Laser printing** – *A4 and A3, charged per page plus computer time.*

- **Colour printing** – *A4 and A2, charged per page plus computer time.*

- **Photocopying** – *A2, A3 and A4, colour and black-and-white, volume discounts and prepaid photocopier cards available.*

- **Scanning and OCR text recognition** – *included in computer time charge.*

- **Staff consultancy charged per hour** – *software installation, disinfecting viruses, recovering trashed disks, advice on machine purchase.*

- **Lamination** – *for frequently used documents like menus.*

- **Faxing** – *per page, rate depends on destination.*

- **Email** – *included in the per-hour computer hire charge.*

- **Digital camera** – *for hire.*

Telecottage statistics

In 1998 the Telework Association supported a survey of telecottage activities by Bill Murray of Small World Connections, and about one-third of the 165 telecentres and telecottages surveyed replied. The results give a snapshot of the 'typical' telecottage which can be useful to those thinking about setting up. All the figures are averages or approximations.

- The average number of drop-in users was 30 regular and 30 occasional users. Only three centres reported that more than ten people other than staff used the centre as a regular place of work. Over two-thirds had no-one using their centre for regular work.
- 40% subcontracted work to local teleworkers.
- Only around 20% saw themselves as 'telecottages'. A further 15% were 'telecentres' with a further 15% describing themselves as 'business centres'; other titles given include Community Resource Centre, Computer Resource Centre, IT Centre, Telematics Centre, Office Bureau.
- The vast majority (88%) were located in villages or small towns (rural villages 38.8%, small towns 36.7%, remote rural areas 12.2%, city centres 4.1%, city suburbs 2.0%, large towns 6.1%).

- Most centres had two full-time staff, one part-timer and one volunteer. Over 60% had no volunteers.
- Half were breaking-even financially, with one-third making a loss (usually the most recently set-up telecottages) and 28% making a profit.
- Facilities varied widely. All had Internet access and 82% had a website. Over half had ISDN lines.
- The main focus was on training and Internet activities. Predictions for the future included an increased emphasis on these topics and on commercial work.
- About 30% of the responding centres were privately owned, with a similar proportion funded mainly by central or local government. The remaining third combined public, voluntary and co-operative structures. Of the privately owned centres, almost all started life that way, suggesting that public centres 'die' rather than go private. Startup funding included grants, equipment or other assistance for almost three-quarters of the centres.
- Income came from commercial operations for over one-third of centres, but 40% relied almost entirely on continued public funding. About a third paid no rent. The median level of grant was £29,750, with median turnover of around £60,000 and income of about £25,000.

Niche business services providing income included: language translation, bookkeeping, recruitment, abstracting, website development and maintenance, computer hire and consultancy, commercial and tourist information provision and, to a lesser extent, call-centre and message-taking services.

Telecottage business ideas

Telecottages usually offer both formal and informal training, computer hire (some offer 'take-away' computers too) and Internet access, photocopiers, printers and faxes. Other facilities include use of workspace and meeting rooms. Trained staff are often available to provide secretarial assistance, word processing and desktop publishing.

Call centres

Some telecottages such as East Clare (*see* p. 125) have successfully started up small 'pocket' call centres offering services such as translation or market research. However, competition from larger, commercially focused outsourced call centres can be fierce, and suitable workstations including an ACD switch and CTI software will be needed.

Conferencing

Telecentres can offer video-conferencing and audio-conferencing facilities. For video conferencing, you need an ISDN telephone line and suitable conferencing hardware and software.

Data input and processing

The simpler end of this kind of work is less available now because most historical data needed by companies has already been entered, and because of strong competition from low labour-cost regions of the world. Data input work is not generally well paid, and is usually quoted as piece-work. However, specialist areas such as the construction of mailing lists, or scanning and processing of specialist data, can be more remunerative.

Faxing/photocopying services

Copying charges average about 10p/sheet for low volume. Fax varies at between £1 and £2.50 per sheet. Colour photocopying or high-quality laser photocopying comes in at about £1/sheet. Think about your location before buying equipment for bureau services. If you are based half-way up a remote valley, are people really going to drop in for a few photocopies? On the other hand, if you have the only decent photocopier on an island, you could be in business.

Equipment rental

This is a minor source of income for many centres. Examples include:

- Hire of computers and software onsite (e.g. for people who want to use word processing, either for private use or to offer a service).
- Hire of computers for private study, for those who want to start using computers on an informal basis – perhaps before attending a formal training course – or who want to use software-based tutorials.
- Hire of access to high-quality laser printers and colour printers.
- Hire of equipment to 'take away' such as portable PCs, small inkjet printers, for occasional teleworkers or overload work.

Sometimes this kind of service can be tied in to an existing shop or business such as a printshop or, in the case of U-compute in Keswick, a post office and craft shop. *See* p. 111.

Office services

Telecottages can be used as accommodation addresses and messaging services by small businesses.

Publishing

Telecottages can act as the focus point for community publishing operations such as local newsletters or business directories.

Skills register

Telecottages sometimes maintain a local skills register of individual teleworkers and can refer work to them. Sometimes the telecentre takes a percentage of the value of the work if a contract is arranged through the telecottage. In others, because the teleworkers are using telecentre equipment, no commission is taken.

Training

Most telecentres offer a variety of training courses introducing people to information technology and sometimes leading to qualifications such as CLAIT or ECDL. Other areas include training in specific software packages (particularly word processing, spreadsheets and databases), training in business skills and special vocational qualifications for teleworkers.

Telecottage case studies

East Clare Telecottage and Training Associates

East Clare Telecottage (ECT) was established in 1991 in Scariff, Co. Clare, beginning with three computers and a printer. Today ECT occupies a town-centre building including a training suite, video-conferencing equipment, an A3+ full-colour laser printer, digital photocoopier and PC network with ISDN Internet access.

ECT has always had a community development role, providing IT access and related facilities in a rural area through its cybercafé. Drop-in access by people wanting to use IT equipment amounts to about 10–15% of the income of the telecottage unit. However, ECT operates on a commercial basis and the services which provide the other 85% of the telecottage's income include:

- Sourcing and management of e-teams for companies outsourcing contract work.
- Training (wide range of courses, run by associated company East Clare Training Associates).
- Translation service using a network of expert translators worldwide.
- Web design and hosting.
- Pocket call centre (3 workstations).
- Office services.

Telecottage manager Nana Luke says ECT has also gained expertise and built up international networks through participation in EU projects, including one to deliver teleworker IT training for the localisation industry, funded through the ADAPT project. Tel: +353 61 921121 Email: bealtaine@bealtaine.ie

Telecroft 2000, Shetland

On the island of Unst in Shetland, Laura Baisley and Josie McMillan run Telecroft 2000, formerly Isles Telecroft. Back in 1991 the Telecroft was set up as a three-year pilot project, initially funded by the Highlands and Islands Enterprise (HIE) and British Telecom along with five other sites in the region. 'One member of our community co-op was keen on IT, which was how we got involved initially,' explains Laura.

Since the first training project (which provided IT training and teleworking experience to four women based on different islands in Shetland), the Telecroft has maintained a policy of providing IT learning opportunities to people whose geographical or domestic circumstances mean that access to conventional learning may be difficult, if not impossible. By being prepared to travel to the homes and workplaces of learners, and providing support to community-based learning centres, the Telecroft has enabled hundreds of people in Shetland to acquire new IT skills.

Much of the training provision has been funded through European Social Fund projects with support from the local enterprise company. As European funds decrease, the Telecroft's charitable status may provide access to other sources of funding. New equipment and furnishing have been funded through the Capital Modernisation Fund, accessed after the Telecroft was branded as a LearnDirect Scotland Learning Centre. This was a welcome change from previous hand-to-mouth upgrade or replacement worries. Remoteness can be a problem, particularly when technical support is required, so Laura and Josie have to be adaptable. A few years ago, they even built three PCs.

The telecottage gets some income from telework services, such as a contract to provide textual descriptions for several thousand photographs in the Shetland Museum's collection. This work is being carried out by a homeworker on Unst who is a previous learner at the Telecroft. Other contracts include administration and payroll work for some Shetland community groups. 'Although business services such as printing, fax and photocopying provide only about 10% of our income, it is a valuable community service and brings in potential new learners through the door,' said Laura.

Since 2001, the Telecroft has also been a learning centre for the Shetland College outreach students, who can use it to access video-conferencing facilities and email contact with tutors at the Telecroft. Recently, the Telecroft received a broadband satellite ADSL connection providing an always-on high-speed Internet service. This has opened up the possibility of on-line learning in a variety of subjects with other providers, but is currently mainly used for surfing the Net, or to provide email access for visitors. Tel: 01957 711224 Email: T2k@telecroft2000.shetland.co.uk

Project Cosmic
'What we were basically was an Internet café,' explained Ian Clifford, Co-ordinator of Project Cosmic, located at Ottery St Mary in East Devon. Ian originally applied to the National Lottery for funds to start up the project in 1997, and received £85,000 over three years on condition that he found matching funding. The cybercafé, which has a fast Internet connection serving eight PCs, was open five-and-a-half days a week and focused on helping young people.

Now things have moved on, the centre has moved to new premises, expanded and developed two complementary businesses offering training and web design. In 2001, Project Cosmic was voted best UKOnline centre in the South West, and it now employs 16 people.

In addition to conventional computer training, Project Cosmic also operates a mobile computer-training lab called the ORBIT project which looks like a small version of the space shuttle on wheels – it has proved highly attractive to its intended audience of children. Tel: 01404 815897 **http://www.cosmic.org.uk**

Community resource centres – Herefordshire and Worcestershire

The Herefordshire and Worcestershire community council began by creating a network of 22 resource centres located in village halls, community centres and schools with help from the county council. The centres were provided for non-profit making organisations, the unemployed, small startup businesses and youth businesses. Most centres are run on a self-help basis by a volunteer co-ordinator, often a retired person, who could show users how to operate the equipment. Opening hours vary and the resource-centre equipment usually consists of a computer, printer, photocopiers, combined scanner/printer, and in some centres, binding and stapling machines.

A funding bid by the Community Council and the Southern Marches Partnership was successful in further supporting nine of the original centres. The Southern Marches Area Rural Telematics project (SMART) was started in 1999 with initial funding of £200,000 for three years aimed at making computers and the Internet accessible to country communities.

Project officer Steve Palframan explains: 'The idea was to introduce computers into rural areas using the existing community resource centres.' The nine centres were already offering services such as photocopying, typing and printing, and each was upgraded with computers, access to the Internet and email. 'The centres are in a variety of locations from village halls to a prefabricated cabin on a caravan park. They are provided by the local community and people use them for typing up work, producing parish magazines, etc. It varies from place to place.'

The SMART project has also provided a lead centre in Ross-on-Wye which is used for training as well as public access to IT. The Larruperz centre has two part-time members of staff and a network of seven PCs. Funding ceased in 2001, and the centre is now self-financing. *See* **http://www.communigate.com**

WREN Telecottage

Once established, a telecottage can act as a platform for various additional services. The WREN Telecottage was founded as Warwickshire's first telecottage in 1991. WREN is a local project of the independent charity ruralnet|uk, and received start-up grants from ARC, BT and Coventry and Warwickshire TEC. Through ruralnet|uk, WREN has both regeneration charity and trading status. Any profits from trading are used to subsidise local services.

WREN pioneered one-stop access to a range of business and community services: IT and the Internet, training, open learning, business services, and local community projects as well as social and networking functions. This jigsaw approach – taking into account both local needs and global opportunities – ensured that WREN has survived in a fast-changing field. It continues to advise on a range of flexible models for similar centres as ideas have developed, and has used its experience to support ruralnet|uk's two-year project for UKOnline centres (*see* **http://www.directsupport.org.uk**).

WREN has moved with the times on limited resources, and is now involved, though ruralnet|uk, in a wide range of projects in both the private and grant-funded sectors. Projects may be short- or long-term, are usually based on partnerships, and often – but not always – use ICTs. A current project involves providing ECDL training for small businesses.

The telecottage has taken part in the DTI's IT for All intiative, has been part of the BBC's Webwise project, and has participated in a range of EU and Lottery-funded projects for the rural voluntary sector. WREN is now a UKOnline centre (*see* **http://www.dfes.gov.uk/ukonlinecentres/**).

WREN's equipment includes the usual computer, office and training facilities but in addition it has a leased line to the Internet, and video-conferencing equipment. The nursery WREN established in 1991 is now a viable independent business. WREN has developed a national and international role as a demonstration telecottage, facilitated by its location at the National Agricultural Centre, Stoneleigh, and by its work in combining community and commercial functions. Tel: 0845 1300 422 Email: wren@ruralnet.org.uk **http://www.ruralnet.org.uk**

Telecottage setup plans and costs

If you are interested in starting up a telecottage or IT access centre, we recommend that you begin by defining your aims. Telecentres can take many different forms and serve a variety of purposes, ranging from community education through economic development to purely commercial ventures.

The first step is to gather together interested people into a management or steering group. Discuss the services that could be offered, and the premises and equipment that will be needed for the services. Don't forget all the bureaucratic issues – planning, insurance, tax, financial structure. Check that you will have access to a digital telephone exchange, and preferably to ISDN services. Get expert help on the equipment issues.

Visit an established telecottage. Many hold occasional open days, including WREN and Moorlands (*see* **http://www.telework.org.uk**).

Assess the need for the centre by performing a market survey. Then prepare a business plan (*see* Chapter 7, *Self employment and startups*) and examine the available funding sources.

SOURCES OF RECONDITIONED PCS

- *Many large computer manufacturers and asset managers now refurbish PCs or take trade-ins including Dell, Technical Asset Management (*http://www.tam.co.uk*) and Frazier International.*

- *The Charities Aid Foundation publishes a directory, Waste Not, listing organisations in need of computers, printers and faxes. Tel: 01732 520000* http://www.caf.org.uk

- *Microsoft has a refurbishment guide at* http://www.microsoft.com/uk/refurbishers/locate.asp

- *The Department of Trade and Industry has launched a handbook to provide advice and help to businesses who want to donate equipment entitled* Unwanted computer equipment: a guide to re-use – *available at* http://www.dti.gov.uk/support/good1.htm

- *A directory of suppliers is available at* http://www.cst.gov.uk/support/dir28032000.pdf

Also try: http://www.icer.org.uk *and* http://www.wastewatch.org.uk

Raising money will involve a search for innovative funding methods. Suggestions include the Lloyds TSB Foundation and National Lottery funding. The LearnDirect scheme also provides funding for organisations providing a range of IT-based training – *see* **http://www.learndirect.co.uk** and the IT training centres section below.

The Regional Development Agencies have taken over some of the grant schemes from the old Rural Development Commission (now replaced by the Countryside Agency). These include small-business grants, redundant building grants and job creation schemes. The Countryside Agency can provide assistance for services that might form part of your plan, such as setting up a shop, post office or village hall. A list of RDAs is on the web at **www.local-regions.detr.gov.uk/rda/info/index.htm** For more contact details call the Department of Environment, Transport and the Regions (Tel: 020 7944 3000).

Rural Community Councils exist in England, with sister organisations in Wales, Scotland and Northern Ireland. RCCs work at parish-council level to assist community development. Some RCCs have become involved in telecentre projects. For details of your local RCC, contact ACRE (the Association of RCCs – Tel: 01285 653477).

IT training centres

Many former telecottages are now IT training centres of one description or another – partly because IT training centres have learned some tricks from telecottages, and partly because telecottages have found training one of the most reliable sources of income.

The LearnDirect scheme developed by the Department for Education and Employment is very much in the ethos of telecottages, and aimed at those who would not normally sign up for formal education. As Gerry Spencer from UFI Ltd, a public/private initiative company which oversees the scheme, explains: 'It's about extending adult learning. There are people out there who would never walk through a college door – but they can log on through the Net or go to a community centre. We don't give out qualifications – so you can't fail – but it will get you up to a level that enables you to go on. It can work out what you do now, and what you need to do. It's like a foundation course.'

As well as its community activities, LearnDirect has a number of courses, case studies and a helpline targeted at the business community. The courses are aimed at specific objectives – such as businesses which have grown to more than five employees and so need to implement a written health and safety policy.

LearnDirect is available from many of the UKOnline Centres (*see* p. 73), and a list of centres that can help you find the one closest to you is at **http://www.dfes.gov.uk/ukonlinecentres/**
Tel: 08000150 750 or **http://www.learndirect.co.uk**

VIRTUAL COMPANIES AND VIRTUAL OFFICES

Virtual companies mean different things to different people. Sometimes people use the term to mean a traditional company which just happens to be geographically distributed, and to do a lot of its communication by electronic means – the 'virtual office'. But sometimes they are referring to a temporary network of people or companies linked by IT to carry out a particular project, which dissolves once the project is completed – the 'virtual company'. Finally, some large companies have brought in the concept of 'self-directed work teams' or SDWTs – groups within the company which come together to solve particular problems or carry out particular tasks, bringing in different company departments as they are needed.

Examples

Ditching the office

Leicestershire-based PR company Word Association ditched its office some three years ago when all seven employees moved to working from home. The company was founded in 1991 by Mark Thomas, and offers a range of PR services including advertising, establishing corporate identity, organising events and exhibitions, producing publications and websites, marketing strategies and media relations. Word Association works mainly in the housing, health and education sectors.

'We moved out of the office as a pilot exercise to see if we could put our theories into practice. It turned out better than we could ever have imagined. We are working more efficiently, hitting our deadlines and keeping our overheads down,' reports Mark. Each person has a fully equipped home office with a PC and modem and dedicated fax and phone lines. A BT Featureline system allows staff to divert calls seamlessly between themselves, despite distances of up to 30 miles, operating as though everyone were connected to a single switchboard.

Mark is convinced that his staff now enjoy a quieter working environment without the stress of a daily commute: 'The secret of our success is the systems we use to communicate with each other and share essential information about the progress of each job. We are particularly careful about passing on vital messages – nothing is left to chance.' Communication methods include daily phone and email content as well as an intranet. There is a Monday morning production meeting, monthly business reviews, and twice-yearly get-togethers.

Recent recruit Julie Horwood comments: 'It was a bit daunting at first because I've always worked in offices where there are people around to bounce ideas off. Now I've got used to it, and I know people are just a phone call or email away. It's great not to have to travel to work.'

See **http://www.wordassociation.co.uk** Tel: 01455 614333

Legal overheads stay virtually down
Christopher Davis set up his company Davis & Co in 1993. After the first couple of years, when the company leased a conventional office, he has consistently managed to keep his overheads more than 35% below those of conventional law firms. Christopher has a strong philosophy behind his business approach: 'It's the idea of moving away from capitalism, where money employs labour, to a structure where people work together – contributing their time, often speculatively, to win and to deliver work.'

This philosophy not only led Christopher to have no employees (although he now has 20 fee-earning associates), but also to avoid offices. Instead, Davis & Co use the Regus serviced offices worldwide, and Regus also operate the central phone number through which clients can reach the Davis teleworkers.

Each fee-earning associate gets stationery, business cards, a Davis & Co email account, support in maintaining their accounts in accordance with Law Society rules, and professional indemnity insurance – an item which would cost them many thousands as sole traders. In return, Davis & Co takes 30% of the fees earned – much lower than the 50% taken as standard by large law firms with premises and staff overheads.

Christopher picks new associates partly on how interested they are in this autonomous way of working, but also on whether they have a client list ('A following, as we call it,') to bring with them. Christopher checks that associates have PCs, email, fax and phone, but not what type of PC or software. 'My experience is that if they find that their systems are too slow, they upgrade themselves.' He also discusses security and possible conflicts in domestic arrangements with potential associates but says that he doesn't even know whether most of them work from home, although he thinks that they do.

Almost all contact in the firm is by phone and email, although there is a social evening once a month in a City wine bar. The nature of the work means that associates form virtual teams which brings them into regular contact and builds relationships. 'We let people get on with it. They are sophisticated, mature people. If they want more camaraderie they will build it.' It seems to work – only a couple of associates have ever gone back to work for a traditional law practice.

See **http://www.davisco.net**

Translating the workers

Comunicado is an interpreting company that can connect you almost instantly to interpreters in over 100 languages, specialising in areas from IT to Art History. The service is provided to corporates, private individuals and to public-sector organisations such as the ambulance service and the police.

The company has over 550 telephone interpreters in the UK, and access to 5500 worldwide. However, all the interpreters are self-employed teleworkers. The company began to use teleworkers out of necessity as a cost-effective service covering all the possible permutations of language and specialism was otherwise impossible.

Interpreters have to have at least a degree in their chosen language and are then assessed through simulated teleconferences, as well as taking a written test. They have to sign up to a code of conduct covering accuracy, impartiality and confidentiality.

Once approved, interpreters are expected to be on-call for at least three shifts a week, and use an online form to register their availability. At the beginning of their shift they must phone in so that a computer can register their availability. Then, when customers call Comunicado's call centre, they can be quickly connected to an interpreter with the right skills. The interpreters aren't paid to be on call but do get paid for time spent on the phone.

Over time the company has found that it's important to provide the interpreters with ways of contacting each other and the company – particularly as some of the public-sector work can be quite stressful. Comunicado holds quarterly training sessions for which it pays travel expenses, but these are arranged partly to encourage social contact. Anyone who misses a session without a cast-iron excuse can't log on for work any more.

http://www.comunicado.com

SELF-ASSESSMENT – SHOULD YOU BE TELEWORKING?

Why do you want to do it?

The first step is to be sure why you want to get involved in teleworking. Here are some common reasons – more than one may apply to your own situation, or you may have a reason not listed here.

- I'm very short of time and looking for ways to be more productive and use my time better.
- The office is too distracting for the sort of work I have to do.
- I want to live in my town/village and not in a city.
- I want to combine work with caring for my children/elderly relative/family member and it will be easier if I can work from home.
- I am spending too much time commuting.
- My customers are all over the place – it's easier to work out of a home base, or to move from one customer to another, than to keep returning to the office.
- I have a disability/illness which affects my work. It would be easier to cope and work as well if I could work at home.
- I'm setting up a business and I need to keep the overhead costs down.
- I want to be more independent and manage my own time and tasks.

How do you want to telework?

Next, you need to think about how you want to telework. There are four main types of teleworking:

- Full-time from home.
- Splitting your time between home and office.
- On the move – at customer sites, in the train, in the car, hotdesking.
- From a telecentre or telecottage.

You may find that more than one of these methods suits your job. Only a small minority of people work full-time at home, and most research shows that if possible you should be spending at least one day a week in the office with your colleagues. Spend some time thinking about how many days or hours you want to telework, and what equipment you will need to carry out your work when you are out of the office – if possible, begin a list.

Are you suitable for teleworking?

The third step is to analyse your situation critically and see if you are suitable for teleworking. The key qualities are:

■ Good self-discipline.
■ Strong communication skills.
■ Ability to work independently.
■ Trustworthiness.
■ Mature attitude.

If you are an employee, your employer will also be considering:
■ Commitment to the company.
■ Personal productivity in the office.
■ The suitability of your line manager to supervise you at a distance.

Is your job suitable for teleworking?

Of course, you have to have a job which has within it some tasks that are suitable for teleworking. The main attributes of job suitability are:
■ High information content.
■ Comprised of autonomous (independent) tasks.
■ Can be supervised by setting objectives, (or time deadlines and financial budgets) rather than by face-to-face contact.

To assess your job, try to keep a log of how you are spending your time during the day, divided up into 30-minute intervals. For each half-hour section, record what you were doing – telephone calls, working alone at your desk, meetings, breaks and so on.

Now score each half-hour section based on the three suitability points above. Give a 1 for low information content, a 5 for high information content and so on. Average your scores to give an overall mark for each of the three points – information content, autonomous tasks and management supervision. If your job is suitable for teleworking, you will get high scores for all three. You may find that if you do a lot of teamwork, your supervision score suggests that your job is not suitable for teleworking – unless you can arrange for certain elements of the job to be carried out on 'at home' days, while others are carried out when you are 'in the office'.

Be realistic about the downsides to teleworking – it doesn't suit everyone. Some people miss the company of their office colleagues. Occasionally teleworkers find that they are overlooked for promotion or training opportunities. More commonly, people find it hard to separate work and home life, so that there is never a space in their lives when they can truly 'switch off'. Once you have read the advice in this chapter, try to outline for yourself how you would cope with some of the negative aspects of teleworking, such as isolation or noise and interruptions.

CONVINCING AN EMPLOYER

Creating a cost/benefit case

Deciding that you would be a good teleworker is less than half the battle: you still have to convince your employer, or, if you are planning self-employment, to create a business plan (*see* Chapter 7, *Self-employment and startups*). The best way to convince an employer is to spend time preparing a cost/benefit case to show that it will benefit the employer too. It may not be possible for you to include all the information you need (for example you may not know what 'overheads' figure your company uses to cover the office space, heating, lighting, and IT facilities that you use while working for them at the moment), but if you can prepare a clear document, employers can fill in the gaps for themselves.

Don't forget that the Employment Act 2002 gives working parents of children aged six and under some new rights in relation to requests for flexible working arrangements that your manager may not be aware of. For more information on these rights, *see* **http://www.dti.gov.uk/er** and page 312.

Research carried out over the past 20 years in Europe and America indicates that teleworkers are:

- More productive (between 10% and 40% more productive).
- More reliable.
- More loyal.
- More likely to produce better-quality work.
- Less likely to take time off.
- Likely to stay with the organisation for longer.

In addition, allowing telework can help an employer to:

- Attract and retain quality staff as part of a work-life-balance human-resources policy.
- Relieve space in cramped offices, if it is combined with a hotdesking policy.
- Reduce office overheads – though the saving will not be large if you are also retaining a central office desk.
- Provide coverage outside normal hours.

Of course there are also costs: you will need IT equipment at home; the employer may need to pay for extra telephone lines or different equipment such as laptop computers and routers to allow remote access to central computers. There will be management time involved in setting up the teleworking arrangement, and it is important that both you and your manager receive appropriate training for teleworking.

Most of the information you will need to prepare a cost/benefit case for your employer is in this book. Keep your document short but spell out:

- A brief introduction explaining teleworking and its spread as a working practice, perhaps giving examples of companies using teleworking in your industry sector.

- Your job and why it is suitable for teleworking.
- Your personal reasons for wishing to telework, if you feel that this is relevant. Bear in mind that under the Employment Act 2002, if you are the parent or guardian of a child aged under six years then your employer must seriously consider flexible working arrangements where these are requested, and provide credible reasons for any refusal (but valid grounds for refusal can include a likely negative effect on the organisation/business – *see* p. 312).
- What sort of teleworking arrangement you are proposing (hours, location, etc.).
- The suitability of your home or other premises for teleworking (covering issues like security, availability of a room for use as a home office, discussions you have held with your family, etc.).
- The benefits to your employer of teleworking.
- Any disadvantages that you foresee both for you and for your employer.
- The cost savings (e.g. if your employer had to replace you, a recruitment company would probably charge 10% of your salary as a finder's fee for your replacement).
- Any extra costs (home-office equipment, telephone charges, training, etc.).

If you think that the teleworking idea is going to be unfamiliar to your manager, it may also be useful to give a brief reference list of books and websites on the subject (*see* p. 367).

When the report is completed, the normal procedure would be first to approach your line manager, and then for the two of you to approach the human-resources department. In exceptional circumstances you may wish to bypass your line manager and approach human resources directly, but bear in mind that if they feel your line manager is unsuitable for supervising a teleworker, or is not fully 'behind' your application, it is quite likely that they will not approve the request unless you can be reassigned to another manager. Management opposition or lack of support is the biggest factor in the failure of teleworking arrangements.

What to do if your boss won't agree

If you think or know that teleworking is not going to be an option with your current employer, you have four choices: put up with the current situation; move to a new employer; take your employer to an appeals tribunal (e.g. if you are the parent of a child aged under six); or go freelance (self-employed). Bear in mind that most employers will initially require you to spend your time in the office so that trust can be developed and you can learn their way of doing things and their corporate culture. There are some occupations where teleworkers are directly recruited (mainly sales and technical field-staff posts) but the majority of companies only offer teleworking to established, experienced employees. If you feel that freelancing might be an option for you, read Chapter 7, *Self-employment and startups*.

TIME AND SELF MANAGEMENT

In articles about teleworking, journalists sometimes ask teleworkers: 'How do you make yourself sit down at the computer and start work in the morning? Why don't you just stay in bed?' Any self-employed teleworker can give them the reason: no work = no pay. You need to pay the rent or mortgage, pay the electricity bill, buy food, buy paper and so on. But behind the simplistic query is a real dilemma: how to organise your work when there is no-one physically hammering on your office door to ask where that report or memo or piece of software has got to. To avoid upsetting clients or employers, teleworkers need to be very good at managing their time and the projects assigned to them.

Time management

One invaluable aid is to use personal organiser software. Microsoft Outlook and Lotus Notes contain a lot of the necessary functions. Not everyone gets on with these packages (and it has to be said that a well-maintained handwritten list or an A4 desk diary used consistently can do the job equally well), but the best of these packages will keep track of your tasks as well as holding information like contact addresses. Microsoft Outlook also has a useful meeting-plan function that automatically sends emails directly from a calendar entry for a meeting inviting the participants to attend.

Typical teleworker tasks that need to be scheduled include:
- Urgent, deadline-based tasks.
- Major projects that may contain a number of sub-tasks.
- Routine work such as monthly reports.
- Regular administrative tasks such as backing up computer data or preparing VAT returns.
- Calls to be made.
- Appointments and meetings.

To carry out this range of tasks you will need:
- A diary function (with meeting alarms and planners).
- A contacts database (addresses, phone, fax and email details).
- A 'to do' list which is prioritised and which allows automatic prompting of regularly scheduled tasks.

It's also a big help if the time manager has a function that allows you to record what time you spent working on which project for billing or cost-centre purposes. Perhaps the most important piece of advice in this chapter is to ensure that you log every hour that you spend working, whether or not you can

claim for it. Do it on the same day, or in the morning of the next day, before you forget. This will also help you to monitor whether you are overworking (or underworking). You can use Microsoft Outlook's journal function and then export the results to an Excel spreadsheet for calculations at intervals, or use specialist software. (For company products suitable for Intranet use, *see* **http://www.timesheet.com**, **http://www.timesheet-software.com** or **www.replicon.com** For a standalone product try projclock at **http://www.cyber-matrix.com**).

Self-management

Motivation is not reported as much of a problem by most teleworkers, but overworking often is (*see* 'Maintaining the worker' section, pages 147–149). One Telework Association contributor said: 'I add up how much I owe my creditors or how much I still owe on the mortgage. This does wonders for my motivation.' Another commented: 'My main incentive to work is the arrival of the childminder, so I know I've got to get stuck in while I've got peace and quiet!' Another experienced teleworker suggests: 'Try and plan your work so that the first thing you have to do in the morning is not difficult or unpleasant. Break off in the evening at a point which leaves you an easy start first thing the next day. This means that if you do run into a problem the following day, you will already be in full swing.'

Here are some other voices of experience:

'I find that it's important to juggle workload according to mood. Some days

TELEWORKERS: SMELLIER BUT THEY COOK MORE?

When away from the office, homeworkers are less likely to shave, wear a fragrance or put on make-up. However, they do not alter the number of baths and showers that they take 'although they do change the time of day somewhat'.

This information is provided by market analysts Datamonitor, who in November 2001 used a creative combination of figures from the UK Labour Force, the European Commission, Eurostat and an online, non-random survey of 300 teleworkers in the UK, the Netherlands and Sweden to come up with a prediction that the EU total of teleworkers will jump to 40 million by 2005.

Datamonitor also say that homeworkers buy more raw ingredients, eat leftovers and aren't as keen on ready-made food. Apparently this dangerous tendency to cook might be halted by the food manufacturers if they produced more light, healthy, ready-made meals for lunchtime consumption. Teleworkers are also more likely to consume alcohol, although apparently this does not mean they are drinking during working hours. Gavin Humphries, Datamonitor's head of analysis comments: 'We found there was a higher propensity of people to go out in the evening for a drink or a meal and a drink if they are at home all day.'

As a result, Datamonitor sees a market opportunity for chain cafés and coffee shops to move into suburbs and villages. To combat the reports of isolation reported by some teleworkers, Humphries feels we should be taking our laptops into Starbucks-type eateries. These and more pearls of wisdom are available from Datamonitor's report *Homeworking*, price £2995 at the time of writing.
http://www.datamonitor.com

I am good for nothing but administrative tasks such as catching up on the bills. When I'm working on something involving major writing or creative input, there is always a stage of displacement activities I have to go through before I can start. This is quite stressful at the time because you are ticking yourself off for cleaning out the fridge when you should be in front of the computer racing a looming deadline, but over the years I have realised it is a necessary part of the creative process – while I clean the fridge, some sort of composting process takes place in the brain and then the structure, idea or phrase will come that allows me to face the blank screen and get going.'

'I used to complete and deliver jobs well ahead of the deadline. Now, I may well finish the job ahead of time but I've learned not to deliver it until close to the deadline. That way, people think I'm busy and leave me alone! It's not a matter of planning your work but of planning your life, setting yourself targets for both the personal and professional spheres and aiming for the proper balance.'

Good tricks for adapting to a new teleworking arrangement include:

- Mark the start and end of the working day – walk the dog, water the plants, read the paper.
- Dress for the office if it helps – even if your audience is a toddler and the cat.
- Understand that teleworking is more productive and intensive than standard office work – give yourself proper breaks for coffee, etc.
- Take a proper break at lunchtime – go for a walk, stretch that back, put your problems into context, take the dog out, burn a few calories!
- Prioritise your tasks: don't try to tackle everything and get depressed by the volume of work undone.
- Set yourself a 'treat' target – if you reach it, you can have the treat.
- Beware of snack attacks and fridges that 'talk' to you while you are trying to concentrate on work. Eat sensibly and try to discipline yourself.
- Understand your personal productivity peaks – have a regular schedule but adapt it to whether you are a 'lark' or an 'owl'.

Don't get hung up on strict rules – do what works for you. US consultant Cynthia Froggatt interviewed 200 'virtual workers' and found that the people who thrive best in the teleworking environment are those who blur the lines between their personal and professional lives.[47]

Start your day by collecting your email, post, and any messages, and working through your 'to do' list in the light of the new messages, prioritising tasks. It is well worth taking the time to eradicate junk mail from the post you have to open by subscribing to the Mailing Preference Service (Freepost 22, London, W1E 7EZ), and its companions the Telephone Preference Service (0845 070 0707 or **http://www.tpsonline.org.uk/**) and the Fax Preference Service (0845 070 0702 or **http://www.fpsonline.org.uk**), so that your name is removed from the marketing databases. For information on preventing or filtering junk email, *see* p. 287.

Next, log your incoming post in a book, or better still on a spreadsheet, so that you have a record of what came in. Stamp it with the date it was received and file it immediately before it clutters up your work surfaces. Your filing system does not have to be complex – it could be just the classic in, out and pending, or action now, action later and information – but if you have one you'll be able to find what you need without having to excavate the piles of paper taking over your home office.

Beating the deadlines

Successful time management is about achieving important goals in your life and in your work. You can't do this unless you know what your goals are. Know your goals – even spend time discussing them with a professional counsellor if needs be – and write them down and read them regularly to keep yourself on track.

HINTS FOR HOMEWORKERS

Homeworking has its good points –
Forget about that bus
And the rush-hour crowds and tube strikes
Have no effect on us.

The downside is the effort
It takes to fill each day
When all you've got ahead of you
Is work to earn your pay.

The routine I've developed
Is big on washing up.
Take each item separately,
Wash, rinse and dry each cup.

Another thing I'd mention
That really helps time pass is
Tightening up those little screws
On specs, if you wear glasses.

Some people check their cheque stubs
Others clean their shoes
Displacement chores are plentiful:
It's up to you to choose.

You'll find your own distractions,
(And don't forget the phone).
There's nothing like a day to fill
When you are on your own.

Simon Rae (first published in Guardian Weekend *section)*

Once you have a list of goals – which can be diffuse, unmanageable items like 'pay off the mortgage' or 'get promoted' – the next step is to divide your goals into smaller, manageable tasks such as 'request performance review meeting' or 'request quotation for early repayment of mortgage'. The tasks then have to be prioritised:

- ■ Important and urgent.
- ■ Important and non-urgent.
- ■ Not important and urgent.
- ■ Not important and not urgent.

Focus only on the first two. Some time-management experts would even suggest that you don't bother with unimportant and non-urgent tasks at all because you'll probably never get round to them.

In addition to task lists, you need to start logging your time – both so that you can get paid, and so that you can spot patterns and plan properly. Do you know what you did yesterday? In detail? Probably not unless you are already logging your time. But it's important because most people underestimate by 10–20% the time that tasks will take. So start working out how long regular tasks are taking – and don't forget to record the time you took for coffee breaks, fixing computer software crashes, and so on. This process will also allow you to begin spotting your peak productivity time. Some people work best early in the day, others only after the coffee break, or late in the evening. By focusing work into these productive periods you can get more done in the same amount of time.

At the end of the day, go through your task lists and plan for tomorrow. Try to keep your list to no more than ten tasks, – otherwise you are probably spending too much time on your lists. Long lists may also mean that some of the items on the list are really non-urgent or unimportant. Try to clear your desk at the end of each day – a lot of leftover, undone tasks at the end of the day can be a turn-off.

Most people's filing tasks can be reduced to three:

- Bin.
- Action – so write it on your task list!
- Filing – do it now, don't just shuffle paper between piles.

Perhaps the hardest part of time management is learning to say no to interruptions unless they are very high priority. 'If you're working to a serious deadline, put the answerphone on. You can always interrupt it if an important call comes in, otherwise you can call back after the deadline work's completed.' Caller line ID displays can also be very useful for screening calls – everyone has at least one client or colleague who can be guaranteed to spend 15 minutes chatting to get one small piece of information across, and this person is to be avoided if it's a deadline day.

Be realistic about your time estimates. If it's obvious that something isn't going to get done by the deadline, inform the customer or client. Often a deadline can be stretched, or the customer or client can rearrange their workload – it is much better to let people know what is happening than to let them down at the last moment.

When agreeing deadlines with clients or managers, don't forget to take account of regular tasks that have to be fitted in to the working day, such as filing, backing up data, accounts and so on, otherwise you will find that these tasks always get pushed into evenings and weekends to make room for deadline work, and you end up overworking.

THE HOUSEKEEPING

Four vital chores

There are four chores that self-employed teleworkers must schedule in if their business is to survive:

- Keeping timesheets should be done daily and the hours added up at least once a month. If you don't know what hours you worked on each project, how can you tell whether you are achieving sufficient reward for your work? And why should your employer or client pay you at all?
- Preparing bills regularly and chasing payments at least once a month. Usually, regular phone calls will ensure prompt payment (bother the accounts department, not your client within the company, who probably has no control whatsoever on when your invoice will be paid). The next step for non-payers is usually a stiff solicitor's letter, which may have to be followed by use of the Small Claims Court.
- Backing up your computer data at least once a week. Most backup programmes can run unattended and automatically, perhaps in the evening after you have finished work for the day. Do not ignore this chore or you will regret it. Sooner or later it will happen to you – your hard disk will fail and you will lose all your data. So make sure that you have backups, that some are kept offsite to avoid fire risk, and that you test and update backups regularly.
- Marketing or researching new opportunities. If you are self-employed you should be devoting somewhere between a quarter and a third of your time to marketing.

For the PAYE teleworker, substantial time should be devoted to keeping in touch with the office, knowing what is going on, and ensuring that people remember you and what you do (*see* 'Career prospects' section, p. 149).

Even teleworkers get sick and go on holiday

If you are unwell or on holiday, let your most active clients and contacts know in advance or leave a message to this effect – but try not to invite burglars through a detailed voicemail message. While you are away, Royal Mail Keepsafe service can hold your mail at a cost of £5.25 for a fortnight or around £15 for two months. One week's notice is required – your local post office can give you the forms.

Kendlebell offer a 'Take a Message' service charged for by the day. For the duration of your absence they will provide you with two or three 'personal assistants' from their list of franchisees who will work together to log and respond to all your calls in your company name. They can organise diaries, take orders, send out brochures and generally run the office over 'intelligent' telephony systems while you are away. If you're an incorrigible workaholic they'll even forward urgent messages to you on your mobile (**http://www.kendlebell.com** or 0800 0727728).

AlldayPA is a call-centre-based service which will handle calls for you or carry out secretarial tasks for a cost of about 59p a minute. You first visit the website at **http://www.alldaypa.com** and register (including the obligatory credit card information). Instantly you are issued with an 0845 number to which you can forward calls, as well as an email address and personal webspace. There is no registration charge. Services include dictation, passing on messages via email or SMS, and forwarding calls. According to the firm's publicity, intelligent routing in the call centre ensures that as far as possible your virtual PA is an agent with experience in your industry sector. The project is the brainchild of Britain's youngest self-made millionaire, Reuben Singh.

Balancing work and family

If you are an employed teleworker, the chances are that you, your manager and your colleagues have received information and training about teleworking – but the family usually gets forgotten. While a formal, written agreement with your family may be excessive, prospective teleworkers should discuss and suggest ground rules on how the family can best help and least hinder the process of working from home. For example, children's voices or pets barking in the background of telephone calls make a bad impression on customers and put strain on the teleworker intent on creating a professional image.

On the positive side, the teleworker is much more available to the family (by virtue of being there in emergencies and no longer spending time commuting). Over time, a greater appreciation by the teleworker's family of what they do usually develops. Here are some starting points for discussion:

- Where is the office?
- Is it out of bounds to partners, children or pets? All the time or just at certain times?
- Who tidies the office?
- Is company equipment available to the family or off-limits?
- Is the teleworker available for domestic chores? Which ones and when?
- Who pays for the extra food needed for the teleworker's lunches and snacks? Who makes sure the food is available?
- Can the teleworker expect help from the family, e.g. with mailings? What's the 'going rate' for help?
- How are business calls and visitors to be handled by members of the family? If the teleworker is out, do they let the answerphone go off, or do they answer the phone?
- How are are any children to be cared for, especially during school holidays?

When planning the home office it may be a good idea to draw up a sketch plan, with paper templates representing the various items to be fitted into the room,

CYBERSUPPORT FOR WORK-AT-HOMES

http://telecommuting.miningco.com/smallbusiness/telecommuting – a list of useful resources.

http://www.wahm.com – short for Work At Home Moms, but watch out for one or two worksearch schemes that could be scams linked from this site.

http://www.en-parent.com – community and career resource for parents looking to use self-employment to balance work and family. The 'en' stands for entrepreneurial.

http://www.homeworking.com – site with info and news and some excellent case studies.

http://www.momsrefuge.com/telecommute – working mothers' focus.

Debra Wierenga's excellent article on the realities of homeworking with small children ('Work-at-Home parents' troubleshooting guide') can be found at the Herman Miller website http://www.jugglezine.com

And don't forget the Telework Association at http://www.telework.org.uk

and get the family to help in designing what should go where. Bear in mind the realities of family life – a loft office could have steep steps where children leave toys to trip up the teleworker, and a room which is a pathway to others will always cause the teleworker to suffer constant interruption. And remember: 'There is never enough room. The paperless office – the biggest joke of all time!'

Discuss how you see the teleworking routine working. Some teleworkers report that they need to keep to a strict schedule in order to maintain their work discipline, while others enjoy the new freedom in their working time. Often at the start of a teleworking arrangement there are interruption problems such as neighbours dropping in during working hours. A contrasting problem can be the 'ogre in the spare room' syndrome, with children creeping round their own house unnaturally quietly because 'Dad's working'.

Most parents find if they are to telework successfully they must either arrange for the children to be out of the house at school or at a childminder's, or else have a childminder present in the home. School holidays are a particular issue for teleworkers. Stresses can also arise if the burden of childcare shifts from one parent to the other and everyone is living and working in the same space. 'I found I couldn't concentrate because I didn't believe my husband was looking after our daughter properly while I was working. She was at a demanding, toddler stage and he would just watch the telly in the same room instead of attending to her. If I heard her crying it was

almost impossible for me to stay in the office. Things improved when we changed the glass door of the office to a solid one so that she couldn't see me working, but it was still stressful for me.'

The support organisation Parents at Work publishes a guide on *Balancing Home and Work* – contact 0207 628 3565 or *see* **http://www.parentsatwork.org.uk** It can be a good idea to decide on a review of the situation after an agreed initial period so that everyone in the family can have their say about whether teleworking works for them.

Housework duties may change as a result of one or both adults teleworking. Ursula Huws, in her 1996 study *Teleworking and Gender*, found that in households with more than one adult, only 11% of men had taken on primary responsibility for housework, whereas around 45% of the men contributed less than half the household income. The women in Huws's sample were more likely than men to work standard office hours, and women were also three times as likely as men to be interrupted by children when working. Men, on the other hand, were three times as likely to be interrupted by friends when working.

On the bright side, once teething troubles have been resolved, teleworking allows far more opportunity to integrate home and work: 'It can be hell when they're small, and friends tell me boys are worse than girls. Always say goodbye and greet them back from school – never be too busy – put the answering machine on instead. Do the taxi runs such as guides, music lessons, etc. Make them feel that there are times when they can use the equipment (under supervision when tiny) and that there are things they must not do (such as "format c:"); but they must also understand that there are times when you are not to be disturbed.'

'Plan your day around the family. There is no point in getting frustrated with the children coming home from school and interrupting you. Plan breaks at times such as these and enjoy them rather than try to battle on irritably. One of the joys of teleworking is surely that you can have more time for the family when it needs your time.'

'I enjoy teleworking because it means I have more time with the family through not having to commute. Also a lovely rural setting and a roomy office make working from home very attractive. The downside is that work is always there, lurking in the corner of your mind and you feel yourself inexorably drawn to it. However, in any conflict with the housework, work wins hands down. I'm often glad of the excuse it gives me to ignore the dust for a bit longer!'

'Not everyone may agree, but interruptions from family members need not necessarily be unwelcome if you organise your work properly and establish ground rules.'

'It is very important when working at home to keep your business and family phones separate. Nothing is as frustrating as continually answering calls for your teenage daughter or discovering that an important caller could not get through because the phone was engaged by family members all afternoon.'

'The most important piece of advice to ensure professional quality, reliability and security for clients while working from home is to produce a large notice to be fixed on the outside of the office door reading "No Kats, No Kids, No Krumbs!".'

MAINTAINING THE WORKER

Keeping comfortable

A number of physiological complaints can result from long-term use of computers and include eye strain, blurred vision, burning eyes, back pain, sore shoulders and repetitive strain injury (RSI). Teleworker home offices need to be designed with appropriate desks and chairs to minimise these problems (*see* Chapter 9, *Staying safe and legal*, p. 295). It usually helps to arrange the workplace to face outwards towards stimulating views, and to take sensible breaks at regular intervals. Controlling food intake when working next to a well-stocked larder can also be a problem. The BT directory-enquiries experiment in Inverness found that although teleworkers suffered less stress than their office-based counterparts, they suffered more snack attacks.

Many teleworkers report stress due to overworking. 'An important problem I find – and it may seem a curious one – is a tendency to overwork. Your work is always there and it is easy to be tempted to do it rather than something else. I think it important, therefore, to have a clear idea of why you are teleworking in the first place (living in the country, more time for the family, etc.) and to carry out periodic audits to see if you are effectively achieving your aims. Resist the temptation to overwork. Make your breaks real breaks away from the computer. Stop and eat; don't nibble and keep going. Plan your social and family life and make your leisure commitments as binding as your professional ones. Comfort yourself with the quantity of work completed rather than worry about the work remaining to be done. Take that walk in the morning if the sun is shining. You can always catch up in the evening when it may well be raining. Set yourself reasonable targets (daily, weekly, monthly) and learn to relax when you have reached them.'

'Don't feel guilty about breaking off to make a drink and relax a little. Working from home is more intense and it is good practice to take a break and unwind.'

These comments are backed up by a Joseph Rowntree Trust report which found that over a quarter of working fathers in Britain already work more than the 48 hours maximum prescribed by the recent European Working Time directive.

It is not unknown for teleworkers to become tedious workaholics, unable to see that what should be a method of introducing freedom and balance into life has become an excuse for self-imposed slavery. An old hand recommends: 'Set yourself a limit on the number of hours a week you will normally work except in exceptional circumstances.'

'Take advantage of the flexibility of teleworking by arranging at least one exercise session a week during "normal" working hours – it breaks up the routine and makes you feel privileged to be a teleworker. You get empty pools, individual attention for horseriding and so on.'

'If you're working alone, put the answerphone on or take the phone off the hook when you go for a toilet break.'

'I've now been a self-employed teleworker for 17 years. During that time I have had periods where I have overworked to the point where my health was affected, and other periods where I found it hard to keep motivated and put in the hours on some projects. My solution on working hours involves using an A4 desk diary with a year-to-view page in the front. I keep detailed records of how I use my time each day and on these two pages, I write down my total hours each day, sum them each week and keep a running total.

I have set myself a target of 1800 hours a year working, of which one-third can be hours where I am doing things I can't bill for directly such as installing new software or chasing work. This amounts to just over our national average of 39 hours per week with nine public holidays and four weeks' holiday (although personally I don't take conventional holidays – just odd days throughout the

TURN IT OFF – CONTROLLING THE 'ANYTIME, ANYWHERE' OFFICE

Gil Gordon, probably the best-known consultant on teleworking worldwide, recently turned his attention to the problem of how to switch off from all the new forms of work. A book by Gil on this subject was published in 2001 accompanied by a website, **http://www.turnitoff.com**

'This technology (voicemail, fax machines, email, laptops, pagers, cellular phones and so on) has changed the way we work – that's the good news. The not-so-good news is that this same technology has made it more difficult to get away from work. We seem to have stretched our workdays and workplaces to the extreme; sometimes we find it hard to leave work behind as much as we'd like, and pay attention to the rest of our lives.

'None of us wakes up one day and decides, "I think I'll give up my free time on weekends, answer my pages during dinner with my spouse and carry my laptop on vacation". That's why I've developed the "turn it off" slogan – to remind us that we do have lives beyond the reach of all that technology. However, this isn't an anti-technology, anti-work, anti-commitment or anti-anything campaign. It's meant to remind us that we'll probably do better work if we get in the habit of letting go of work even for a little while now and then.'

Gil's prescription to improve things involves creating a grid of all the hours in a week, and dividing this into three basic categories: core working time when you are available and on-duty; mid-duty periods when it is acceptable for colleagues to contact you if something requires your immediate attention; and off-duty periods. The book also contains invaluable suggestions on negotiating and communicating this schedule to colleagues and family.

year and about ten days' break at Christmas). This system doesn't stop me once in every couple of years having to do an all-nighter to meet a deadline, but it does ensure that I know I am earning enough without overworking while also reassuring me that I am not letting things slip. I think it's really helped improve my work-life balance and increased my creativity and value to clients.'

Anecdotal evidence indicates that overworking tends to affect those who have just begun teleworking. After a while most teleworkers realise that people in conventional workplaces don't work as hard as they do, take longer to get to work, then have a bitch with colleagues about the management and go through a settling-down routine before they actually do anything.

Career prospects

While it's a myth that teleworkers are 'out of sight, out of mind' to their managers, it is important to be proactive in trying to manage your career. Andrea Whittle, a PhD researcher from Brunel University, gave *Teleworker Magazine* 12 tips for career management for employed teleworkers:

1. Actions speak louder than words – deliver on your promises and deadlines and show you can be trusted to work autonomously.
2. Set clear objectives that are achievable but challenging – agree them with your manager and review them regularly.
3. Develop your 'emotional intelligence' – communication, listening, empathy and teamworking skills.
4. Communicate regularly with your manager but be sensitive to their workload – don't copy them in on every email.
5. Manage your manager's expectations – if you are falling behind, let them know early, don't delay and dump a nasty surprise on their desk.
6. Don't forget the power of the human touch – meet with people to develop trust when needed rather than relying on email and phone.
7. Work to develop a network of contacts you can turn to for help and advice – and don't forget to return the favours.
8. Develop your own portfolio of skills and experience – make yourself indispensable to the people you work for.
9. Be informed about latest developments in your field – it could ensure that you are at the centre of the next big project.
10. Things change rapidly, so work to ensure that you get the training and development you need to keep your CV current.
11. Use face-to-face time in the office effectively, seeing the people who have the greatest role in assessing your work and furthering your career.
12. Be in the driving seat – don't wait until your boss suggests a career move, as it may never happen.

Training

After a period of years teleworking, it is likely to be core skills such as software packages and professional qualifications that will need updating. For the self-employed, this means planning budget and time to take courses. For PAYE employees, training should be regularly discussed with your manager to ensure that you don't end up in a skills backwater. *See* Chapter 11, *Training for teleworkers*, for more detailed information.

Loneliness of the long-distance teleworker

Teleworkers, particularly those who are disabled or based in rural areas, can suffer from isolation if they work from home for long periods. Professional associations such as the Telework Association that provide helplines and conferences can also assist in reducing isolation. Telecottages and telecentres provide an alternative workspace with human contact. Some teleworkers choose to share an office with a neighbour or colleague who is teleworking – for companionship, and because they find that being 'observed' makes them work, even though their companion is not their boss and may well work in a completely different field.

ALAN DENBIGH'S SEVEN SURVIVAL TIPS FOR STRESS-FREE TELEWORKING

Telework Association executive director Alan Denbigh has been teleworking for 12 years. This is what it's taught him:

1. 'Never on a Monday.' Never install software in the morning, particularly on a Monday.

2. Teach the family to 'shaddit' when you're on the dog-and-bone.

3. Build in some exercise or you'll become a tubby-teleworker.

4. Avoid meetings. Use phone, email, fax and post but don't waste time on meetings except at the start of a business relationship.

5. Don't meet customers at home or you'll suffer extra stress trying to give the entire house and office an instant makeover (unless you need something to force you to get tidy).

6. Le Weekend is Sacred. Yes, you can enter the 24-hour society and spend your entire life working now that you're a teleworker, but your partner will leave and the kids will run away when the strange creature from the home office comes to call.

7. Start the day by writing a list. Always include something you don't want to do. Feel smug when ticking items off.

'Based on my experience as a freelance translator, I found the relative lack of praise and positive feedback when working alone was a problem. Customers call when there is a panic to sort out, or when they want an urgent piece of work, or when they get a bill and want to whinge. I think lone workers suffer from a lack of professional backslapping.'

'I make a point of getting out to see someone in a business capacity at least once a week, face-to-face. It doesn't really matter who they are – client, suspect, prospect, supplier – but it meets the need for face-to-face networking and avoids teleworking cabin fever, especially during the early spring.'

'There was one occasion when I was tempted to use the Samaritans' online service. I was owed a lot of money, the work was piling up and my concentration was just shot to pieces. I found I was just reading and rereading my email messages instead of getting anything done and things were getting out of control. In the end I went to my GP and that solved the problem, but the Samaritans' email address is jo@samaritans.org for anyone else who gets that way.'

'I've been a teleworker for more than a decade and have prided myself on being able to keep customers through a good working relationship. A few years ago a grant from an enterprise group allowed me to bring over two people from an export customer and I was amazed what a difference it made to work

THE TIDESWELL GROUP

The Tideswell group at their usual venue, the Star pub.

Freelance journalist Pete Hawkins, who is based in the Peak National Park, describes the setup of the Tideswell Group. 'Two Christmases ago I started to get worried about loneliness when I realised that around the country, thousands of employees were having Christmas parties and I was at home with a cup of tea and a biscuit. Sometimes the daily walk to school with the kids is my only link with the outside world. So I put a note into the village newsletter calling anyone interested to a meeting in the local pub – the Star Inn. Half a dozen folk turned up and we spent an enjoyable evening sinking pints and chatting about what we all did.

'At the second meeting we discovered that one person had managed to access special Peak Park grants towards the cost of their home office. A visit from the local business adviser to the third meeting has led to a number of small grants and training projects accessed through the local TEC. Some of us have also cooperated to set up a website despite our eclectic mix of professions. We realised there were groups of us who had similar skill areas. A website framework was designed, we committed to putting in £100 each and started to call ourselves the Tideswell Group. We've also found some situations where we can team up – I recently worked with a management trainer to run a training course for a firm of solicitors, and the graphic designer has produced marketing materials for other group members.

'However, we decided we didn't want the group to be organised formally – we were there to have fun. If we wanted to have formal meetings with chairs and secretaries, then we could have stayed as employees. The most important thing is that the sense of isolation has gone. I have the benefit of working from home but now I have links with others who are willing to bash ideas around. I have access to information and training through Business Link and another excuse to go to the pub once a month! Last Christmas we all met one lunchtime and after a pub meal toured our individual offices, eating mince pies and drinking sherry around the filing cabinets. Almost like every other office party.'

Pete's website is **http://www.walkingholidays.org.uk**

with them face-to-face and then go out and relax over a good meal. It's surprising how much you can get the wrong impression of people over email and the phone – now our calls are much more relaxed and chatty.'

Other activities that can help to reduce isolation include attending workshops, exhibitions and seminars, joining professional associations, and seeking out discussion groups on the Internet.

SUPPORT ORGANISATIONS

Some support groups are special-interest websites, some are more conventional types of support such as trade unions, and there are also specialist associations like the Telework Association, which celebrated its tenth anniversary in 2003. Examples include:

- Trade unions that support self-employed and freelance workers such as the NUJ, the CWU and Amicus-MSF section. Trade unions can usually offer discounted benefits such as insurance and legal assistance in addition to their traditional roles in representing members.
- Recruitment companies with 'approval' schemes such as **http://www.smarterwork.com** which try to provide a supply of work for those who join up. Smarterwork charges around £250 per year.
- Member-driven not-for-profit associations such as the Telework Association provide discounted benefits, representation and information.
- Local groups such as the Tideswell group (*see* p. 152) which try to provide opportunities for social contact with others working in a similar way, and may also cooperate to obtain work or equipment.
- Website-based sources of shared information and resources such as **http://www.homeworker.com** and **http://www.smarteric.com**

The Telework Association

The Association has around 2000 members, including individuals, corporate members, telecentres and telecottages. The aim of the Association is to make teleworking an accepted way of working. Much of the information available from the Association is aimed at the individual, but we also encourage the corporate world by emphasising the business benefits. The Association has been something of a pioneer – the *Teleworking Handbook* has been adapted and translated into French and Italian, *Teleworker Magazine* received a European Teleworking Award, and the first independently accredited teleworking qualification was also supported by the Association, which also lobbies and campaigns, and runs projects that seek to advance the cause of teleworking.

Individuals pay around £30 to join and receive this *Handbook*, the bimonthly colour magazine *Teleworker*, and the weekly e-zine *Telework Online* which provides regular news updates and information on work opportunities. Members have access to a web forum and get discounts on events as well as being able to consult the Association helpline. The Telework Association is a not-for-profit organisation and supports itself through membership, product and consultancy income.

Tel: 0800 616008 **http://www.telework.org.uk**

6

Implementation in organisations

This chapter covers introducing teleworking to companies (for PAYE employees), and gives a 'route map' for a conventional, planned introduction of teleworking, with a formal trial or pilot project followed by a rollout plan for the whole organisation. Chapter 1, Overview *contains information on the advantages and disadvantages of teleworking from an employer's viewpoint and this is not repeated here.* Chapter 2, Self-employment and startups *deals with starting up and maintaining a teleworking business as a self-employed person. Please note the disclaimer in the preface to this book – we have done our best to collate information on issues like company teleworking policies and agreements, but it is up to individuals and organisations to check documents with their professional advisers where appropriate.*

Teleworking is no different from other changes that are introduced within organisations. It has to be justified, planned, and carried out with the consent of the people it will affect. There is a valid argument in favour of informal experimentation: enough companies have successfully carried out trials that there is little point in repeating the activity, since we already know that teleworkers are usually happier and more productive than average employees – so just get on with implementing the practice in your company as quickly as you can. The counterargument is that a trial is necessary in every company, as it allows problems to be ironed out without incurring excessive costs or disruption.

It is clearly overkill to do a formal trial or to develop a complete personnel policy for one person who occasionally takes a laptop home to complete a report, or for someone who occasionally accesses the company network to pick up messages while travelling abroad. Informal experimentation is a good way to get a feel for whether teleworking will suit your company without making major investments of time or money. It allows different styles of telework to evolve for different situations.

In many organisations the reality is that teleworking spreads silently and informally, often through the practices of a group of managers or professionals who grant themselves the equipment and permission to telework after hours or on the road. Other good places to look for groups of staff who may already be teleworking, and might perhaps share their expertise, are travelling sales or engineering staff. In some organisations, particularly teaching and professional practices, teleworking may already have spread informally throughout the organisation to create an established tradition of flexible working.

What is appropriate for your organisation is for you to judge, and most will 'pick and mix' to suit themselves from the suggestions in this chapter. But even where teleworking is apparently already spreading and working well, there can be arguments for considering a planned implementation. Otherwise teleworking can come to be seen as a perk for the favoured few, or else some easily avoidable scenarios may cause the organisation to reverse its relaxed attitude. Here are a few examples:

- What happens to home-based IT equipment belonging to the organisation if someone leaves? How is it to be returned? (US case-law indicates that the employer has the responsibility of retrieving the equipment from the home office in the absence of a written agreement otherwise.)
- How will your IT staff respond to a call from Paris saying that a laptop with remote network access was stolen in the airport?
- How will you respond to a valued member of staff whose job is not suitable for teleworking, but who requests working from home and can point to examples of other staff members who are already teleworking?
- A member of staff already working considerably reduced hours has developed a disability and asked to be allowed to work from home. The figures don't add up for the cost of implementing the technology needed for the low number of hours worked. Are you entitled to refuse the option? (UK law says you must give a good business reason; US law says the employee must show that the 'working at home' option is cost-effective and that duties can be adequately performed from that location. Many disability organisations would frown upon an employer who did not try to accommodate homeworking where appropriate, with a concomitant risk of bad public relations.)
- Your network administrator was working from home to fix a network crash on a Sunday afternoon when a heavy file she was lifting fell from a shelf above the desk, crushing her hand and damaging her laptop keyboard. Your insurer won't pay because they had not been notified of work taking place outside office premises.
- The marketing manager arrives late for a strategy meeting on Monday morning – he got a virus on his home PC at the weekend from the Internet, which trashed his hard disk including the presentation he was supposed to give at the meeting.

Your organisation probably needs to establish a set of rules on how to respond to such scenarios (a policy) as well as a clear idea of how teleworking might alter the legal agreement with your employees (amendments to their contracts). These documents don't need to be long or complex, but if you are to get the most from teleworking, consistent guidelines help to make implementation trouble-free.

TRYING OUT TELEWORKING

The 'full menu' procedure is as follows:
- Carry out a feasibility study, looking at any existing telework in the organisation plus costs and benefits of implementing teleworking.

REASONS NOT TO ADOPT A FLEXIBLE WORKING POLICY

- *If you do not have efficient people and a result-oriented performance management system.*
- *If you do not have the appropriate technology infrastructure.*
- *If you do not have adequate operating policies, procedures and systems.*
- *If you do not value your people or have a culture of trust and empowerment.*
- *If you are out of touch with lifestyle and demographic changes.*
- *If you are unconcerned about market and competitor trends.*
- *If your company's values do not recognise imagination, creativity and responsiveness.*

Extracted from a presentation by Adryan Bell of architectural consultancy DEGW

- Research existing sample telework policies and individual employee agreements (*see* p. 170).
- Consult employees, unions and employee representatives to draw up draft policies and agreements.
- Carry out a pilot project to assess a change to teleworking, using a small group (*see* box on p. 162).
- Monitor and evaluate the pilot project and decide whether a larger rollout will be beneficial to the organisation.

Feasibility studies

The feasibility study should outline the business case, including the operational, strategic, cost or employee advantages to be gained. It should also include a draft implementation plan with timescales and draft budgets.

The first thing your colleagues are likely to need are good reasons for making the change. Or, as in the box on the previous page, you may need to get people thinking whether there are any good reasons for not adopting a flexible working policy like teleworking. This is not as tongue-in-cheek as it seems – some organisations are unrealistic about their suitability for this kind of organisational change, particularly in relation to technology.

If you think this approach won't work, you might try assessing the existing level of tacit teleworking. Many personnel and human-resources departments have no idea of the extent of teleworking going on in their organisations. A celebrated exercise at the World Bank indicated that there were no teleworkers according to the human-resources department, but a different story was told by the IT department – over 1000 telecoms links being used for around 240,000

Some organisations using teleworkers in Britain (October 2002)

This table is intended to show the breadth of business areas now covered. It is not intended as a comprehensive guide, or as a work-finding guide for prospective teleworkers.

Company	Type of work	Numbers
Local Authorities		
Aberdeen City Council	IT, Economic Development, Legal and Corporate	25
Cambridgeshire County Council	Social services, registration of old people's homes, touchdown centres	300-400
Dorset County Council	Various	20
East Riding Council	Housing Benefits officers	21
Hertfordshire County Council	Property Department	30
Horsham District Council	Councillors	12 plus
Kent County Council	Social services, occupational therapists, educational psychologists, consultants	100
Leicester City Council	Computing and telecoms	3
London Borough of Brent	Social workers	8
London Borough of Enfield	Various	47
London Borough of Lewisham	Various social services	18
London Borough of Sutton	Planning introduction	
North Wiltshire District Council	Councillors and IT staff	55-60
Oxfordshire County Council	Various	Hundreds
Sefton MB Council	Education, social services	19
South Hams District Council	All departments	50 p/t
Stoke-on-Trent City Council	Various IT	12
Suffolk County Council	Social services, trading standards, technical and professional workers	290+
Surrey County Council	Teachers, personnel officers, social services, environmental health, planners and business support	100
Wakefield MBC	From clerical to CEO	23
Wiltshire County Council	Education welfare officers	Dozens
Financial Services		
Alliance and Leicester	Call centre	12
Barclays Bank	Various	Dozens
Britannia Building Society	Word processing	3
Co-operative Bank	Debt collection and others	10
Lloyds TSB	'Work options' scheme open to all staff	27,000
Marsh Insurance Brokers	Technical processing	14
Nationwide Building Society	Recruitment consultants, buildings administration, technical, retail	114
Prudential	Life and pensions back-office	50
Royal Bank of Scotland	Various	About 29
Royal Sun Alliance	Sales, claims advisers, engineers	1800
Scottish Widows	Sales staff	200
Skandia Life	Managers, senior personnel	5

Company	Type of work	Numbers
Technology		
BT	Various	5000
Cable & Wireless	Telesales, fault handling, 999	
	Business Sales and others	3,000
Cisco	Sales	360
Hewlett Packard	Sales, training, engineers, professionals	100
IBM	Various, worldwide	53,000
Unisys	Various	10
Miscellaneous		
ACAS	Conciliation staff	500
Automobile Association	Call-centre operators	150
British Gas plus	Field-service engineers, managers	7,000
Classic FM	Presenter	1
Comunicado	Translators and interpreters	550
Davis & Co. Solicitors	Solicitors	40
Design for Learning	Training, research, distance-learning	60
Evergreen Business Services	Dictation. press review, translation	13
Infogenie	Expert advisers (medical, computer support)	130
Multiple Sclerosis Society	Helpline staff	35
Ofsted	Childcare inspectors	1000
Open University	Sales force and academics	75
Rank Xerox	Sales team	300
Telework Association	All staff, some freelance	7
The Experience Corps	Animators, local co-ordinators	90
WWF	Regional organisers	15
Word Association	PR, events co-ordinators	8

man days per year. If you don't have the time or resources for a formal staff survey, do your own simple research – check the date and time stamps on emails you receive from colleagues. How many of these are happening outside working hours? How do you know if they were sending the emails from the office or from home?

The feasibility study should recommend whether to set up a formal or an informal introduction of telework. If you opt for an informal approach, some simple precautions will avoid the more predictable types of failure:

- Select teleworkers who are experienced, trusted members of staff with good skills in IT, time management and communication.
- Ensure that the teleworkers' line managers are supportive of the experiment, and check that managers have adequate IT skills.
- The teleworkers must be satisfied that they have suitable equipment and skills. Employers are still responsible for employee health and safety outside the office, and have a duty to provide adequate training for all work-tasks.

FINANCIAL SERVICES SECTOR SAVES COSTS

The Nationwide Building Society has joined a growing group of financial services companies taking advantage of teleworking to retain skilled staff, saving training and recruiting costs. Employee relations manager Denise Walker explains: 'We employ teleworkers because we want to try and access people with experience who prefer to work from home – such as mothers with small children.'

Nationwide has had a policy of allowing employees to request the option of homeworking from their managers for several years. There are about 85 full-time employees on formal homeworking-conditions contracts, made up of 40 staff in three regional mortgage-lending control teams, and additional staff in the technology division and the retail recruiting division. The Nationwide staff union has agreed a homeworking allowance of £104 pa and has provided input to the teleworking resources pack.

Walker stresses: 'Teleworking needs a different type of manager – who can manage people they can't see, remembering, for instance, to include all teleworking employees in messages which are automatically circulated.' Pauline Henderson of the corporate personnel department, who drew up the company's homeworking policies, says that managers have to answer a lengthy checklist of questions including describing how the homeworker's performance will be monitored, how the individual will be made to feel part of the team, how communications between the office and home office will take place, and whether the company will benefit from the arrangement.

Applications have to be approved by the Homeworkers' User Group, which brings together people from different parts of Nationwide including the personnel divisions, technical services and property services. Pauline comments: 'I wouldn't advocate 100% homeworking. We still want our homeworkers to interface physically with the rest of their team. Typically, they'll be homeworking three days out of five and hotdesking the rest.'

At the Prudential insurance company a pilot scheme for telesales consultants began in summer 1998 with five 'guinea pigs' selling home insurance. Teleworking allowed one of the five, Kamini Govindasamy, to double her hours and wages. 'Before I worked in a big office with 60–80 other people. Now I can give a hundred percent to the customer because it is quiet and I can have a one-to-one relationship with them without asking them to repeat things because I can't hear.'

The Prudential teleworkers have monthly meetings with their line manager to discuss progress. Jean Tomlin, director of sales and operations, says the telesales consultants have reduced their unproductive time and in some cases this has lead to increased hours. The teleworkers were supplied with PCs and ISDN or Kilostream links to the Pru's main database at the call centre in Essex.

POWERGEN PREPARES FOR HOMEWORKING

Energy supplier Powergen has taken advantage of tax breaks which allow computers up to the value of £500 per year to be supplied to employees for home use without being taxed as a benefit in kind.

In autumn 2001 more than 4000 employees (over 80%) signed up to be given a PC, monitor, and printer under the company's Clicks@home scheme. Powergen has leased the PCs at a cost of around £2.25 million from PeoplePC, a company that operates similar schemes for large US employers like Ford and Delta Airlines. Powergen is subsidising 75% of the cost of the machines, while its employees pay approximately £8 a month. They also receive a computer-based training package to help IT novices get started.

Employees also get a CD-ROM with software for an Internet connection via Powergen's own ISP – but the company does not subsidise their connections, and there is no access to the corporate network available. Powergen does not have a formal teleworking policy but the number of people working at home on an occasional basis is expected to increase, and IT Performance Manager Paul Lambert admits that the intention of the scheme is partly to create an infrastructure that would make it easier to roll out formal homeworking in future.

- Have some system for reporting back what went right or wrong.
- Monitor costs, however informally.
- Communicate the experiment clearly to colleagues, supervisors and employee representatives such as unions, so that they know that it's happening and don't think that it's a suspicious secret or a perk available to a privileged few.
- Make sure that the teleworkers know how to indicate if they want to give up the experiment. Reassure them there will be no repercussions if they do give up.

If the informal approach works, you will need to think about whether to expand teleworking, and if any formal trials or procedures are required.

Estimating costs and benefits

A textual description of various advantages and disadvantages of teleworking for companies can be found in Chapter 1, *Overview*. This section focuses on establishing a rough estimate and methodology for financial costs and benefits which is likely to be needed before a company will agree to run a pilot teleworking programme. It draws on some material from the dated but valuable book *Teleworking Explained* (1993) by Mike Gray, Gil Gordon and Noel Hodson, as well as on material available on the websites of Gil Gordon and Jack

SETTING UP A PILOT TELEWORKING PROJECT

- *Set up a steering group or project team.*
- *Identify the planned costs and benefits to the company.*
- *Identify suitable jobs for teleworking.*
- *Select suitable staff members.*
- *Draft and agree changes to contracts and agreements.*
- *Arrange training for teleworkers and their managers.*
- *Install equipment for the home office, mobile office or hotdesking system.*
- *Provide continuing support to teleworkers.*
- *Monitor and evaluate the pilot.*

What is your exit strategy for the pilot? Both the US Patent Office and BT in its original 1994 trial for directory-enquiries staff found that those involved wanted to continue teleworking, but for different reasons this was not possible, resulting in frustrated workforces and considerable dissatisfaction.

Nilles (*see* references). Some equipment suppliers, such as Cisco, provide online cost calculators (*see* **http://www.cisco.com** and search for the ROI calculator).

A straightforward monetary cost/benefit is given in the box on p. 164. However, the calculation will depend on individual company circumstances. For example, some organisations will see a quantifiable benefit in providing family-friendly policies leading to improved staff retention. Others may be concerned to show a contribution towards environmental factors such as savings in energy, or reductions in commuter traffic. Where introduction of teleworking results in savings on office space (through desksharing or hotdesking), there will be a direct financial benefit which will not apply to an organisation where the teleworkers retain their previous workspaces onsite.

Because the main payback for most companies is either increased productive hours per week for a staff member, or increased productivity, the calculations will be more favourable for senior staff members with a correspondingly high pay rate or chargeout rate per hour than for staff with more basic skills.

Many of the published case studies of teleworking are for pilots carried out in IT departments where ability to use teleworking equipment starts from a high base level, and hourly rates are also high. The payback for basic clerical staff with lower pay rates who will also need more IT training may not look so advantageous from a purely cost-based point of view. Paybacks for part-time home-based teleworkers will obviously take longer if a home equipment setup duplicates office equipment but both equipment sets are only used part-time.

First, estimate the one-off costs of change such as:

- Equipment for the home office (PCs, phone lines, chairs, desks, filing).
- Training for the teleworkers (consultants or in-house?).
- Training for their managers.
- Lost productive time during the setup period for teleworkers and their managers.
- Time spent by HR department designing telework policy, establishing new agreements and procedures and monitoring the trial.
- Time spent by IT department specifying, installing, testing and supporting the teleworker equipment.
- Health and safety inspection procedure for home offices.

Next, look for costs that you will be able to measure both before and after the teleworking pilot, and work out how to obtain these figures. The topics to be examined will include measurements of:

- Output ('deliverables') of the teleworker – quality and quantity, hours worked, targets and deadlines met, satisfaction with their working life, stress levels.
- Changes in employment costs – salary, expenses, support staff, office space and overheads, training costs, recruitment and retention, sick leave.
- Travel costs – company car expenses, season tickets, time spent travelling, communications costs while travelling, air tickets, hotel bills (some of these costs are borne by the employer and some by the employee – so the costs and benefits to each need to be distinguished).
- Environmental issues – energy consumption, waste production, traffic reduction (if these are important to the company's objectives).

This should enable an estimation of annual running costs to add to the one-off setup costs. The payback periods for those telework programmes which have been published are in the region of 18–24 months but vary widely. It is important to periodically review the cost/benefit analysis. Some companies try to protect their investment for the payback period by making it clear to staff that if they take up the teleworking option, they will be expected to continue it for at least two years.

Identifying suitable teleworking jobs

Jobs suitable for teleworking include those with: clear objectives and measurable outputs; and minimal requirements for supervision or face-to-face teamwork. For each job, assess how much of it can be done remotely in order to help in setting expectations for the amount of time that can be spent outside the conventional office.

TELEWORKING IMPLEMENTATION COSTS

Durham County Council reports its 2002 homeworker costs as:

PC, printer and software	£1000
Network connection	£300 plus £360/year running costs
Router	£400
Faxphone answering machine	£200
Total	**£1900**

Nortel provides two offerings for its employees who wish to telework – part-time and full-time – and supplies a cost/benefit justification adapted to each country where it offers teleworking. The figures for Ireland for 2000 are given here (using a year 2000 average $/£ conversion figure of 1.51). Conventional office-space charge assumption (against which cost avoidance is measured) was £21,192 per employee per year – £1766 per month. Call costs assume 800 min/month remote access part-time and 1600 min/month full-time using eircom lines.

Setup charges	Part-time	Full-time
ISDN installation	£292	£292
HOMEbase equipment	£659	£659
HP 65 combined printer/fax copier		£397
Furniture		£993
Subtotal	**£951**	**£2341**

Monthly charges	Part-time	Full-time
Office space (cost of central-office facilities)	£1060	£353
Technical support	£83	£83
ISDN line rental	£24	£24
Call charges	£56	£111
Subtotal	**£1223**	**£571**

Cost avoidance year/teleworker	**£6516**	**£14,340**

Booz Allen Hamilton, in an extensive report for the US Government's General Services Agency, compared 'per seat' IT costs due to home-based telework as follows (costs annualised and converted from dollars to sterling at 2001 rates):

General office baseline	£2402
1–2 days per week, laptop PC with dial-up access	£2882 (+20%)
3–4 days per week, laptop PC and 50% rebate for DSL line	£3222 (+34%)
Full time, desktop PC, 100% rebate for DSL Line	£3083 (+28%)

Gartner Group estimated in 1999 that hard-core 'road warriors' cost around $5500 (£3416) each year in support costs, compared to $3500 (£2173) for a standard desktop user.

Enterprise Ireland (EI), an Irish government business development agency, sponsored trials of teleworking in eight companies. From the equipment costs of these trials, EI estimated in 2000 that the average cost for a home office was about £3,150 sterling plus recurring costs including communications, training and IT support of about £800 sterling per annum.

SETTING UP A PILOT PROJECT

The steering group

The first step is to establish a team or steering group for the teleworking pilot. You will need a project manager, clear responsibilities and reporting arrangements, and links to a sponsoring board member.

One important reason for ensuring that there is a steering group is 'corporate amnesia'. If the telework programme is the territory of one individual, and that person moves job or company, there is a strong likelihood that the programme will die when they leave. There are many examples of good programmes that have withered after losing their champion, so try to set up a structure that will be resilient.

A second important reason is to ensure an integrated approach that has commitment and leadership with links at high levels within the company (e.g. at board level). IBM Global Services comment that this is the most important lesson it has learned in implementing 'mobile office' for 100,000 employees: 'If the mobile office is treated, for example, as a real-estate or IT responsibility, then problems may arise in other areas and the initiative will be seen as a failure.'

Decide on benchmarks

The second step is to identify the parameters that will be used to assess the success of the pilot – without clear measures of success or failure, it will be hard to spread teleworking beyond the pilot study to other areas. A more detailed working of the initial cost/benefits case using the specific examples of the prospective pilot teleworkers should reveal what measurements are both useful and feasible.

Common problems

Don't attempt the pilot project too quickly – a realistic schedule allows time for problems to develop and be resolved without constant 'firefighting' and anxieties among those involved. The project should build-in opportunities for individual and group meetings to review progress in order to identify and resolve teething problems quickly.

The problem most widely encountered in teleworking trials is 'middle-management syndrome', which describes the difficulties encountered in management cultures where status depends on the number of people reporting to a manager. These managers prefer to see staff sitting at their desks or attending constant face-to-face meetings, and find it hard to make the change from 'eyeball' management to managing by results – often due to concerns about their own position and effectiveness. Another source of resistance can be managers who themselves are not happy using IT; they can become a major obstacle to an effective trial. When considering these issues, also look at the reverse side of the coin – teleworking can act as a spur to change management culture and improve IT literacy among staff.

Staff selection

There are five qualifying factors which must be in place before an employee should be selected for teleworking:

- Job description (or tasks within job description which can be 'clumped' together to be carried out on teleworking days).
- Personality and experience of the employee.
- Personality and supportive attitude of their line manager.
- Supportive team colleagues.
- Space and facilities for home office or mobile working.

It may be that teleworking is being offered to staff with caring responsibilities or with a particular reason to want to work from home – in which case the staff will be self-selecting. Where the pilot project can choose the prospective teleworkers, it is important to select people suited to the demands that teleworking may place on them. Introverted people who are poor communicators are unlikely to adapt easily but may be attracted by the solitary workstyle. Some companies have used psychometric tests and counselling to ensure that applicants are likely to make a success of the change. The key personality traits to watch for are:

- Self-discipline.
- Good decision-making and problem-solving skills.
- Good self-management and time-management abilities.
- Good communication skills.
- Ability to cope with reduced social contact.

Some employers consider that established, mature staff are more likely to want to telework and to be successful at it. In practice there is a clear prevalence of experienced workers. A survey of 1953 technology professionals by the website **http://home.techies.com** in 2001 found that only 32% of entry-level workers practise any form of telecommuting, but that for those with ten years or more experience the figure was 67% telecommuting at least a few hours each week.

Kevin Curran and Geoff Williams[48] emphasise that, although there are no personality inventories on the market which specifically measure suitability for working at home, several provide information about traits essential for remote working such as level of need for contact with others, self-discipline and preference for certain kinds of work. These inventories include the Work Environment Scale, the Myers-Briggs Type Indicator and the Work Style Reference Inventory. However, use of psychometric testing is considered controversial and unfair by some HR professionals and many trade unions. Problems might arise if someone who is keen on teleworking is denied the chance to participate in a trial due to unfavourable personality traits. Clear and open policies on teleworker selection can help to overcome such difficulties.

Policies, agreements and unions

A survey carried out in 2001[49] by IRS and *Flexible Working* magazine found that less than half of respondents had drafted formal policies on teleworking, and only one quarter had negotiated agreements with recognised trade unions.

At the pilot project stage it is advisable to draft a company telework policy for discussion with employees, employee representatives and unions, which can also be revised to take account of the findings of the pilot project. Guidelines and examples to assist in preparing telework policies and individual telework agreements are given later in this chapter.

Setting up a home office

This topic is covered in more detail in Chapter 4, *Alternative workplaces*. The pilot project team must establish what equipment will be needed by teleworkers to carry out their work-tasks at home. The IT department will probably want to establish a standard 'home office' or 'mobile worker' kit. Bear in mind that needs vary with the job description. At the Irish airports authority Aer Rianta, the pilot teleworking trial quickly discovered that their standard equipment specification, although high-level and including ISDN lines and a combined printer/fax/scanner/copier, was not suitable for two buyers who frequently needed to be logged into the company's retail management system while sending a fax and talking on the phone simultaneously. The ISDN connection would only allow two of these three operations at any one time so extra voice lines had to be installed.

The team should establish that the prospective teleworker has a suitable home office available – ideally in a separate room. If the teleworking arrangement is planned as a regular one, employers should check that the teleworker has a computer workstation and adjustable chair that comply with health and safety legislation – regardless of whether the equipment belongs to the employer or employee. A visit by a manager or health and safety specialist is recommended prior to beginning a telework trial to assess any problems such as inadequate supply of power points, as well as to investigate the local telecoms infrastructure. Some areas may not have digital exchanges, or else line quality to a teleworker's home may be poor due to long runs of overhead poles. Availability of ISDN services should also be checked if needed. (*See* Chapter 4, *Alternative workplaces* and Chapter 9, *Technology and techniques*.)

Any disruption to the home caused by installation of equipment should be kept to a minimum and negotiated with the staff member and their family in advance. Some issues which need to be borne in mind in designing the home-office are covered in Chapter 7, *Staying safe and legal*. There is a checklist of home-office equipment on p. 292.

Funding the setup of the home office can happen in a number of ways. The employer may provide equipment, or supply a budget and allow the employee to make the purchases. In some situations employees may provide their own equipment. Whatever the arrangement, a risk assessment, which may be carried out by the employer, or a self-assessment checklist procedure carried out by the employee, is advisable to comply with health and safety legislation.

Training

Managers, prospective teleworkers and their colleagues remaining in the conventional office will all need training in order to adapt to the new circumstances. Much of this will focus on effective communication. Managers may need to adapt to a new culture – managing by results – which requires skills in the areas of delegation, co-ordination and orchestration. Traditional techniques – particularly persuading people to do things by force of personality – may not be effective in managing teleworkers. The common thread to the new management skills is improving interpersonal skills for a work environment involving less authority and more trust.

The general consensus among teleworking consultants is that an initial induction or information session is needed first – to cover what teleworking is, the business case for introducing it, and the likely advantages and pitfalls. This induction will usually take place at an early stage of the pilot project and is often part of the selection process: it allows those interested in taking part to get enough information to make a decision on whether to pursue their interest, and offers opportunities for discussion with their line manager. It can also double as a training session for members of the steering group or project team, and bring forward issues for their consideration.

Once staff selection for the final project has taken place, a second training session is needed. Opinions are divided on whether the second session should take teleworkers and managers as separate groups, or combine them – practical issues such as availability and size of training room will probably decide this. The second session should:

- Indicate top-level support for the trial and spell out the business benefits to the company.
- Introduce any documentation such as survey forms, or communication agreements, or the company telework policy.
- Discuss the changes needed for management by results.
- Look at any practical issues such as how to forward calls to the home office, how to schedule meetings which need the teleworker's presence, and how to ensure that computer files are appropriately updated in different locations (synchronising data).
- Look at HR issues such as insurance cover in the home office, security policies and the exit procedure if the trial is not working out.
- Explain to the teleworkers and their managers the plan for monitoring the trial and the criteria for success.
- Encourage manager/teleworker pairs to complete a communications agreement covering issues like how often email and voicemail should be

checked, what should happen in the event of the teleworker being needed
urgently in the company office, what core hours the teleworker must be
available for, and so on.
- Check for training needs – any skills the prospective teleworkers feel they
lack, such as time management or specific IT skills.
- Provide plenty of opportunities for discussion.

Further training material for managers may also be needed to cover:
- Specifying aims and criteria clearly.
- Agreeing and negotiating work-tasks.
- Relating pay to performance (where appropriate).
- Developing conflict resolution skills for remotely based teams.

Colleagues will also need to be informed of the teleworking initiative,
including the company's reasons for introducing it, who is managing the
project and what the outcomes are likely to be, as well as how they will be
measured. Open information should dampen speculation about the long-term
teleworking intentions of the company and also assist the teleworkers in their
communications with non-teleworking colleagues.

A commonly reported problem for new teleworkers is that their colleagues
don't phone with important information for fear of disturbing them 'at home'
with work calls – something that can usually be sorted out through a clear
agreement among everyone involved about the need to establish core work
hours, regardless of location, and the use of voicemail outside those hours.
There is also a strong argument for introducing 'follow me' telephone systems,
where dialling one central number automatically switches through to the
teleworker's current location, before starting on a telework programme, in
order to reduce any impact on colleagues.

Other training strategies may include a programme of workshops for new
teleworkers, allowing them to shadow more experienced colleagues, and
allocating them mentors. Specific IT training modules will probably be
required, such as the use of dial-up network connections and procedures for
maintaining data security.

It is important not to assume that prospective teleworkers are competent IT
users. Check and assess that they are happy using the software and hardware
needed in their job, and remedy skills gaps before beginning a trial – otherwise
you will be measuring IT training deficits, not the effects of teleworking. Some
companies have found that providing basic training in 'do it yourself' technical
support for IT equipment provides a good return in reduced support costs.
Others instruct teleworkers not to attempt to repair equipment but to return it
to the office, for health and safety reasons.

Look at the context of any other organisational changes which may be
occurring at the same time. Often teleworking is introduced as part of a series

of changes, and may occasionally be seen as taking things a step too far. One corporate that pioneered teleworking reported that during its introduction of teleworking, there were 14 different change programmes going on within the company. The teleworking trial suffered from the level of confusion caused by the number of simultaneous changes occurring.

HR ISSUES

Work-life balance

Teleworking is often introduced as one of a range of measures to improve work-life balance. Computer company Compaq (since merged with HP) approached work-life balance issues by surveying 250 managers about the different options which could be offered. The company's motivation was to recruit and retain the best staff, and to help manage their health and wellbeing.

The survey was used to rationalise 12 possible options down to the five which were offered. Individuals can now propose themselves for any of the five arrangements using forms and background information from the company intranet. The five options can be used to vary:

- Length of time worked (including part-time working or reduced hours).
- When the work is undertaken (flexible start times and nine-day fortnights).
- Where the work is undertaken (homeworking contracts and occasional homeworking).
- Breaks from work (career breaks).

Compaq found its six-month timeframe to review, build and implement the scheme too short. HR Director Christine Watson reported that some managers could not be persuaded to support the scheme and referred to it as 'nothing but a shirker's charter'. Christine also pointed out that of all the options available, the only one where savings were fairly easy to measure was homeworking.

Policies and agreements

This section extracts some common issues which need to be addressed, drawing in part on work carried out by Cathy Murray of the Small World Connections consultancy, published in *Flexible Working* magazine in January 1997, and in part on the Irish government's Code of Practice for teleworking which contains a policy template (**http://www.e-work.ie/uploads/code.pdf**). These sources may well be superseded by a UK Code of Practice currently under consideration by a working group – check the Telework Association website **http://www.telework.org.uk** for an update. The EuroTelework project also has an archive of sample contracts at **http://www.euro-telework.org**

CONFESSIONS OF A TELEWORKING CONVERT

Like many managers, Ian Jones thought teleworking was great – especially as the company he directed sold home-office insurance policies – but not for him, just for independent small businesses. That was until he was forced to try it after his baby daughter was diagnosed with a potentially fatal illness.

'I thought that the office wouldn't cope without me for two or three days a week, that staff would run riot, clients would wonder who was in charge, and colleagues would believe I had lost touch.

'Then after my daughter's diagnosis, what was, I suppose, a normal family life became one interrupted by a series of hospital visits building up to a bone-marrow transplant operation. Thankfully my fellow directors were very understanding and for most of two months I commuted to and from the hospital and, with the assistance of ISDN and a laptop, continued with some work and kept in touch with the office.

'I was surprised at how easy it was to overcome the possible disadvantages of teleworking – distractions, lack of motivation, feelings of isolation – and at how quickly I realised the personal advantages such as reduced commuting, increased leisure and family time. From a business point of view I find my time is better managed and the split between home and office is an advantage rather than a hindrance.

'As a result I believe that I have been more productive and that working from home has not undermined me as an individual, or undermined the effective management of the company. Quite simply, teleworking has worked – and I am now in the fortunate position of honestly being able to claim that I understand my clients because for two days a week, I'm one of them.'
http://www.tolsonmessenger.com

General issues

Teleworking can be required as part of an employee's job description, or it can be introduced as a voluntary arrangement. Where the arrangement is voluntary, the policy should set out the provisions for suspending or terminating the arrangement and returning to conventional office working.

Usually this involves identifying a period of notice by either side, which is often one month. Other issues, such as the return of company-owned home-office equipment, will also need to be specified.

It is usual for teleworking agreements to specify a number of core hours when the teleworker is available for telephone contact by colleagues. Outside these hours, it is up to the teleworker to decide their pattern of work in order to achieve the tasks they have been set. Otherwise working hours are not altered by teleworking, although there may need to be variations to the procedure by which overtime and sick pay are agreed, claimed and monitored by the employer. A procedure for the teleworker to report for meetings at the office as required should also be included.

Employers normally provide all relevant IT equipment (computers, faxes, scanners, photocopiers, modems, etc.) and supply and pay for a separate telephone line, often with an answerphone or voicemail to buffer 'after hours' calls without disturbing the employee. Whether the equipment belongs to the employee or the employer, the policy should spell out the situation on:

- Provision and ownership of equipment and furniture.
- Arrangements for maintenance and technical support.
- Insurance.
- Personal use.
- Provisions against misuse (this may already be covered in the company's IT security policy).
- Arrangements for returning items if the teleworker changes jobs or returns to office-based work.

Suitable jobs and teleworker selection

The effect of teleworking on colleagues remaining in the office, and on customers should be considered alongside issues of employee and job-description suitability. Oxfordshire County Council's policy stipulates that there should be no adverse effects on the level and quality of service, or increases in the workload of non-teleworking colleagues. It is important to avoid any unfair extra workload, either on those who are teleworking or on those who are 'back at the office'.

Sometimes teleworking is introduced as part of a company disability policy or equal opportunities policy. In relation to disability, consideration should be given to appropriate support mechanisms such as specialised equipment which may be required by individual employees. It is possible that excluding certain workers from teleworking could have equality and industrial relations implications, so laying out clear criteria on selection in the company teleworking policy is important. The US General Accounting Office has warned in a report on barriers to telecommuting that employers who discriminate against non-disabled teleworkers could be at risk in relation to equal opportunities legislation.

The home office

The company policy should list a procedure for establishing whether a suitable home office or other teleworking workplace is available.

In large organisations it is usual for there to be an inventory system for the equipment provided to the home office, including labelling, and procedures for returning the equipment if the teleworking arrangement is ended, for replacement if the equipment is lost, stolen or damaged, and for repair when necessary. If an arrangement is made for the teleworker to use their own equipment rather than the company's, then it is important that the teleworker check their home-insurance policy to ensure that the equipment is covered for such usage and that they inform their insurer of their plans.

Employers with well-established schemes, such as mmO$_2$ (formerly Cellnet), may pay for courier delivery of a batch of paper files, reference material and stationery to the home at the start of the teleworking arrangement.[50] With regard to furniture, some employers (such as GlaxoWellcome) expect the teleworker to supply their own furniture, whereas others – particularly those whose employees may be involved in long hours at the computer – choose to supply suitable ergonomic office furniture so that they are certain they are carrying out their health and safety responsibilities. Another solution is to provide an allowance for the purchase of suitable furniture (Shell UK provides this as an option for teleworking employees – the amount granted is £300).

Stationery and other office consumables will also be needed in the home office. In some companies these are provided from central stores; in others a stationery/postage allowance is paid, or expenses are reclaimed.

A number of employers who have long-standing telework schemes include in their guidelines a request that those instigating the arrangement plan to keep costs down, e.g. by using existing office furniture or IT equipment to furnish the home office.

Privacy for employees working at home is another issue which should be clarified in a company policy. The privacy clause should indicate procedures regarding any home visits for health and safety inspections, such as requirements for a written request to inspect the home office, or to collect equipment if an employee leaves the company. Mechanisms for telephone and mail redirection to protect privacy should also be provided if required.

Oxfordshire County Council recognises the right of its employees to keep their home telephone numbers and addresses confidential – something which is not difficult if a separate telephone line paid for by the employer is used, and if the postal address remains at the main office. For reasons of personal security Surrey County Council advises its teleworkers not to hold meetings with clients in their homes but to use council premises instead. Employers are divided on whether managers should meet with staff in the home, but according to the IRS survey[51] around two-thirds do not permit teleworkers to hold home meetings at all. Durham County Council recommends monthly home visits by managers, during which general office and work issues should be discussed to help counter any feelings of isolation. Mobile phone company mmO$_2$ encourages managers to undertake a home visit as part of the teleworker induction process, to help maintain the working relationship and to enhance understanding of the employee's situation and working environment.[52]

Additionally, companies should discourage situations where a home phone number is given out – rather, they should ensure that telephone calls are received at their central office and redirected to teleworkers so that if a staff

member who teleworks leaves, their calls can be redirected easily to their replacement without confusion.

The area of childcare can be problematic to cover in a teleworking policy. Some agreements specify that the teleworker must have adequate childcare during working hours – teleworking is no substitute for childcare, despite the media stereotype of the toddler cuddled on mummy's knee while she taps at the keyboard. But all parents will be familiar with the problems of the suddenly sick or distressed child, and since one of the aims of a teleworking agreement is to provide flexible work practices which allow better balance between home and working life, agreements which are draconian in this area can be self-negating. A statement to the effect that employees must complete their assignments on time, and that the company expects children to be cared for while the employee is working, particularly during school holidays, is probably sufficient. It should also be noted that a strong statement in this area combined with a teleworker group that is all female might conceivably lead to equal opportunities problems.

Some agreements also specify the duty of the teleworker to maintain their home-office area safely for themselves, and for others, including family members or work colleagues who may enter it.

The company is normally responsible for insuring the worker while they are using the home office. Some employers, such as AT&T, specify that they are not liable for accidents involving third parties or family members, and that the teleworker should take out their own insurance to cover such eventualities. There are many examples of insurers providing cover for employees working at home, but in the case of Stoke City Council, it was found necessary to agree with the insurance company a 'cordon' around the working area which is clearly specified. For employer liability purposes, the insurer/employer is responsible for this work area. Outside this area the employer is not liable (e.g. if the worker falls down the stairs and suffers injury). On electrical supply, the guidance from the Health and Safety Executive is that the employer's liability stops where their equipment plugs into the wall socket in a home office, but many health and safety departments would recommend that wiring is checked for reasons of practicality (voltage fluctuations causing problems with equipment) as well as safety.

Health and safety

Because of the employer's health and safety responsibilities, some companies insist on initial and periodic inspection visits to the home office. Others take a 'self-certification' approach, providing advice and training and a checklist to the teleworker and asking them to carry out their own inspection. This is an issue which must be handled with some sensitivity due to the difficult border between home and work. Family members may resent being 'on parade' for the boss's visit, while teleworkers may feel stressed by the need to present in as good a light as possible their entire home and family, not just the home office, to their employer. Usually a period of notice before a home visit is specified in writing.

Shell UK provides its teleworkers with detailed guidance on teleworker health and safety, covering the following issues:

- Equipment layout.
- Positioning of cables.
- Lighting.
- Ventilation.
- Handling and carrying equipment.
- Suitable chairs.
- Lighting levels.
- Noise levels.
- Ventilation and humidity.
- Fire safety issues such as the fitting of smoke detectors and access to an extinguisher.
- Inadvisability of allowing children to play with a company PC.

This level of detail may not be required in some situations, but it is important that employers specify how they will check and monitor the health and safety of the employee's working environment. IBM Global Services makes the point that there may be a relationship between using a self-certification approach to health and safety and whether the arrangement is voluntary: 'An enterprise which requires its employees to work at home would need to take more direct responsibility for the employees' working conditions.'

Oxfordshire County Council issues a health and safety checklist to employees for completion, while Glaxo Group Research includes in its teleworking contract that 'the individual must provide a working environment which satisfies company security and health and safety requirements'. Health and safety issues are covered in more detail in Chapter 7, *Staying safe and legal*, pages 295–303.

Communication procedures

Effective communication is the key factor for successful teleworking. The change to teleworking requires replacement of many of the informal communications methods of the traditional workplace, so it can be useful to clarify how the teleworker is expected to use different methods (phone, fax, email) to avoid misunderstandings and communication difficulties. If the company already has detailed reporting procedures or communications guidelines between colleagues or between managers and subordinates, these may need some revision to incorporate teleworking. It is normal to find that there are no communications guidelines in place, in which case it is probably worthwhile to ask teleworkers and their managers to sit down with a draft communications agreement and come up with a structure which suits them.

The issues that should be addressed in the communications agreement, which is usually a separate, informal document between the manager and teleworker and copied to the HR department for information, include:

- Location of the home office or other remote workplace, and contact details.
- Use of fax, phone, email (including frequency of checking email), collection of voicemail, and common-sense guidelines such as not carrying on commercially sensitive conversations using mobile phones outside the office in places where they can be overheard.
- Agreed core contact times – reporting-in arrangements, arrangements for teleworker to receive work instructions, arrangements for informing manager of task completion, and arrangements to keep the office informed of the whereabouts of a remote employee.
- Arrangements for access to technical support for equipment or software problems.
- Arrangements for scheduling meetings with colleagues and managers.
- Delivery of internal communications (memos, newsletters) and post to the teleworker.
- Access to any specialist technology such as intranets, computerised diaries, or conferencing software.
- Arrangements for monitoring work performance (if keystroke monitoring or call-listening methods are used, the employee must be informed of their use).
- Procedures for reporting problems such as harrassment via email or other abuse of company communications systems.
- Any arrangements for non-teleworking colleagues to act as 'office buddy' or mentor for the teleworker.

■ Arrangements for reviewing the teleworking arrangement and dealing with any training needs.

Career development and training

A training assessment should be carried out for teleworkers. Likely topics will include:

■ IT skills such as dial-up remote access and Internet usage.
■ Self-management skills, e.g. priority-setting, time management.
■ Ability to recognise and deal with symptoms of isolation and demotivation.
■ Training needs of the teleworker's manager – e.g. management by results, goal-setting, progress-monitoring, giving feedback.
■ Health and safety training (this may already be covered in standard company induction training) – the responsibility of the employer for health and safety of employees, and the responsibility of employees to take reasonable care of their health and safety, and to report defects in equipment or working conditions leading to risks.

Some potential teleworkers worry that they may miss out on opportunities for promotion or training, and become isolated from the company. In consequence, many agreements or policies contain a clause stipulating that entitlements and arrangements for career development, training and performance appraisals will be unchanged by a teleworking arrangement. In practical terms, it is important for HR staff to realise that remote workers are widely distributed and rarely available at the same time, making it harder and more expensive to arrange conventional classroom training and perhaps requiring further movement in the direction of delivering some materials through e-learning.

Security

Security procedures for teleworking are usually similar to the company's existing security procedures, but may require adjustment. For example, if secure-document waste is normally shredded, but the teleworker has no access to a shredder, it may be necessary for documents to be returned to the office for shredding. Issues to consider include:

■ Dealing with secure-document waste.
■ Locking the home office/password-protecting the home computer.
■ Checking for computer viruses.
■ Ensuring that software installed complies with licences (non-duplication).
■ Keeping data backups (it is advisable for one set of backups to be held at the central office site in case of damage or theft at the home office).
■ Confidentiality and non-disclosure agreements.

S*ee* Chapter 9, S*taying safe and legal* for further security guidelines, and Chapter 8, *Technology and techniques* for more on data security.

Terms and conditions

An employee who teleworks has the same employment rights, and is protected by the same employment legislation, as all other employees. However, some clarification of elements of terms and conditions may be needed, such as:

- What core hours must be worked (if any)?
- Which hours or days are to be worked in the office and which teleworked?
- The procedure for agreeing and monitoring working time, overtime, sickness and holiday arrangements.
- Any change to the application of bonus systems.
- Any element of piecework – if so, how is this applied?
- Reimbursement of expenses (*see* below) for heat, light, cleaning of the home office, stationery, postage, telecommunications, travel.
- Any effect on premium payments for night or weekend working.
- Benefit-in-kind – any information on taxation implications of personal use of equipment such as PCs.
- Fringe benefits – any change in their application.

Most companies pay allowances to teleworkers to cover their home-office costs. For smaller organisations, a system of reimbursing receipted expenses, plus payments covering any increased costs are the norm. For larger organisations with many teleworkers, the administrative burden of handling individual receipts may be uneconomic, in which case an annual or monthly agreed allowance will be preferable.

A fixed amount payable to the employee and revisable on a yearly basis is perhaps the neatest way of proceeding. The sums involved may be based on before-and-after usage or on an apportionment in relation to space used for work within the home. In the latter case, the basis of the allowance should be an analysis of the running costs of the house (mainly heat and light) divided by the proportion of the house used for business. These amounts should be declared on the annual P11D form returned by the employer. Alternatively, dispensation for the amounts should be agreed with both the Inspector of Taxes and the Contributions Agency. Employees could be liable for tax if the employer pays more than can be shown to be a justifiable amount.

Shell UK pays an allowance to its teleworkers of between £1040 and £1860 depending on the number of days spent working at home. Oxfordshire County Council pays £50 per month for wear and tear on the home office plus increased energy usage. Durham County Council provides a fixed lump-sum payment of £100 a year. At the other end of the scale, GlaxoWellcome Research Group believes that added expenses for teleworkers are balanced out by savings on travel and does not make any payment. This was also the position

OXFORDSHIRE COUNTY COUNCIL'S FLEXIPLACE SCHEME

Oxfordshire County Council employs about 16,700 people (11,800 full-time equivalents). The majority are female, and 58% are part-timers, many of whom work flexitime. In 1992 the Council introduced a Flexiplace scheme, as part of a bottom-up, grassroots initiative to allow working from home where appropriate. Now, although no detailed figures are kept, Flexiplace is mainstream for Oxfordshire, with a large proportion of the workforce occasionally homeworking.

Chief Executive Richard Shaw has turned the County Hall restaurant into a large café with tables suitable for meetings, and comfortable chairs. There are also facilities for people to use their laptops in the café. Some hotdesking is taking place although there is no formal policy as yet. Personnel officer Lucy Freeman reports: 'I have noticed several people using the café facilities instead of trying to find a free desk as the environment is comfortable and spacious.'

The prime consideration has been that there should be no effects on the level and quality of the service provided. Lucy reports that there has not been a problem with in-office colleagues having to take teleworkers' phone calls: 'So much is done by email now that the person who is not in the office still personally fields the contact that someone is trying to make with them.' To date the scheme has been largely 'budget neutral' – costs have to be met from the normal operating budget of the relevant department, and there have been no major workspace savings. However, there have been reductions in journeys and their associated costs which are important because the council wants to reduce any unnecessary journeys.

Hilary Simpson, originally responsible for introducing the Flexiplace scheme, says the development of the scheme was 'pleasingly non-eventful', but that by now everyone who was going to volunteer probably has done so. 'We let it grow and when we started, the technology probably wasn't sufficient to support what we were doing.' Hilary stresses that giving employees flexibility about where they work is 'an efficiency issue, an environmental issue and an equal opportunities issue' and that people design their own work patterns. The Council pays employees who regularly work a substantial proportion of their time at home a £50-a-month allowance to cover increased energy costs and household wear and tear. Currently this allowance is paid to only 18 people but many more work from home on occasion.

Example 1
An animal health inspector can now drive straight from home to markets in North Oxfordshire without reporting to the head office in South Oxfordshire first. The Council is making major savings on the cost of journeys back to base, freeing the inspectors to devote more of their time to looking after animal welfare.

Example 2
A management accountant in the department of leisure and arts works a 30-hour week contract, of which ten hours are now home-based. 'I tend to work in the office between the hours when my children are at school. Then at home I usually work in the evenings when I can really get my head down.'

of Britannia Building Society when it trialled teleworking – heating costs would be balanced out by travel savings. Another variation on this theme is mobile phone company mm0$_2$, which allows employees to calculate heating and lighting costs according to a set formula up to a maximum of £150 a year, or else to claim a flat £78 tax-free without the need to provide receipts.

Benefit in kind

Regardless of the method of payment, allowances for teleworking expenses have tax implications. All non-cash benefits and expenses provided to employees in the course of their employment are normally taxed. For this reason many employers include statements in teleworking agreements forbidding personal use of equipment, or advising the teleworker that it is their responsibility to seek advice on the tax implications of personal use. The 1999 British budget included a measure to exempt teleworking equipment provided by employers from being treated as a perk or 'benefit in kind'. Computers, scanners, software, modems and printers are now exempt up to a maximum benefit of £500 a year (which means in effect any PC not exceeding a value of £2500) but there is a catch – it only applies to companies which do not restrict the provision of equipment just to senior staff and directors. Fax machines are not included but will not incur a liability if they are used only for business purposes. The equipment also has to remain the property of the company. Where a telephone line is provided, there is no liability if it is used only for business purposes. The Finance Act 2000 relaxed the rules further so that assets or services provided solely for work use by the employer in the employee's home are not taxable if private use is not significant (this could include the provision of garden offices – *see* p. 94). Employers can also contract and pay for Internet connections and rental fees without fear of BIK problems.

Teleworker Magazine also quizzed the Inland Revenue about a situation where the employer pays for a broadband Internet connection with no separate billing or record of calls (because it is an always-on connection) and no breakdown between work and private bills is possible. They agreed that to the extent that there are significant employment duties required to be carried out by the employee at home, and the cost is not increased due to private use, this situation does fall within the Finance Act 2000 exemption.

The situation for mobile phones is complicated. Ideally the employer should provide the phone and pay for calls – if the employee owns the phone and the employer pays the bills, things get sticky both in regard to the apportionment of private and work use, and in relation to tax on the rental charge.

Furniture provided by an employer is subject to benefit-in-kind and strictly speaking should be recorded on the annual P11D form, though the low value of standard office furniture is unlikely to excite great interest from most tax officials. *See* **http://www.inlandrevenue.com**

In relation to running expenses, costs can be recovered from the employer without incurring tax only where it can be shown that there is an 'objective' reason why the work is being carried out from home. This has been strictly interpreted recently by the Inland Revenue, so proceed with caution and check carefully before assuming that such payments are tax-exempt. In some situations, the employer and employee may wish an allowance to be paid but to be declared for tax. In relation to heating and lighting, the costs can only be recovered without incurring tax for the proportion of the house which is used for work (say one room in six or one-sixth). Other costs, such as rent, council tax and cleaning, can only be claimed where a separate room is dedicated as the home office (but *see* pages 305–309 on possible business-rates implications of dedicated rooms).

Advice should be sought before making any one-off payment to compensate for a change in working practices, since these can also be deemed a taxable benefit. More information about taxation isues is given in Chapter 7, *Staying safe and legal*.

An employee who must work at home can argue that the home is the real place of work and hence travel to the office is business travel and reimbursable tax-free. Again, the 'objective need' test for work at home applies, and the employee must be instructed in writing by the employer to work in this way. For mobile teleworkers such as salesforce staff, or engineers who must use home as a base and travel mainly to customer premises, the situation is a little clearer and generally all their business travel costs will be reimbursable. However, there have been situations where a regular trip to office premises (perhaps to attend a weekly meeting) has still been interpreted as a commuting trip which cannot be reimbursed without tax consequences. Even where the distance travelled to attend the regular meeting is large, it can be considered a 'commute'.

Self-employed teleworking contractors

Once companies begin to allow their own employees to telework, it is often the case that they become happier with the idea of using contractors who work at a distance as well, because they are more familiar with managing at a distance. Employers need to ensure that they do not, through the nature of their arrangement with the contractor, establish an employee-employer relationship without intending to. Simply creating an agreement which absolves the employer of any responsibility for the contractor's tax and national insurance payments is unlikely to be valid if the conditions are not agreed by the relevant authorities. Further guidance is given in Chapter 9, *Staying safe and legal*.

ACAS TELEBUDDIES PAIR UP FOR PROFESSIONALISM

ACAS, the Advisory, Conciliation and Arbitration Service, has about 600 employees. Staff are involved in resolving disputes between individuals and their employers and in resolving large-scale industrial disputes, covering a wide geographical area and travelling between ACAS offices as well as to client sites. A considerable level of informal homeworking had developed, so ACAS decided to run a pilot project in one region to gauge effects on staff and service levels. ACAS also commissioned research from the Institute of Employment Studies on the best method of developing good practice in homeworking.

The IES survey interviewed 273 homeworkers. Some 24% were designated full-time homeworkers, 15% had free choice on when they work in the home and when they work in the office, 23% occasionally took work home and 39% had an informal arrangement to take work home. Nearly two-thirds (66%) worked from home only 1–2 days a month, but about 20% worked from home for more than half of the time.

ACAS teleworkers get a PC and ISDN line, a small laser printer and a fax/phone costing about £3500. ACAS also pays up to £200 for a new desk, or alternatively homeworkers get one from the office. ACAS insists on a proper office chair, and the homeworker can also be supplied with a two-drawer filing cabinet. The cost of any extra electrical sockets is covered by ACAS but must be installed by a qualified electrician. The cost of adding a few shelves for storage is also covered. The average cost of the non-IT elements of homeworker setup was £500.

The main problem found in the pilot project was IT maintenance and support. The procedure for getting technical support was cumbersome, and the need to make trips to individual homeworker premises was extremely time-consuming. There were also technical teething problems with the network and with homeworkers' connections to the network. Despite feedback from office-based staff suggesting that the impact had been negative due to problems persuading homeworkers to cover office duties, analysis of work diaries found no difference between the time spent by office-based conciliators and their homeworking pairs on non-conciliation work.

Just over one-third of the homeworkers reported experiencing social isolation 'occasionally', while 13% 'often' felt isolated, and 3% were 'very often' isolated. There was some evidence that managers found teleworkers harder to manage, but that this was a training issue since only 22% agreed that homeworkers themselves put greater demands on management time. Managers were also generally fairly neutral about whether homeworkers were more productive than office workers.

A case study based on the IES work has been published which emphasises telebuddies as one of the most successful features of the ACAS scheme. Everyone is paired with a buddy who is kept in touch with current work. Because they are fully briefed on each others' caseload, buddies can stand in for each other in case of sickness or if their buddy is on holiday or overbooked. The buddy is also first port of call if someone needs information or advice, or just wants to talk through a difficult problem.
http://www.acas.org.uk

DRAFT TELEWORKING AGREEMENT

While a company telework policy will answer most issues which could arise between a teleworker and the company, a specific agreement signed by the teleworker is also advisable. This can refer to the company policy in places, or specify exactly the arrangements for that teleworker. It will usually be drafted as a variation to the employee's existing contract of employment. The draft given below can be varied to take account of individual circumstances, and likely topics for inclusion are italicised. We have not included realistic spaces for answers due to space restrictions.

Name --

Address(es) at which the telework/distance work will be performed --------------------

Telephone number --

Mobile telephone number ---

Details of position/nature of work --

Hours of work *(office-based hours, home-based hours, core hours, flexible hours, recording of working time, overtime, etc.)*

Communications structures *(core contact times, arrangements for meetings, feedback, mentoring, etc.)* ---

Reporting-in procedures ---

Home-office arrangements *(technical requirements, provision of equipment and furniture, maintenance arrangements, prevention of misuse, personal use of equipment, health and safety, insurance)*

Training *(induction training, technology training, self-management skills, etc.)* ------

----

Security and confidentiality arrangements
(any differences from standard company policies)

Terms and conditions *(any differences from standard company arrangements)*

Arrangements for suspension/termination of teleworking

Monitoring and review process

• I have read and understood the company policy on teleworking and agree to a teleworking arrangement as set out above.

• I have agreed that a health-and-safety risk assessment will be required on the proposed workplace for teleworking.

• I will operate in accordance with the company safety statement.

• I have informed my mortgage/insurance company that I intend to use my home for business purposes.

• I understand that teleworking is not a substitute for childcare.

• I understand that the teleworking arrangement does not affect my status as an employee.

• I understand the arrangement for termination of the teleworking agreement by myself or by the company.

Signed (employee) --

Signed (company) --

Date --

TRADE UNIONS AND CONSULTATION

For a teleworking agreement to be successful, it must be widely supported and agreed by both management and workers. This is likely to depend on three factors:

■ Consultation – often happens through a trade union.
■ Voluntary nature of the agreement – anyone who becomes dissatisfied with the arrangement should have available to them a clear route back to the main office (unless they were recruited into a position which specified teleworking).
■ Timescale – all involved will need time to consider the issues and for discussion before any decisions are made or agreements signed.

The agreed position between European employers and unions is set out in the 2002 European Framework Agreement on teleworking (*see* p. 65). It is likely that in the UK there will be an agreed Code of Practice setting out how employers and unions can best implement the framework agreement.

Unions with considerable experience in teleworking issues and negotiating teleworking agreements include Amicus-MSF, Unison, BIFU, the NUJ and the CWU.

IT REQUIREMENTS AND SUPPORT

Planning

Early involvement of the company's IT department in the teleworking pilot is vital, and an IT staff member should be included in the steering group. IT staff are likely to be involved in specifying home-office equipment, enabling remote access to company networks, installing and checking equipment at the home office, providing training in use of remote dial-up connections, and providing continued technical support. The website **http://www.cio.com** contains a wide range of articles about remote access issues which are written with IT staff in mind.

Equipment specification

It is helpful both in costing and in providing telephone support if the IT department creates a standard specification for teleworking equipment, and keeps a duplicate set-up including communications equipment onsite for testing and diagnosis of problems. However, this should not mean that one size fits all teleworkers. First of all, users have different requirements in terms of performance and software. Secondly, there are different forms of teleworking (home-based, remote, occasional) which may require different solutions (budget desktop, laptop with docking station or port replicator, etc.) Most large companies end up with two or three standard telework equipment specifications to meet different user needs – and with the advent of smartphones and PDAs, the list is getting longer.

To keep costs down, some employers with large-scale schemes have guidelines in place on what equipment is to be used in the home office. Durham County Council specifies that wherever possible an existing office PC is taken home.[53]

Telecommunication access charges can easily get out of hand if users are not educated appropriately: they may stay online for hours carrying out tasks which could just as easily be done offline with a downloaded file, because they perceive the access to be 'free' – at least to them. The advent of always-on connections where the fee charged does not depend on the amount of time used may help to provide predictability on communications charges. If a high proportion of remote users are outside the local call-charge area of the main office, it is worth looking into outsourcing remote-access facilities. However, direct dial-up is likely to be cheaper than outsourcing where most users are within the local call-charge area.

Remote technical support

Most IT staff already provide some support via a telephone helpdesk, but they may not be used to some of the problems that arise when you can't just nip up the stairs and directly check out the offending screen. Therefore clear guidance on provision of support to the teleworkers, and conditions under which a home visit might be appropriate, or where the teleworker may have to return their equipment for repair or upgrade, need to be set out. The IT department staff may themselves require further training in telephone helpdesk operation. Extra budget may be required where home visits are needed.

Security

Telework programmes sometimes require existing company information to be revised. Issues such as security policies, and procedures for data backups, encryption of files, keyboard locking and passwords for home-based PCs may also need checking.

The IT department will need to work out a policy on data backup for information held on remote machines such as PCs in the home office. This may involve backing up to another medium, such as a Zip drive, tape drive or CD, at the trial stage. Companies with a large number of teleworkers must think in detail about issues of data backup and synchronisation. Some use software which compresses any changed files and then uploads the compressed files to an online data repository. Software tools for backing up laptops using compressed data are also available from Veritas and Computer Associates.

Users must be trained to understand the increased data-security risks posed by remote working, so that they understand how the security systems work and why it is important to accept any minor frustrations which they may cause (mainly relating to connection speed or logon procedures).

There is a trade-off between usability and protecting data which will differ between companies. For example, one industry commentator believes you would need to be dealing in 'nuclear secrets' before it is worth installing file encryption. At the other end of the scale, most companies accept that there are considerable security risks attached to laptop use. 3Com group reported that laptop theft had become its largest category of property theft worldwide – and airports are a common location for theft to occur, particularly around security-check conveyor belts.

There are some measures which can be taken in relation to laptop theft, such as provision of cable locks to mobile staff so that they can lock laptops to furniture in hotel rooms, or installation of hidden transmitters or of tracking software (e.g. Absolute Software's CompuTrace, which automatically reports the location of the laptop any time it is connected to the Internet). British Gas even marks its PDAs with 'smart water' – a liquid which, when dabbed onto equipment, leaves an individual, invisible marking which can be used to identify stolen property at a later date. *See* Chapter 9, *Technology and techniques*, for more on data security.

Outsourcing

It is worth looking at outsourcing remote-access telecommunications where there are many mobile users operating outside the local call-charge area, or if VPN solutions are in use, or where online usage is high, since many outsourced packages are charged on a flat-rate basis. Outsourcing can prevent considerable IT staff resources being spent on 'modem management' and basic user training, which are not considered particularly creative or career-enhancing by many IT professionals.

To make a decision on outsourcing, IT staff need to know:

- Size of user population.
- Percentage of users dialling in more than once per month.
- Who accesses the system remotely most often.
- Whether the calls are local or long distance.

The IT staff will also need to agree a clear service-level agreement with any outsourcing company, covering issues such as back-end network availability, dial availability and latency. These figures must be related to the user population figures outlined above, not to the outsourcer's general population of users.

There should also be guaranteed response times and procedures for reporting and resolving different types of problems (e.g. those which affect only a small group of users, or more serious setbacks that could knock out all the remote users). Reporting arrangements will also be needed to document user activity, problems and failed connections, broken down by division or business unit.

Outsourcing hardware supply and support is also a tactic considered by many large organisations who have remote workers. Laptops are generally considered more difficult to configure, support and maintain than desktops. Sun Microsystems, which has over 7000 laptop users, has had to consider how to offer support on a global basis. The company first saw an explosion in laptop users in the mid-1990s. Then the IT department used to send people around the country fixing laptops – until the costs of the system were examined in detail.

Now Sun has what it describes as a 'filling station model', outsourcing the hardware problems to Vanstar Corporation. If a hardware problem needs fixing or a software upgrade has to be carried out, the laptop is shipped to Vanstar. This has allowed Sun to reallocate a team of 10–15 IT staffers who previously looked after the teleworkers. However, the company still operates a 24 x 7 telephone helpdesk. In addition, Sun has standardised on three configurations of laptop, all supplied by Toshiba.

Monitoring software

Software that monitors employee activity is sometimes requested in relation to the introduction of teleworking. Generally this is not necessary as teleworkers

THE MOVE FROM HOMEWORKING TO TOUCHDOWN SPACE

Abbey National launched home-based teleworking in 1998, with 20 volunteers from the e-commerce department. Wiith the help of their outsourced equipment and consultancy partners BT, that initial group of 20 was up and running within four months. The bank increased the number to 70 teleworkers by autumn 2000, and reported that 90% found that the teleworking project had had a positive impact on their lives. Recently, members of the bank's executive committee have been provided with dial-in access from home.

ISDN lines were used to link staff into the corporate intranet, and to provide 'follow me' portable numbers. Staff were issued with a laptop, a desk phone and a mobile phone. Technical support was provided by a helpdesk which assesses the problem and refers it either internally or to BT, which maintains the hardware, software and communications specific to teleworking.

Laptops can be fixed or replaced by BT within four hours where necessary. The teleworking agreement specifies that all equipment provided by the company may be serviced only by approved engineers. Abbey National made a conscious decision not to provide printers for teleworkers at home, encouraging as much material as possible to be scanned and reducing the amount of paper in use. Post is distributed from central facilities in returnable pouches.

Two touchdown areas have been established at the company's offices in London and Milton Keynes, providing power cables, LAN connectivity and phone lines. Desks at the touchdown centre can be booked using Microsoft Schedule. In the Milton Keynes office, the touchdown centre has freed up space which is now occupied by another department of 19 people.

Workshops were laid on for the teleworkers and their managers to deal with communications issues and social contact. Health and safety guidelines were also supplied to each triallist, and managers were required to confirm that the home workplace conformed to the required standard. Online forms were used to get teleworkers to comment weekly and provide monitoring data. Over three-quarters (77%) agreed that the equipment supplied was appropriate while 79% reported adequate support from their manager.

Productivity increases were measured at an average reported rise of 21%. Some 85% of respondents felt that their productivity had improved, and this was backed up by their line managers. An even higher 87% reported that home-based working was a factor that would influence any decision to change jobs.

tend to be monitored through their output (results) and not by the hours they spend at their keyboards. Peter Skyte, former national secretary of the IT Professional Association, part of the Amicus-MSF union, comments: 'Old-fashioned employers still adopt command and control policies treating employees as the greatest threat, rather than, as their rhetoric would suggest, the greatest asset.'

If such software is found to be necessary, Iontas have a product called PC Focus which monitors activity without recording the content of documents or of emails. The company points out that if staff spend half an hour on personal use of their PCs, this amounts to 2.5 hours a week and can turn out to be a significant drain on company resources (*see* **http://www.iontas.com**). Scalable Software have a product called Time Manager which can be used to show teleworker activity on the company network (logged-in time, idle time, active time, applications used, etc.) and can compare this with in-office workers (*see* **http://www.scalablesoftware.com**)

Companies should be aware that the Human Rights Act 1998 Article 8 states: 'Everyone has the right to respect for their private and family life, their home and their correspondence.' The Institute of Management (IM) guidelines on the Human Rights Act warns that unauthorised monitoring of an employee's telephone calls and emails on company premises could be in contravention of Article 8, even when the employer suspects that a member of staff is using its resources in a personal capacity. The IM says that interception could probably be considered reasonable if the employee had been told that such behaviour was a disciplinary offence and that checks would be made where appropriate to detect breaches of company regulations.

In some situations, monitoring software can be extremely useful to help plan and record activities for companies with large mobile workforces. Teleware, a software supplier specialising in remote work applications, provides systems which can monitor the whereabouts of an employee to assist in forwarding calls. Teleware's systems can also be used to log activity.

For example, a service engineer can be allocated jobs with information being sent to a PDA. The engineer can respond with a status such as 'job accepted', or 'on route' with an estimated time of arrival. The job status is updated on arrival, and again on job completion. The software can include options to indicate parts used either by the use of dropdown menus, or an attached barcode reader. The PDA can also be used to allow the customer to sign for completion. All this information can be processed both to provide invoicing information, and for employee time records relating to payroll – and Teleware even have an application which checks staff records for compliance with the European Working Time Directive, producing an automatic report of problems for HR staff.

Another example where Teleware have a practical scheme in operation involves local-authority home carers. When the carer arrives at a client's home, they use a toll-free number to let the central system know where they are. This can be particularly important where a time-critical duty is involved such as administration of insulin injections. *See* **http://www.teleware.co.uk**

From the horse's mouth

Two IT managers in large organisations, one in the private sector and one in the public sector, give their advice on supporting teleworkers.

Equipment
'Historically, our home-office machines were end-of-life desktop machines but we've now decided to give new homeworkers the same spec as office machines. The specs for mobile workers are lower, but only because laptops tend to be slower.' 'Most of our teleworkers have more or less the same PC as they would have in the office. The mobile workers have a standard laptop.' Both reported that they don't encourage employee-owned equipment, but realise sometimes this causes space problems so sharing peripherals is allowed. One commented, 'VPN and thin client solves this too....'

Support
'Telephone support is the first line – hours have been extended to cover evenings because of homeworking. Support is generally on a return-to-base arrangement but onsite service is being considered.' 'We do it through telephone support. If that doesn't solve the problem, mobile workers have to bring the kit in. For the homeworkers, there are a number of companies that can supply a home-visit service.' Both said that although they log support calls, they haven't yet analysed whether any special problems are arising for the teleworkers, and reported that the main problems seem to be performance and speed of online connections.

Upgrades
'We build and ship to provide the teleworkers with a fixed PC. We do have some update software but it's often quicker to get them to bring the PC in.' 'It's mostly return-to-base, but CD-ROM upgrades are being introduced for software. Anti-virus updates are online and regular!'

Security
One reported that they were looking at the use of Citrix to access corporate solutions, rather than loading sensitive material onto the teleworker's PC. Both said that their procedures were stringent and that they considered teleworkers' machines to be more vulnerable than those on the internal network. One is looking at using smaller laptops which can fit in a standard briefcase rather than in a special computer bag to avoid attracting the attention of thieves or muggers.

Connections
One reported that connections were mostly standard dial-up, with some ISDN and awaiting broadband. The other reported that most teleworkers now have

ADSL and, where this is not available, ISDN. On telecoms costs, one reported that costs were still high but coming down and that they had estimated the costs in advance. The other reported that most work is done offline with occasional sessions for email exchange. Diverting costs from the office to a mobile was seen as a significant cost burden and as justification for installing a landline for working from home.

Budget

One reported that occasional homeworking comes from a central budget, with a business case based around desksharing. The other reported that costs were shared between departments and IT, but that no budget had been provided for the extra support costs of teleworking.

Training

One reported that the needs were largely having the right mindset to work remotely, and that taking prospective teleworkers through Microsoft Office in some detail paid dividends in improved confidence and the ability to try 'workarounds' rather than calling support. Both reported providing technical training on remote access. One reported that they initially missed the advantage of learning from their sales staff, who have always worked remotely and had developed a lot of good techniques. They now have a remote office room in-house where people can 'try out' teleworking.

ROLLOUT ISSUES

Equal access to a fair process

Lloyds TSB bank offers flexible working options including teleworking to its 71,000 staff. Joanna Slevin of Lloyds TSB drafted this policy of access to the new work options, published in the company's Work Options pack.

- Meeting business goals will remain our priority. Requests will be evaluated on their impact for the business, and the needs of customers and colleagues will be considered first. The impact of the scheme will be expected to have a neutral or positive effect on the business.
- Flexibility is a different way of working which is not an entitlement or a way of conferring preferential treatment. Managers will approve requests that are consistent with business needs. If the arrangement does not work for the business, it will not be approved.
- Equity means equal access to a fair process. There are standard request forms to help you think through the proposed arrangements and how they will affect you, our customers and your colleagues. Your manager has to make a sound business decision and the aim of the policy is to ensure that this is done fairly. The same process is available to everyone but it does not promise the same outcome for all.

- Working in partnership: you and your manager should work together to get the best from any proposed work option. You should understand how well it will affect the business. The process will be monitored centrally to ensure that it is consistently and fairly applied.
- Job performance is relevant. Managers will consider job performance when evaluating a request. For example, staff who have shown that they are able to work well without supervision are more likely to adjust successfully to working offsite. For those who have weak time-management or communications skills, this option may not be appropriate.

Ford UK is also offering teleworking to all salaried employees. A company spokesperson said: 'It's obviously practically difficult for those in the manufacturing areas. People can apply to telecommute from 1–4 days per week. Everyone is eligible, but it's not an entitlement, it's at management discretion. Information about the scheme is available on the company intranet, but we are limiting the option to 2% of salaried employees to start with.' Ford sees the move as helping to attract and retain staff.

Benchmarking

Because many organisations are still trialling telework, it can be hard to get a handle on standard or best practice for teleworking. However, a survey of 68 organisations (which represented the 32% of respondents who reported home-based teleworking), covering a total of 9500 teleworking employees carried out for IRS in 2001[54] found:

- The main motivations for introducing teleworking were improving work-life balance, saving office space and boosting productivity. However, only 20 out of 64 organisations reported that they had measured productivity.
- Most employers provide PCs and a large majority pay for printers and extra phone lines.
- About half of employers supply a desk and chair.
- Only one-third compensate for other homeworking costs – one in four pay an annual allowance to reflect costs of heating and lighting, cleaning and wear and tear on the home offices. Commonly the figure for this allowance is between £400 and £500.
- The annual savings per teleworker per year were approximately £1000 to £2500 in most cases.
- Two out of three give all teleworkers remote dial-up access to their intranets. Less than one-third provide high-speed ISDN or ADSL connections. About a third will pay for broadband facilities for selected teleworkers deemed to need them.
- Only six out of 68 organisations were using video conferencing.
- Two-thirds ask at least some of their teleworkers to hotdesk when in the office. A quarter have introduced desksharing for teleworkers.

- Two-thirds require at least half the week to be spent in the office.
- On health and safety, three-fifths provide training in safe practices. Half ask employees to carry out a risk assessment of the home office. One-quarter arrange for a home-office inspection by a manager or health and safety specialist. Nine of the 68 did not carry out any risk assessment at all.
- Half of the organisations have altered their employees' contracts of employment to include a change of work location. In general this was for teleworkers who spent the majority of their time at home. One in four of those organisations with union recognition had agreements covering home-based employees.
- Most report modest numbers of teleworkers (35 on average, though this was skewed by two very large employers with over 1000 employees). Five out of six plan to increase teleworker numbers.
- Reservations expressed, due to problems experienced, concerned technology problems (14 employers), teleworkers experiencing isolation (13 employers), maintaining contact with teleworkers (nine employers) and problems in changing management attitudes (13 employers). Other categories such as overwork attracted few reports (three employers).
- Less than a quarter (16%) reported providing management training.
- Five out of six plan to increase the number of employees teleworking, and of those who could estimate the increase, the average increase planned was 50%.

IBM report that 'consumable items can be disproportionately hard to manage, with employees spending far too much time trying to find out how to order a stapler or more paper. An e-procurement system can be an important aid in this context, and some suppliers now specialise in supporting the homeworker's office needs'. BT have gone a step further and put almost all such activities on the company intranet – you can order a company car or a personal franking machine for your home office on the BT intranet, which is said to be the largest and most comprehensive company intranet operating in Europe.

Prudential in the US felt that training was the key and implemented a system where no staff member could be issued with a laptop until they had attended two days of training. This training was partly carried out by existing field agents, who were recruited by the IT department to become part of the training course, giving tips from their practical experience as mobile teleworkers. A new system for rollout of software upgrades was also implemented. These are now sent out to teleworkers on CD-ROM for guided self-installation, but spread out over a five-day period so that the helpdesk is not overwhelmed by simultaneous calls.

Don't forget that teleworkers have training needs other than those directly related to their teleworking. Make explicit the mechanisms for informing teleworkers about training and development opportunities.

Voluntarism

The new European Framework Agreement has enshrined the principle that teleworking should be voluntary, unless it is included in the original job description. This is not only so that employees are not forced into arrangements which don't suit them, radically blurring the distinction between work and home, but also to prevent discrimination against those who may not have suitable physical or family situations that can support teleworking.

Senior human resources staff at IBM point out that: 'IBM's policy is designed to encourage mobile office working where the job permits, but never to force this initiative on employees. Although we are committed to making our real estate leaner and more flexible, [our] policy recognises that some IBM employees find it important to meet colleagues regularly or may not have a suitable working environment – they may lack space or be prone to constant interruptions at home.'[55]

The point about voluntarism depending on the original job description is important, as in some sectors – such as financial services, where branch structures have been largely demolished – many jobs now depend on the ability to telework, and there is no office to return to.

Territorial disputes

In a recent paper based on IBM's corporate experience and aimed at human-resource managers,[56] the authors point out that the introduction of a 'mobile working strategy' may result in some costs rising as well some costs which decrease. While all may agree that the goal is an overall reduction in costs to the company, individual departments may resist investing in technology to enable their employees to work at home if they do not see the resulting reduction in office costs. Therefore it is important that those steering the rollout ensure that clear information is presented to departments which might otherwise resist the change.

Monitoring progress

Although both managers and teleworkers may find the monitoring process a chore, without information to indicate any changes in levels of productivity or job satisfaction, it will be hard to make the case for widespread introduction of teleworking. The level of monitoring will vary according to business needs, but could include:

- Running costs – e.g. stationery, telecommunications.
- Productivity – deadlines and work-targets met and unmet, ability to deal with multiple priorities.
- Effect on colleagues, customers and levels of service – e.g. extended hours of customer service, reduced telephone hold-time for customers.
- Changes in work activity – e.g. a reduction in breadth of tasks due to only a proportion being suitable to teleworking.

- Working hours, sick leave and absence, staff turnover.
- Satisfaction and stress-levels in working life.
- Changes in motivations for teleworking – e.g. childcare, reduced distractions, etc.
- Relationship between teleworker and manager.
- Changes in communication patterns.
- Technical support and IT issues.
- Issues of isolation or demotivation.

In measuring productivity, remember that hours worked may not be an appropriate measure for knowledge workers, since overwork can often lead to reduced productivity – people are not machines. Measuring the costs is usually much easier than assessing the benefits.

Another area that needs checking is staff-management ratios. Existing evidence on whether teleworking leads to changes in staff-management ratios is contradictory, according to a review of teleworking carried out by Ursula Huws for the Local Government Management Board in Britain. She notes that the FI group, a software company using home-based workers, employed one manager for every five programmers, one for every eight systems designers and one for every ten systems analysts, which was more than twice the industry standard at the time.

Providing continuing support

In the initial stages of a teleworking programme it can be helpful to arrange meetings so that teleworkers can swap experiences and give feedback. Meetings held once a quarter, or once every six months, are usually sufficient.

Those who have been teleworking for some years report that a lack of positive feedback becomes an increasing problem. Often, teleworkers only receive feedback when there is a problem to be solved or a deadline to be met – they can get left out of team back-slapping when a contract is won, or a customer's letter of satisfaction is posted on the office noticeboard. Rank Xerox, veteran of long-term widescale use of teleworkers, ensured that teleworkers were kept on circulation lists, listed in the company directory, and invited to departmental meetings and to social functions.

The teleworking organisation can lack much of the informal communication that comes from people working in close proximity, and needs to find a way of replacing the useful parts of this. In addition, the introduction of teleworking for part of a department can lead to a 'them and us' situation. Management may need to think of measures to discourage this split (one employer encouraged a lottery syndicate to encompass all team-members rather than just those 'in the office'). Typical strategies include trying to ensure that teleworkers attend the office for regular meetings and training, and allowing extra time for informal social contact with colleagues during these sessions.

Companies which have moved a long way down the route towards becoming 'virtual', with a high proportion of staff working at different locations, report that they need to instigate new team-building measures – such as internal HR staff known as 'talent managers' who meet with staff individually to discuss and respond to training and technology needs, and to ensure they understand company policies, as well as to pick up any feedback or suggestions for improvement. A system where senior managers meet informally but regularly with different staff members has also been reported to be extremely useful in maintaining corporate culture in distributed organisations.

Senior HR staff at IBM report that: 'A weekly conference call or e-meeting may take the place of a face-to-face meeting. Chairing these requires different skills from conducting face-to-face meetings – managers need to take the time to learn these skills and to practise them well. It is also very tempting for busy employees to opt out of a remote meeting that they would attend were they in the office. Managers may need to make it clear that remote meetings are important, and follow up on absentees. Many managers will require regular face-to-face meetings with remote workers coming into the office once a fortnight or once a month. Without this it is hard to prevent office and remote workers from feeling they have a different status within the company.'[57]

Experienced telework managers have also reported the need to develop a 'sixth sense' about detecting during telephone conversations when teleworkers have a personal problem. Don't forget that teleworking does not necessarily mean working at home in isolation full-time. A sensible teleworking programme should include regular face-to-face management meetings as well as opportunities for colleagues to mix at the office.

The telework project team should create a support function to deal with any technical and managerial issues arising from the project in the future. The team should specify the arrangements both for monitoring of telework arrangements, and for review of the telework policy itself.

THE PUBLIC SECTOR

Employer and supplier

A report by teleworking expert Ursula Huws for the Local Government Management Board[58] sums up the pros and cons of teleworking for public-sector organisations:

- Savings and costs on office space could be up to 50% but there may be hidden costs of refurbishment, infrastructure and staff retraining.
- Initial setup costs will probably be around £1500 per worker but will vary depending on telecommunications in place and the availability of competing providers.
- Continuing costs will include telecoms, maintenance and technical support, insurance and health and safety checks.

BBC TRIAL MAKES MONITORING SENSE

The BBC completed a six-month trial of teleworking for 17 staff in 1999. Project manager Geoff Adams-Spink set clear objectives:

- *To establish the potential for savings in accommodation and other costs.*

- *To determine which areas of the production process would lend themselves to teleworking.*

- *To establish whether there are 'soft' benefits, such as improving sickness rates and staff retention.*

- *To test the effect on the creative process of some staff working remotely.*

Monitoring took place through a combination of surveys and interviews: the teleworkers returned a weekly survey to the project. Both teleworkers and their line managers completed surveys half-way through, and at the end of the pilot.

Benefits included improved morale and staff retention. The vast majority (82%) said that they would be attracted to a post or would consider staying in a post if teleworking were part of the package. Staff were also more willing to work antisocial hours such as early mornings or Christmas Day because it didn't involve a long commute to the office.

Downsides included technical support, with only 54% of teleworkers saying that the IT support they received at home was as good or better than the service in the office. One teleworker said that they felt invisible while working from home, but others overcame problems by regular visits to the office. The teleworkers involved in daily radio programmes were least successful. Geoff comments that for teleworking to succeed in the daily radio sector will require substantial re-education for peers and managers.

Of the original 17, 14 continued teleworking. Geoff believes the issue of accommodation and cost-saving is open to question. 'In order to release space, most departments would need to offer the teleworking option to a substantial number of staff, and very careful planning would be necessary to avoid undue congestion in the office when staff are required back at base.' On the soft issues, he's quite convinced: teleworking delivers improved morale, enhanced productivity, reduced sickness rates, greater loyalty and better retention.

- Management and training costs will be incurred, but are an investment in staff development which should lead to productivity increases.
- The impact of teleworking on productivity varies considerably and is likely to be between 10% and 30% for local-authority workers.
- Work-life balance for employees – often a major motivator – will be improved.

■ Staff retention may improve – teleworking increases staff commitment, important when public administration is competing against higher private-sector wages.

Huws concludes that local authorities need to recognise the diversity of teleworking forms and use them appropriately; and that they must take a cross-departmental strategic overview approach. The main difference between public-sector bodies and private companies (other than limited resources and issues of staff retention) is usually that public-sector bodies have multiple roles – both as suppliers and providers – which they need to consider in relation to their teleworking strategy. Local authorities may wish to ensure consistency between their own teleworking policies, and other council policies relating to transport, environment and planning. Despite these drivers towards teleworking, it is much less prevalent in the public sector. Analysis of the 1998 US Current Population Survey figures[59] indicates that less than 10% of teleworkers are to be found in the public sector.

Teleworking can attract more applicants to job adverts in a time of skills shortages (London Borough of Enfield got over 1000 replies the first time they advertised posts with a teleworking option) and can bring about reductions in traffic congestion (Cambridgeshire County Council estimated a 4–8% reduction in time and distances travelled if teleworking were available to all managers and administrative staff). There may also be economic development benefits in using teleworkers located within the council's area where tasks need to be outsourced or 'e-lanced'. Grampian Regional Council set up a telework centre in a remote area of its region to carry out administrative tasks. In addition to servicing Grampian, the Forres centre also carried out work for other councils based in south-east England, and created extra jobs in an area of high unemployment.

The EU Target project carried out pilots at several public bodies in the Yorkshire and Humber region, funded through the Interreg. IIc North Sea Region programme (*see* p. 204). From their experiences, an excellent set of guidelines for public-sector organisations has been produced, available by email from alison.pilling@wypte.gov.uk. Part of the guide, giving a step-by-step procedure for telework implementation, is reproduced here.

20 steps to teleworking success for public-sector organisations

Set out below are the 20 steps you will need to take in order to develop a pilot scheme to introduce teleworking at home into an organisation, based on our experience of delivering the pilot.

Step 1 Identify the priorities for teleworking for your authority – e.g. financial, environmental, employee welfare.

Step 2 Form an informal working group of interested key players – to raise awareness and work up a proposal. The working group could include:
- politicians if appropriate;
- senior management;
- corporate accommodation staff;
- trade union representatives;
- human resources/personnel representatives;
- ICT support services.

Step 3 Identify a pilot project and develop a business case (identify costs/benefits).

Step 4 Discuss the proposals/concepts with trade unions and management.
Trade unions: It is very important to have an open dialogue with the trade unions, as there will be concerns about extending working days and detrimental impacts on conditions of service. You will need to negotiate any changes (temporary or permanent) to contracts and working conditions.
Management: Traditional management styles are declining, with more managers accepting that staff will no longer need to be 'in view' at all times. Modern management techniques are focusing on better communications and team development, irrespective of location. Managers will need to be supported in developing this new approach to people management. There will need to be a greater focus on ensuring that staff attend workplace meetings to engender team spirit and reduce organisational isolation.

Step 5   Present the proposal to senior officers/cabinet/council.

Step 6   Identify a budget and a minimalist administration process to support activities.

Step 7   Hold awareness-raising seminars to inform all staff in the pilot area of the proposal, including purpose/pilot duration/training/monitoring. Keep the message simple – the focus is on people and their jobs, not the technology. Circulate simple information to all staff and hold short presentations (15 min).

Step 8   Invite volunteers.

Step 9   Assess volunteers, e.g. job suitability, adequate space at home, management agreement – ensure representational cross-section. It is critical to the pilot that the volunteers chosen/selected should be a representative sample of all workers and should not be drawn solely from management.

Step 10   Verify volunteers' eligibility for pilot and ascertain ICT needs (not wants).

Step 11   Draft and agree with trade unions a 'temporary variation to contract' document – binding for the duration of the pilot. Ensure that volunteers sign and comply. Volunteers must sign a legal document which varies their existing contract. This provides clarity for all parties.

Step 12   Produce a volunteer guidance pack for claims, tax, insurance, health and safety, etc. (*see* full guidelines for suggestions and examples of what to include). Managers of home-based teleworkers should familiarise themselves with the contents of the pack.

Step 13   Hold volunteer and manager 'induction days' (separately). Issue volunteers with the guidance pack and deal with perceived expectations/problems.

Step 14   Procure ICT and other equipment, install and check onsite. Don't underestimate time and resources required for the setup stages:

• Confirm with volunteers a suitable date, time and location for installation.
• Agree any minor works (e.g. phone cable extensions) that are required to be installed. Programme the installation after the new telephone lines are installed and operational.
• Ensure compatibility of software between home and office
• Produce an inventory of all equipment and supplies required, including printer paper.
• Arrange vehicle and staff to transport and install equipment. There are private companies who will carry out this work, but at a premium rate.
• Test that ICT systems are fully functioning at the point of installation.
• Allow the volunteers to test the system before departing.
• You can expect a small amount of minor IT 'snagging' work.
• If possible, teleworkers at home should be given access to the organisation's network, as any other arrangement can severely limit the potential for independent working. Security issues were successfully overcome by some of the partners in the Target project.

ICT communications are vital for the exchange both of data and of verbal interaction between work colleagues. It is important to identify the type of work to be undertaken and the ICT required. This will vary considerably, according to the organisation's ICT commitment, available telecoms arrangements, the amount of data involved in work-activities and whether it is time-critical (requires real-time updating).

Ensure that the IT and communications networks can carry the data (e.g. not all BT exchanges have been upgraded for ISDN, etc.). Office furniture may be required and must comply with the current EU/UK workstation health and safety guidelines. A good-quality chair is essential.

The use of laptop computers for regular work should be discouraged as the machines are not ergonomically designed for daily long-term use, whereas tablet PCs and Palmtops are more portable. You should seek advice on the options available to you from your in-house IT specialists with reference to your health and safety advisers.

Step 15   Health and safety inspection in volunteers' homes: once the workstations have been fully installed, arrange health and safety inspections of all homework stations by a qualified/competent person. It is suggested that this should not be a self-assessment. Guidance about workstations should be issued to all volunteers (*see* full guidelines). The layout of the home workstations should be inspected and records kept, and volunteers advised that they should not alter the workstation.

Step 16   Commence trial and contact volunteers with offer of support.

Step 17   Check quarterly with volunteers – keep in contact. Monitor costs, progress and impact of teleworking on volunteers. Identify what you intend to monitor, and ensure that the data is collected regularly – preferably on a monthly basis from volunteers. Explain that it is conditional for their continuation in the project (*see* full guidelines for monitoring proforma). After a reasonable 'settling period', it is suggested that an informal short feedback session is held with an offer of limited ICT training/exchange of tips, etc. Offer further support and encourage confidential honesty (especially for fault-reporting, bad experiences, isolation, etc.).

Step 18   Provide an annual update to management on initial findings.

Step 19   Produce a final report. Verify the business case – e.g. reduced accommodation/travel costs. Report your findings, including problems encountered, to all stakeholders and especially to senior management and the trade unions. It is as important to highlight negative as well as positive issues. Disseminate your findings to all appropriate levels within your organisation, especially the corporate working group. Encourage discussion and support for the concept in your organisation.

Step 20   Initiate discussions between trade unions and human resources to mainstream teleworking.

The dissemination of your project should provide the platform to propose a rolling-out/mainstreaming across the organisation. It should certainly raise interest and create a debate in the organisation. The working group should provide effective support to ensure the successful adoption of this new way of working. Ensure that robust procedures and documentation are in place and are agreed by trade unions to support the rolling-out programme. Business cases should be provided, either at a corporate or a departmental level, to ensure that the proposed benefits (including non-financial) are identified.

Case studies

County Council telecentre leads to major Workstyles change
Surrey County Council opened its Epsom neighbourhood telecentre in September 1997 as the first step in its Workstyles programme. By 1998, the telecentre had proved so successful that a major programme to reduce property costs but maintain service-levels was launched. Since then, 90 buildings amounting to 627,000 sq ft have been reduced to 21 buildings with 400,000 sq ft of space, saving £11m capital costs plus £0.5m annually.

The council's 3750 office-based staff have also been helped to take charge of when, where and how they work. About 700 staff have dial-in access and council-provided IT equipment, but only about 50–100 spend most of their time at home, including the educational personnel consultants and the secretaries to the child-protection panels. A further 700 work flexibly, taking work home to do on their home PCs – about 50 of these have secure webmail access. There are also 96 bookable hotdesks at five locations around the county. The hotdesks are often used by people who want to reduce their travel by working closer to home, or by people looking for a quiet, distraction-free space away from the hustle and bustle of team areas.

Caroline Cheales explains: 'We don't have the resources to set up everyone who would like to work from home with the right equipment and connections. Recognising this, we allow the use of home PCs, provided that our security and data-protection procedures are followed. We also provide limited webmail access to the council network. We have a very flexible attitude to homeworking, and try to think in terms of tasks rather than jobs which are suitable, though we do provide equipment for heavy-duty homeworking. In our experience there is a surge of interest every Christmas as people get new or upgraded PCs – we're expecting a similar surge this year as people get broadband connections. We do refund call costs and provide charge cards for this purpose.

'The Workstyles programme has helped us considerably with retention – you actually hear people referring to better working conditions. The unions have been generally in favour, but weren't happy with the reduction in parking places which took place for planning reasons. In fact, I would advise other authorities to extend the benefits of flexible working schemes to the union offices early on – we set up roaming profiles with follow-me phones for officials

One of Moto's motorway touchdown centres

to allow them to dip in to the new work practices. They become unexpected champions, wanting to know why people are being left out of the scheme, and feeding back informal niggles we would otherwise have missed. We should have done it earlier.

'Not all requests for homeworking are supported, perhaps because the team isn't ready, or we feel it's being proposed as a childcare alternative, but the "no" is never final – we look for ways to work towards it being possible. We have a one-stop-shop guide on becoming a homeworker, and managing homeworkers, and there is a formal HR policy guide as well.'

See **http://www.surreycc.gov.uk**

Cambridgeshire County Council

In 2001 Cambridgeshire approved the development of a series of touchdown centres for staff use. Caroline Stanger, head of modernisation for the council explains: 'The idea is that we prevent people from sitting in queues on the roads if they have a meeting in the south and they're in the north of the county.' The centres are also intended to rationalise property use, and to help with rural development. 'We are very split – the south is booming and the north is very different (rural and in some decline), so another aim is to get employment out into the county,' says Caroline.

The centres form part of the council's overall strategy to provide public access to all council services by Internet or phone by 2005, through a network of one-stop shops and broadband access points. Cambridgeshire also has a homeworking scheme for staff and the touchdown centres are intended to assist homeworkers too: 'Staff will have access to all the information and systems they need wherever they are – whether working at home, in their main office, or at one of the touchdown centres,' reports Caroline.

Commuting savings

In 1999 a European-funded project allowed four local authorities in the Yorkshire & Humber region to experiment with teleworking. The Target project was aimed at travel-awareness issues, and had participation from European partners in Bremen, Germany and Göteborg, Sweden as well as from City of Wakefield, Kirklees, South Yorkshire Passenger Transport Executive and West Yorkshire Passenger Transport Executive.

The pilot involved 23 employees in the UK and each volunteer worked at home for one day a week. It proved successful for all except one, who suffered difficulties due to overwork. Now three of the councils are working to make teleworking part of their corporate policy, and a best practice guide has been produced (*see* p. 199).

James Stephenson of Wakefield Council led the pilot scheme, and explains: 'In practical terms this project will translate into deskshare arrangements (2.5 days a week) so that people retain a workplace presence but the organisation benefits from a reduction in accommodation. The way to develop teleworking in all large organisations is incrementally, to move from one day per week into a desksharing arrangement.'

The 23 volunteers saved travel distances estimated at 50,195 kilometres a year. Reactions to the project in the different organisations ranged from full management support to negative, reluctant acceptance. Stephenson believes that substantial work needs to be undertaken to convince management and unions of the benefits of allowing workers more flexibility. A key, unresolved issue is whether the 'champion' of the project should be an HR or an IT professional.

The pilot was relatively small-scale and as such, financial benefits could not be extrapolated. As a result of the pilot, the passenger transport executives are looking at the possiblity of their helpline service agents working from home. Wakefield and Kirklees councils are planning a formal implementation of teleworking. *See* **http://www.target.net**

The key findings of the project were:

- ■ Volunteers enjoyed the flexibility of mixing their working hours with other commitments.
- ■ Productivity was reported to have increased, primarily due to fewer interruptions than in an office.
- ■ Management became more accepting as the pilot progressed.
- ■ Insufficient work-breaks were taken by the teleworkers.
- ■ Volunteers reported a reduction in stress-levels, particularly in relation to journey-to-work time.

■ As expected, the reduction in car travel as a result of the pilot realised savings in carbon dioxide emissions.

Recruitment and retention

The East Riding of Yorkshire Council has been using teleworking to improve its staff retention figures. The project began in November 2000 with a pilot of 12 teleworkers in the Revenue Services Division. Bernice Lade, Service Development Manager for the council, explains that it had become very demoralising to train a housing benefits officer for six months only to see them leave almost as soon as their training was complete.

Now, every piece of paper used by the department is scanned-in and available to teleworkers online, and the teleworkers can input their information directly to the central processing system.

The telework initiative reduced staff turnover from 30% to 8% in 12 months and improved productivity by 20–30%. The time taken to process a new claim has been reduced from 103 days to 26 days. Sickness levels were 50% lower, and these figures were sustained over the 12-month pilot period.

'It has been an incredible success. We have trouble getting them into the office now. Initially they were coming in once a fortnight but now it's once a month. They are in regular contact with managers and colleagues via email and each has a mobile phone. All the feedback has been positive. We have had no reports of people feeling isolated.'

Staff get a fully equipped home office, in most cases including an ISDN connection to the council network. They have access to the same software as their in-office colleagues and carry out the same duties. The average setup cost is £2770, and the council estimates that having 45 staff working from home will provide a net saving of £42,987 a year.

The council estimates that there is also potential for 150 teleworkers in the Social Services, Public Protection and Housing section, plus a further 140 in the Finance and IT section. Ray Ward, the head of the Revenue Services section comments: 'One other thing that has helped us to succeed is that we don't force anyone to telework. Interestingly, some staff who were subsequently interested did not express that interest at the start, as they were concerned about what their managers would think.' Ray has found that monthly team briefings work best: 'If you try to get them in more regularly, it doesn't add benefit for them or us and it won't be popular.'

Avoiding long hours at Sefton

Sefton Metropolitan Borough Council won a BT eWell-being award for its teleworking scheme in 2002. The European-funded scheme was a trial for 19 of the council's 3000 office-based employees, allowing them to work at home. Volunteers came from a number of departments including housing, social services, education, personnel, technical services and finance. All got training in time management, planning and priority-setting, as well as workflow management and health and safety.

Project manager Sue Philpott emphasises the importance of the induction process for managers and colleagues as well as teleworkers: 'Everyone has to fully understand the operational arrangements and likely impact,' she says.

Unison branch secretary Nigel Flanagan, who was also involved in the Sefton project, points up the danger of teleworking being seen as a perk: 'We believe that teleworking would suit a lot of our members, providing certain safeguards are in place. But it only suits certain types of occupation, so it can be seen by blue-collar workers as a white-collar perk.' Nigel is concerned that once it becomes possible for call-centre jobs to be carried out from home, this could cause problems of intrusion if out-of-hours work is also involved. 'Unions have to be vigilant about taking work home becoming part of the culture. It's not easy to see that people are being overworked if the extra, uncontracted work is done at home.'

At the end of the trial, ten of the group continued to telework. Twelve felt that the experience had been positive, but six said it would be difficult for them to continue because of work demands back at the office. The council acknowledged that it had taken a year to provide suitable IT access to all those who needed it – exactly the kind of problem pilots are intended to iron out.

7

Self-employment and startups

This chapter is aimed at teleworkers who are, or wish to be, self-employed or run a small business. It is not relevant to companies implementing telework for employees (see *Chapter 6,* Implementation in organisations). *If you are already employed and wish to remain in your job but begin teleworking, you need to read Chapters 4 and 5, and then draft a cost/benefit case for teleworking to put to your employer.*

GETTING WORK AS A TELEWORKER

Where are you now?

At the moment you probably fall into one of four categories:

- You know what you want to do and probably already have a specialist skill and experience, but want help with the details of setting up a business. We suggest that you read all of this chapter.
- You don't know what you want to do, you just know you'd rather be independent and working from home than in your current situation. Start off by reading the business ideas section. Sorry, but you are in the category of people least likely to succeed – this is because people use teleworkers whom they trust or who clearly have the right skills. If you go into an area where you have no track record and no contacts you have worked with previously, your task will be harder. Try to find a business idea that fits closely with your existing experience, or else plan to apprentice yourself in some way to someone already working in the field.
- You plan to approach your manager in your existing to job to ask for a teleworking option, but if they say no, you are thinking about leaving and setting up a business. If you haven't already, read Chapter 5, *For teleworkers and wannabees*, which contains information to help you persuade your manager. Then read all of this chapter and spend some time assessing whether you have the qualities it takes to make self-employment work. Don't forget the stark figures – two out of three small businesses fail within five years.
- You already have a small teleworking business set up but would like to have more customers or make more money. Read the introductory section and then the Marketing, Advertising, Press and PR section.

Whatever your situation, you are going to need to get work, and that means marketing. Many teleworkers have excellent skills in their areas of expertise, but know little about sales and marketing and lack self-confidence to start the process of 'selling themselves' to get work. Yet this is an activity which experienced self-employed teleworkers advise should take up at least a quarter of your working time if you are to have a regular stream of work providing adequate income. So think about getting professional help with marketing if the whole idea makes you nervous. In the UK, your local Business Link would be a good place to look for help. In Ireland, talk to the Enterprise Line (1850 353333), FÁS and your local County Enterprise Board or LEADER group.

Check your mindset

Perhaps the first thing you need to do is adjust your mindset. From your customers' point of view, they probably aren't interested in whether you are a teleworker, even though you may see teleworking as a central issue. So begin your marketing review by heeding the advice of Gill Price of Evergreen Business Support, who manages a network of teleworkers: 'Working at home is your bonus and has many advantages, both financial and personal. But don't be so keen to point out to new customers that you work from home, as it's not always viewed in such a positive light. The proof of the pudding is in the eating – months down the line you might decide to share the information with your customer, who will of course be so pleased with your services by that stage that the news will be inconsequential. Had the customer had to consider that you were working from home when you tendered for the business, it could have put you on a less-than-level pegging with a competitor.'

The big issue for most prospective customers is not technology – it's whether they trust you, because they probably aren't that used to working with people at a distance. They need to know that you have the skills, that you are reliable, that you will turn the work in on time, will be easy to deal with and will complete the job within the estimate or budget. They don't want to end up looking stupid in front of their colleagues or customers for having used your service. So you need to provide them with plenty of reassurance about your competence.

The third change in mindset you need to make concerns marketing. Marketing is not selling or public relations. Marketing is the process of adjusting what you are selling (your product or service) to best fit the demands of your customers. It can cover all kinds of strategies, including the timing and method of delivery of work, the pricing and the technical details of the work (such as the software packages used). Successful marketing is the key to a successful small business.

What your customers are probably searching for is higher quality and lower cost than they can get elsewhere, or for a job completed within a timescale they cannot manage themselves in-house. How are you going to convince them that you can achieve this? Here are some quotes from a Telework Association conference on marketing teleworking:

'If people are sending work out of their office, they expect it to be done better than if it were done in-house. Everything has to be slicker and more efficient. You have to have a control system that makes absolutely sure work doesn't get mixed up, that it's done in the right order, on time and accurately. You have to be more careful than if you were working for one

LOCATION, LOCATION, LOCATION

There are plenty of case studies giving examples of people working far from their clients or employers, such as programmers working from Australia, or Irish call centres servicing the North American market. Teleworking can allow work to be independent of distance. But all the evidence is that most companies prefer to use teleworkers who are located close enough to be able to pop in and discuss work face-to-face when needed. The TeleFutures study in Ireland (1996) found that over 80% of companies would prefer their teleworkers to be situated within 25 miles. The exception to this is people with rare skills or combinations of skills, who can usually lay down their own conditions on how they will work. Some people promote teleworking by having two different prices for their work – a lower price if the job can be teleworked without onsite client meetings. Overall, the lower your skillset (e.g. secretarial), the more likely it is that your clientèle will be local, so build this factor into your business plan.

particular business.' (Judith Verity, Office Ghosts)

'I looked at what the competition was charging for their reports and tried to get in at that sort of level. People tend not to take you seriously if you are not expensive enough. And when people ring to place an order, we answer the telephone in exactly the same way. To the customer it is a unified response, although it may be a different voice. It is like a corporate image over the telephone line.' (Anthony Capstick, Instant Search)

Establish your objectives

Objectives can be difficult to define for teleworkers. Some want a way of working which allows them more time with their families. Others are concerned with improving profits through lowering overheads. Others may be motivated by the desire to avoid commuting to work or office politics. This chapter limits itself to looking at business objectives, but anyone considering starting up a teleworking small business should consult the bibliography, and spend some time with their family working out a set of objectives. These might cover profits needed to meet living expenses, number of hours to be worked each week, circumstances under which the teleworker can be disturbed in the home office – and everyone in the family should understand and agree to them. You need a clear business idea and set of objectives before you start thinking about marketing. Equipping yourself with a computer and an Internet connection is not enough; there are a lot of other things you need to think through. For example:

- What services will be offered?
- Who is going to use the service?
- How do people buy it? By phone and fax or over the web? Then pay

attention to voicemail messages, website performance and fax presentation – the 'shop window' of a teleworked business.

- When do people buy it? Are there peak periods (such as pre-Christmas) that need to be covered in terms of staff levels?
- Where do people buy it from? Through the Yellow Pages, or through a personal recommendation, or from their PC over the web?
- Do others already offer a similar product or service? Is your service an improvement on these competitors? Is there any evidence that customers want an improvement?
- How much is it going to cost? Are you going to be cheaper, on a par with, or more expensive than your competitors?
- What is the business going to be called? The name will depend upon your target market. People offering a professional service may prefer to use a version of their own name as the business name, since the clients are essentially 'hiring' that person.
- What happens if a contract goes badly wrong? Do you need professional indemnity insurance in case a customer sues you? (*Note* It is often a condition of such policies that you do not tell your customers that you are insured because that could make them more likely to sue.) Do you need legal help to prepare a standard contract for signature with clients?

Brian O'Kane's guide *Starting a Business in Ireland* suggests two exercises which may help to further clarify your business idea.

1. Write your own CV for the position of managing director/administrator of your business. What are your skills and experience? Build on these. Look at your technical, personal and business skills.
2. Write a short description of the processes which must be completed before you have something for which you can invoice a customer (e.g. receive enquiry, discuss with client, give quotation, use software package on computer and so on). Throughout, keep a list of every item which will be required, from paper to printer right down to the chair you sit on.

BUSINESS IDEAS

Many occupations not listed here, ranging from quality management to market research, can be teleworked; but you must already have the relevant skills and industry contacts to make them work. General issues of how to sell teleworking services are covered later in this chapter. When considering what services to offer, be careful to evaluate the cost of software that will be required, and avoid substantial investments in this area without thorough market research on the demand for the proposed service. Note that ideas suitable for telecentres and telecottages are given in Chapter 4, *Alternative workplaces*.

USEFUL WEBSITES FOR MARKETING INFORMATION AND CONTACTS

There are many websites aimed at people who are starting up small businesses working from home. The official take is available at **http://www.businessadviceonline.org** (the government's small business service) but the site is rather slow and stodgy. There is a link to help you find your local Business Link office.

http://www.taforum.org.uk is an exhaustive guide to British industry and trade associations. Enter your search term into the 'description' section of the search engine to find all kinds of useful organisations you did not know existed.

Information on specific companies is at **http://www.companieshouse.co.uk** – details of 1.5 million registered UK businesses including company reports, directors' details, dissolved companies, disqualified directors, insolvency details, etc. plus detailed guides to company registration processes.

The SOHO Guidebook at **www.toolkit.cch.com** is highly recommended.

The homeworking site has lots of interesting case studies and examples of personal experience – **http://www.homeworking.com** There is useful stuff on the 4anything site **http://www.4telecommuting.com** but quite a few of the links don't seem to be working anymore.

And of course, try the Telework Association itself – **http://www.telework.org.uk**

For people planning a business which is very sales-based there are a number of sites that give advice on marketing techniques. Try **http://www.webmarketingtoday.com** – the linked doctorebiz site at **http://www.doctorebiz.com** is quite interesting.

For people who need some coaching in basic selling techniques, there is a lot of free and useful advice available at **http://www.smalltownmarketing.com**

Abstracting, editing, proofreading and indexing

Skills in the publishing area include copy editing, proofreading and indexing. There is strong demand for these skills if they are combined with the ability to handle scientific subjects. However, rates of pay for work in non-technical sectors can be low. Preparing press cuttings to clients' briefs is another related niche business area – you may have to work slightly unsocial hours and be in a region where you can get the relevant papers or magazines early.

Audio typing, remote typing, document formatting

This market is under threat from advances in systems which allow direct dictation to computer. However, there is still scope for audio dictation in specialist areas such as medical and legal transcription, where a detailed knowledge of terminology may be required. Also, in any situation where accuracy or human intelligence is important, or where the quality of the audio recording is poor, humans are needed for the transcription process. If you plan to go into this area you will need to specialise or add value to your transcription services, and consider related tasks such as proofreading, indexing, editing, and translation.

Work arrives by fax or email (.wav sound files for example), or on audio cassettes, is transcribed onto computer and returned as disk, printout, email or all three. For audio typing you may need a transcribing machine. This is a tape recorder with a foot pedal for playing the tape, stopping it and rewinding where necessary while leaving the hands free for typing. There are three main sizes of tape: standard audio (C-size), Philips mini cassette and Dictaphone mini cassette, so talk to your prospective customers about the size(s) they use before buying. There is also specialist software that can be used to receive and play compressed voice files for transcription. The work can range from correspondence to whole books or conference proceedings. Perhaps you could link up with conference organisers in your area?

Bookkeeping and accountancy services

Accountants may be prepared to send out the more tedious areas of their work, such as putting purchase receipts and invoices onto spreadsheets. To succeed in this area you will need specialist accountancy skills such as an accountancy technician or bookkeeping qualification. There is a multitude of software packages in this area, and every company has its personal favourite. Be careful to check this out before investing in expensive software. Accountants who plan to telework from home themselves need to take account of the likelihood of client visits and whether this will require them to get planning permission, as well as the need to provide suitable parking facilities and insurance cover.

Computer programming/software support

Small computer dealers sometimes diversify to offer tailor-made programming services to customers as well as software training and support. Offering technical support over the telephone to new computer users could also be a winner. But beware – you should think about getting professional indemnity insurance to cover yourself in case your advice leads to a financial loss for one of your customers – what would happen if you recommended a backup procedure that led to the loss of vital data? This kind of insurance can be expensive. Specialist areas for computer programming and software include CAD/CAM (computer-aided design and manufacturing), computer design of PCBs (printed circuit boards), mathematical and financial modelling, stress calculations for engineers, quantity surveying and project management.

EVERGREEN – THE BENEFIT OF 25 YEARS EXPERIENCE

Gill Price of Evergreen Business Support has employed several of her staff two or three times over: firstly in the financial-services industry, where Gill worked for Equitable Life; and secondly when she set up the Scottish Widows 'virtual life office', a network of teleworkers carrying out back-office administration. When changes in technology led to the closure of the virtual life office, Gill set up Evergreen and re-employed some of her former colleagues again.

'We now have 12 full-time employees, all teleworkers, located all over the country. We've specialised in three areas I know well – transcription, press review and translation services. The transcription services involve a remote windows-based dictation service that customers phone. Evergreen staff produce the documents as required and return the work via email, post, courier and fax. On the press reviewing, we screen many quality and popular titles in the early morning, seven days a week and 365 days a year. The press clippings are taken to fit detailed client briefings, and because we have been focusing on financial services, we find that Wednesdays and the weekends are the busiest days. With translation, we're providing a one-stop shop with text proofing, accuracy and speed. One regular contract involves the transcription of confidential legal work, and we've had to strengthen our existing confidentiality agreements with the clients and with our employees to take account of the sensitivity of the work, as well as looking at our data-protection and data-security measures in order to comply with the Data Protection Act.'

Gill believes that a 'virtual' organisation is a big advantage. 'My literature does not refer to home-based staff because to some people it would be perceived as a distinct disadvantage.' She also thinks her long track record in the financial-services industry has been a big advantage in winning work: 'Outsourcing is the future. I am convinced that more companies will become virtual and simply buy-in the services they require. But I find it's too complicated to explain exactly what I do, so I treat the business more as a collection of three niche services, and just explain the particular service required. In the main we get work through word of mouth, although I do some advertising.'

However, she hasn't quite managed to relax into a flexible workstyle in her Wakefield office. 'In the final analysis, I am responsible for everything, so the hours are long; and in addition I like to actually do some of the work myself on new jobs so that I understand what the staff are being asked to do, where the problems lie and how to be more efficient.' Gill also believes that her large-company experience helped her to set up effective systems for Evergreen: 'Although we are still a fairly small company, I have always used written contracts, procedure notes, health and safety assessments, so we just continued and found it worked well for us.'

Gill gets all her staff together twice a year. 'We usually start in the morning with a business agenda, but then we have a nice lunch and catch up – many of us have been working together for over a decade. I also send out a monthly newsletter to keep everyone in touch.'
http://www.evergreenbusinesssupport.com

IDP: DOES EXACTLY WHAT IT SAYS ON THE TIN...

Jennifer Boyle is head of International Data Processing (IDP), a company with 22 staff in Dublin and 12 in Listowel, a market town in rural Co. Kerry. Eight of the Dublin staff telework, as do all of the Kerry employees, although there is also a central office in Listowel. IDP's work includes creating billing files for clients, gathering statistics, and extracting and entering data from paper-based forms. In recent years Jennifer has focused on the transcription market, specialising in conference proceedings for US clients.

'I have been working in this area for 20 years now, and the business has been in operation for ten years. In the old days it was basic data entry, but things have changed. Clients' requirements are much more sophisticated, and they require high levels of skill. We now do a lot of image processing where the clients themselves scan the document into a graphic image and transmit it to us, rather than airfreighting paper around the world, but we provide the skilled human input needed to interpret the image and turn it into the correct data record.'

In Listowel IDP occupied an office formerly operated by the American data-processing company Neodata. Neodata closed down its operation in 1997, at which point Jennifer took over the 20 staff and premises, retraining them for her work. Twelve of the 20 still work for IDP, but the company is now in town-centre premises. She explains: 'They all have PCs at home but sometimes we work on contracts where clients are concerned about confidentiality and don't want to see information leaving the central office building. It's interesting that sometimes clients with highly confidential information don't seem to be much concerned about teleworking, while others whose data is less sensitive set much higher non-disclosure standards.'

Jennifer has a number of clients in the public sector in Ireland, mainly government departments, as well as her US clients. 'Initially my presence in Dublin and face-to-face contacts were important. These days we have a long track record and a good reputation, and I have been able to relocate to Listowel myself, visiting Dublin once a week to meet clients and staff. There are two other companies with similar operations in Dubin but we all have our own niche services and particular client bases, and we often collaborate. A typical job for us would be a major international courier company – they freight documents from all over Europe into Dublin every morning which we turn into billing records for them. That's a service we have developed over the years in close co-operation with them. Competitors do spring up every now and then but generally they die off quite quickly too.'
mailto:jennifer@idp.iol.ie Tel: 00 353 66 976 8561

Information-broking and advice services

Almost every business sector needs facts of some description. Information brokers are experts at accessing paper and online information sources and distilling the results into a product they can sell to clients. Most brokers are specialists who know intimately the resources in a particular subject area. Good personal contacts are also important. Charges are usually via an hourly or daily rate, or by subscription to a briefing document.

Internet-based services

Internet services offer a wide range of opportunities for the dedicated (and technically knowledgeable) pioneer. *See* p. 344 for the example of Mark Francis-Jones and his jewellery business. Many consultants and workers in the publishing industry use the Internet to market their services. Others advertise and sell rare goods. See if you can find John Eagle, who sells his dramatic photographs, posters and postcards of Irish lighthouses over the Internet – he's based in a remote village where employment opportunities are few. He doesn't even bother to have his own website but gets other lighthouse enthusiasts to put his photographs on their sites – his business operates with just an email address. For an example of a slightly bizarre but successful niche Internet service, try **http://www.dogbooties.com** – only in America (with thanks to Joanne Pratt).

The main problem with Internet-based services is charging mechanisms. More people are now prepared to send their credit-card numbers to 'secure' commercial Internet sites, but there is still concern about this area, so providing a scheme for alternative payment methods is vital.

Office services

A number of virtual office services have grown up over the past five years, providing an official 'front' for businesses including telephone answering, accommodation addresses and meeting space. These services aim to fulfil all the functions of a traditional receptionist/secretary, without of course the expense.

Kendlebell offers work opportunities on a franchise basis to provide personal call-handling services for businesses that don't want to use voicemail. Franchises cost from £25,000 for one or two people working from home up to £75,000 for a centre. The cost to the clients is from £29 to £250 per month (**http://www.kendlebell.co.uk** or 0800 0727 728).

Publishing, design and multimedia

There are a number of areas where teleworkers can be involved in publishing, including preparing diagrams, editing text, layout work, proofreading and graphic design. In addition, new media areas such as the creation of multimedia CDs offer opportunities that are highly suitable for teleworking. However, they all require specialist skills. It is not just a case of buying the desktop-publishing software!

SUSSING OUT THE SCAMS

People looking for telework business ideas can be vulnerable to a number of well-tried and tested homeworking scams. One such scam, successfully prosecuted in Staffordshire, netted over £1m in registration fees. The National Group on Homeworking identifies a number of common types, and warns that there is no legislation to protect you from misleading schemes:

- *Kit scams usually appear as ads in local press and shops. They invite you to send money for a kit costing anything from £20 to £200. Whatever you send back, they will reject on the grounds of inadequate quality and you will not be paid.*

- *Recruitment scams usually involve you in placing ads in local shops. Let's say you pay £15 to join the scheme. For each extra person you persuade to part with £15, you get about 30p. So the only way you can recoup your £15 is to help the company rip off a further 50 or so people.*

- *Directory scams are often targeted at teleworkers. The ads ask you to send in the typical £15 fee, and in exchange they will send you a directory of companies offering work to homeworkers. This turns out to be photocopied addresses, each of which in turn ask a registration fee of a further £10 to £200.*

For advice on how to deal with any scams you discover, or to check out a company, contact the National Group on Homeworking (0800 174 095) or **http://www.gn.apc.org/homeworking** The group runs a homeworking helpline, as well as providing free legal advice for members. Remember – never pay to get work. Be wary of box numbers and ads which don't give a phone number.

Telemarketing

Telemarketing has a bad image of monotonous work for poor pay, doing ghastly tasks like selling double-glazing to householders in the evenings. Contrary to the stereotype, most telemarketing work is business-to-business and happens during the day. It's an occupation well suited to teleworking. Opportunities in this area can be found in many publications and on many websites. If you already have customer-service experience and are well-organised, this could be for you. Related work includes setting appointments and gathering market information – such as ringing a database of companies to find out what fire safety equipment they use.

Translation services

Translation services are increasingly in demand, and translation work is often received and delivered via email these days. Translations can be tied in with word-processing and desktop-publishing services. By connecting together a

TROUBLESHOOTER AND FIREMAN

Marcus Harvey took voluntary early retirement from his former job for a bank in Belfast, as a team-leader in IT security after 15 years. He thought that becoming a computer consultant at home would just be an extension of the same work. However, he found that the key was building up trust, and dealing with new customers in a personalised way.

'I found that the best way of starting a business from home which involved frequent contact with people was to start by offering my service to family, friends, and friends of friends. Now I offer a wide range of services, from support and advice to repair, maintenance, updates, website design, accounts packages, networking, Internet connectivity and e-commerce.'

The result is that Marcus has to be prepared to jump into the car at a moment's notice. He says: 'I suppose in a way I'm a cross between a trouble-shooter and a fireman. Coming from Belfast, that seems to go with the territory! The other day I was on my way to rescue a tax consultant whose laptop had crashed after a power failure when I got a call from Perth, Western Australia. "Gud Day mate – a friend told me you could do a really good website design job at a reasonable price – I'm tired of being ripped off by big companies who don't care about small businesses like mine, so I thought I'd give you a whirl." That's the sort of job I pick up now. Anything from a laptop spec for a student to helping a freelance journalist who works from home and can't afford for his systems to go down just before a weekly deadline.'

Marcus finds himself working at strange hours of the day or night, but it's all part of the job. 'I wouldn't do it if I didn't enjoy the work. I can always say no. If I'm really under pressure I'll call in a subcontractor, someone I trust. That way I still keep my reputation.'
Email: rm.harvey@ntlworld.com

number of language teleworkers, telecentres or web-based businesses can provide a complete European service.

Word processing and desktop publishing

Word-processing (typing) services can be offered to homeworkers, businesses, political parties and pressure groups, community newsletters and societies. If you are in a university area, see if you can get involved in typing theses and academic papers. Another area which is more within the skills range of most teleworkers than full-blown publishing services is the use of desktop publishing

GOT A QUESTION?

Infogenie is a virtual call centre that links enquirers to experts in the fields of computing, medicine, games, Internet, natural health, veterinary medicine, the law and taxation. The service was founded in Berlin in 1996 and now operates in the UK, France and Italy as well.

Infogenie connects several hundred experts around Europe, including about 130 in the UK. Tom Casey, Expert Services and Recruitment Manager, explains: 'We operate a set shift pattern with some services operating 24 x 7. Others provide a dynamic service. Our doctors and lawyers sometimes log on for just 15 minutes at a time. If the system encounters a severe overload, it will dial up experts automatically and ask them to log on for work.'

Infogenie operates Norwich Union's Healthcare advice line which provides instant access to policy-holders to speak to a GP at any time. The system achieved 98.5% of all calls being answered within service levels, including service levels for soft skills such as accessibility and friendliness. All the experts are screened and are required to have indemnity insurance as well as the relevant professional certification.

Another service offered by the company is PC technical support, which also requires experts to be able to talk on the phone and access the Internet simultaneously.

For the premium-rate services that Infogenie offers, experts are trained not just in soft skills but also in the ICSTIS guidelines for the operation of premium-rate services.

Andy Manning, a games support helpline worker, has been working for Infogenie for just over a year, although he says he only ever lasted 5–6 months in conventional call-centre work: 'Here you don't have someone looking over your shoulder all the time!' Andy has a heart condition which prevents him from driving, and also has to attend a lot of hospital appointments, so the flexibility offered by Infogenie is important – he can sign off at any time. Most days he signs on and tells the system how many hours he plans to do, and sometimes logs in for extra hours at the weekend. He says the only downside is that there is no-one to share difficult calls with.
http://www.infogenie.co.uk

to prepare simple brochures, newsletters, pricelists and instruction leaflets for local companies.

Web-page design

The production of web pages is something that many teleworkers have tried their hands at. It is still 'flavour of the month', with many businesses requiring help to advertise their services on the web. To produce web pages, you need appropriate authoring software and a working knowledge of HTML, the programming language used. It is a big help if you have graphic-design or information-editing skills, as many client companies are not good at putting together clear information, or understanding how to structure it for use with hypertext. Some websites include forms and other areas for users to enter information. Programming skills in cgi scripting, database-related languages such as ASP, and in Java, the programming language used to send small, self-running programmes over the Internet, are in high demand but the market for basic web-page design is highly competitive.

MARKET RESEARCH

Once you have your business idea, you need to do some market research. If you are applying for any kind of outside assistance in starting up a small business, the questions which grant-giving bodies or banks will want answered include:

- What is the total market for this service, and what are the overall trends in this market area (static, expanding, contracting)? Look for national surveys on market share and size – many are available from good reference libraries or on the web.

- How much of that total market is practically accessible to your service (e.g. if it is a geographically limited service, check out what percentage of the national market is in your 'catchment area')? Research basic figures in your local library or on the web, such as the population in your area, the percentage of people unemployed, the breakdown of types of employment into service, manufacturing, agriculture, and so on.

- How much of the accessible market could you reasonably hope to capture? This answer should take into account practical constraints (e.g. maximum number of productive hours in a year which you expect to work), and will look more convincing if you give a minimum and a maximum and then show that you are selecting a fairly conservative figure between the two.

- What competitors do you have? What are their strengths and weaknesses? How much do they charge? To provide information on costs, there is little alternative to ringing around competitor companies to check out prices – few give this kind of detail on their websites. This is a horrible job but vital. Make sure you have a 'project' for them to quote on or they will quickly realise that you are not a *bona fide* customer. Look through the Yellow Pages to see how many companies are working in your area. Don't forget that your competitors may be listed in different sections of the telephone directory such as secretarial services, computer graphics, desktop publishing, computer training, computer consultancy and so on.

- Ask existing customers, family, friends. Why would (or do) people use your services?

BEATING THE BARRISTERS TO THE BAR

Jan Wood is an independent barrister's clerk who works from her home in Exeter, clerking for a number of barristers located in different areas of the country. The title of 'clerk' she regards as a bit misleading to those not familiar with the legal profession. 'You're more like a media agent, providing a shop window for barristers to get work,' she explains. And of course, she also collects the fees.

'I actually started as an independent clerk in 1997 when the chambers I worked for closed overnight. I thought, "What if I do it from home for myself instead? With the Internet you don't need libraries – you've got CD-ROMs." I checked it out with the Bar Council and got the OK to set up as a virtual clerk.'

Barristers work with a virtual clerk much as they have always done. Bookings and messages, as well as background papers, are forwarded by email, phone or fax. The barristers can work at home and then email their pleadings to the instructing solicitors. Conference facilities (for meeting with clients) can be made available at the instructing solicitor's offices. When the work is complete, Jan receives a 'work record sheet' from the barristers by email. She uses ACE software to generate the fee notes (invoices) for solicitors, and then has to chase up payment.

The results is that chambers overheads and travel expenses are avoided, and administration costs kept to a minimum. In return, Jan receives a nominal monthly clerking fee plus a percentage of the fees received. Jan's website, which was created by her son, has created interest from as far away as Hong Kong and Turkey.

http://www.the-virtual-clerk.co.uk

The information from your market research will be used to prepare your business plan.

BUSINESS PLANNING

Business-plan structure

There are many books and guides available which will help you to put together a formal business plan (*see* bibliography). Many Business Links have advisers who can help with business plans, as do high-street banks. The purpose of a business plan is to produce a document, probably only around ten pages in length for a simple small business, which has four basic functions:

- To help you clarify your thinking – focusing your thoughts and making sure you have done the calculations needed to ensure that your plan is realistic.
- To establish that your business idea is financially viable.
- To provide an accessible, clear document which contains all the relevant information about your business idea for outsiders, including advisers such

THE SALES SOLUTION

Telework Association member Bernadette Eaglestone left an excellent job and career behind her after the birth of her son. 'The decision to leave was probably the worst and best decision I have ever made.' She came across the Telework Association website while searching for information on homeworking on the web. 'I joined the Association on a Wednesday morning. My membership details came through the following Monday and by the end of that week I had my first assignment through the Association's listings of telework opportunities.' Bernadette started out doing database cleaning – phoning to check contact details. Since then she has moved on to appointment fixing, sales and telemarketing and is branching out into market research. All these areas were ones in which she had some experience from her previous job. 'I refuse to use the call-centre approach and work with a script. You personalise the service so they don't think of you as a nameless person sitting in a faceless office – you are actually interested in them. I try and listen to what people aren't saying as well. I will leave it a while after a negative response and then ring back. Situations and people change continuously. A "no" today could be a "yes" tomorrow.'

Helen Legg is also a Telework Association member and had worked in a high-street bank as a customer-services manager. Then her branch closed, requiring a long commute to a new location at a time when she had young children. She tried freelance telemarketing from home instead and has worked on various contracts selling water coolers, mortgages, printing services, website design and financial advice. She's had some bad experiences, including a company that refused to pay her for two months' work, leaving her with a £2000 phone bill. Helen advises checking the contract on offer and trying to keep payment terms fairly short so you aren't running up a bill, and reports she is now happy working with Turnover Plus.

Nigel Francis of Turnover Plus says that they deliberately employ more mature people in their 40s to 60s for their appointment-setting business. They have several people on their books, mainly working on commission, and operate an office with staff who deal with account-handling and administration. Nigel says 'maturity, persuasiveness, self-motivation and tenacity are the main qualities required'. Prospective telemarketers need relevant experience (in market research or telemarketing) and a PC capable of email and handling Excel spreadsheets, so they can receive databases of client contacts. The range of earnings for full-time equivalent telemarketers is £16,000 to £20,000 on average, but most work part-time. 'The average is about three days per week. Part-timers seem to do better at this kind of telemarketing – it can be quite soul-destroying to make a hundred calls before you manage to set an appointment, so short bursts are better than full-time working,' explains Nigel. The telemarketers cover their own phone costs and are paid on commission for the number of appointments they manage to set. Nigel has started organising IT training courses and some coaching exercises in telemarketing techniques such as overcoming objections and getting to the key decision-maker. 'We'll definitely be running the training again – it was very successful,' he reports. http://www.turnoverplus.com

THE VIRTUAL ASSISTANT

Angela Willis worked for other people for 20 years. Along the way, one employer went bust and another got taken over by an American company that 'rationalised' it. Angela decided she could have a more secure existence by having a number of clients of her own. 'I wanted to be more in control of my own working life and have more flexibility.'

Despite variations in workload, Angela now has a greater degree of stability, carrying out tasks for a portfolio of eight clients, including proofreading and editing, database management and even web design. Most of her clients are referred by word of mouth, and come from the local area, and she hopes that a forthcoming profile in the local newspaper will provide some more leads.

The way that work is delivered has also changed in the five years that Angela has been a virtual assistant. 'Some of it I pick up, but a lot of the work arrives by email and disk,' she says. 'Five years ago it couldn't have been done but now I can even offer a "virtual branch" to overseas companies wanting a presence in the UK.'

'A lot of small-business people are looking for support. I am a small business myself so I understand their problems,' she says. 'The advantages to them are enormous. To employ someone leads to all the problems associated with PAYE and NI, not to mention finding space and equipment for them. A virtual assistant works as and when they are needed, from their own office with their own equipment. They get to know their business, their clients and their way of doing things.' However, Angela does find that organisation is vital in balancing client needs. 'Because you are multi-tasking, you have to be able to prioritise and keep track of everything.'

Angela is a member of an online support group for virtual assistants, ukvirtualassistants@yahoogroups.com. Email: angela@acwresource.co.uk or Web: **http://www.acwresources.co.uk**

as accountants, and people you want to invest in your business such as bank managers.
- To provide a baseline against which the progress of your business can be measured.

There are many different structures for business plans. Here is a simple one which covers the basics.

1. Principals: who are you? Why should anyone believe you can do this? Brief history and objective of your business. Past performance (if available).
2. Product: what will you sell, and what processes are involved before you have something to sell to the customer? How is it different from other competing services? Is it ready to sell now or do you need to develop it in some way?

3. Location: where will you carry out the business? Why have you chosen that location and how does it fit in with how you need to carry out your business? Do you have specific premises in mind? Indicate the cost of purchase or rental. If you are working from home, estimate the reduction in overheads compared to a conventional office.

4. Equipment: what is needed for your product or service? Give cost estimates and indicate if you already possess any of the relevant equipment.

5. Are any raw materials or consumables needed?

6. Employment: who will be employed by the business? On what basis? Full-time, part-time, subcontracted? Don't forget you will need to cover the administrative tasks vital to continued successful operation, such as chasing debts and completing VAT returns.

7. Management: what will the management structure be? Outline the qualifications and experience of the key personnel.

8. Finance: where will you get the money from? How much will be invested by the principals? How much will be borrowed and on what terms? How much are you looking for in terms of grants (if any)?

9. Profitability: the figures bit. Provide audited accounts for the last two years if you have them. Give projected profit and loss acounts and balance sheets for the first two years of the project.

10. Marketing: how will your products or services be sold? Do you have any firm contracts or orders? Market surveys? Competitors?

Setting prices and quoting

Preparing a business plan can seem to be a bit of a circular process – how can you know how much to charge until you know what the running costs are that you will have to cover? Or how successful your service will be? But in fact, a combination of estimating running costs and researching the prices charged by others for similar services will give you a fairly good guide to what you should be charging. This may, in turn, get you to refine your ideas about your start-up costs – what you will really need to get going.

So start by doing the cashflows and other business calculations to find out what you need to earn to cover your running costs. If you aren't sure of how to do this, refer to some of the small-business guides in the bibliography or get professional help from an accountant or business adviser. Your selling price must be higher than this breakeven cost. Selling price in turn affects your choice of target market, means of communication, choice of name and so on.

Many teleworkers find quoting for jobs nerve-wracking initially. Applying common sense is the best advice. If you aren't sure, ask to prepare a small section of the work as a 'free sample'. Work out how long it takes you, and multiply up to the size of the whole job. Use the trial section of work to get the exact details of the job agreed with the customer. Novices tend to underquote –

so think about adding on 20% to the final amount you arrive at. Some customers find it reassuring to know the underlying cost per hour that you are calculating from. Others want you to quote a fixed price for the whole job. Ask other established teleworkers for advice on quotes.

Legal structure

There are four basic structures for a startup business.

Sole trader

A sole trader has sole responsibility for their business, is self-employed and can trade under their own name, or any name of their choice (a 'trading name'). If you use a trading name you must display it along with your own name and address on all business premises and stationery. The sole-trader option is inexpensive because although you have to make income tax returns, you can do this yourself and do not need to have a formal audit or even use an accountant (though unless you have experience in this field, professional advice during the startup period is recommended). The disadvantage of this option is that if your business fails, all your assets including your home, if you have one, can be sold to pay your creditors. You need to file a registration form with your local tax office within the first three months of trading – the form is contained in the information pack PSE 1, entitled 'Thinking of Working for Yourself', available from the tax office. You will start paying most of your income tax and some of your national insurance contributions in advance after your first year of trading.

Limited liability company

A limited liability company creates a separate trading identity, which in turn limits your liability for debts to the amount you have invested in the company unless it can be shown that you have 'traded recklessly'. However, banks sometimes ask for personal guarantees for loans from directors which are not limited liability. The company's owners are its shareholders. Private limited companies only need to have one shareholder and cannot publicly trade their shares, which are usually held by employees, other businesses, family members and acquaintances. There must be at least one director and a separate company secretary. You have to register with Companies House (providing a Memorandum and Articles of Association, plus forms 10 and 12). You also have to have a meeting of the board of directors at least once a year, and your company accounts must be returned to Companies House each year. However, these accounts only have to be audited by an accountant if your company turns over more than £1m in a financial year. If there any changes in director, these also have to be notified. You can buy an 'off the shelf' company where all these forms have been pre-registered for under £500. So you get protection, but at a price of reduced independence and increased bureaucracy and accounting fees. You pay tax on any income you draw from the company, and any profits remaining are also taxed. Directors performing administrative duties for the company must be paid as employees unless it can be shown that they have a separate business performing that same service. There is a special form of limited company called a company 'limited by guarantee', which is normally used by voluntary organisations that do not distribute profits. Here the liability is limited to a nominal contribution such as £1.

Partnership

This is the form usually used by groups of professionals who work together. The format is similar to sole traders except that the partners are 'jointly and severally liable' for any debts of the partnership – again, personal possessions and houses can be sold to pay off creditors. As with sole traders, partners are taxed as individuals on the income they receive and must make national insurance contributions. There is usually a written partnership agreement which can cover a number of topics and which should address an 'exit route' for partners who wish to terminate the arrangement. If partners do not draw up their own deed of partnership, then the way the partnership operates will be governed by the Partnership Act which states that profits must be shared equally. Partnerships are easily set up and cannot be taken over. There is no requirement to produce audited accounts, though a profit-and-loss balance sheet is produced, and the Inland Revenue informed. On the downside, an individual can make a business decision without informing the other partners. Partnerships must be dissolved on the death, resignation or bankruptcy of a partner.

Limited liability partnership

This is a new form of company structure introduced in 2001 and intended to provide partnerships with a form of organisation that limits their personal liability. LLPs are taxed and structured as partnerships but in other respects are treated as companies. Charities and non-profit-making organisations cannot use the LLP structure – it is only available to businesses seeking to make a profit. LLPs are formed by members, like companies, rather than partners. There must be at least two members, and there are no restrictions on the maximum number of members. If one member behaves negligently, they will still be liable for debts, but the liability of the other members will be limited. LLPs have to disclose information on their finances and membership to Companies House but the partnership agreement remains confidential. The partnership agreement determines the relationship between the members of the LLP, and provides more flexibility in this relationship than a limited company, which is governed by the Companies Act 1985. Tax and national insurance contributions are also lower than for a limited company. Incorporating an LLP is also simpler, and the administrative overheads are less than for a limited company.

RAISING FINANCE

How much do I need?

Once you have a business plan, the next step is to raise the necessary finance for starting up. Double-check your business-plan figures against the checklist of items that you may need (*see* p. 292 at the end of Chapter 8, *Technology and techniques*). Decide which are priority items, and which non-priority or unnecessary. Can you reduce costs by buying secondhand or borrowing? Remember to include VAT in the prices unless you are VAT-registered, in which case you will be able to reclaim many VAT amounts.

One important item you will need to decide on with your accountant or financial adviser is whether to register for VAT. You are required to register for VAT if your business turns over more than £54,000 in the UK, or more than €25,500 in Ireland for service-based businesses (the Irish manufacturing threshold is €51,000 but teleworkers by definition will be service providers). However, it may be worth your while registering even if your turnover is lower in some circumstances. For most teleworkers, the issues are:

- If you register then you can reclaim VAT on equipment that you purchase.
- If your customers are VAT-registered, the fact that you charge VAT will not inconvenience them; but if they are mainly not registered (private clients), then it is actually going to cost them more to use you if you do register.
- If you register, you will need to learn how to set up and keep VAT accounts and make regular returns. In some ways this is a pain; in others it is a blessing in disguise because it forces you to keep your accounts up to date.

- Some prospective clients may regard VAT registration as a badge of credibility since it implies that your turnover exceeds £54,000 (or €25,500).

You are more likely to be successful if you take a conservative approach to startup costs and 'make do' rather than going for expensive items and incurring large financing charges, but beware: a common error is to underestimate startup costs.

Your financing will also need to include working capital – the money you need to start up and keep going until the first cheques come in. Bear in mind that, unless you are doing basic secretarial work where people call in to collect their work, and you can extract the money as you deliver the work, you are unlikely to be paid until at least 30 days from the date on which you invoice a customer. In many cases the delay between completion of the job and invoicing, and payment of the invoice, will be 45 or 60 days. Don't strangle your business at birth by failing to finance these delays adequately. The most common cause of business failure is cashflow – so make sure that you invoice at the earliest possible instance, follow up with a statement to remind them, and then chase payment.

Where do I get it?

The options for raising finance are:
1. Your own equity (ability to buy shares in the business).
2. Other people's equity (other shareholders apart from yourself).
3. Borrowing money.
4. Grants (almost without exception, grant-making bodies will require that you raise at least half of the cost yourself).

Start by thinking about what finance you yourself can raise, and by taking a careful look at which of your assets you would need to retain if your business went under. You may not want to mortgage your house as collateral for a business bank-loan, but if you are lucky you may have other assets you are prepared to risk such as shares, jewellery, paintings, cars or land.

Now consider the possibility of investment (other people's equity). In general, small businesses have difficulty raising equity capital or venture capital except from friends and relatives, because the amount of money is too small (normally around £500,000 is the minimum that professional investors want to look at because of the expense of checking and setting up the operation). Whatever the source of your equity finance, be very clear on the following points as outlined in Brian O'Kane's book:
- Are you prepared to allow other people to own (and therefore control) part of your business?
- What reward can they reasonably expect for their investment?
- Can your business realistically offer the kind of return that would attract outside investors?

The amount of debt finance which you can raise will almost certainly be defined by what your bank manager is prepared to lend you, and will be based on your business plan and available security. Bank managers are looking for the three Cs – character (your track record), collateral (security against any inability to repay) and cashflow (evidence that your business is financially viable). Arnold S. Goldstein's book *Starting on a Shoestring* suggests that unless you know the answer to the following points before you go to see your bank manager, you may not get very far:

- Why do you need the amount requested?
- What will you do with it?
- How do you know that it's enough?
- How much less can you live with?
- Who else will you borrow from?
- How do you propose to repay it?
- How can you prove that you can repay it?
- What collateral can you offer?

Don't overlook banks as a potential source of finance – most of the high-street banks have overhauled their services to small businesses within the last few years and many produce packs of useful information.

Telework Association member Edwina Clough provided the following useful tip: 'If you are planning to become self-employed and you need finance, try and get it before you leave your existing job as you will be able to get a personal loan rather than a business loan, and the interest rates can be more favourable.'

MARKETING, ADVERTISING, PRESS AND PR

Very few startup businesses include sufficient budget for marketing and PR in their business plans. Begin by formulating some idea of whom you need to address, breaking down the audience into distinct groups. You need to create a short, clear explanation of how your service will work, be charged for, have its quality guaranteed, be delivered and so on. Then work out the most cost-effective method of contacting the different audiences – postal mailing, phone, website, email, listings in directories, trade shows or a combination.

Antony Capstick of Instant Search gives the following advice: 'With PR and journalism, one has to think of a peg to hang the idea on when you are selling it to journalists. When Companies House opened up its service to people from the outside, I marketed the idea for my Instant Search business through that "peg". I sent faxes off to the newsdesks saying: "Companies House has opened their computer to the outside; however, you can get the service if you don't have a PC because Instant Search are offering it as a mail-order instant-access service." The best publicity I got from that was the *Manchester Evening News*.

BUSINESS ADVICE AND FUNDING FOR TELEWORKERS

Business Link advice centres – check the website
http://www.businessadviceonline.org to find your local centre, plus lots of
online advice on funding – but be warned, this website is slow. A subsection of
the site, the Small Business Service section **http://www.sbs.gov.uk** is rather
better and contains information on the Small Firms Loan Guarantee scheme,
which is available to those unable to obtain conventional finance due to a lack
of security or track record. This scheme provides loans of £5000–£100,000 (and
up to £250,000 for established businesses) over a period of two to ten years
(Tel: 0114 2597308/9).

Chambers of Trade/Commerce – details of your local organisation are available
from British Chambers of Commerce Tel: 020 7565 2000
http://www.britishchambers.org.uk/

Most high-street banks offer direct loan schemes on an 'instant decision',
unsecured, phoneloan basis for amounts between £1000 and £15,000, and
supply packs of advice and information for customers or prospective customers
thinking of starting their own businesses.

Prince's Youth Business Trust – assistance for businesses being set up by people
aged under 30. Tel: 0800 842842 or *see* **http://www.princes-trust.org.uk**

Age Concern has set up PRIME, an advice service for the over-50s 'grey
entrepreneurs' – *see* **http://www.primeinitiative.org.uk**

A useful website to check out is **http://www.j4b.co.uk** – 'our goal is to provide
SMEs with a transparent, honest interface between grant applicants and grant
providers'. Lots of information on grants, awards and soft loans (loans with
subsidised interest rates or reduced security requirements).

They quoted me and I was flooded with calls from Manchester, lots of orders –
it was very good.

It also helps in background credibility if your name is mentioned, for
example in the FT or another quality paper; somehow people think you are
better. There may be direct sales as a result of editorial coverage, but it also
helps when you approach people directly if they have already heard of you.'

You may want to advertise so that customers will be aware of your existence.
This will depend on what kind of service you are offering. Many teleworkers
have found conventional advertising or mailing too expensive in the long term,
and insufficiently rewarding. This is probably due to the trust issue. People
need to feel they know you before they are going to trust you enough to send
work out.

The people who already trust you are those who have worked with you
before – whether on a face-to-face or a teleworking basis. So your time and
money may be better spent on chasing up former colleagues and employers

MEASURING ADVERTISING RESPONSE

Anthony Capstick of Instant Search comments: 'The next area I went into was direct advertising in newspapers. I tried all the national newspapers – the *Sunday Times*, *The Times*, *Telegraph* and the *Observer*, particularly the small-ad section in the back.

For example, we run a six-line ad in the *Sunday Times* advertising our services. This costs something like £70, resulting in something like ten or 15 orders per week, and it's generally busy Monday or Tuesday. You need to run the ad for a specific period of time. I went in and out a couple of times at the beginning because I didn't want to spend too much. But I did notice that when I left it in, I was getting a much better response. People often browse papers, and may see the same ad again and again. The fourth or fifth time they may ring you up. If they have just see the advert once they may think the company is not very reliable. Persistence pays.

'But the whole thing is wasted if you do not ask every single person who rings in where they saw your service advertised, where you got that enquiry. Otherwise you are just throwing money away. I constructed a spreadsheet with the cost of the advert, when it appeared, the number of enquiries and the number of conversions from that enquiry. When people call in and their orders are taken, a code is entered about where they saw Instant Search advertised. At the end of the month, when I'm booking the next level of advertising, I can see, for example, that a £200 ad in the *Sunday Times* brought in £500 of business, whereas the *Daily Telegraph* cost me £80 but brought in only £60 of business. Stick to the Sunday papers if your business can go overseas – we have agents in Moscow picked up from a three-line ad in the *Sunday Times*.'

(e.g. through web searches for their names, or just asking around about where they may have moved on to), or on networking (attending and speaking at relevant conferences, for example).

The best of all advertising is word-of-mouth. Keep up the quality of your service and you will be repaid by personal recommendations. On the downside, it has been estimated that if a customer has a bad experience of your service, he or she will probably report this to 26 other people.

If your service is something that would benefit from traditional advertising, think carefully about which media (newspapers, local radio) will work best for you, and compare prices. Contact details for most publications are available at **http://www.mediauk.com/directory/** The basic options are:

- Newspapers.
- Trade magazines.
- Web – include costs for professional design, search-engine registration and maintenance, and help with publicising your website unless you are already an expert in this area. *See* p. 239 for further advice.

- Local radio.
- TV (if your budget is huge).

Try to think about how you will measure response to your adverts so that you will know where to spend your money next time. Keep asking new customers where they heard about you and record their replies.

Directories and networks

Many businesses use directories to market their services. The best known and most widely accessible publication is the telephone directory (Yellow Pages, or Golden Pages in Ireland). Before advertising in Yellow Pages take a good look at the entries for your area. A problem that many teleworking businesses come across is that there is no obvious place for their services in Yellow Pages at present – or rather too many. Some teleworkers would need to make entries in a number of categories to cover all their services. For this reason Yellow Pages may be a good option if your business fits into a niche – such as market research – but very expensive if you cover a range of categories. Remember that you are entitled to a free basic text entry in Yellow Pages if you pay the business, rather than residential, tariff on your telephone. Make sure that you get that, and that it is correctly worded – Yellow Pages entries for the whole country are now widely available on the web (**http://www.yell.com**) and via CD-ROM, so this constitutes a useful form of advertising with nationwide coverage.

If you decide to pay for a more complex Yellow Pages ad, think through the different options and prices. Often a plain text advert in bold type will be more cost-effective and practical than a graphic. In general, companies are more concerned about reference clients than they are about the size of your Yellow Pages advert. Think of it in plumbing terms. If you are looking for a plumber, you might use Yellow Pages to find the number of a particular plumber, but you are more likely to select that plumber based on personal recommendation or reference from friends and neighbours than 'cold' through any directory. So while it's important to have your contact details accessible, it may not be so important to take a large ad.

Local business directories may also be worth buying entries for – your local chamber of commerce or library should be able to give you information on the directories operating in your area. Chambers of commerce and other business networking organisations also publish local directories themselves, and encourage their members to use the services of other members.

Individual teleworkers may find it worthwhile to register with employment agencies or recruitment websites, as some are now taking on board the task of getting in contract work for teleworkers – though some will require you to set up your own limited company (*see* sections on employment-agency law and IR35 in Chapter 9, *Staying safe and legal*). A number of agencies advertise on the

Internet, but most of the requests are for permanent staff, not for temps or teleworkers.

Informal networks

Telework Association member Gill Price points out that there are many informal networks that you can use for PR purposes.

'If you have school-age children, become involved in the PTA group. You meet other working parents, and I have made a few interesting work-related contacts via this route. Parents talk to a lot of other parents – this is a useful networking area which costs nothing and can spread very wide. I have also found that teachers network with other schools – another useful link.

'Sponsoring local sports teams can be another helpful route. Last year I sponsored a junior football club and next year I'm sponsoring a dance festival. I send press releases to the local publications telling them all about it – and most local clubs are delighted with relatively small sponsorship sums such as £50 towards a trophy.'

Malcolm Newdick of Riverbank IT Management, which provides IT support, develops the idea: 'My top tip is selling by referral. We have got our best opportunities by forging alliances with similar but non-competitive businesses in the same market. For us it's a training company and a web-design company. We refer customers to each other. Referrals are a recommendation – you are welcomed as a trusted supplier, not a cold-calling salesman; and you're usually bidding alone, not up against five other possible suppliers.'

Responding to enquiries

Whatever the package of information you decide to distribute, you will need to collect responses – perhaps by phone or through a website contact form – and process any work enquiries, usually by providing a quote. Some of the responses will include fears, some criticisms, some good ideas, etc. They need to be analysed and responded to appropriately and promptly. Your prospective customers may list a number of common anxieties about using teleworkers. You need to have some responses thought out for their worries – for example:

- Computer viruses – can you guarantee that the disks you send to your customers are virus-free?
- Equipment backup – what would happen if your computer went down? Is alternative equipment available quickly? Do you have ample data backups of work in progress in case of disaster?
- People backup – if you are a small operation, how will you deal with the inevitable peaks and troughs in demand? What happens if you are flattened by 'flu? You might deal with fluctuations in workload through a network of associated teleworkers, or perhaps through online networks such as the Telework Association email broadcast list. Set the system up before you are in a crisis!

THE IMPORTANCE OF BEING ANSWERED

Anthony Capstick of Instant Search comments: 'One of the most important things we decided was that we would answer the telephone in a uniform way. Our standard greeting became: "Good morning, Instant Search, Anthony speaking, how can I help?". When you are working remotely from your customers it is vital to give the right impression. It is a bit like the impression you get going into a shop or restaurant. You are completely put off the place if there is a full ashtray sitting on the counter or a black plastic bag full of smelly rubbish in the doorway.

'In the same way it is completely unacceptable to answer the telephone by simply saying "hello" or without introducing yourself. It gives off an amateurish air. Same goes for children screaming, dogs barking, doorbells ringing in the background. Completely unacceptable, along with voicemail messages that say "Please leave a message and we'll get back to you" – oh yeah? In which century?'

Anthony Capstick's book *How to Change your Life with Technology* can be ordered at **http://www.instant-search.com**

- Confidentiality – what happens if another teleworker accesses commercially sensitive information? Could somebody unscrupulous get hold of your client-company's stationery?
- Data security – make sure that your computer system is secure. Use security features such as passwords and file-locking to prevent unauthorised access of clients' files. Make sure that your office is secure. Lock away customers' stationery and files if they are sensitive.
- Presentation – look at your website, fax cover sheets, letterheads, business cards. Do they reflect a professional image? How does your office look if a customer drops in unexpectedly? Can customers hear radios, kids or pets in the background when they ring up? Are all staff trained in telephone-answering?

These issues are related to quality control which is covered in more detail at the end of this chapter. Think up a system for tracking progress on all jobs undertaken (which could be as simple as a whiteboard list). Measure your response time and always prioritise new work-enquiries unless you have reason to believe they are not serious.

Using the press

Properly handled, your relations with the local and business press can be one of the most cost-effective forms of marketing. However, they need to be seen as part of your marketing strategy. Just as with direct mail or advertising campaigns, identify the target and then look at the most effective means of reaching it. To get to your target you must first convince an intermediary target – the journalist. The key to success is to treat press relations as a partnership in which both you and the journalist want to reach the same people. The journalist wants to give them an interesting, useful read; you want to make the audience aware of your product or service. Helping journalists to achieve their objective is the secret of success.

Step 1: identify the publication. It could be a business-to-business title, or a specialist trade paper. Be careful not to confuse business and consumer counterparts – mountain bikers don't necessarily read *Cycle Trader*, and turkey farmers may not have much interest in *BBC Good Food* magazine. If you're unsure, the reference bible is the voluminous and expensive monthly *BRAD* (British Rates and Data) which gives information on almost every periodical in Great Britain, and some in Northern Ireland and the Republic of Ireland (also try **http://www.mediauk.com/directory/** and *Willings Press Guide*, available in many libraries).

Step 2: draft your press release, always keeping in mind the famous acronym KISS – Keep It Simple, Stupid:
- Try not to exceed one page of generously spaced A4 on your business letterhead.
- Use a short, clear headline that sums up the story in a few words.
- Get all the main details into the first paragraph. Further down include an interesting quote.
- Avoid journalese – you are writing to attract the journalist's attention, not to do their job for them. Expunge words like 'revealed' or 'shocked' and keep in mind the news angle – why might your story generate interest?
- Avoid jargon and stick to clear, quantifiable facts such as 'this is the third government contract won by Anytown Design in two months' rather than 'this places Anytown Design as an industry market-leader'.
- Try and make it interesting. Avoid burying the story in paragraph six.
- If you enclose a photo, try to ensure that it is a print, not a transparency. Label it clearly on the back with the name and job title of each person, and briefly describe what they are doing. Do not use felt pen or biro for this label – in a pile of photographs the ink may come off the back of your photograph and on to the front of the one below, and biros can also cause indentations that damage the photograph. Use pencil or a typed label. Don't expect to see the photo again, whether or not it is published.
- Date it and include your contact details and telephone number at the bottom.
- Most journalists now prefer press information by email – but don't send the information as an attachment such as a Word file. Use plain text in the body

of the email because you don't know what software attachments they can read, and they may not bother to find out if they can read yours. Also, some won't accept unrequested attachments for fear of email viruses. If you have had a photo scanned, ask first if they would like you to send it by email; don't send it unannounced or their antivirus/antispam regime may bin your message. If the image file is very large, they will not thank you for blocking up their email connection.

Step 3: make sure you're sending it to the right person. A call to the paper to find out, for example, who covers local business may get you a name. If you don't have a name, send it to a relevant-sounding job title such as Industrial Correspondent.

Step 4: if a journalist calls you for further details, remember that they don't bite!

- Be courteous and don't patronise in explaining your story. Today's trainee journalist could be a valuable contact on a national paper in a few years' time.

- Don't lie or exaggerate – journalists aren't particularly interested in the skeletons in your cupboard until you lie to conceal them.

- Avoid going 'off the record' – giving information which you do not wish to be published. Although journalists rarely abuse this privilege, mistakes sometimes happen.

- Understand that you have no veto over what is printed – there is little point in demanding to see an article before it's published.

- Don't antagonise journalists by complaining. Errors are sometimes made – if they are trivial let it lie rather than be branded as a time-waster. For a major mistake, write a polite letter to the editor.

Step 5: if at first you don't succeed, try again. Keep your name in the eye of the public, and in the eye of other journalists. If there's a subject in which you have expertise, you may gradually become established as what's unkindly known as a 'rentaquote' – so that whenever a feature in your area comes along, you're the first person who comes to mind as an interviewee.

Internet marketing

There are several ways that you can use the Internet for marketing.

- Find companies which might give you work, by using Internet search-engines and then inspecting their websites.

- Use targeted email shots to advertise your services to prospective customers.

- Use web-based recruitment agencies and worksearch companies (jobsites).

- Create your own web page to advertise your services.

- Use personal emails to good prospects to advertise your services.

THE TELEWORKER'S GUIDE TO INSTANT PR

Here are some tips from our editorial team with nearly 20 years of experience between them as top teleworking rentaquotes.

- *If you are going to pay for coverage, do it through targeted, professional PR – it's usually better value than advertising, particularly for placing press releases through better contacts and getting someone else to harass publications for you.*
- *Local media are usually quite easy to get into because you have the local angle, and they have space to fill. But is your market local?*
- *Get a decent photo, scan it and make sure it's available as a good quality .jpg file.*
- *Almost all publicity is good publicity. But think about the coverage you are likely to get from an interview – the Association once did an article in a tabloid and got a huge response which cost a lot to deal with, but which brought in almost no new memberships.*
- *We have found that broadsheet newspapers are the best format to get across a complex message, because people can re-read the information, leading to a more considered response. The same applies to the TV and radio programme you target.*
- *Don't keep going for the same newspaper just because you have contacts there – the readers will get bored with you and you won't get any enquiries.*
- *For radio or TV interviews, make sure you have some idea what the programme is about so that you can strike the right tone.*
- *If you are being interviewed over the phone, just concentrate on what the interviewer is asking and think of it as talking to one person, not to millions.*
- *Note down one or two key points or statistics in advance if you think you'll need them, but don't read out an essay or rustle papers.*
- *If it's a group interview, write down the names of the other interviewees to avoid having to refer to 'the bloke with the deep voice'.*
- *Try to get your plug in early without being too blatant. Be careful with websites – introduce them as a source of further information. Make sure the URL is short and try to avoid having to spell it out – boring!*
- *TV interviews can be very disconcerting. You're probably perched in an uncomfortable location with lots of external noise, your earpiece threatening to drop out, and sweating from the lights. When you see the result, particularly if it's pre-recorded, you'll be amazed how little space they crammed the item into. Response from TV is often poor quality as people don't seem to listen properly.*
- *Partnerships are a great idea – team up with other organisations that have a common interest, especially those with their own press department.*
- *Used carefully, letters of support from famous people can be very effective.*
- *Trust the press despite their press – mostly they are just trying to do a job. Yes, occasionally you will get misrepresented but there's little point in complaining unless the problem is serious – you will need that contact again some day.*
- *Don't talk about things you don't know about. It will come back to haunt you.*

■ Use e-zines to inform existing and prospective customers about your services.

First, a warning: do not send unsolicited CVs to people by email. It is most unlikely to result in any work but will probably annoy the person you send it to. If you think, perhaps from looking at their website, that they are likely to have suitable telework to outsource, send a short, polite enquiry first (not more than two paragraphs) explaining your skills and asking if you can send your details.

The obvious exception to this warning is a jobsite that asks you to upload your CV. Many of the more sophisticated jobsites have features where you can specify what kind of work you are looking for and receive email notifications or alerts when any suitable job comes up. Unfortunately, few of the jobsites specify whether jobs are suitable for teleworking, so dealing with the resulting email can be time-consuming.

The Telework Association runs its own mailing list, detailing teleworking job opportunities. This is published weekly and is part of the Telework Association subscription. For more details *see* **http://www.telework.org.uk** or ring 0800 616008. Telework Association Online also provides news items on teleworking, and lists press coverage relating to teleworking.

The jobsites listed in this chapter all have some relevant opportunities at the time of writing. However, do take care – there are also many 'get rich quick' sites, as American telecommuting expert Gil Gordon summarises.

'I think there are three things going on:

1. Because demand for these jobs – sometimes from legitimately desperate people – vastly exceeds the supply, alarm bells go off for every sleazy operator under the sun. I think it is nothing less than unethical preying on the desperation of others.

2. Slowly but surely there are some semi-legitimate sites developing, mostly in the area of freelance networks of sorts. They try to act as brokers or intermediaries rather than information-providers. But these are few and far between.

3. Nobody is monitoring all of this. The sleazeballs operate well below the radar of the enforcement agencies. By the time someone makes a complaint to a local authority, it's too little too late.

'What really surprises me more than anything is that here in the US, where the unemployment rate is under 4%, you would think that even the dumbest employer would wake up to the fact that there are scads of willing and able people out there who won't make themselves available for full-time, in-office work. But it's not hard to overestimate the intelligence of most employers.

'Oddly, one of the missing links is that neither the employers nor the would-be telecommuters know how to make the marriage. The workers envision that they can magically submit their resumé to a company clear across the country

TELEWORK ASSOCIATION ONLINE – WEEKLY NEWS AND WORK OPPORTUNITIES

The Telework Association produces a weekly email bulletin of news and telework opportunities, compiled by executive director Alan Denbigh. Telework Association Online goes to around 1000 Telework Association subscribers – if you are a member of the Telework Association, joining instructions can be found on the website. In addition to summarising any news coverage of teleworking issues, Telework Association Online also provides two-way communication between the Association and its members. If an issue arises, Telework Association Online provides a quick way for the Telework Association to find out whether it is something affecting a lot of teleworkers or only a few.

The work opportunities are also listed in the Telework Association's bimonthly magazine *Teleworker*. One employer commented: 'It's very encouraging. We were really struggling to find people to work in a remote position, and when you put something in the magazine we had a stream of good people. The quality of what was coming through was very good indeed.'

and then start working for a huge salary from the comfort of their bedroom. The employers envision that this same unknown entity will want to live cross-country and will never show up.'

Gil's website contains a compendium of work-opportunity links – but as he says, 'I have a bunch of these listed and have tried to screen them, but I don't vouch for them.' *See* **http://www.gilgordon.com**

After a lobbying campaign by the Telework Association, the UK government's Employment Service is now to include an indicator to show jobs which can be teleworked. However, the change is not deemed a priority and is unlikely to take place until 2003. Check out **http://www.jobcentreplus.gov.uk**

Sites aimed at freelance teleworkers seem to fall into three categories:

- Auction sites, where a project is listed and teleworkers 'bid' for the contract.
- Job-sifting sites that go through everyone else's jobsites, pick out the teleworking ones and often charge you for providing the details.
- 'Support' sites offering access to work opportunities alongside forums for teleworkers, access to distance learning, etc.

Many of the sites do charge and it can be hard to work out what you are being charged for. Almost all require you to 'register' your contact details before you can access most of the site features. Some have clear privacy policies, but others may make some of their income by selling email addresses. Overall, as with all homeworking schemes, the advice must be that any site which looks for the worker (rather than the job advertiser) to pay a fee should be treated with caution. Also beware of getting involved in contracts outside your area of expertise, as it will hard to be sure that you are getting the appropriate remuneration or that you can provide a competent service.

One possible exception to the warning above is some of the specialist work-broking sites such as Smarterwork.com. Originally an auction site for work, Smarterwork has decided to go 'upmarket' by charging teleworkers €250 to become 'service providers'. According to CEO Milton Lewis, 'One of the things that service providers like is the fact that they can prove they have been through our certification process, obtained the Smarterwork certificate and share our value for professionalism and customer service. This aids client confidence and helps differentiate the providers from their competition.' Smarterwork itself has recently downsized again and is now practising what it preaches, going from 30 full-time staff to 17 freelance staff and 5 full-time.

Creating web pages

The Internet is the focus of a great deal of marketing activity because it is cheaper than conventional print advertising or direct mail, and because the content of the 'advert' can be altered at any time – although it is still extremely hard to measure the response to web advertising, or 'cost per hit'. Many websites are really PR activities rather than conventional marketing tools, despite the 'buzz' about e-commerce and online trading.

Web pages are normally 'hosted' by an Internet service provider (ISP) – they have to be available 24 hours a day, so renting space on existing servers is cheaper than setting up your own. ISPs will also design pages for you if you don't want to learn to use HTML authoring tools or don't have graphic-design and editing skills. Most people use an authoring package which allows you to specify the structure of the document (heading levels, graphics and so on), and then inserts the correct codes to produce the desired effect, checking for adherence to the HTML rules as it goes along. Web-authoring tools include:

- Adobe GoLive
  http://www.adobe.com/products/golive/overview.html
- Macromedia Homesite
  http://www.macromedia.com/software/homesite/
- Macromedia Dreamweaver
  http://www.macromedia.com/software/dreamweaver/
- Microsoft Frontpage
  http://www.microsoft.com/FrontPage/

In addition to web-authoring software, you will also need 'ftp' software which is used to upload the finished pages on to your ISP's web server. There are several pieces of shareware which can carry out this task such as WS_FTP (**http://www.ipswitch.com**).

When designing web pages, it is important to keep information short and well structured, and not to go overboard with complex graphics which slow

A GUIDE TO LOOKING FOR WORK ON THE WEB

We have kept a watching brief on various 'telework websites' for several years now, and have concluded that most of them are of little use. Skills registers have also proved something of a waste of space. Many of these projects have been carried out over the last decade; most have languished, except where they have:

- *aimed at high-level skills;*
- *actively sold the teleworkers through a dedicated marketing operation;*
- *taken steps to control the work-quality of the teleworkers on the register.*

Instead, we recommend using search techniques on the conventional jobsites. Try entering 'from home' or 'at home' or even 'telework' as a jobsearch criterion – and don't forget 'teleworking' and 'homeworking'. Be prepared to spend time sifting through the results.

Register for the *Telework Online* e-zine at **http://www.telework.org.uk**

http://jobs.guardian.co.uk – try the searches above and expect to find a number of voluntary-sector jobs (not-for-profit organisations) that are based from home with some degree of travel.
http://www.nfp.org.uk – again, voluntary-sector jobs, some based from home.
http://www.fish4jobs.com – a reasonable number of hits but also one or two 'too good to be true' ads. Watch out for ads which require response to an expensive 09 or 0870 number. Try also searching for telephone canvassers/telemarketers, as some of these are home-based.
http://www.jobsite.co.uk – consulting engineers, recruitment consultants, sales and some IT opportunities.
http://www.jobserve.com – well organised into different sectors.
http://www.monster.com
http://www.peoplebank.com – you have to register.
http://www.topjobs.ie – good search facility but no telework jobs when we looked.
http://www.totaljobs.com – about 44,000 US vacancies, of which we found around 50 appeared to offer work-at-home opportunities. Mostly in IT, some human resources, some construction/project management. Management consultancy, marketing, advertising, PR, creative and media also had some entries. Oh, and a post for a chat-line operator to talk to male callers.
http://www.working-options.co.uk – part-time work, particularly in the legal profession.
http://www.flexecutive.co.uk – including part-time work and jobshares for marketing and HR staff.
http://dir.yahoo.com/Society_and_Culture/Issues_and_Causes/Employment_and_Workplace_Issues/Telecommuting/ – catalogue where you may find other sites.

down browsing for the user. Use the facility of hypertext – instead of creating very long pages, make smaller, separate pages with logical links that users can select to get more information on a particular topic.

The Internet also provides facilities to create online forms for collecting feedback from users. The information in these forms has to be processed on the computer where the web pages are hosted, so if you want to use forms you will need to create what is known as a 'cgi script' to process the form information. Because such scripts can cause havoc on the local server if they go wrong, most ISPs won't let you use this approach without some help from them in ensuring that the script is bug-free.

Most people can learn quite easily to create simple web pages. But if you need to create an extensive website with much interaction between pages – and especially if you do not have experience with graphics, information provision, cgi scripting and HTML – you should consider paying someone to prepare the pages for you.

Also bear in mind that a number of disabled rights group are campaigning to ensure that business websites don't discriminate against disabled people. The practical effect of this is that your HTML must be programmed correctly so that software tools for processing HTML and 'reading' the contents through an artificial voice can function correctly. To check your pages for accessibility, try the free Bobby software downloadable from **http://www.cast.org/bobby**

Reaching your audience

Once you have created your pages, you need to signpost them so that people can find you. You can use a service like Jimtools (**http://www.jimtools.com**) to do a number of search engines automatically – and the list of similar services is growing. Some require that you pay a small fee although Jimtools is free. Some of the most important search engines need to be completed 'by hand', i.e. by visiting the site and submitting a URL by answering a series of questions, including Altavista and Yahoo. Many search engines make use of the Open Directory Site **http://www.dmoz.com** so you should also submit your URL to this website directly.

Whichever search engine you are dealing with, before posting details of your site make sure that you have used the metatags features in HTML to indicate (invisibly to the user) the content and keywords of your site on your home page – this will help search engines to index your pages properly. Use of the metatags should be explained in your HTML editing package, and there is a short tutorial on metatags on most of the search-engine help pages – such as the straightforward explanation at **http://www.jimtools.com** The specialist website **http://www.searchenginewatch.com** keeps tabs on how the search engines rank sites to help you keep at the top of their listings.

E-commerce

Because this is a complex subject with many pitfalls, and one that changes constantly, it is not covered in any detail in this book – although a number of references to useful books and websites are given at the end of this chapter. Bear in mind that you do not have to have a secure site with credit-card details to make money from the web. By skilfully presenting your services and products, but combining this with traditional invoice/cheque or faxed order methods, you can provide a fast response without the financial and technical burden of running a true e-commerce site. There is a DTI guide to the various European directives that those involved in e-commerce must be aware of at **http://www.ukonlineforbusiness.gov.uk/cms/template/popup-content.jsp?id=94836**

Affiliate marketing

It is possible to set up links from your web page to other people's sites that will earn commission for you. A much-used example is Amazon – links direct to a book on Amazon will net you about 15% of the price the book sells at. Another method is to have banner adverts on your page which earn you a few pence any time a visitor clicks them.

Think hard before doing this. Your website is for you to contact your customers. Only you are in a position to judge whether affiliate links will annoy, or be useful to, your customers.

Useful websites for affiliate marketers include:

> TradeDoubler **http://www.tradedoubler.com**
> Commission Junction **http://www.cj.com**
> Ukaffiliates **http://www.ukaffiliates.com**
> Yourcheque **http://www.yourcheque.com**

Email marketing

There is a very fine line between the responsible use of email as a business tool and blatant 'spam'. Collecting email addresses is something which has to be done tactfully and constantly – always request permission to add an address to your database. Ask customers to fill in registration forms on your website – but bear in mind that this may put some people off using the site at all. Include a query on email addresses with your bills. If you are exchanging business cards, ask if you can add them to your list.

Try to ensure that you are giving something useful in return for permission to send material to an email address. And keep your list current – at the moment about 50% of people change email addresses every two years. The figures are even more drastic for web-based email services like Hotmail.

Email marketing expert Denise Cox (**http://www.allrealgood.com**) gives the following advice:

'You should ensure that your email software sends plain text ASCII_messages without HTML or RTF formatting, because some of your customers won't be able to read the formatting. The emails should be about 65 characters per line with a hard break following each line. Avoid using the tab key – use spaces if you have to – and don't use columns. To ensure that email software creates 'live' links where you have entered a URL or an email address, put mailto: before the email address and http:// in front of the URL (e.g. mailto:info@newteleworker.co.uk or http://www.newteleworker.co.uk). Avoid sending uninvited attachments (especially if these are large). Do include automatic signature text which gives all your contact details (most email software has a signature function).'

Denise suggests you might consider using the following email communications with your customers:

- Updates – new services or contacts.
- Special-interest mailings – subdivide your customers and provide them with useful, relevant information.
- Order confirmations – many people find that they get no response to enquiries sent to websites, and are unsure whether or not their order has been accepted. Follow up by email.
- Autoresponders – if you receive too much email to provide a suitably speedy personal response, use autoresponders to give information or to let the customer know that there will be a delay before they receive a reply.
- Participating in, or originating, discussion groups.
- E-zines (email magazines) – but make sure that the information is useful and give people an easy way to unsubscribe if they don't want it. Limit the size to 15k (maximum 2500 words).

Newsgroups and discussion forums

Paul E. Bennett is a Telework Association member who specialises in electronic systems design engineering. He has found that participating in online discussions can also be a fruitful form of marketing.

'The best method to get known is to be seen to be helpful to others while being careful not to offer too much for free. After a while, people on news-groups will come to know you as helpful and offering sound advice, and they may feel inclined to pay you for your personal attention to specific problems.

'It is important not to be too blatantly or forcefully commercial and to follow good netiquette at all times.

'I have had some interesting work come in over the past five years from newsgroups including a European assignment in Brussels, one for medical systems, two in the energy sector and three in rail systems. To make this work you should:

- Have a short but informative email signature that includes your website details on all your newsgroup posts.

■ Make responses to selected requests for help in the form of indicators to the general direction of the solution, but don't give the whole solution (which is what you want to be paid for). If the questioner needs more assistance they'll ask and you can discuss terms.

■ Don't be disappointed if they shy away from spending money. The Internet is full of people who are basically freeloaders, but the results when you do weed out genuine potential payers are worth it!'

Mailing lists

Traditional postal mailing lists may not sound as exciting as Internet marketing but they work when used intelligently. Software tools allow records of contacts to be easily held, and the production of vast quantities of marketing materials that can be personalised to the addressee. However, mailshots can have a negative effect if they are not correctly written and targeted, or waste your resources if they are not well planned.

First, you need to know whom you are going to contact and why. Use your business plan and market research to build up a profile of the likely customer. If you are selling to businesses, your next step will probably be to purchase a mailing list from a specialist company that holds regularly updated and indexed lists of companies such as Kompass (**http://www.kompass.com**). As you pay 'per name' you will need to build up a brief for the mailing-list company which may include parameters such as:

■ Number of employees.

■ Market sector (most mailing-list companies have a series of ID codes for different market sectors).

■ Person to contact within the company (e.g. finance director, human resources/personnel).

■ Service, manufacturing, or export sector.

■ Number of years established.

■ Ownership (e.g. foreign-owned or domestic).

■ Geographical location.

■ Telephone number (vital for qualifying the list – *see* opposite page).

Mailing-list companies want to get you to buy as many names as possible, whereas you want the smallest number that will give you a good rate of response. To avoid this poacher/gamekeeper conflict you may wish to use a mailing-list broker. Bill Moss, an experienced broker, explains: 'Mailing-list brokers get a discount from suppliers because they buy in bulk. They also know the various mailing lists extremely well. So you can get professional advice from a mailing-list broker to produce a well-defined list, get the broker to obtain the list for you, and pay the same amount as you would have done buying direct – the broker pockets the difference between the discount and the standard retail price as the fee for his or her advice.' (**http://www.bill-moss.com**)

CRIME AND PUNISHMENT FOR AFFILIATES

Telework Association member Guy Clapperton runs several websites, including one for crime books – at **http://www.crimebookshop.co.uk** He comments on the importance of providing value for your customers if you use affiliate schemes:

'I make no claim to publish, pack or dispatch any books at all. I just read loads, review and recommend the best, get input from authors when I'm lucky and find customers the best discounts from a basket of booksellers. Consider why you've set up your website and don't divert from that, but do add value where you can – the punters will like it and you can make some beer money.'

Guy's tips and suggestions are:

- *Keep other companies off your front page unless there's a reason not to, such as needing a graphic. Where you do use the front page, make it a pay-per-click scheme rather than a commission scheme that won't produce income unless their product is selling.*

- *Keep all affiliate schemes relevant to the topic of your website.*

- *Look for complementary rather than competing schemes.*

- *Keep any links in positions where they will appear on the first screen of information so that users don't have to scroll down to find them.*

- *Beware of US schemes – there are VAT implications.*

- *Be realistic about the returns – this is beer money, not winning the lottery.*

Guy's main website is **http://www.clapperton.co.uk**

The broker will also be able to help you ensure that you get the names in a format that you can use. The safest format to ask for is CSV (comma separated variable), which will work with most spreadsheet and word-processing programmes. You will probably need to put the list into spreadsheet format while you qualify and sort it before using it with your word-processing mail-merge feature. Some suppliers will provide lists in mail-merge format for specified word-processing packages.

Bill has a checklist for those buying mailing lists, whether direct or through a broker:

- Does it matter where the client is located?
- What contact name (job function) is needed, if any?
- Do you need telephone or fax numbers?
- How is the list you are buying compiled, and how old is it?
- Is the list owner registered for data protection?
- Is the list owner a member of the country's Direct Marketing Association? If not, think twice about employing them.

THE TELEWORKING HANDBOOK

Before you even consider the logistics of sending out your mailing, you must qualify the list. This is a tedious process which consists of telephoning the company and checking that the person on your list is indeed still the managing director, human resources manager or whatever; that you have their correct title; and that they are responsible for the area of activity you are interested in.

Be polite, patient and persistent with receptionists – they get many such calls each day and sometimes can be a bit short with the latest enquirer, whom they think is either a salesman or yet another jobseeker. If they offer to put you through to the person in question, grasp the opportunity. Briefly explain why you are contacting them and tell them you will be sending a mailing shortly. Don't get depressed if they express no interest – you've just saved yourself a wasted stamp and follow-up call.

The next step is to set up a sensible schedule for mailing and follow-up. Be realistic – most mail-outs have a very low response-rate of around 3%, so build this into your workload projections. For business-to-business services it is highly unproductive to send out several thousand mailings at once, a large proportion of which will go straight into the bin. Instead, send out small batches in stages, and follow up by telephoning again a few days after the mailing to ask whether the mailing was received, and whether they are interested in your product or service. If they are not interested, ask whether they would mind explaining why, so that you can better target your marketing in future. This approach may elicit useful information about what's wrong with your service; however, some respondents will treat this tactic as a hard-sell technique and refuse to elucidate – don't push.

For consumer or retail services, it may be more effective to use geographical mailings to all houses in a district, usually organised through the post office on a cost-per-copy basis. Such campaigns are almost always more effective if press coverage or advertising is used at the same time. Most post offices can arrange to frank large mailings for you, but normally you will have to prepare the mailings with all envelopes the right way round. For mailings of over 2000 you can use the 'Mailsort' service which considerably reduces postal costs, but is only available if the postcode is clearly included in the address labels. Some companies can act as bureau services for Mailsort. In Ireland, franked mailing is available at main sorting offices only and must be paid for in cash or by banker's draft – no cheques.

In either case, before embarking on a mailshot be sure you have costed it properly and that you have put aside resources for the follow-up, and for capturing details of any prospective customers who contact you as a result. Among the costs are:

- Mailing-list purchase.
- Time and telephone costs for qualifying the mailing list.
- Design, editing and printing of the mailshot material.

- Envelopes, laser labels and postage.
- Responding to enquiries.

As a rule of thumb, you should expect around a 10–15% response-rate if you also follow up the mailshot by phone – have you planned for the expected increase in demand for your services? If you send out 100 mailings, and you get 10 jobs as a result, will half the new contacts be wasted because you aren't able to give a timely service due to overwork?

As well as keeping track of your responses, you will need to have some method of estimating the overall conversion rate between the money you have spent on the mailing and the increased business which directly results from it.

Avoid fax shots because the level of negative reactions from people receiving unsolicited faxes outweighs the cost.

TYING UP THE LOOSE ENDS

So you've made the sale, agreed the brief for the job and the price – what next? In some situations – for example if you are working for a large company or government agency – they will probably send you two copies of a contract outlining the work, the payment schedule and other factors. You read it and sign on the dotted line if you agree, returning one copy to the customer. But for most business-to-business transactions, unless you act to ensure that there is a written agreement, the job may go ahead on an ad hoc basis which leaves you in an extremely vulnerable position.

The Irish government's Code of Practice on Teleworking suggests that you draw up your own description of the job, including the following information as appropriate.

- Clear contacts information identifying the purchaser and supplier and their addresses.
- General description of the work to be carried out, including purpose and scope, timetable, delivery format and delivery date.
- Details of the payment and payment timetable during or following the completion of the work, including VAT liability.
- Details of any systems or procedures to ensure the confidentiality and security of the work, e.g. responsibilities under the Data Protection Act.
- Statement on the ownership of any resulting copyright or intellectual property rights.
- Arrangements for loan or supply of equipment, including insurance.
- Arrangements for cover in the event of illness, incapacity, holidays or other absences, and for subcontracting if permitted.
- Quality assurance procedures. If group working is involved, identify the individual responsible for quality within the group.

It may be worthwhile to ask your solicitor to help you to draw up a 'template' contract document. Send the document to your client by fax, post or email, ask them to read it, sign a copy and return it to you to indicate their agreement before you start work. This kind of clear written agreement will help you to avoid disputes, unnecessary stress and nonpayment of bills.

Before you do sign on the dotted line, if you are dealing with a limited liability company, consider a trip to the Companies House website at **http://www.companieshouse.org.uk** It costs nothing and you can check to see how long the business has been going, and whether the accounts are overdue which could save you from a payment problem in the long run. The Thomson's Directory CD lets you see how long a company has been in the same building. Be a little suspicious of sole traders who set up as limited companies – there is generally no reason to do this other than to avoid losses due to bankruptcy. If you feel that they need you more than you need them, you might consider adding a clause into any agreement or contract stating that one of the directors of the limited liability company is personally liable for any monies owing to you in the event of company liquidation.

Keeping your customers

Working long-term for a company but not being an employee requires diplomatic, constant attention. The rule of thumb is that 80% of your new business leads will come from existing customers, so look after them! If your contact moves job or leaves, you've probably lost the contract, so if you can, try to pick up work from other people in the same company to make your position more resilient. This should be easier than approaching new companies because you already have a reference client (the first contact) to establish that you are competent and trustworthy.

Keep a good eye on corporate politics if you can – who's in, who's out, who's moving departments. Spend extra time building up relationships with new staff – go in for face-to-face meetings, and explain in detail what you are doing by email because they probably know less about the procedures in place than you do. They may also be new to managing teleworkers so you have to politely train them in what information you need so that you can get your part of the job done. Overcommunicate and reassure them of your reliability. Assess their level of competence in IT and email – if the new person only likes to deal by fax, then that is what you are going to have to use because they are the customer, even if you think it's timewasting.

Also keep your receipts – archive all email and other communications so that if there is a dispute about an instruction or any aspect of a job, you can show exactly what communication you received from the client. It's an unfortunate fact that self-employed teleworkers can end up in the middle of in-office disputes because they are in a weak position and are 'expendable'. Once people know that you always keep your receipts they are much less likely to try to scapegoat you for any problems encountered.

Cultivate receptionists, secretaries and accountancy staff – make their lives as easy as possible and ensure that they have a favourable opinion of you. Be sure you understand the client-company's purchase-order and billing systems and stick to them. If they only do one cheque-run on the last day of each month, then don't bother hassling for a cheque in the middle of the month unless there's some overriding reason why you need that money. If they require your invoices or quotations in a certain format in order to assign them to a particular cost centre in the company, make sure that that information is clearly printed on every document.

If your business is one where customers are likely to have a number of transactions, build a customer database. Give everyone a customer ID and let them know their number so that when they phone or email you can have their record in front of your immediately.

QUALITY CONTROL FOR TELEWORKERS

One of the key characteristics of successful businesses is a 'culture of quality' – the participation of all staff to ensure that the product or service delivered constantly satisfies or exceeds the customer's expectations. Most teleworkers have limited time for sales and marketing, so building strong customer relationships and encouraging repeat business makes sense.

Many small businesses carry out work at superlative levels of quality without needing to think about these issues – quality is inherent in their method of working. But as businesses get larger, or where a company is part of a more complex supply chain, then it often becomes important to address quality-management issues if consistent levels of customer satisfaction are to be achieved.

All businesses, whatever their size, should adopt some quality-management measures. This might be as simple as putting in place some basic mechanisms for carrying out the main business functions which may not necessarily be documented. At the other end of the scale, a company may use a formal, documented quality-management system (QMS) that has been audited by an independent organisation and shown to comply with a recognised standard such as ISO9000. The approach will vary depending on the nature and size of the business.

Where do I start?

The first step in putting in place a quality-control system is to understand the key processes operating within the business. Then you can put in place mechanisms to manage these processes if needed. For a self-employed teleworker, there are various key processes:

- Estimating/quotations/tendering.
- Handling of sales orders.
- Tracking the progress of work.
- Despatch and invoicing.
- Document version control.
- Checking of work before despatch.

For a one-person business operating from home, there may be no need to formally document these procedures. A simple system could be established based on a hard-copy order book, or on spreadsheets for recording and progressing enquiries and sales orders. In larger businesses where teleworkers are operating in a variety of locations and where work co-ordination is an issue, having the procedures documented and understood by everyone becomes essential. Larger businesses are also likely to have a broader range of key processes that need to be managed, such as:

- Purchasing.
- Assessment of supplier performance.
- Material inspections.
- Management of subcontractors.
- Payroll/HR.
- Project planning.
- Handling of customer returns/complaints.

Quality requirements need to be built into the working methods and procedures of the business. A properly designed quality-management system need not be a burden, but an inappropriate system can become a bureaucratic overload that is expensive for a small business to maintain. Such systems are inflexible and stifle creativity and innovation. Improving internal procedures should instead result in greater efficiency, improved customer service and improved customer satisfaction.

GLOBAL CUSTOMER CARE?

Phil Hart, formerly a UK resident, teleworks from Australia for researchers in Arizona, Australia and the UK, designing software. Over the years he has developed a number of useful techniques for keeping customers.

'About three-quarters of my time is spent at home, building and testing software. A small part of my time is spent managing my own business – IT issues, accounts and training. The remainder is spent meeting existing and potential clients.

'With larger organisations, I find it useful to assume that people do not talk to each other. If a manager tells you something significant, s/he might not have told your regular contact the same thing. Checking can save embarrassment for everybody. I also find it helps to report back to each active client on a fortnightly basis – this can be informal or formal, depending on the client organisation.

'Getting paid can require tact. When I'm working through an agency it's easy – I send in timesheets, the money appears in my bank account. When dealing directly with clients I find it helps to discuss my invoice with the client before sending it in.

'Logging time is very important – if I'm not careful, something I thought would take five minutes so I didn't need to log it can take two hours and need invoicing. But if I make a silly mistake that involves four hours of rectification work, I don't charge the client.

'You need to consciously replace being on the grapevine to pick up informal information. Also security arrangements (power protection, backups, encryption, etc.), physical resources such as hardware and software, and training, are now your responsibility. This means a data backup system, a LAN, a CD-writer, up-to-date anti-virus software and regularly visiting the websites of the big players in my specialist area to keep informed of changes and events.'

What are the quality standards?

If you feel your business needs formal certification of its quality standards, you will need to produce and apply a system that conforms to the internationally accepted quality standards, known as the ISO9000 series. The ISO standards comprise a number of model quality systems together with guidance notes indicating which quality-management system is applicable, depending on the key processes within the business. Most teleworking businesses fall under ISO9002 except for those involving design/software activities that will also need to take note of the design control requirements of ISO9001:1994.

These standards provide a useful measure of best practice, and for many companies it will be sufficient to base their quality-management system on an ISO9000 standard without going for certification. However, some customers require that an independent check or certification is made of the quality-management system. This check is usually by means of an audit carried out either by the customer or by a third party. There are a number of third-party organisations accredited by the DTI to carry out these audits and a successful audit results in your company becoming 'registered' to ISO9000.

Is quality management different for teleworkers?

In a standard industrial quality system, a company controls its subcontractors or suppliers by insisting that they deliver in accordance with a documented specification defining the scope, timescale and standards applicable to the materials or service supplied. Teleworking often relies on less formal, and more personal, relationships with customers. Many teleworkers operate on a reimbursable contract basis, receiving payment at an agreed rate for the number of hours, or days, worked. Under such arrangements, the teleworker is likely to be operating under the customer's QMS, almost as an employee, rather than working under their own quality system.

Simon Burke of ISO9001-registered company Intermec Ireland agrees that ISO9000 is probably inapplicable to individual teleworkers or very small businesses of fewer than five people. 'The effort involved and the corresponding documentation of the business processes could be enough to kill the business.' Instead, Simon recommends making sure that you can comply with your client's vendor-assessment procedures. 'A company like ours divides its purchases of goods and services into primary items that can affect the quality of our own products and services, such as software developments. Other purchases are secondary, such as office stationery and consumables. All primary goods and services must be purchased from other companies that are listed on an internal Qualified Vendor List. This list is compiled by the company, usually on the basis of a quality-related questionnaire, sometimes called a Vendor Appraisal Form. This must be completed prior to trade between the two companies. If the vendor is ISO9000-registered then there is no problem. If not, samples of goods or services will be tested, or they will be accepted through a reputable third-party recommendation. A vendor is normally on the list only for a given product or service. If a vendor is qualified to supply one item, it does not qualify them to supply everything.'

So for small teleworking businesses, the best advice may be to be aware of your client's vendor-assessment forms and make sure you can comply with their quality-management system.

Telework Association member and document image-processing consultant Geoff Preston of clickManuals Ltd also points out that by preparing documentation on your procedures as Windows Help files, you can ensure that they are easily searchable and accessible (as opposed to files gathering dust on shelves), and make them available to employees or contractors at other locations. There are a number of software products available for authoring Windows Help files including Robohelp and Doc-to-Help.

CHECKLIST

There's a lot to be considered when starting up a small business. Here's a short checklist to help you measure your progress along the way.

Plan the business

- Assess your own strengths and weaknesses, e.g. write your own CV or job application.
- Establish your business and personal goals, e.g. where do you want to be, how many hours do you want to work and how much do you need to earn?
- Assess your financial resources and sources of risk.
- Determine the startup costs.
- Decide on your business location – home?
- Identify possible business ideas.
- Do market research.
- Identify customers.
- Identify competitors.
- Identify running costs.
- Discuss your conclusions with family and other people whose advice you respect.
- Write a business plan.

Get professional advice

- Pick a solicitor.
- Choose the form of business organisation (limited company, sole trader, partnership, etc.) and register if necessary.
- Pick an accountant.
- Prepare a business plan.
- Pick a bank.
- Open a business account/apply for business loans/apply for overdraft facility.

Practical necessities

- Get insurance.
- Get business cards.
- Make sure you have planning permission for your premises if required (this is not usually an issue for single home-based teleworkers).
- Notify mortgage company and home insurer if working from home.
- Get furniture and equipment (*see* p. 292).

- Get suitable software to prepare VAT accounts (if needed) and tax accounts.
- Get memberships of relevant professional associations.
- Set a starting date and arrange your marketing plan around it.

And finally, don't forget that many large surveys, such as those run by the European Foundation for the Improvement of Living and Working Conditions, show that self-employed people work longer hours and have less access to training than those who are employed. On the other hand they have a lot more control over their time and often report higher levels of satisfaction with their working life. Is this the trade-off you want to make? Be sure to look before you leap.

8

Technology and techniques

A NOTE ON PRICES

Technology changes dramatically, and prices with it. Sample prices are only given here if they are considerably higher or lower than you might expect. Often the prices stated by equipment manufacturers in advertisements are slightly higher than the 'street prices' which you will actually have to pay. To get an idea of the likely street price, check a number of retailers' advertisements for the same product, and take an average. Web-based retailers often offer a further discount for purchases made through a website by credit card, because these sales are administratively less expensive for them. Remember that quoted prices for office products often don't include VAT.

HOW AND WHERE TO BUY

When you are deciding what to buy, try to get quotes and advice from more than one source. Do some research on the web, and talk to other users of similar equipment. Look for tips in relevant newsgroups and ask fellow subscribers for advice. We've included a checklist at the end of this chapter to help you collate and cost your equipment needs.

Pick up a computer magazine at your local newsagent. For PCs, *Personal Computer World* (**http://www.pcw.co.uk**), *Computer Shopper* (**http://www.shopper.zdnet.com**) and *PC Advisor* (**http://www.pcadvisor.co.uk**) magazines are among the best for comparing advertised prices as well as useful information. For Macs, *MacUser* (**http://www.macuser.co.uk**), *MacWorld* (**http://www.macworld.co.uk**) and *Mac Format* (**http://www.macformat.co.uk**) are good, reliable titles and carry thorough product surveys. Their websites include review articles from past editions, which can be useful, as well as message boards where you can post queries and comments.

Computers and office equipment are available from various sources:

- Independent local retailers can give you a personal service but may be relatively expensive.
- High-street chains such as Dixons.
- Computer superstores such as PC World and Compustore.
- Direct by phone or over the web from manufacturing companies such as Dell, HP and Apple.
- Direct by phone or web from retailers such as Time or other direct-sales organisations like Viking Direct, which mainly provides stationery but also sells some computers.

Buying by mail order or over the web using a credit card may protect you against defective goods or suppliers going into liquidation. On the other hand,

SCAM SCUPPERS TELEWORKING HOPES

Ann Roberts has found it extremely hard to work due to severe arthritis of the spine which restricts her movement. Although it would be easier for her to give in to her disability and spend her life on benefit, she prefers to have a job and had planned to start a teleworking service offering office work, website design, accounts and printing.

'I am doing my hardest to try to get out of this poverty trap,' she said. 'I'm not fit enough to go out to work but if I could work from home, I could work for hours. I have worked hard all my life and it's depressing and frustrating to have to live on £74 a week.'

In pursuit of her teleworking aim, Ann sent off £300 to a computer company which promised to provide a cut-price PC, printer and scanner. All Ann had to do was fill in a questionnaire once a month which the company would then sell on to its clients as market research. After two months, no PC had arrived. Ann then discovered that the company had been investigated by the Department of Trade and Industry and forced into liquidation.

'It doesn't look like I am going to get my money back. It's a lot of money to me. I wouldn't normally be suckered into anything like this. It's so galling to lose that sort of money when you can ill afford it.'

interest charges can make this an expensive method of payment if you don't clear your balance quickly. Some magazines are members of the Mail Order Protection Scheme – look for the MOPS logo – which offers you limited protection against problems with advertisers.

For complex items such as computers, a low purchase cost is no bargain if you are getting poor advice or limited after-sales service. Is onsite repair offered, or will you have to bear the expense of returning the equipment for repair? Is there a guaranteed response time? What is the service offered beyond the standard guarantee period (usually 60 or 90 days)? Some computer dealers offer access to technical support through premium-rate telephone lines, but manufacturers like Dell offer low-cost phone support if you can supply your customer reference number.

Consider whether you should rent or lease equipment, or buy it outright; the first two options are more expensive in total cash terms, but your accountant may decide it will save you more tax, and if money is tight at first, it reduces your startup costs. If you buy, then you pay upfront and you can only claim a percentage of that cost each year (around a quarter) against tax. If you buy you will also probably need to negotiate a loan with your bank to cover the purchase cost upfront. If you rent or lease, the whole amount can be claimed against tax, and you do not have to stump up large amounts of money upfront. However, there are complexities – you don't actually own the equipment,

OUR SIXPENNYWORTH FOR SUCCESS WHEN BUYING AND USING PCS

Here are our tips for buying and using PCs, based on 29 years of hard experience.

- *Accept that you're not going to get it right 100% of the time. We have had both good and bad experiences with direct sales operations like Dell, and with local dealers. Unfortunately this is one area where past performance is not much of a guide to future results.*

- *Try to anticipate the future. If in doubt as to whether or not you'll need something (e.g. more hard disk space) get it built into the new PC because it will cost more and cause more disruption to retro-fit it.*

- *Assume that it will take you at least 40 hours, spread over a period of weeks, to specify, finance, order, chase up, install and completely customise a new PC for your purposes – researching magazines, comparing prices, dealing with the bank or leasing company, backing up and moving data, creating shortcuts, getting everything just so. The chances are the lost earning hours spent doing this will cost as much as the PC itself.*

- *Always take at least two backups before moving data onto a new PC.*

- *Never load games on your work machine.*

- *Avoid clever little utilities that you can download free off the web or get given by friends unless they are really clever – they usually turn out to be the thing that's causing the crashes, data problems, etc.*

- *Use up-to-date virus software which you can update regularly from a website. It is professionally very embarrassing to find you have passed on a virus to a customer or client. Set Outlook so it doesn't preview attachments, and delete any email with an attachment that you weren't expecting.*

- *Get a utilities programme such as Norton Utilities to help you tidy up after system crashes and for moving programmes.*

- *Learn how to use data synchronisation utilities like Windows Briefcase – this can provide a 'belt and braces' extra backup facility if you also have a second office computer, as many experienced teleworkers do.*

- *Check out PC support suppliers in your area. Sometimes no phone helpline, however good, can replace the effectiveness of paying someone by the hour to come in and haul you out of trouble.*

- *Have a plan (like an arrangement with a teleworking neighbour) for what you're going to do if the hard disk crashes or the printer jams irrevocably when you're working to a deadline, or the electricity board helpfully decides to cut your power off for the day.*

- *If you can afford it, have multiple methods of getting online (e.g. ISDN and a dial-up modem, a Hotmail or Freeserve account and a business dial-up account) to ensure you can stay in contact.*

- *Keep spare stock of printer cartridges, disks, backup tapes, etc. at all times.*

though there is usually a method of buying it at the end of the lease. Leases do provide a degree of security – usually they can't be withdrawn or curtailed by credit squeezes or changes in economic conditions, and are not repayable on demand like an overdraft. To work out the best option for you, consult your financial adviser and bank.

Many equipment purchases have hidden costs. Printers require expenditure on toner and paper; mobile phones and portable PCs often require extra sets of batteries to maximise their usefulness. If you're travelling abroad, you'll need power and telecoms adapters for any portable equipment. These costs are often impossible to assess precisely as your use of the equipment will change over time, but an informed estimate will save you some unpleasant shocks.

MOBILES, MESSAGING AND PDAS

Cordless phones

These handsets allow you to roam around within about 100 metres of the base station, able to answer the phone speedily without your client knowing that you were watering the garden, not sitting at your desk. Cordless headset phones that free your hands for keyboard work or to reach up to that awkward file are also now available (double-check that the handset you've ordered is the correct model that will work with the headset – they usually need two additional connection points. There is a useful table of cordless handset features at **http://www.freedom-mobiles.co.uk/dect.htm** and **http://www.headsetco.co.uk**). If the wireless technology Bluetooth ever gets off the ground it's possible that cordless headsets may even become fashion accessories – Motorola already has a slinky offering on the market.

Mobile phones and PDAs

Mobile phone charges are continually reducing but can be pricey if you opt for a pre-paid 'ready to go' type of phone. Most services offer a choice of connection or 'airtime' contracts, ranging from a low basic charge with high charges for each individual call, to a high standing-charge offset by lower call rates. This is one area too complex and fast-moving for detailed coverage in a book, but it pays to be more than usually suspicious of advertising. Try to imagine in advance how many hours per month you'll typically be using a mobile, and calculate costs of the different contracts on this basis. Watch out for hidden higher costs of dialling people on other mobile networks.

Most mobile phones can accept the SMS (short message service) text messages of up to 160 characters. SMS can automatically alert a remote worker when email has arrived in the office, and is considerably cheaper than voice GSM calls.

Matching your up mobile with a personal digital assistant (PDA) can provide a perfect toolset for remote workers. You can use the phone as normal, send and receive SMS messages, and download Internet content into the PDA – either via a GSM modem card that fits into a PCMCIA type II or III slot, or through built-in GSM or GPRS capabilities. PDAs have a much lower power consumption than laptops, and weigh a lot less. Their main limitation is that their keyboards are tiny or in some cases non-existent. If you also invest in an add-on keyboard, many of the recent PDAs can actually be used as a laptop replacement as long as all you need is basic word-processing/email/contacts-database/spreadsheet functions. *See* **http://www.thinkoutside.com** and **http://www.gotype.com** for keyboards that work with PDAs.

Offerings in this area include the Palm Computing range (PDAs providing a contacts database, email and diary facilities, with greyscale or colour screens, and typically between 2 Mb and 8 Mb of RAM). The Palm machines also have a 'synchronising cradle' to connect them to a desktop PC, ensuring that the data carried around is always the most current version. Palm machines can communicate with mobile phones via an infrared port. There are also offerings from companies like HP and Toshiba that use the PocketPC operating system (a cut-down version of Windows). Some PDAs can double as phones (these are sometimes called 'combos' or even smartphones) such as the Nokia Communicator. PDAs range in price from around £180 to £500.

One to watch is the Blackberry GPRS always-on wireless device which looks like a large pager with a keyboard (*see* p. 107). This device can be programmed with special applications using Java, and has proved extremely popular with mobile teleworkers. However, overall PDAs have been suffering from a drop in sales in the past couple of years and there is no consensus yet on whether and how the pocket PC and mobile phone markets may combine.

Unified messaging

A number of services now provide seamless or 'unified' messaging for people on the move, through the use of personal numbers and other technologies. Unified messaging provides access to voice, email and fax from anywhere using any device at any time. Usually the messages are compiled into a single 'inbox' that can be accessed from a PC or by telephone. Various options are available, such as listening to a recording of an email message and then returning the call by voice. Many use SMS to send alerts to a mobile phone whenever a message arrives at the inbox.

Telephone chargecards

If you travel around frequently, think about a low-tech piece of technology – the telephone chargecard, offered by most major telephone companies. This can be used both in public cardphones and on any private telephones where you wish the call-charge to be made to your own account rather than to that phone (useful when your mobile has unexpectedly died). International chargecards are also available, though some transfer the bill to your credit-card account rather than to your phone bill. Ordinary credit cards can also be used in many British and foreign payphones.

COMPUTERS

Computers change so quickly that it is never the perfect time to buy the perfect machine, and there are two schools of thought that both claim to minimise the disadvantages. One is that you should buy the most powerful computer you can afford, as you will always outstrip its capacity during its lifetime. The other is that if you require your computer to perform relatively simple tasks, it is not necessary to go for the latest technology, and secondhand or low-specification computers provide a substantial cost saving.

Part of the argument rests on the rapid depreciation of computer equipment – in accounting terms, a computer which is more than three years old is likely to be worthless. However, recent increases in processing power have extended computer lives a little. But even when you've only had the machine a year, and it is still useful to you, in monetary terms its value will have plummeted. This factor weighs towards the 'buy expensive' option – an expensive computer may still be useful to you after three years, whereas a cheap computer not only has no financial value but becomes obsolete in practical terms more quickly because it is old and slow. Buying firsthand also often means that you get some quite powerful software bundled in which would cost a lot to purchase individually. On the other hand, if your resources are limited, you probably have no choice but to go for the 'buy cheap or secondhand' option.

Another issue to consider is plain old one-upmanship. If you work in a technology field, you may, for the purposes of credibility, need to keep up with the latest stuff whether or not you really need it. In reality, the easiest way to buy a computer is first to consider the software you'll need and not the computer itself – the programs with which you and your PC can actually accomplish something. Decide what task you want the computer to do, identify the software that does it, and then buy a suitable computer on which to run that software – at the same time making sure that it will be easy to add other software, extra memory and other enhancements to it. This is easy advice to follow if you are using specialist software such as CAD drafting packages, but if your needs are fairly general, you will find the major software packages for word processing, desktop publishing and so on are supported on almost all computers, so you may still find the choice confusing.

The good news is that you can now buy a firsthand computer with an impressive technical specification for under £1000. These machines will handle applications such as spreadsheets and databases with relative comfort. Machines costing less than £1000 will usually have 'budget' processors, and less memory cache. They will not be able to load software packages as fast as the more expensive processors, and won't perform as well with number crunching or graphics applications as their more expensive big brothers.

Start by reviewing whether you need a laptop (more expensive) or whether you will be able to do what you need to do with a desktop. Then check out the websites of computer manufacturers such as Dell, IBM and HP as most contain good support material to help you come to a decision. By comparing the configurations and prices on different websites you will be able to collate a list of questions (such as, do I need a DVD-ROM drive?) which you can then find answers to on the computer magazine websites. Most manufacturer websites now have pages where you can 'configure' (choose options) for your PC and see instantly how this will affect the price. Before you buy from a website, try taking your specification to a local dealer or a high-street store in order to get an idea of their offerings and prices.

Portable computing

Portables (laptops or notebooks) are standard for mobile workers. Consider the weight of the whole device, including cables, spare batteries, carrying case, etc. if you will be doing a lot of travelling. Seven pounds may not sound like much but feels a lot heavier when you've toted it through three airports. Recharging mobile batteries can become a chore; check how long the batteries will last between recharges and if necessary get a second battery – they tend to die before the machine itself and can be hard to obtain except when making the original purchase. After all, isn't the reason why you are buying a notebook because you're looking for a road-warrior machine? If you will be moving between home, office and travel, consider getting docking stations to provide larger keyboards and screens when you want to carry out concerted periods of work. Many companies now provide docking stations for laptops in their 'touchdown' or 'hotdesking' facilities. Where money is tight, look at using 'port replicators' rather than docking stations.

Unravelling the jargon

The operating system or 'platform'

This is the software supplied with the computer that manages its basic functions. Most likely, your choice will be between Windows XP, Windows 2000 and the Apple Mac OS, although the 'free' operating system Linux is currently the dark horse approaching fast on the inside rail. The difference between operating systems is much like that between petrol and diesel fuel: though they do much the same things, they do them in entirely different ways, and you can no more use a program written for the Mac OS operating system on a Windows PC than you can run a diesel car on unleaded. (OK, you can run Windows on a Mac, but only if it has plenty of processing power and a special emulation programme installed.)

The processor type

The central processing unit (CPU) chip is the 'brains' of the computer and powers all that it does. Intel produces over 90% of the world's PC processors, and most PC users currently buy a Pentium 4 processor with a special instruction set for improving streaming media and better graphics.

The processor speed

Gordon Moore created Moore's Law in 1965 – it says that processor power for computers doubles every 18–24 months. So far it has held. The faster the speed, measured in MHz, the more expensive, and usually the better the performance. Before you go mad on processor speed, bear in mind that if your software has not been developed to use the greater speed it won't make much difference to you. But if you use graphic-intensive software such as Photoshop or CAD packages a lot, go for the highest speed you can afford. It's wise to try out real-world tests of the sort of work you normally do, or to speak to a good dealer. In some situations, a PC with a lower processor speed but more RAM may actually go 'faster' – it depends what you're asking it to do. Graphics cards and hard disks also affect performance.

The RAM or memory

Measured in megabytes (Mb), this – along with the processor specification – is the vital determinant of a computer's speed and its capability to run the latest software. A standard offering now is 128 Mb but get as much as you can afford. It won't go to waste and it will extend the computer's lifespan.

The hard disk size

Measured in gigabytes, hard disks have become enormous. It is not surprising to find a 40 Gb hard disk in a computer now, and the standard offering is 20 Gb. That shouldn't prevent you from managing to fill the hard disk with 'useful stuff' long before the computer's useful life has expired.

CD-ROM drive

CD-ROM drives in computers are rapidly being replaced by DVD-ROM drives, though they remain standard in most laptop PCs. Also, most software packages are still distributed on CD-ROM. A CD-ROM can store about 650 Mb of data. The key thing to look for is the speed. Recent drives are '40 speed' – 40 times the speed of the first ones. Ordinary CD-ROM drives will only read data. If you want to write to CDs you will need a CD-recordable drive, though these come as standard with some more expensive PCs. A basic CD recordable drive (CD-RW) costs around £100 but is cheaper if you buy it configured into a new PC than as a standalone.

DVD-ROM drive

DVD stands for Digital Versatile Disk. DVDs use smaller tracks than CDs and so can store much more data. These narrower tracks need special lasers to read them so they are not directly compatible with CD-ROMs or with audio CDs. DVD-ROM drives in PCs have two lasers – one reads the DVD data and the other CD data, so that the drive in a PC is backwards compatible with CDs. DVD disks hold about 4.7 Gb of data – around seven times more than a CD-ROM – and can store a full-length movie.

External storage

External hard disks or magneto-optical drives can provide space to backup data from your PC or to help you transfer data to other people. Many PCs come with a Zip drive – there are various different capacities from 100 Mb to 750 Mb. Floppy disks are still built into most PCs, but their days are numbered. Tape drives are still vital for regular backup devices that can accept a copy of your entire hard disk. New forms of storage include a variety of minidiscs and memory sticks. Try to stick with the mainstream forms of data storage otherwise in ten years time you will have large archives of data on formats for which there is no longer any drive available to read the stored information.

Screen (monitor)

If you are going to be spending long hours at your PC, a large screen with good resolution is vital: 17-inch is now standard, but 19-inch is more comfortable.

Another option to consider, if you have the budget, is an LCD screen (flat panel screen) which can save a lot of space in a cramped home office – they have reduced in price recently. In the end, it will be a compromise between space, screen resolution and size, and price.

Another option if space is limited is an all-in-one PC which packs everything – display, storage, motherboard, etc. – into one single unit. The iMac and IBM's NetVista X series are examples of this approach.

Peripherals and other add-ons

Printers

Choose a printer based on what and how often you want to print. Letters, bills and reports will probably be needed regularly and only require a black-and-white printer; while greetings cards, invitations, photographs and posters may be occasional items which need colour. Strangely, if you need both, it may actually be cheaper to buy two printers – a standard laser printer for the black-and-white work and an inkjet or similar for the colour work. Look at the cost of consumables, and the speed of the printer when making your decision, and have some idea of how many pages you are likely to want to print each month.

If your home office is small, you may prefer to get a combined scanner, copier, printer and fax machine, also known as a multi-function device or MFD for short. In the past MFDs tended to be a little unreliable – usually being good at one or two functions and fairly average at the others – but they have improved markedly in recent times. Again, you'll need to decide between monochrome, laser high-volume models or colour, inkjet, lower-volume models. You may need a second mobile printer that you can take with you if you are travelling – battery-operated inkjets or bubblejets are available for less than £300.

If you are doing professional desktop publishing or graphics, you will need a PostScript-compatible printer – these models are slightly more expensive than standard printers. You might also want to consider an A3 model for printing large layouts.

Networks

A small network can increase productivity in a home or small office where more than one computer is in use, by allowing file and printer sharing, internal email and the division of Internet bandwidth equally among users. You will need network cards for each PC, which are available from a wide range of manufacturers. These cards fit into a free PCI or ISA slot in a desktop PC, or into a PCMCIA slot on a laptop PC. Prices vary from £25 to £60 depending on the manufacturer.

To connect two PCs together, a thin piece of Ethernet cabling, two T-connectors and two terminators are required, which can be picked up from electronics stores and catalogues. This is known as a cross-over cable. To connect more than two PCs you will need switches and hubs. A switch reads the destination of each packet of data and forwards it to the correct port on the hub.

The hub is a collection of ports which act as a connection point for different devices on the network. Each PC is connected to the hub or switch, which then acts as a gateway connecting to the Internet, or to a local area network (LAN), thus forming a wide area network (WAN). For under £100 is possible to buy an eight-port 10/100mbit/s auto switching hub, which allows a network of PCs to be built up. 3Com's OfficeConnect FastEthernet Networking kit provides everything that you need to connect four or more PCs to a network. The kit includes two 10/100 network interface cards, a four-port hub, Ethernet cables and networking software.

If you have access to a broadband Internet connection, you could also consider a broadband router, which connects several computers to either an ADSL or a cable modem connection. The better models include a basic firewall and network address translation facilities (NAT). Expect to pay around £200. Similar devices can be used to share ISDN connections.

Wi-Fi in the home

Another attractive option for a home office is a wireless network. Intel's Anypoint connection system costs as little as £100 and can offer wireless network connections between PCs at distances of up to 45 metres within the home using 10 Mb/second USB connections – but most network hardware companies also offer competing products. The Windows XP operating system supports wireless networking.

Modems

New desktop PCs, and most laptops, come with a 56k modem already installed (an internal modem). Think through what you are planning to use for your Internet connectivity. It is always a good idea to get a PC with a standard dial-up modem because even if you plan to get DSL or ISDN, there will be times when your system isn't working and you need to resort to the good old-fashioned dial-up modem. Generally the faster types of Internet connectivity just plug into the USB port on your computer, but check who is supplying the modem for satellite, DSL or ISDN, how it connects to your computer, and whether it can be operated alongside an old-fashioned dial-up connection.

Fax

The spread of email is gradually making fax redundant – especially standalone fax machines which are being replaced both by fax modems in PCs and by combined fax/printer/scanner/copier devices. If you go for a PC-based fax, remember that while you can receive faxes containing graphics, you won't be able to send graphics unless they are artwork already on your computer, or unless you have a scanner to read in a hand-drawn graphic.

Scanners

Scanners are used for three purposes: to scan text, to scan line graphics such as logos; and to scan photographs. For text scanning, you will need a flatbed scanner with an automatic feeder, and OCR (optical character reading) software. Text scanning works well on clean, typed manuscripts. It does not cope well with heavily edited typescripts, or with handwriting (yet). For scanning line graphics such as simple company logos, a cheap flatbed scanner will be sufficient. To scan photographs at high resolution you need a high-quality scanner, and specialist knowledge of printing processes such as halftoning to get best results. For colour reproduction, expensive colour separation drum scanners are used. These are normally provided on a bureau basis by reprographics or typesetting companies. Standard desktop colour scanners do not provide sufficiently good quality for high-volume colour printing, although they are excellent for adding interest to short-print-run documents such as report covers, local newsletters and brochures.

Digital cameras

Anyone involved in the publishing area is likely to benefit from the ability to take their own pictures and use them in publications. For reviews and advice on purchase try **http://www.vnunet.com/Products/Hardware/Camera** or **http://www.image-acquire.com**

Web cams

Unless you have a high-speed Internet connection, web cams are really more of a gimmick than a business tool. They are certainly inexpensive and can be used with a wide variety of software, but with a standard dial-up connection the refresh rate for a moving image is really too slow to provide anything but the novelty of transferring images. Expect this area to expand rapidly once broadband Internet connections become more widespread.

Software

Getting suitable software is just as important as buying the right computer, and it would be impossible to do justice to such a complex subject here. There are thousands of packages in existence, and most are updated every year or so with new versions.

You may wish to avoid being used as an unpaid software tester by the manufacturing companies. To avoid the worst software bugs, don't buy new versions of software until they have been on the market for three to six months, at which stage patches will be available to fix the bugs which all those other people discovered to their cost.

'Office' suites

The most popular business applications are usually included in the price of higher-priced desktop PCs, as bundled 'office' suites providing all the basic software functions that most businesses will need. Microsoft leads the way with Office while Lotus and Corel are worthy but trailing competitors with their Smartsuite and WordPerfect suites. Less expensive PCs tend to include a version of Microsoft Works suite which includes word processing, a basic spreadsheet programme, home management, graphics and reference software. Which is fine until you need to send your Works file to someone who uses one of the business standard suites such as Office, produced by the same manufacturer, and you have the deep joy of trying to convert your files to a usable format. Not recommended.

Graphics

Graphics software is slightly different from DTP in that it's usually employed to create or manipulate single images or illustrations, such as logos or cover designs, rather than entire publications. There is a vast gap between hobbyist and professional-level software, and knowledge of printing processes is required to get best final results. The best-known professional packages are Corel Draw, Adobe Illustrator and Macromedia Freehand. For preparing Internet graphics, the most widely used professional packages are Macromedia Fireworks and Adobe Photoshop.

Because of the wide range of graphics packages which have been developed there is also a wide range of graphics file formats. It is worth knowing that the professional illustration packages such as Adobe Illustrator provide quite an effective way of transferring graphics from one format to another when this is needed. Another trick is to import the recalcitrant graphic into a professional desktop-publishing package like QuarkXPress and then export the whole layout page, including the graphic – usually this can provide a method of conversion to .pdf or .eps formats.

Avoid drawing complex graphics in Microsoft Word unless it is unlikely you will ever need to use them except as part of Word documents, as it is almost impossible to successfully export Word Art files to other formats.

Groupware

Groupware tools are used to help people collaborate over a network or over the Internet. Groupware facilities can include editing of documents by multiple authors, shared electronic diaries, contacts databases, email conferencing, task lists, access to networked databases and electronic forms (e.g. to record customer contacts).

COMPUTER SECURITY

Anti-virus software

Anti-virus programmes now also rely on 'heuristic' technologies, which means that they look for virus-type behaviour.

There are well-known commercial packages such as Symantec Antivirus which will provide almost complete protection for your PC. With online facilities such as Symantec's LiveUpdate available over the Internet, anti-virus protection can be constantly updated to guard against recently invented viruses for a nominal fee. A single occurrence of a computer virus could damage vital data and, if you passed it onto a client, might cost you your good name.

Data security

Teleworking changes information-security risks for companies. Allowing remote access requires a company effectively to extend their network to the teleworker's home, or to provide them with a method of updating centrally held files such as databases via modems or ISDN connections.

The risk to data security depends on the value and sensitivity of the data being handled. Start by reviewing existing procedures and identifying processes which introduce an additional hazard by virtue of being remote. Procedures should cover the use of PCs, remote access to central computing facilities, data transmission, backup procedures (data integrity) and viruses.

In the old days (before broadband), the main risk to most corporate networks was teleworkers bringing floppy disks from their home PCs into work which carried computer viruses. Now the advent of ADSL Internet connections in the home which are 'always on' provides a juicy target for hackers who have longer connection sessions in which to target a particular PC. The PC is also often assigned the same IP number for its connection on a broadband connection, in contrast to dial-up Internet connections which are assigned a dynamic (changing) IP number for each connection session. The latest Windows and Mac operating systems, Windows XP and Mac OS-X, contain built-in firewalls which will no doubt become built-in challenges for the next generation of hackers. Firewalls are filters on all incoming and outgoing data which operate according to predetermined rules, designed to prevent most hacker-attacks. Most are not set on by default when you switch on a new machine – configuration can be complex and is best handled by an expert.

The proliferation of inexpensive wireless (WiFi) networks in company buildings, and even of WiFi hotspots in public places, can also increase security risks. Any PC fitted with a WiFi card will automatically seek out and connect to any base station within range (which can be up to several hundred metres). Standard WiFi installations do not even switch on the basic security supplied with the system, known as WEP. WEP itself has caused some security headaches, and can be cracked with effort, but something is better than

KEEPING THOSE EMAIL VIRUSES AWAY

Eric Chien, Chief Researcher for Symantec, gives this advice: 'The first line of defence is a bit of common sense. Be cautious about emails from people you don't know. I would delete attachments from anonymous users, and even where you know the sender, be suspicious – did you expect to receive an attachment? Remember that in general it is only by opening attachments that you will run into problems.'

If you use Microsoft Outlook and you receive a message you are not sure you want to open, it is worth right-clicking the message header and choosing 'Options'. This allows you to look at the header of the message – which shows you the return address, and the route by which it made its way to your computer. This extra information will often help you decide whether to delete the email unopened – either because you think it might have a virus, or because you think it's timewasting spam.

Helpline Computer's Sue Phillips adds: 'Never boot your computer from a floppy disk unless you personally created it, write-protected it and it has been hidden in your sock drawer ever since; and never open a document with macros enabled.'

In summary, Eric advises:

- *Only open attachments that you expect to receive.*

- *Keep your virus software updated regularly.*

- *Set up your virus software to detect viruses arriving by email.*

- *Scan your entire hard disk for viruses on a regular basis.*

- *Keep an eye on your web interface software (browser).*

Our editorial team add that you should watch out for anything with no subject line, or with 'Re: (blank)', as there is a good chance it has been generated by a virus replicating itself on someone else's system. Also look out for general subjects like 'About your message' or 'We thought you'd like this'. A recent sneaky tactic is to emulate the standard messages which appear when your email to someone else bounces (e.g. messages that appear to come from 'Postmaster' or '@mailer-daemon'. In Outlook, right-click the suspect message and choose Options to read the message header before opening such files, especially if they have attachments.

nothing. Companies are advised both to ensure this system is switched on, and to register the unique media access control (MAC) addresses of the WiFi network interface cards in laptops that access their WiFi networks. It is also recommended that WiFi base stations should not be located on external walls as they will then be broadcast outside the building. In terms of their network architecture, they should be placed 'outside' the corporate firewall.

Other increased security risks are posed by laptops which may have been 'got at' by hackers or computer viruses while connected from home, and which are then brought into company premises and logged on to the company network 'inside' the corporate firewall where they can 'sniff' for corporate user IDs and passwords or carry out further attacks. As a result, large companies with significant numbers of remote workers are tending to install personal firewalls on all PCs – distributing and extending the firewall protection to machines which are taken offsite.

Although security threats often daunt IT staff when faced with implementing a telework programme, they should not be discouraged because there are a wide range of suitable products available ranging from the inexpensive to the bullet-proof. In all cases it is important to carry out a risk assessment in order to balance the budget required with the appropriate security technology to reduce the risk. One pragmatic approach to the problem may be to specify that certain tasks may not be teleworked – their associated data must remain within the company offices.

Companies normally require teleworkers to secure their computers with access passwords, so that the machine cannot be used at all except by someone who knows the correct password to enter as the machine boots up. Passwords can also be individually applied to sensitive files to prevent unauthorised access. Blanking screen savers which switch in whenever a PC is not in active use are another common device to try to minimise the risks of people overlooking sensitive information on computer screens in public places. Unfortunately, most people don't change their password until forced to, and it is not unusual to find passwords written on yellow stickies attached to the computer casing.

A teleworker who stores email messages and other documents on their laptop's hard drive can present a risk to information security if the laptop is stolen or lost. One way to reduce this risk is to encrypt sensitive data so that only authorised users with access keys can unlock and decrypt the data. Typically, an extra drive letter is created on the laptop. Any file saved to that drive is automatically encrypted and cannot be accessed without the relevant password. Normally only data files are encrypted (reports, spreadsheets, emails, etc.). If software products like the Microsoft Office applications are also encrypted, there is a significant deterioration in the speed at which they operate.

One such encryption product is SafeHouse, available from **http://www.pcydynamics.com** Of course, users often forget passwords, which requires there to be a remote method of resetting the password, usually based around an encryption of the machine's serial number and often involving considerable expenditure of time by the company helpdesk.

Company networks can offer some protection by first identifying users through passwords when they log on, and subsequently restricting their accounts to allow them to read and write data only to certain areas of a network. But in many cases simple 'user authorisation' is not enough.

Where the company provides remote access via modem or ISDN, anyone in possession of the company's remote access number can try to connect. The standard telephone system (PSTN) allows no real checks to determine the identity of the user. ISDN has two checks – Caller Line ID and also Chap/PaP (machine handshakes which confirm that the caller is allowed to make a connection). This can confirm the identity of the remote computer through which the connection is being made, but still does not prove the identity of the person who is using the remote computer.

User IDs and passwords are usually stored in the dial-up networking software of the desktop or laptop, so using a password to identify an individual is meaningless. If the PC is stolen and sold on, the person receiving the stolen machine could try the dial-up networking and would find that the access number, user ID and password were all saved in the machine – thus an unauthorised person might gain access. Passwords are also fairly easy to crack, and if cracked, the computer system has no way of determining who is a legitimate user – all it sees is the authorised username and password.

To overcome these difficulties many companies now ensure that a method of strong authentication is used for remote access to networks. This involves two pieces of information to identify the user. Typically, in addition to knowing a password or PIN number, the user has to carry some form of physical token (such as a card, or a device that can display numbers) which creates one-off passwords. The combination of both pieces of information (the user's PIN and the one-off password) is much harder for unauthorised users to simulate.

MICROSOFT SOURCE CODE HACKED VIA TELEWORKER'S PC

A top news story in 2000 was the successful attack by a hacker on the Microsoft network. The intruder used a hacker tool known as the QAZ Trojan which allegedly emailed stolen passwords from an employee's home machine to a drop point in Russia.

There is some confusion about the exact details, but it appears that the Microsoft network may at that time have been protected only by static passwords, rather than through the use of strong authentication methods such as access tokens. It was also a matter of speculation that the employee's home PC did not have up-to-date anti-virus software in place.

There are two types of two-factor authentication systems: time-based and challenge-response. Time-based authentication systems generate a password every 60 seconds that is valid for only one minute. This means that a user must send the password over the network within that time period in order to gain access to the system. The market leader in this area is RSA Security Inc's SecurID card. Each card has a unique identifier known to the server to be linked to a specific user/password combination. Using this identifier and a very accurate timing device, the card generates a random number every minute, which the server can match. So for a period of 60 seconds, if user ID, password and the number displayed on the SecurID card match, the user can be authorised to log on to the network.

Challenge-response systems generate a Data Encryption Standard (DES) encrypted password good only for a single use. DES is harder to defeat than other security methods, since passwords are dynamic, and they are good for travelling workers who may use different computers from different locations. Schlumberger, a company that specialises in highly confidential maps and databases of oil-well information, has a high-security system where all PCs require a smart-card physically sitting in a smart-card reader attached to a PC to be in place, as well as certificate authentication challenges (requests for username and a DES password) every 15 minutes – distracting but highly secure. In addition, applications reside only on corporate servers and cannot be placed on remote machines.

One form of security that is now 'out of fashion' is dial-back. In this system the user would dial in and give a username and password. The network would then disconnect and dial back to a pre-defined telephone number for that person. This had the advantage of ensuring that the telephone costs were picked up by the company, but the disadvantage that it only worked for people based in one place (e.g. at home), and not for roving teleworkers. However, with current telephone systems it is now simple to redirect the dial-back number to another location and an unauthorised machine, so this method is not considered secure.

Many small businesses use the Symantec software PC Anywhere to connect to remote PCs directly via a dial-up modem. This can be a practical remote-access solution for very small organisations, and allows you to 'take over' the remote machine, running all the programmes and retrieving any data you have forgotten to take with you. However, this is not a very secure method of access when only a simple username and password are in use.

People now telework from home, from hotel rooms, on trains and at client premises, so the requirements for flexibility and reduced telecoms costs have increased. Some large telecoms and IT companies have established themselves as providers of global 'points of presence' or POPs for connecting people to corporate networks. Using Virtual Private Networking (VPN) the teleworkers can establish a secure link from their laptop or desktop PC, through the POP and right into a dedicated box or server on their company network. VPN uses advanced cryptography to establish the point-to-point connection and encrypt all data during transit, preventing other users of the POPs from 'eavesdropping'.

The encryption systems use keys which reside on the company's host servers and on the teleworker's machines and are not generally available, so many companies only use a password to authenticate VPN links. As before, this can be risky since you are identifying the computer, but not the person who is using the machine – VPNs also need to be bolstered by the 'strong authentication' methods described above. Many VPN products also include firewall capabilities. Unfortunately, VPN takes a heavy toll on performance when used to connect to a network remotely. Sometimes this results in unusably slow response times.

A solution which is increasing in popularity is to use what are known as 'corporate portal solutions'. These provide much of the functionality required by remote users but do not actually allow them direct access to the network. Normally the user logs in to a web page using 128 bit SSL encryption (and sometimes also strong authentication). Applications are delivered through the web browser. Companies which provide these type of solutions include Novell, Yahoo, Ericsson and PeopleSoft. Yahoo has quite a comprehensive offering including consulting, software-development and hosted/management arrangements.

There are also managed outsourced solutions run by companies such as AT&T and Fiberlink. The users connect through POPs provided by the solution-providers into a VPN. Fiberlink's product also supports PDAs. However, at the moment these type of solutions tend to be prohibitively expensive unless you have 150 or more remote users.

Other security issues

The Telework Association's contacts with members indicate that you should also consider the following security risks:

KEEP LAYERING-ON THE SECURITY

If a teleworker allows their PC to become virus-infected, or utilised by a hacker, and that teleworker has access to a company network, then the remote PC can act as a 'back door' allowing access to the company network. These risks are increasing as broadband always-on Internet connections become more common, and as the number of apparently speculative attacks on computers connected to the Internet (even through dial-up connections) increases.

Jon Willert, a computer security expert with 15 years' experience, has an excellent article on the comprehensive and informative specialist security SANS Institute website, covering security practices for telecommuters (see **http://rrr.sans.org** and look in the Home Office section). In his view the key point is to have lots of different layers of security. The article makes the point that all the layers must be properly configured and updated regularly. Jon recommends:

1. *Use current anti-virus software and change the default settings to ensure that all files are checked, not just program files and documents* (e.g. Norton Antivirus **http://www.symantec.com**).
2. *Use a software-based personal firewall (e.g. Zone Alarm* **http://www.zonelab.com**).
3. *Use a router/firewall device for your Internet connection.*
4. *Update your operating system with security patches – see* **http://www.microsoft.com/privacy/safeinternet/security/best_practices/ updates.htm**
5. *Update your applications with security patches.*
6. *Keep updating your own skills and knowledge on security issues.*

Of these steps, the only expensive or difficult one is number 3, as it requires some knowledge to select and configure the firewall device, and the equipment costs between $200 and $850. Jon suggests you look for devices and software that are certified by ICSA Labs (**http://www.icsalabs.com/**).

Jon also recommends testing your computer security using facilities at sites like **http://www.dslreports.com** or **http://www.sonicwall.com** 'These tests should not be able to penetrate your layered security and should produce timely and easy-to-understand alerts!'

- Employees or colleagues who might set up in competition with you. Use password-protection systems on your computer or network. Keep a close eye on what is being taken in and out of the office.
- Children who may gain access to your computer. Access-control software is needed to protect business-related files and directories – it's easy for play to accidentally delete or alter files.
- Stationery that could be misused (for example, you might have a

pharmaceutical company's headed paper that could be used to obtain samples of controlled substances). Lock it up if necessary.

■ Physical damage both to computer systems and to backed-up data. Store a set of data backups offsite (at the central office site, or if you are self-employed, with a friend) lest fire, theft or flood should destroy both computer and backups.

■ Shredding of confidential paper waste or erasure of old disks. Don't allow sensitive material to end up on your local council dump. Take measures to ensure appropriate destruction or storage. If you are selling on or giving away old computers, ensure that data has been thoroughly erased, not just deleted (in which case it can still be retrieved).

Keeping data up to date – synchronisation

Most teleworkers who use more than one computing device need to carry out two synchronisation tasks. First, they need to be sure that they are working on the most current version of that vital report, database or account. Second, they need to keep their personal-organiser information up to date – contacts databases, diaries, 'to do' lists and so on – as they switch from one device to another.

Internet security websites abound with tales of the temporary student employee who synchronised his PDA with the corporate address book and overwrote several thousand contacts with details of his friends and family. Such stories are mostly apocryphal, but they do point out the need for procedures that maintain the integrity of important information while allowing updates from different sources. Typically, a remote user will be able to update their own personal contacts database on their office PC, but will not have access rights to change any centrally held network information.

It is also normal for corporate networks to have effective anti-virus software, so that a machine which has become virus-infected while in use outside the office cannot be brought in and 'synchronised' with the network, allowing further infection to take place.

For many people who have a laptop and a PC, the Windows Briefcase facility can do the trick in ensuring that crucial files are up to date, and its use is clearly explained in the Windows helpfiles. If your computers aren't directly connected, then the night before you are due to work at home, you copy all the files you'll need into the briefcase, and then copy the briefcase onto a transferrable medium such as a Zip disk or CD-ROM. When you get home, you put the briefcase onto the home PC, work on those files, and at the end of the day, copy the briefcase back onto the disk. Back in the office, you copy the briefcase across and then tell Windows to update with the files in the briefcase. If you are able to dock your laptop or otherwise connect the two computers together, there are some automatic synchronisation options available and these should be selected with care (otherwise your logons can become painfully slow while the system checks and updates a number of files). The Windows Briefcase interface is not the most transparent piece of software ever written, so handle with care.

Windows 2000 has a rather better synchronisation manager utility which allows people who connect intermittently to a network to work on a specific file offline from a remote location, and then choose how to synchronise it with the original, network-based file (so for example, it can be synchronised whenever you log on, or according to a schedule, or only when you choose). Again, use of this technique is covered in detail through the Windows help system.

In relation to contacts databases, most people use versions of Microsoft Outlook, and most PDA devices have synchronisation software such as Palm Desktop, or ActiveSync for PDAs that use the PocketPC operating system, which can be set to automatically update Outlook between a number of devices. For those who use other contacts databases, there are proprietary systems available such as Intellisync from Pumatech (**http://www.intellisync.com**) or PDASync from Laplink (**http://www.laplink.co.uk**). These systems are mainly used by people who need to synchronise Lotus Notes data on Palm devices. If you need to synchronise a Mac with a Sony PDA try
http://www.markspace.com/missingsync.htm

Another approach is to synchronise data through specialised websites or application service providers. This can allow synchronisation between a whole series of devices (desktop, laptop, PDA and cellphone), or for members of a remote team to share calendars. *See* **http://www.fusionone.com** or **http://www.wesync.com** or **http://calendar.yahoo.com**

Security for shared facilities

Where a number of people use a shared facility such as a telecentre, there are various ways of improving data security. If the location is company-owned, basic physical-access precautions such as security-swipe cards should be in place so that only authorised staff members can use the IT facilities. IT equipment may also need to be physically locked to desks.

Where access cannot be controlled to the same extent, such as in a cybercafé or telecentre where customers walk in off the street, other options are available. Infrared mice and keyboards can be used which are physically locked away unless issued to a particular user. Or, as in the case of the easyEverything cybercafés, the PCs can be configured so that they allow access only to web-browser software – there is no other software available to users.

ALL YOU NEED TO KNOW ABOUT THE INTERNET

The speed/cost equation

Teleworkers rely on good-quality Internet access for their livelihood, so unless you are a bit of a techie yourself, choose a paid-for service with good technical

Park bench with integral Internet and power connections at Bury St Edmunds

support rather than a 'free' service which is designed to provide basic access without the frills – and which makes its money either through your telephone calls to the ISP, or through expensive technical support over premium-rate lines if you hit a problem.

Business services with a good reputation at the time of writing (this is a market in a state of constant flux) include Virgin Net (**http://www.virgin.net**), Claranet (**http://www.claranet.com**) and, for high-speed connections, Telewest (**http://www.blueyonder.co.uk**). If you do decide to go for a 'free' service, the best-known offering is Freeserve (**http://www.freeserve.com**). *Internet* magazine gives up-to-date reviews of British ISPs, their rates and contact numbers at **http://www.internet-magazine.com/isp/top10.asp**

If you go for a paid-for service, the other decision you need to make is whether you should be paying on a usage basis (cheaper for those who don't connect to the Internet intensively), or whether you should pay a fixed fee per month or year for unlimited usage. Fixed-fee services are offered by a variety of ISPs, although check the details as most have a 'cap' on your total usage (for example, BT Openworld limits usage to 150 hours per month).

Assuming that you have a reasonably fast modem and a clear telephone line, your access speed to the Internet is likely to be faster if your Internet Service Provider (ISP) has a low use-modem ratio and a high bandwidth connection to the Internet. The best sources of information about this are the magazines that do regular benchmarks of all the major providers. Using the right search engine, and learning how to frame accurate searches, will also speed up access to the information you need. And remember – if you did opt for a 'free' service you can't really complain about its quality.

Email facilities

The 'free' services usually offer free email, but this is often web-based, which means that you browse to your ISP's homepage, enter your user ID and password and can then view your mail. What you can't do is view and store your email in a business email application like Outlook, Pegasus or Eudora. Some free services do offer 'POP3 mailboxes', and these are the ones to look for as you will be able to set up a 'POP3' email account and use a proper email package such as Outlook. This is also vital if you want to view your email over a mobile phone, through a unified messaging system or from a number of different locations. On a Mac, look for IMAP, which does something similar for the .Mac mail service.

Some packages such as Microsoft Outlook are set up by default to use more sophisticated email formats such as 'RTF' or 'HTML' so that messages can be made to look more attractive with different fonts, bold and italic, special backgrounds and so on. Switch them off. You don't know if the person at the other end has suitable software to be able to read these formats – they could be trying to access their email from a mobile phone or PDA. Stick to plain vanilla ASCII text wherever possible. Also turn off the .vcf virtual business card option if you are using Outlook. This sends a small attachment with all your emails which can be very annoying for the recipient. Some companies with strong data-security policies even instruct staff to trash all mails with unsolicited attachments without reading them.

Transferring large amounts of data

If you are planning to use email to send large text and graphics files, you will need to obtain a compacting utility such as PKZIP for the PC (**http://www.pkware.com**) or Aladdin Dropzip and Stuffit Expander for the Mac (**http://www.aladdinsys.com**). These programmes squash your files, commonly to about half their original size. You can then email the 'stuffed' or 'zipped' file in half the time, and with any luck save half the phone-call costs.

If you send your file in this form, the recipient needs to have the appropriate programme in order to unpack the file to its original size. Some compacting programmes allow you to create 'self-expanding' files – the recipient double-clicks on the compacted file and it expands itself back to normal size without the need for the correct unpacking software to be installed on their machine.

There are also some applications where a direct modem-to-modem link or an ISDN link is cheaper than using an email system. For example, dtp files for a four-colour magazine can easily exceed 10 Mb in size – larger than many ISPs will allow. Typesetting bureaux sometimes offer their own high-speed direct links to keep the cost of transferring such large amounts of data down. If you are involved in large-scale file transfer, it is worth comparing prices between different analogue modem speeds, ISDN lines, ADSL and high-speed cable modems to work out the cheapest methods for different file sizes. This will allow you to see whether the additional installation and rental costs are justified in your situation (*see* p. 282).

Web space

Most providers throw in free web space on which to create your own website, but whether this is useful depends on what kind of site you want to build. You can put together a simple site on your own (*see* p. 239), but for many applications such as customer response forms or e-commerce, you may need some help from your ISP, which is unlikely to be free. You might be better off going to a provider who offers a specific amount of web space at a sensible price including support, rather than one that offers you free space with no support for it.

The paid services can also host your own domain name (such as myowncompany.com or myfirm.co.uk) which always looks more impressive to customers than piggybacking off the ISP's name (e.g. mycompany@ISPname.net). You can check and buy domain names online but do this with the domain registration authorities, not with companies that sell or register domains (**http://www.nominet.net** is the authority for all domains ending .uk, while **http://www.iedr.ie** handles Irish domains ending .ie and InterNIC handles .com and .net domains at **http://www.internic.net/whois.html**). Some of the commercial sites have been rumoured to actually pre-register sites you enquire about in order to extract funds from you if you really want that domain – *see* p. 330.

A bit of backup

If you are likely to do more than just send a few email messages and surf a bit, it's well worth considering using two providers, to give you backup in case of a problem at one ISP. You can send email in an emergency or when you are on the move using one of the web-based services such as Hotmail (**http://www.hotmail.com**) or Web2mail (**http://www.web2mail.com**).

High-speed connection

Most teleworkers access the Internet using dial-up modems. But a standard 56 kilobit per second (kbps) modem struggles when you are sending email with large attachments such as graphics or multimedia files. ISDN lines are widely available and offer slightly faster speeds (64 kbps or 128 kbps if you link the two lines together, though this costs more per call). Businesses that need serious bandwidth for sending data across the Internet sometimes invest in expensive T1 leased lines, giving speeds of up to 1.5 mbs depending on the time of day and weight of Internet traffic. In between the extremes of T1 and dial-up or ISDN are various flavours of 'broadband' connection.

PEAK DISTRICT SATELLITE OFFICE

Michael Oliver's company e-1st specialises in e-commerce solutions including hosting, so he needs to be online almost constantly – but he lives in the Peak District near Sheffield, and is unlikely ever to have access to cable or ADSL connections.

'I would certainly describe our Internet use as extensive. We have to upload information to customer sites, send a lot of emails and check the websites of our competitors frequently. That means two PCs online constantly, and in use around ten hours a day. I think we probably transfer about 9 gigabits of data each month,' he comments.

'Using a dial-up connection was a nightmare. We'd been used to broadband before we moved to Sheffield and the speed problems, combined with the cost of high-intensity use meant we were in danger of going out of business. We couldn't afford the unreliability and blocking problems of the unlimited-usage offerings – and using a rapid-dial connection instead resulted in very high call-charges,' remembers Michael.

The solution was a broadband satellite connection from BT Openworld. Michael paid £860 plus VAT for installation of a dish, cabling, satellite modem and a satellite router. He describes the system: 'The dish is similar in size to a TV satellite dish, and we paid for installation, although we could have done it ourselves, in order not to encounter any technical problems. Now we pay about £56 a month in running costs, and the only issues we have had are related to reduced performance in bad weather such as thunderstorms.'

So why did he move to Sheffield in the first place? 'Lifestyle. I had sold shares in an Internet business at the right moment, and wanted a life in the countryside with less pressure. I have that now – in essence I do the same job, but customer expectations aren't so drastic with my current business,' he concludes.

Michael reckons that you need to have a requirement to be online for over three hours a day before satellite becomes an economic option: 'I don't think you could justify it just for browsing and occasional emails.'
http://www. e-1st.co.uk

Broadband

High-speed Internet technologies are becoming more affordable and widespread in Britain and Ireland except in rural areas. The term 'broadband' simply refers to connection speed – most broadband technologies run at 500 kbps or above, around ten times faster than a standard dial-up modem. There are four basic flavours:

xDSL

This includes ADSL, but there are several flavours of DSL – hence, the x. DSL is short for digital subscriber line and means that instead of the last section of telephone-line into your home running in old-fashioned analogue mode, it is upgraded so that you have a fully digital connection.

First, you have to have a local telephone exchange that has been upgraded to DSL. BT operates a website where you can enter your postcode to find out the status in your area at

http://www.bt.co.uk/broadband_information/index.html

Second, you have to be fairly close to the exchange, as the line runs (not as the crow flies). Figures vary according to where you read them. BT say you must be within 3.8 kilometres of the exchange (about the same distance as for ISDN). Others say 4 km or even 5.5 km – but the bottom line is that if you live at the end of a muddy lane miles from anywhere, you probably won't get DSL for some years (if ever).

Finally you will need an ADSL splitter which you plug into the digital line and connect to your computer, usually through the USB port. The result: a fast, always-on Internet connection so you don't have to make a call to your service provider every time you want to access the Internet, and you don't run the risk of dropped calls and broken connection. One possible problem is that if you already have an ISDN line but are upgrading to ADSL, the line must first be converted back to analogue and tested – and it may not pass the line-quality tests for ADSL. The practical, if expensive, solution is to first order a fresh analogue line and then convert that. Other countries offer ADSL over ISDN lines, but not the UK. *Typical download speed 512 kbps. Typical upload speed 128–256 kbps.*

Cable

NTL (**http://www.ntl.co.uk**) and Telewest (**http://www.blueyonder.co.uk**) offer broadband Internet access over their cable TV networks in some areas of Britain. Cable, whichever company operates in your area, is generally only available in cities. Cable modems can slow down depending on the time of day and number of people accessing the Internet simultaneously, unlike xDSL. Cable Internet access is also an 'always on' connection. *Typical download speed 500 kbps. Typical upload speed 128–256 kbps.* However, both providers also have 1Mbps offerings.

Satellite

If you live in a rural area, this may be your only option for a high-speed connection at the moment. Data is sent to a satellite dish at your home. You also need a satellite receiver card and satellite modem; and some systems also require that you have a standard dial-up connection as well to send the upload information (mainly your mouse-clicks). *Typical download speed 500 kbps but can be higher. Typical upload speed 150 kbps.*

> http://www.aramiska.net
> http://www.bridgebroadband.co.uk
> http://www.beamsolutions.net
> http://www.btopenworld.com/satellite

Wireless cable

This is an extension of cable where the cable signal is broadcast locally over a microwave radio system. You need a receiver aerial on the roof of your building plus a transceiver which converts the signal to Ethernet. Not widely available at present. *Typical speed 512 kbps.*

The broadband information website **http://www.broadband4uk.com** gives speed comparisons for different connection methods but doesn't include prices. We have added some guideline prices for July 2002, but of course they will probably be obsolete by the time you read this book.

Speed and price guide

Technology	Megabytes downloaded per hour	Time to download a 1 Mb file	Price (approximate, July 2002)
Cable 1Mbps	440 Mb	8 seconds	£39.99/month
Cable 512 kbps	220 Mb	16 seconds	£25/month
Satellite 512 kbps	220 Mb	16 seconds	£59.99/month but £899 installation fee
ADSL 512 kbps	220 Mb	16 seconds	£32.99/month
ISDN 128k	55 Mb	65 seconds	Depends on number of calls – note two lines in use, so double 56k cost
56k modem	18.5 Mb	192 seconds	Depends on number of calls

Finding what you want on the web

With over a million new pages being uploaded onto the web each day, it's getting harder to find the information you want. The web is not a well-organised library, but an aggregate of content both good and bad. Fortunately it has automated 'librarians' in the form of search engines. Upon receipt of a simple query and mouse-click they will go off and search the web, returning results both relevant and irrelevant.

The most widely used search engine worldwide is Google (**http://www.google.com**). A typical one-word search query on most search engines will return about half a million 'hits', or possibly relevant web references – so be sure to search on combinations of words or phrases. Most search engines allow you to search for words in a particular order (e.g. 'canned meat' but not 'meat canned') by enclosing the words in double quotes. Some have sophisticated advance search facilities where you can search for 'red' and 'dwarf' but exclude where these occur accompanied by 'snow' and 'white'. Take time to read the search tips provided.

Entries on most search engines are collected by 'robots' or 'spiders', software tools which roam the web indexing what they find automatically. Web designers enter text on their pages in the source code that the robots use (also called metatags). Some unscrupulous people unfortunately include entirely irrelevant text on their pages to boost their search-engine ratings.

Yahoo! (**http://www.yahoo.co.uk**) remains the most popular of the directory-based sites. These organise entries by category, and also use human evaluation to supplement the robots and spiders. Yahoo! has categories on everything under the sun from business and economy to society and culture.

Netiquette

The general etiquette of online services (network etiquette, or 'netiquette' for short) is one of consideration for other users. Most breaches of netiquette are due to ignorance, rather than any desire to offend. A simple example would be that typing in capital letters is the online equivalent of SHOUTING. Instead _underscore_ words or *asterisk* phrases. Because online communications do not allow body language such as ironic grins and shoulder shrugs, some people use symbols such as <bg> for big grin and 'emoticons' such as the smiley face :-) (look at it sideways) or {%—)) (cross-eyed smiling man with hat and double chin) to embellish their messages. There are also a number of acronyms such as IMHO (in my humble opinion), AFAIK (as far as I know) and BTW (by the way) in common usage.

Probably the most important piece of netiquette to understand is that blatant commercialism and marketing is disapproved of, at least in Europe. Sales messages are likely to result in your being 'flamed' – sent a hailstorm of rude replies.

A less obvious form of netiquette stems from the world-wide nature of the web. Words that have a quite innocent meaning in one country can mean something altogether more sinister or obscene in another. A UK group with a common interest in lace-making found this out to their cost when they discovered that the term has a pornographic meaning in the US. It's important

HIGH-SPEED HOMEWORKING

Microsoft is to be the first corporate customer for BT's Agile Office broadband offering. Most of Microsoft's 1500 UK staff will be equipped with home DSL routers to allow them to work securely on the company's internal network, sending and receiving data at high speed.

Microsoft does not employ any permanently home-based workers, but allows staff to work at home when they choose. The new system should provide faster, cheaper connections because the broadband connection is 'always on'.

BT has announced that it also plans to transfer its own 5500 home-based staff to Agile Office, beginning with 2700 retail division staff. The company believes it will save £1m for each 1000 teleworkers it migrates to the new system.

to realise that other people may have sensitivities of which you are unaware. It is also unfortunately true that many websites carry material that you might find at best distasteful, and that might be seriously injurious to children. It is possible to buy software (often from your ISP) which will screen sites for pornography, or other illicit material, and which will enable you to put out of bounds altogether, sites that you do not want your children to see. Filtering software has the ability to block IRC chat, email, newsgroups and selected sites. Well-known products include Microsystem Cyberpatrol (**http://www.cyberpatrol.co.uk**), Solid Oak CYBERsitter (**http://www.solidoak.com**) and Net Nanny (**http://www.netnanny.co.uk**).

Instant messaging

According to Gartner group, around 90% of businesses will start to use Instant Messaging (IM)by the end of 2003, spurred on by the inclusion of Windows Messenger in Microsoft's new operating system Windows XP. IM is not the same as SMS messaging on mobile phones (although a version for mobiles is being developed and is expected in Europe during 2003). It is a way of text messaging other PC users logged on to the Internet. It's generally cheap or free after you have paid your Internet service provider subscription and telephone call. The software itself is also usually free to download – but of course there is currently the usual turf war of incompatible standards that blights most IT developments.

Most IM packages allow you to register a user name and set up lists of other users with whom you are willing to chat. Whenever you log on to the Internet, the IM software starts up but stays in the background. You can see when your IM-using clients, colleagues or friends are online, and they can see you. In many packages you can then initiate a communication by voice, video or text, and send files or photos. There are also whiteboard facilities in a number of IM packages.

At the moment IM is tending to enter organisations by stealth, although some companies have found they have critical masses of users which tends to cause the IT manager either to want to ban it altogether for security reasons (it might provide a hacker with a back door into the corporate network), or to want to set up their own IM server in order to provide better reliability. Some companies have built custom applications using IM technology to provide archived records of chats. The prediction is that IM will eat into current email and telephone traffic, while providing teleworkers with another IT tool to prevent isolation.

Providers include:

http://www.aol.com/aim/
http://www.messenger.msn.com
http://messenger.yahoo.com
http://www.icq.com/download

A standards dispute is in place between different manufacturers' offerings as users wait to find out which offering will win over the competition.

CONFERENCING

This section defines conferencing very broadly as any form of transmitted, changing data shared between colleagues. There are four basic flavours: datasharing screens over PCs; point-to-point video conferencing (videophoning); video conferencing between more than two locations; and webcasting.

Data sharing or computer conferencing

Many companies use audio conferencing alongside a datasharing package to allow participants to view and collaborate on documents – control for editing the document can be passed among participants, for example, which can be a lot faster than emailing versions to colleagues for comment and correction. These facilities usually function best if a separate phone-based audio conference is held alongside the datasharing, but the good news is that generally, datasharing works fine with a standard 56k dial-up connection. Getting a static IP connection from your ISP can also make conferencing a lot easier (most dial-up connections are dynamic, i.e. you receive a new IP address each time you dial in).

Conferencing packages can be downloaded from the web – Microsoft Netmeeting is the most popular and is free from Microsoft (**http://www.microsoft.com/windows/netmeeting/**). Most conferencing software also has 'electronic whiteboard' features which allow you to cut, copy, paste and annotate information from other software packages such as word processors and spreadsheets to be viewed by the other conference participants. The whiteboard can be saved for future reference. Netmeeting also has a 'chat' feature for swapping concise text messages, but it is usually used in practice with a simultaneous audio conference. There are also file-transfer facilities so that you can send text, audio and video files to the other participants during the conference. Advanced features allow a conference to be initiated through sending an email message to the other participants.

Other datashare/conferencing packages include **http://www.webex.com**, **http://www.conferencing.com**, which offers meeting-space online, and GroupSystems for Windows, which has special brainstorming and categorisation tools.

Videophoning

What most people think of as video conferencing – a point-to-point video link – is really videophoning, but the distinction has largely been lost in recent years. Video conferencing can allow effective meetings while avoiding travel costs, but has not taken off into widespread usage yet except to allow contributions at conferences from people who cannot be physically present, or for point-to-point communications (such as recruitment companies carrying out interviews at a distance). Although the technical standard of affordable systems today is no replacement for face-to-face meetings, it offers an improvement over the audio conference, especially for delicate meetings or negotiations where a face-to-face meeting is not possible and voice would not be enough. Otherwise, audio conferencing is more functional and cost-effective as well as being less distracting and time-consuming.

The entire video-conferencing sector has lurched between predictions of speedy growth and reports of imminent death for over a decade. However, with the advent of high-speed cable and DSL connections, it may finally be here to stay. Most systems are still based on ISDN, although there are low-end solutions using web-cam cameras and standard dial-up lines using software such as CUSeeMe. ISDN systems can be a little jerky so you need to learn to moderate your body language – no wild gestures. Also, on many systems only one person can 'speak' at one time (rather like a VHF radio system). In this situation it helps the flow of the conversation if you can indicate clearly by your tone of voice or by gesture when you have finished making a point. Otherwise, conversations can either degenerate into a staccato cutting from one participant to another as you accidentally interrupt each other, or to a Quaker-like silence at the end of each point while the person at the other end tries to work out if you've finished talking.

For a basic point-to-point system you need a sound card in your PC (most are built with one these days); a camera, preferably with USB plug-and-play port, costing less than £100; a microphone; speakers; an Internet connection; and conferencing software that runs the H.323 standard (for users connected by a LAN), H.324 standard (for users connected by an ordinary telephone line) or H.320 (for ISDN or leased-line connections).

SPAM, SPAM, SPAM, SPAM, SPAM, SPAM, SPAM, SPAM, SPAM

Spam – or unsolicited, junk email – borrows its name from the famous Monty Python sketch. It was first used in the Internet context to describe the practice of posting the same message repeatedly on different discussion lists or chat rooms. Now it has become a catch-all description for unwanted email. Spammers believe that they are just helping direct marketing to evolve. In fact, spam wastes valuable time, clogs networks and slows down the operation of the Internet – one in three US emails is now thought to be spam, while one in seven UK emails falls into the unwanted category (see **http://news.independent.co.uk/digital/features/story.jsp? story=319529 29/7/2002**).

It will theoretically be illegal to send spam in the European Union from the end of 2003, though no-one is entirely clear how the EU plans to enforce this directive, especially in relation to spam sent from Eastern Europe and Asia. The new directive will enforce an 'opt-in' policy where spammers must get permission before emailing, and websites must notify users and get permission before storing 'cookies' of information about them. The directive anticipates the move to mobile technologies by ensuring that owners of mobile phones will be able to block information about their location if they wish.

Some people are under the misapprehension that they get spam as a result of visiting websites. This is usually untrue unless you have used a form or contact link on a website to give your email address. In fact, most spam is either automatically generated by guessing likely email addresses, or else collected by small 'robot' programmes which roam the web picking up email addresses from discussion boards or websites. Generally, the amount of spam you receive is proportional to the amount of time you have spent using the Internet and the number of places that your email address is recorded. So just because you were sent some awful pornographic spam does not mean that your children are necessarily visiting porn sites using your email address.

To foil spam, use a different email address (such as a Yahoo! or Hotmail address) for any public postings and website registrations, saving your main address for messaging colleagues, friends and family. The spam will pile up in the public account and can be regularly trashed. Always examine the privacy policy of a website before offering any personal information such as your email address, and be sure to opt out by unchecking that box on the form if you don't want to receive marketing information. Don't bother to reply to spam asking to be removed from a mailing list – all you are doing is confirming to the spammer that the email address is active, in which case they will probably send you more.

Many ISPs offer spam-filtering options, but some filters may also remove legitimate email such as that from mailing lists. Most email packages such as Outlook, Netscape Messenger or Eudora allow you to set up rules to sift out mail likely to be junk and send it to a separate folder (such as mail with no subject line or $$$ or Viagra or sex in the subject line).

...continued overleaf

Spam continued...

You can then, if you wish, review it before sending it to the trash. There are also anti-spam software packages which can work with your email software to weed out marketing scams and other offal, as well as messages from known spammers – try Mailwasher (**http://www.mailwasher.net**). Some ISPs have spam-filtering in place which subscribers can avail themselves of – *see* **http://www.cloudnet.com** which uses Spam Assassin.

If you suspect a message could be spam or a virus, another good trick is to use your email software to look at the full header of the message without opening it (this is particularly wise if it is unexpected mail that contains an attachment which could be a virus). In Outlook, right-click the message and choose options. Then use your judgement to assess the true return address on the email – anything with a strange Pacific or Eastern European domain name or a webmail address such as Hotmail or Yahoo! ought to arouse your suspicions.

A nasty development in spamming is the use of real email addresses (such as yours) as the false return address on the spam, so that you suddenly receive 100 failure messages from email servers for spam which has been sent to invalid addresses. There is almost nothing you can do about this. If you have your own domain but only use a small number of email addresses on that domain, you can ask your ISP to block all other mail addresses on that domain.

Newsgroups are a bad source of spam. If possible use a different email address for contributions to newsgroups. If you have to use your regular email address, then use your email software to insert no-spam in the From: or Reply to: parts of the email (e.g. no-spam-jane-smith@bigisp.com). Any junk mail sent to that address can be returned to the sender.

The Irish Times journalist Karlin Lillington recommends that for detailed information on what spam is, why you get it, how spammers work and how to block spam check out **http://www.junkbusters.com** and consumer group **http://www.cauce.org** To deal with spam without timewasting, try Mailwasher at **http://www.mailwasher.net**

In addition to holding 'face to face' conversations and collaborating with colleagues and clients regardless of location, you can also send video images, and use the camera to view items. Netmeeting includes video-conferencing facilities, but these are not very satisfactory unless you have a high-speed connection.

Video conferencing

Bandwidth is important for video links – the more you have the better, and it's generally considered that systems which run at less than 128 kb and 30 frames per second are inadequate for business use. Systems that run at 384 kbps (three linked ISDN lines) are more than usable, while systems which run at 768 kbps (six linked ISDN lines) give quality equivalent to good TV. One way to improve things if you have to run on a low-speed line is to restrict the size of the window that the video link takes up on your screen – the smaller the window, the less the speed and processing required to update it. A basic ISDN-based video-conferencing system costs about £4000.

Because of speed restrictions, video quality tends to be poor unless ISDN connections are available (or unless you are running links within a company across a high-speed ethernet network or intranet).

Based on bitter experience, be careful about trying to run conferences with video contributions in venues which do not already have a tried and trusted video-conferencing system. The ISDN lines will probably go in the day before the event, and the equipment, if it works at all, will do so just 30 seconds before you need it, causing dangerously high blood pressure to the organisers. Also, almost because the technology makes it easier for speakers to contribute, they seem to be less committed when working on video links than when contributing face to face, and become more likely to duck out on you at the last minute.

Room or group video-conferencing systems are much more expensive (around £15,000) and are best used where there are several people in each location. They can be used to link up international meetings or to deliver training presentations. If you are involved in a group or one-to-many video conferences, experts advise having a separate audio (sound-only) link as a backup, in case technical gremlins cause problems with the video transmission. Where a number of ISDN lines are available they can be 'bonded' together to provide extra facilities, such as the ability for a speaker to send down presentation slides to a separate screen using part of the bandwidth. Telephone companies, some colleges and commercial conferencing firms can provide bureau facilities for high-quality video conferencing, as can some telecentres. Picturetel have a portable high-end system that weighs less than ten pounds (**http://www.picturetel.com**).

Where a multipoint conference with more than two locations is required, you will probably need to use the services of a company that can join the lines and switch the video through a conferencing network service.

Webcasting

Webcasting involves taking a video and/or audio feed and compressing it into data formats which can be 'broadcast' over the Internet for viewing on PCs via a special web browser. It is widely used to record conference presentations for future viewing, in training and to make animated Powerpoint presentations available.

Almost all webcasting uses the RealOne Player software from RealNetworks, although there is also a Microsoft offering called Netshow. The RealOne player browser is free to download. The webcasting software is also available free for personal use (which may encompass a one-off event) but the professional versions must be purchased for providing webcasting services. Many ISPs offer some streaming facilities alongside their webspace offerings, though sometimes this is Windows Media Player rather than Real. Apple provides its Quicktime streaming software free with its servers and server software – an alternative worth looking at for corporate users. Webcasting services need to sit on a server with good bandwidth if you are expecting simultaneous connections from your users.

It is possible to separate the RealOne Player audio and video streams (e.g. to have the same presentation with commentary in different languages that the viewer can select). It is also possible to divide the feed so that you get a 'talking head' presenter beside a Powerpoint slide presentation. *See* **http://europe.real.com**

TECHNICAL SUPPORT

Issues relating to technical support of teleworkers by companies are dealt with in the IT issues section of Chapter 6, *Implementation in organisations.*

As computer manufacturers tighten their belts worldwide to cope with the IT recession, many self-employed people are finding that formerly reliable technical support is hard to come by and involves infuriating and fruitless hours spent in call centre 'wonderland'.

This has left a market gap for independent providers of technical support. The new remote-assistance function in the Windows XP operating system may help provide more opportunities for authorised third parties to connect to your computer over the Internet, chat with you, observe your computer screen and if required, take over control of your PC temporarily. The problem is knowing which suppliers of support are any good.

For some years the Telework Association office has used Sue Phillips of Helpline Computers, who has 20 years of experience in rescuing computers. What follows are her tips for trouble-free PC maintenance – but delivered with the caveat that there are many different flavours of PC and operating system out there, so you use this information at your own risk.

Do it yourself – sensible precautions

A backup system that works
First and most important: back up your data. Tape systems are the best because they are the only economic way to get your whole system backed up by pressing one button and leaving the PC to do its backup while you go to the pub. If you have to put a 20 Gb system onto 650 Mb CD-ROMs, slotting them in and out, you just won't do it, or not regularly. What you'll do is think that backing up just your work files will do. It is only when you've spent an entire week reinstalling all your software programs that the attractions of a full tape backup

will really become clear to you.

A working backup system is the best anti-virus recovery system, the best uninstaller for troublesome software and the best solution to 'oops I didn't mean to press that button'. A tape backup means you can restore everything onto a blank hard drive in a few hours, or even just select one single vital file for backup. You do need to test the backup system (try recovering a specific but harmless file) and you should try to do a backup once a week. You'll sleep easier – try to make it part of your end-of-week routine on a Friday night.

The Emergency Recovery Disk

Many manufacturers have their own version of this which you get instructions for making when you unpack the computer and boot it up for the first time. It contains all the files Windows needs to boot, and also normally your vital Windows Registry files. There is a generic version of this type of programme called ERS (*see* **http://www.backtec.com**) if you don't already have such a disk. Make a second emergency recovery disk once you have installed all your application software and are happy with the machine's operation (say, after the first calendar month), as some settings will have changed due to the installations.

An awful lot of apparently irrecoverable problems can be rescued by reinstalling Windows over itself, but problems with a corrupt Windows Registry cannot be fixed – unless you have a backup of your Registry files, and preferably, a full backup of your PC.

Anti-virus software

There is a separate section discussing anti-virus software and techniques in more detail. The main point is, you must have it and you should schedule the anti-virus software to scan your disk for viruses at least once a week. You should also set the software to scan whenever you boot up the PC. As new viruses are constantly being invented, you also need to regularly update your virus definitions. Most of the current packages will do this over the Internet for you, such as Symantec's automatic LiveUpdate facility.

Regular housekeeping

These tasks should be done once a month, or whenever you find that performance is slowing.
- Close all programs and reboot the computer.
- You can now safely delete the contents of the \windows\temp folder which is where Windows stores a lot of 'stuff that might come in handy later' and which it sometimes fails to clear up properly.
- Empty the recycle bin – right-click the bin and select Empty. These are all the files you deleted which Windows has helpfully kept in the bin in case you change your mind.

EQUIPMENT AND SERVICES CHECKLIST

Item	Priority	Cost new	Cost secondhand
Desktop or laptop computer			
Software			
Modem and Internet connection – high speed?			
Telephone/mobile (and headset? speakerphone? separate data line?)			
Call plus services (diversion, caller line ID, call waiting, etc.)			
Answerphone (or voicemail service)			
Printer			
Fax (or fax software for computer)			
Scanner			
Photocopier (or facilities using scanner/printer)			
Repair contract			
Tape drive (or other device) for backup			
Surge-supressed power sockets			
Consumables (paper, ink cartridges, etc.)			
Disks and disk storage, CD-ROMs, etc.			
Insurance			
Files, tabs and labels			
Shelves			
Advertising costs (directories, website)			
Desks			
Chairs			
Filing cabinets – lockable?			
Suspension files for filing cabinet			
Wastebasket			
Fire extinguisher			
Smoke alarm			
First-aid kit			
Heating, lighting, ventilation, power sockets			
Address labels			

Item	Priority	Cost new	Cost secondhand
Postal scales			
Desk light			
Pinboard			
Reference books			
Stationery – paperclips and pens			
Envelopes			
Postage stamps			
Business cards			
Compliments slips			
Letterheads			
Brochures			
Professional fees (accountant, solicitor)			

■ On the Start menu, choose Settings and then Taskbar and Start Menu. On
the Advanced tab you will find an option to clear recent documents,
programmes and web settings. This will remove any temporary Internet
pages stored on your PC but will also clear the lists of recent documents
and programmes. You can clear just the Internet files by going to Start –
Settings – Control Panel – Internet Options. On the General tab you will
find options to clear your Internet pages history and Internet temporary
files.

USEFUL URLS FOR DIY TECHNICAL SUPPORT

Microsoft: **http://www.microsoft.com/support**
Corel: **http://www.corel.com/support**
Lotus: **http://www-3.ibm.com/software/lotus/support**
Symantec: **http://www.symantec.com/techsupp**
Bulletin boards on Windows, DOS and Linux issues: **http://www.virtualdr.com**
Web-based substitute for company helpdesk: **http://www.pcsupport.com**
Free help, step-by-step walkthroughs, dictionary:
http://www.computerhope.com
Helping Mac users since 1994: **http://www.macintouch.com**

With thanks to Irish computer magazine *PC Live* (**http://www.techcentral.com**)

There are other tasks often recommended in computer magazines, such as defragmenting disks, but here we're trying to provide you with a minimal list of sensible but safe actions to carry out.

Never use a recovery CD
Technical support helpdesks will sometimes authoritatively state that whatever is wrong with your PC is so dire that you must use the recovery CD supplied with the computer. NEVER do this without seeking a second opinion because, even if successful, it will restore your PC to the state in which it left the factory – i.e. the programmes that you installed and all your data will be gone. These disks make life simple for the call-centre agent but can be a disaster from your point of view.

Store PC gubbins safely
Have a dust-free place for safety storage of all the manuals, CDs, serial numbers, etc. which belong to your computer(s), so that when asked for the disk or information by a helpdesk agent you have it to hand.

This section is intended for all those involved in teleworking – employers, employed and self-employed.

Some of the legislation that affects teleworkers, such as that covering business rates, is a bit of a grey area. Elsewhere, a little interpretation is required – for example, does a home-office risk assessment require an independent home visit, or can a suitably trained teleworking employee self-certify? In general, the advice must be to inform yourself and use your common sense – few authorities want the headache of regulating home offices in detail. Get yourself a good accountant and solicitor, and ask for advice about anything you're not sure of – either from your advisers or from the relevant authorities. If you encounter a problem that is not easily solved, let the Telework Association know about it so that we can try to help and warn others who may be affected.

HEALTH AND SAFETY

Health and safety authorities have wide powers of inspection and enforcement, and all HSE legislation includes workplaces in the home. Strictly speaking, all workplaces, including those in the home, should have a written health and safety risk assessment.

Any equipment used by the employee in the course of their employment should be deemed safe by the employer. In general it is advisable that the employer should provide the teleworker with all equipment, and ensure that the equipment is inspected and checked on a regular basis and in accordance with the company's on-site practice. This is also the recommendation of the European Framework Agreement between employers and trade unions.

Unfortunately, this is not always the case in practice. A 1999 web-based survey by infrastructure specialists Sulzer of 362 homeworkers and 123 managers found that only 63% received health and safety advice when they started to work at home. Just under half received no advice, assistance or money to assist with remote working. Their working conditions at home were less than ideal – 30% were working in part of a living room and 5% in the kitchen (**http://www.si-cbx.com**).

Employers with more than five workers have a legal requirement to carry out a conventional health and safety workplace risk assessment on teleworkers' home offices. This involves:

1. Identifying hazards that may cause harm, however small (such as keeping potentially harmful substances out of the reach of children).
2. Deciding who might be harmed and how (e.g. the homeworker, members of the household, visitors).
3. Assessing the risks and taking appropriate action (e.g. deciding what steps

must be taken to eliminate or reduce the identified risks, such as training teleworkers to recognise and eliminate hazards like trailing cables, or the early symptoms of upper-limb disorders caused by bad posture).

4. Recording the findings – what steps have been taken to reduce or eliminate risks? Inform the homeworker, or anyone else affected by the work, of the findings.
5. Check the risks from time to time and take steps if needed, especially if there is a change in working procedures (e.g. institute an annual review of the homeworking conditions).

The Health and Safety Executive produces a booklet on safety for homeworkers at **http://www.hse.gov.uk/pubns/indg226.pdf** The Institute of Occupational Health and Safety has an excellent datasheet including a telework premises assessment form on its website, stressing the importance of adequate training and of regular reassessment of the risks at **http://www.iosh.co.uk/files/technical/teleworking.pdf**

Employers should put in place a system for their teleworkers to report accidents or hazards, just as they would in a conventional workplace. This can usually be adapted with little alteration from standard office accident-reporting procedures.

Home-office health and safety

The minimum acceptable space for working is normally 11 cubic metres, which is equivalent to floorspace of about 4.5 square metres (about 15 square feet). Work surfaces for PCs (desks, etc.) need to be at least 80 cm deep if they are to take a traditional computer monitor, which is quite deep. Around 70 cm of legspace under the desk or worksurface will be needed. There must be enough space for it to be possible to move and adjust the arrangement of screen, keyboard, documents and any other equipment needed for work.

Beware of spaces which may lack natural light (cellars and attics) or where temperature control and ventilation could be variable or insuffficient (sheds, garages, cellars, attics).

In order to reduce risk of RSI or other injuries due to poor work furniture, the employer is also advised to supply all working furniture. The main law relevant to teleworkers is the Display Screen Directive 90/270/EEC which requires:

- Clear and stable screen, bright and free from glare, which should swivel and tilt easily.
- Adequate arrangement of keyboard characters, adjustable keyboard with sufficient space to support the hands and arms of the user.
- Sufficient user space in which to change positions and vary movements. Work desk sufficiently large; document-holder adjustable and stable.
- Satisfactory lighting conditions. Light levels should be about 350 lm m^{-2}.

HSBC TAKES IT SERIOUSLY

'Our duty of care follows them home, so we have to take it seriously,' says Trevor Morriss, head of compensation and benefits at HSBC Asset Finance. The company has about 100 regional sales staff who work from home, backed up by a sales support staff in Birmingham who forward post and stationery. There are monthly team meetings in hotels, but the teleworkers rarely vist the corporate offices. Teleworkers are supplied with a PC and printer, business phone line and home workstation.

Since the early 1990s, when reorganisation first sent the sales staff out on their own around the country, Trevor has worked first to prepare a comprehensive guide for HSBC's homeworkers, and then to get the booklet transferred to the HSBC intranet for use from any location. 'In the early years there was no easy way for teleworkers to find out what to do if, say, their mobile phone was stolen, or they wanted information on pension entitlements,' reports Trevor.

On home offices, HSBC carries out a self-assessment procedure. 'We say, we are not going to demand to inspect your home because we respect your privacy, so you do it for us.' Natural common sense means that most of the assessments throw up no problems, but there are exceptions. 'One of our people explained how he had to trail a wire across from one room to another up the stairs when he wanted to use the phone,' reports Trevor, 'and he had young children. We told him he had to wire it in and we would pay for it.'

Trevor was also responsible for a company policy banning the use of mobile phones in company cars, even using hands-free. He reports that the 'shock-horror' response was strongest among the home-based sales staff. He has also been working to ensure that the 48-hour working-week limit in the Working Time Directive is met. 'We have made significant progress in persuading managers that it's not the cleverest thing in the world to send emails at midnight or ring people at 8.00 a.m., or expect them to be available at 8.00 p.m. Just because they are workaholics doesn't mean their staff have to be the same,' he notes.

HSBC teleworkers get a £300 allowance each year to offset extra expenses due to teleworking and to compensate for issues like light and heat. Senior teleworker Ken Braddock points out this is hardly major compensation for the loss of the use of a spare room when guests arrive.

Despite the success of the sales team, HSBC has no plans to extend teleworking, 'but it has made us totally amenable to the idea that people can work at home when they need to', concludes Trevor.

- Minimised glare and reflection at the workstation, and minimisation of radiation levels.
- Work chair adjustable in height, including the back rest.
- A foot-rest available if required.

■ Environmental factors should be minimised, including effects of reflection/glare, noise, heat and humidity.

Practical experience within the Telework Association suggests that the following health and safety issues need to be attended to:

■ Insufficient power sockets leading to overuse of extension leads, trailing cables and adaptors. Home offices may need rewiring for more sockets – get the installation checked by an electrician. The employer is not responsible for the electricity supply in the home, but some request and pay for an inspection in order to ensure better safety and reduce the chance of employer-owned equipment malfunctioning.

■ Shelves situated inconveniently so that when heavy files are frequently placed and replaced there is risk of stress on the spine and of overbalancing.

■ Inadequate office chairs and tables which are not the appropriate height or adjustability for long periods of work.

■ Reading glasses not the correct prescription for close work. Anyone working with computers should have their eyes tested, and the optician should be informed of the computer work.

■ Psychologically, most teleworkers prefer to be situated so that they can see out of a window if possible, although it is important to avoid problems with glare and reflection on computer screens.

■ Lighting – spotlights and anglepoises are generally less tiring than fluorescents in small spaces. Screens should be positioned at right-angles to windows, although if suitable blinds are available some may prefer to position them parallel to a wall containing a window. Blinds to prevent sunlight from making screens hard to read should be installed where needed.

■ Temperatures should be as near as possible to 18.5 degrees centigrade. Small home offices can easily overheat because IT equipment generates heat – temperatures may become uncomfortably hot in summer unless adequate ventilation can be provided.

■ Adequate ventilation is also important where equipment such as laser printers may give off ozone or other fumes.

■ The use of IT equipment usually requires two additional power outlets, and one or two telecoms sockets.

■ Safely stowing cabling is important.

■ Electrical equipment needs to be checked for safety (e.g. all cable grips in place, no burn marks on plugs or cracked sockets).

Health and safety on the road

For mobile workers, there are some additional risks which must be taken into account including:

DURHAM COUNTY COUNCIL'S CODE OF PRACTICE

- *A suitable and sufficient assessment will be made of the risks to the health and safety of employees working at home.*

- *Employing departments will provide all appropriate employees with comprehensive and relevant information on the risks to their health and safety as identified by the assessment.*

- *Suitable action will be taken to ensure that workspace and workstations are suitable and sufficient to secure the health, safety and welfare of teleworkers.*

- *Employing departments will provide, and where necessary install, equipment suitable for home use and ensure that it is regularly tested for electrical safety.*

- *Where electrical equipment requires additional power sockets, employing departments will arrange for modifications of electrical power outlets to be carried out by competent persons.*

- *Employing departments will provide, all employees with appropriate health and safety training or information before they begin to use any teleworking equipment; they will also provide retraining if and when any changes in working practices occur.*

- *Employees will be made aware of safe systems of work for teleworking operations.*

- *Teleworkers will be given sufficient guidance and assistance to enable them to organise their work to break up continuous periods of keyboard work.*

- *Teleworkers will receive regular managerial support and guidance.*

- *Teleworkers will be given suitable and sufficient access to first-aid materials and emergency services.*

- *Arrangements will be made for teleworking employees to report accidents through normal departmental channels.*

- *Where display-screen use is a significant part of employees' duties, managers or supervisors will, at the request of the employee, arrange for eyesight screening to be carried out by the occupational health unit. If neccessary, the occupational health unit will recommend that the employing department arranges to pay for a test by an optician.*

- *If corrective appliances are required specifically for display-screen use, the employing department will arrange to pay the cost of lenses and a suitable basic frame; if the employee chooses to purchase frames that are more expensive, the employment department will make a payment equal to the cost of basic frames and lenses.*

LAPTOP SAFETY CHECKLIST

● *Access to a full-size keyboard, separate mouse and screen, or to a docking station.*

● *Access to appropriate, stable worksurfaces.*

● *Information provided on the need to take regular breaks from laptop work and to use stable worksurfaces.*

● *Action taken to discourage prolonged laptop use.*

● *Measurement of laptop weight (including power cables, etc.) taken.*

● *Safe lifting training given.*

● *Suitable carrying bag supplied (e.g. backpack type rather than briefcase bag type, preferably without any identifying computer logo).*

● *Training given on action to take if approached by a thief.*

(Adapted from Wustemann L, *IRS Handbook of Flexible Working Law and Practice*, IRS 2000)

■ Risk of road accidents (a company policy on the use of mobile phones in cars, including the use of hands-free kits, will be needed).

■ Problems with poor ergonomic working conditions (sometimes a docking station for a laptop, providing a full-size screen and keyboard can help).

■ The possibility of equipment being stolen, and the employee being harmed in the process (employees should be trained always to give up the equipment, and to ensure that backup disks are stored separately from the laptop so they are not stolen at the same time).

■ Problems with lifting large or heavy equipment around, including laptops.

Issues specific to laptops include the inability to adjust the keyboard and monitor, and the trade-off between having the keyboard in the right place for your fingers, as against having the screen in the right place for your eyes – something of a problem when keyboard and screen are attached to each other. In addition, screen text is sometimes small, and people can be tempted to use laptops in unsuitable situations such as on knees or on aircraft seatback tables. Where people choose to work in such unsuitable situations, more frequent breaks will probably be needed.

There is currently some uncertainty about the law in relation to mobile phone usage in cars – whether hands-free or otherwise. The sensible advice must be that drivers should pull over if they want to use a mobile phone because of the distraction to driving that conversation causes. However, this advice will be hard to follow for many 'road warriors'.

The good news is that a survey in 1999 for the Health and Safety Executive found that hotdesking does not pose a risk of increased stress-level for staff in comparison to the traditional office.[60] However, desks and chairs provided for touchdown space do need to be adjustable – and there must be easy access to clear instructions on how to adjust the furniture. Another health and safety issue for touchdown space is ensuring that power and data sockets are located above the worksurface, rather than near the floor, requiring ergonomically unsound grovelling under desks to achieve a connection.

Posture and telephonitis

Prolonged computer work can cause discomfort and fatigue to the back, shoulders, neck, head, eyes, buttocks, legs and wrists. Maintaining posture in a static position also causes blood flow to the muscles to be restricted. Ergonomics expert Éilis Duggan of Workright Consultants offers the following guidelines to maintaining a comfortable and efficient work posture.

- Feet should be flat on the floor with knees bent at 90° or 100° angle.
- The front edge of the chair seat should not touch the back of the knee or press into the underside of the thigh, as increased pressure on the back of the leg may lead to numbness, fatigue or knee swelling.
- It should be possible to tilt the chair seat forward slightly by 5–15°, to lift your hips so that they are slightly higher than your knees.
- The chair-seat to chair-back angle should be slightly backwards (10–20°). Try to maintain contact between your own back and that of the chair.
- Any document you are working on should be placed by the screen at the same distance and height, and as close as possible.

HEADSET RESEARCH INDICATES HEALTH BENEFITS

Research commissioned by headset manufacturer Plantronics indicates risks of health problems from non-headset telephone use if you are on the phone for more than two hours a day.

The research was detailed but used a small sample. A team from Surrey University surveyed 26 workers from a variety of occupational groups (legal, secretarial, computer support, PA, financial and administration) analysing posture and health problems followed by a cross-over study where the participants used headsets.

Nearly two-thirds rarely or never had a headache when using the headset compared to 65% sometimes or frequently using a standard handset – a reduction of 27% overall. Headset use also reduced neck pains by 31%, lower-back pain by 16% and upper-back pain by 9%.

The Chartered Society of Physiotherapy reports an increasingly common form of repetitive strain injury (RSI) – telephonitis, caused by wedging the telephone between head and shoulder. Research by the Californian Institute for Treatment and Prevention of Repetitive Motion Injuries warns that anyone combining telephone calls with other tasks can increase neck and shoulder muscle tension by up to 41%.

- Elbows should be at a 90° angle and shoulders relaxed and dropped.
- Change body position frequently, moving feet up and down, adjusting chair and/or keyboard height.
- Organise work so that you can take 'mini-breaks' to stretch muscles.
- Exercise regularly and eat well – take the dog out for a walk at lunchtime?

Ian Fletcher-Price of ergonomic office suppliers Posturite UK advises: 'The minimum requirement for a chair is one with a five-star base, swivel action, gas height adjustment and a tilt mechanism for the seat. The chair back must also be height-adjustable to support your lower back. If you are constantly looking between your source material and the computer screen, a document holder avoids repetitive neck motions and constant refocusing of the eyes which can lead to headaches.'

A booklet on taking care of your back at work is published by the charity BackCare. Tips include changing the height of your chair so that your forearms are level with your desk, and hands at keyboard height. For a copy ring 0800 652 1110.

TELEWORKER, ASSESS THYSELF

The Nationwide Building Society, which has about 85 teleworkers who work at home, has, in common with many large employers, developed a self-administered risk-assessment procedure for home offices. In addition to completing this form, the teleworker must also take a photograph of their proposed work area. Including a photograph of the workspace is a common requirement of self-assessment programmes.

The risk assessment forms part of the application process for teleworking, and if the application is approved, the exercise is repeated after the teleworking equipment has been installed. The Nationwide reserves the right to inspect teleworkers' homes, but in practice operates a self-assessment scheme. 'It's a sensitive issue – managers feel they are intruding,' reported Pauline Henderson of the Nationwide's Homeworkers User Group, who now works with the DTI Work/Life Balance unit. She reports that some applications are turned down on health and safety grounds, such as one case where an employee proposed using his laptop at home: 'We said no; if homeworking is to be done formally, we can't condone using a laptop. He was asked to go back to his manager and rethink the way he could work,' says Pauline.

In the US, the Occupational Safety and Health Administration announced in 2002 that it would not inspect home offices for violations of federal safety and health rules, and that employers are not expected to conduct home inspections either.

HOME OFFICES – OTHER ISSUES

Planning and building regulations

Setting up a home office can constitute a 'change of use' in strict planning terms. However, as far as planning departments are concerned, the average teleworker is unlikely to require planning permission, particularly if they are not creating a nuisance to neighbours. Surrey County Council provides the following advice to its own teleworking staff: 'Teleworking at or from home does not represent a significant change of use of a building likely to cause a nuisance or hazard to your neighbours. Unless you intend to make structural alterations to accommodate your working area, or extra noise, pollution, etc. is generated because you are working at/from home, there is no requirement for planning permission.'

Some other councils differ on whether home offices constitute a 'material' or an 'ancillary' change of use (turning an outhouse into a garage and car-repair workshop is rather more 'material' than putting a computer into a spare bedroom). Material changes of use require permission; ancillary changes or temporary changes probably don't. Decisions on whether the change of use is 'material' are based on whether it will cause increased traffic, changes to the visible appearance of the property, nuisance such as noise or smells, or unsocial working hours.

Oldham Borough Council, in contrast, formally recognises teleworking in its planning guidelines, and regards home offices as ancillary changes of use. The Oldham document is available to other planning authorities, who can use it as a blueprint for their own guidelines if they wish. Babergh District Council in Suffolk prepared its own leaflet Working from Home – balancing the issues because 'we often get asked questions about homeworking and we are aware that there are people who don't really want to ask the question'.

The Department of Environment, Transport and the Regions issued revised guidelines in 2001 which request local authorities to encourage teleworking. The document, Planning Policy Guidance 13 (PPG13), can be viewed at **http://www.planning.odpm.gov.uk/ppg/ppg13/pdf/ppg13.pdf** and contains recommendations for local authorities to 'be alert to the possibilities for harnessing the use of new technologies to encourage local employment opportunities which reduce the need to travel. They should take a flexible approach to the use of residential properties for homeworking, consistent with the need to protect the amenity of the area for any neighbouring residential uses'.

In Ireland, the Department of the Environment has issued the following guidance:

'**1.** Teleworking/telecommuting from home (either part-time or full-time where all that is involved is a computer terminal). In relation to teleworking, it would be difficult to argue that there is any material change of use here and accordingly it would not be an issue from a planning point of view.

2. Home as an office with staff and dedicated space for use. This is quite a different concept and would involve a material change of use and would consequently come within the scope of the planning code.'

Building a workspace

If the establishment of the home office involves any building work, such as conversion of a loft space, there are strict building regulations which must be adhered to, mainly relating to means of escape in case of fire. Loft ladders and space-saver stairs are not favoured, according to Paul Kalbskopf, building control officer at Stroud District Council, because they require familiarity of use for safe passage. Roof lights should also act as a means of escape, so that you could get out, or a fire officer could get in. You may also need to upgrade the floor between the loft and the rest of the house to give half an hour of fire resistance. Kalbskopf advises contacting an architect, and then approaching building control and planning departments for advice before starting work.

Another alternative to a loft conversion is a garden office (*see* p. 94).

WHEN TELEWORKING UPSETS THE NEIGHBOURS – VICTIMS OF SUCCESS

Systems ReMarketing started off in 1990, when Michael Cahen, his wife Maggie and partner Chris Jones began a business from the study in Michael's house. The business involved sourcing repaired, secondhand or mildly obsolete computers; advertising the stock by email to a trade audience; and providing all ordering and other information over the Internet as well.

'Our biggest competitor at the time employed almost 200 people and couldn't provide the same level of service. By keeping the distribution costs to an absolute minimum, the business grew very rapidly. Before long, the team of three had grown to six. The atmosphere was great. The house overlooks a golf course, the alfresco lunches, the odd bottle of wine and a very civilised working environment suited almost everyone,' Michael explains.

Except the neighbours. Although the bulk of the warehousing and despatch was done from a different site, a few spares were kept at Michael's house for emergencies, and were collected by courier companies for delivery to customers. One of the neighbours in Michael's quiet, residential cul-de-sac complained to the council that a business was being run from a residential address. Following an unannounced visit from the council, SRM was threatened with an enforcement order unless the business moved or ceased trading. A planning application was made and rejected. Michael's wife Maggie was concerned about bad relations with the neighbours. If the planning application had succeeded, the cost of partial business rating would have been considerable. In the end, a small office was rented in Marlow, and the centre of the business moved there, with the Surrey office becoming a remote site.

Mortgages

Anyone with a mortgage who is planning to use a home office regularly must notify their mortgage provider. It is particularly important to make this notification if you are also moving into self-employment. A few building societies do offer packages with a built-in payment holiday or the option to reduce payments for a period of time. Those which don't would rather discuss the situation with you now than end up with a repossession on their hands. A typical letter might run something like this:

Dear Sir/Madam

Re: Working from Home

I am about to begin working from home, initially for X day(s) per week, in connection with my employment for Y organisation. I would be grateful if you can let me know of any details/conditions that I need to take action on and/or confirmation of your agreement to the above arrangements.

Yours faithfully
Etc.

Business rates

If you do go through the process of receiving official planning permission for your home office, then you may be liable for commercial rates or council tax on the portion of your house that you are using for work.

In the UK, as far as liability for business rates is concerned, a large grey area exists. The accepted advice is typified by internal Treasury guidelines issued for the management of its own homeworkers: 'Generally when part of a home is used as a workplace where the non-domestic activity precludes the use at any time of that part of the property for living accommodation, the part will be non-domestic and therefore subject to the business rate. In practice where domestic use can take place after work has finished, it is unlikely that liability for the business rate will arise.'

A council rating department spokesman commented: 'This is a grey area for everyone, and will become more of an issue. We don't actively go looking for people working at home. It is difficult to enforce unless it is a separate building that cannot be used for other purposes.' This view was confirmed by another local rating officer: 'We apply what we call a six o'clock rule. If, after six, the room reverts back to domestic use, then it would not be subject to business rates. Generally, as most home businesses wouldn't need planning permission, we would only get to hear about this if a neighbour complained. It is highly unlikely that a home-office business would require business rating.' However, the same officer described an example of a publisher operating from home and using two rooms – one entirely for stock and the other as a computer room – which resulted in an amicably agreed annual rate of around £300. Telework Association member Geoffrey Carter, who uses one room with a computer and a few files to which the family have access in the evenings, found himself with a bill for £450 for part-use of the room after a visit by the valuation officer. After intervention by the Telework Association, the rating against Geoffrey was dropped. Another case, Fotheringham v. Wood ([1995] RA315, LT) found

RESTRICTIVE COVENANTS

Some properties, particularly estate houses and flats, may be subject to covenants which could in theory restrict working from home. The origin of these covenants is usually a condition put in place by a vendor selling development land to prevent business rather than residential developments. A Telework Association member discovered that his flat was affected by a covenant imposed by a local authority when selling land to a builder, and intended to prevent business use other than by a dentist or doctor. Another Telework Association member, Peter Fowler – a solicitor working on business-related legal matters and commercial property – has kindly provided some background information on the two types of covenant, freehold and leasehold (see **http://www.peterjfowler.co.uk**).

Freehold covenants

A typical restriction on a housing estate would be that no trade or business could be carried out on the property, and no use is permitted other than as a private dwelling house. The power of enforcement lies with the original estate-owner or his successors, and in some cases owners of other properties on the estate who could be affected by physical damage or a fall in value of property. Most teleworkers are unlikely to cause damage as they are working entirely inside their home, although some problems could be envisaged (excessive parking obstruction from multiple visitors to a business). In general, it will be a case of common sense and keeping disturbance to neighbours to a minimum. Sometimes old estates may flex their muscles and request payment for a licence to vary the original covenant, but often they have no direct right of enforcement and may no longer own any nearby property which could be affected. The threat of action is likely to be a bluff as the cost of enforcement could be prohibitive. They could also face a substantial claim from the teleworker if their claim failed, but in the interim the teleworker had been prevented from working by their injunction.

Leasehold covenants

Houses on very long leases such as 999-year leases will fall into the same category as freehold, and the above comments apply. However, some small developments of houses or blocks of flats on long leases with ground rents pose a different problem. There will probably be an existing landlord or management company (possibly owned by the residents) who could enforce the covenants – although, as before, they will have to prove that damage is being caused. Such proof is easier where covenants have been established for the common good. All that is needed to cause a problem is one resident who has been inconvenienced and an active residents' committee.

In general, if you are prudent and do not cause any nuisance from your business, even if you are in technical breach of an estate covenant, you will probably be safe enough to carry on teleworking.

Tenancy agreements

If you rent accommodation you should also check your tenancy agreement for restrictions on working from home.

against an accountant working from home on the basis that the room was wholly or mainly used as an office, and use of the room as living accommodation could not be envisaged. Even in this situation, usually the room cannot be business rated unless it is adapted for the needs of anyone you might employ to work there – e.g. it has separate access, toilet and handwashing facilities from those used by the family.

Capital Gains Tax

If you classify part of your house for business purposes, and claim costs such as mortgage interest, then the 'work' part of the house is potentially liable for Capital Gains Tax. 'Although the domestic portion of a house is exempt, CGT could be due on the proportion of the gain related to the rooms used. If you used two rooms in a 12-room house, then one-sixth of the gain would be due. But as the exempt band is £7100 per person, and gains are inflation-adjusted, realistically the problem will probably only occur when the gain happens in a year when other CGT gain items have been realised,' says Mark Dyer, accountant and Telework Association member. The Dyer website at **http://www.netaccountants.com** gives further information on CGT – which may be worth consulting for those with rapidly appreciating London properties. In Ireland there is no CGT risk due to teleworking according to Revenue guidance leaflet IT69.

WHEN IS A PHONE LINE NOT A PHONE LINE?

Ken O'Brien moved to Porkellis in Cornwall and planned to set up a computer business from home. He was stunned to find that he could not connect to the Internet. BT informed him that Porkellis was on a line-concentrator which allows 90 subscribers in the village to be routed through 14 trunk lines. The company told Ken that although they could provide him with a direct line, they weren't prepared to because of the cost. The response galled Ken because the village primary school has an Internet connection as does a cottage two doors away which, through an accident of history, has a direct line. Ken did enquire about an ISDN line, but was told his house was over four miles from the local telephone exchange so neither ISDN nor BT's Homehighway service were available.

Oftel advised that there is no requirement for BT to provide anything other than a voice service. BT said that as a line-concentrator is a recognised method of providing speech transmission, the line will not be removed from this equipment. On previous occasions BT have commented to the Telework Association that, although their liability was limited to voice, they encourage use of the phone for teleworking, fax services and so on. If you have difficulty with line quality they recommend asking for the complaints review manager of the unit and requesting a thorough quality check on the line.

Both rates and CGT can be avoided where a room is not exclusively used for work. However, in a typical taxation conundrum, for those who are employed and must work mainly from home (where there is an 'objective need' for teleworking and written instruction from the employer), the extra tax reliefs available on rent, cleaning, council tax, etc. cannot be claimed unless a room is exclusively used.

'Business' charges by public utilities

Regulations in the Finance Act 2000 indicate that an electricity supply is considered domestic if at least 60% of the fuel is used for domestic purposes. If you use less than 33 kilowatt hours per day, even if some of it is for business purposes, you will also escape business tariffs. You will need to supply information on what percentage of the bill is domestic, and beware – they are supposed to charge you VAT on the business portion.

For telephone service, BT does not compel people to use the business rate, but points out that the business service has the advantage of a Yellow Pages entry, and a Business Pages entry. BT also puts business users on a higher priority for fault correction than residential users. In both cases compensation is paid if the fault is not repaired within 24 hours.

INCOME TAX

So what expenses can you claim for your home office? If you are employed, p. 180 has information on taxable allowances, travel costs and benefit-in-kind. If you are self-employed, the best advice is to talk through the issues with your tax adviser, but you can probably claim expenses for heating, lighting, telephone, depreciation of the fixtures and fittings, installation of extra power points, cleaning costs, business insurance, refurbishment, office equipment, postage and stationery, repair of IT-related equipment, work-related publications such as books and magazines, and membership of professional associations. For startup small businesses, 100% capital allowances on investments in information and communications technology such as computers and software have been available for the three years from 1 April 2000. *See* **http://www.inlandrevenue.gov.uk/manuals/capitalmanual/CA20000/ ca23130.htm**

EMPLOYED OR SELF-EMPLOYED?

Many teleworkers and telecottages have reported confusions and difficulties when they wish to get help from other teleworkers to complete work. The difficulty comes over whether the other teleworkers are employed (PAYE) or self-employed. The definition used to distinguish between self-employment and PAYE-employment is that of a contract for service against a contract of service:

■ Contracts for service are agreements for a specified piece of work to be completed. In teleworking terms these normally consist of the completion

ARE YOU EMPLOYED OR SELF-EMPLOYED?

The main criteria are listed in a free Inland Revenue booklet entitled *Employed or Self-Employed?* (**http://www.inlandrevenue.gov.uk/pdfs/ir56.htm**) which states that if you can answer yes to the following questions, it will 'usually' mean that you are self-employed.

- *Do you have the final say in how the business is run?*

- *Do you risk your own money in the business?*

- *Are you responsible for meeting the losses as well as taking profits?*

- *Do you provide the major items of equipment you need to do your job, not just the small tools which many employees provide for themselves?*

- *Are you free to hire other people, on terms of your own choice, to do the work that you have taken on? Do you pay them out of your own pocket?*

- *Do you have to correct unsatisfactory work in your own time and at your own expense?*

If you answer 'yes' to the following, then you are 'probably' an employee:

- *Do you have to do the work rather than hire someone else to do it for you?*

- *Can someone tell you at any time what to do or when and how to do it?*

- *Are you paid by the hour, week or month? Can you get overtime pay?*

- *Do you work set hours, or a given number of hours a week or month?*

- *Do you work at the premises of the person you are working for, or at a place or places that they decide?*

Another key issue, though not decisive, is how many clients you have if you are self-employed. In general, longer contracts with one 'client' will indicate employment, while several, simultaneous contracts with different clients suggest self-employment.

Ann Collins of Proto-type, a Telework Association member, has successfully established a situation where the four teleworkers she works with are classified as self-employed. Proto-type is a remote word-processing service based in Essex and operating for city-based firms. The company's main client is a quantity surveying group. Handwritten documents and audio tapes are received by fax and post, typed and returned by modem. Ann explains: 'We started off with just myself and we are still small, using four teleworkers, with very tight margins. The additional cost and the time in administering PAYE and national insurance for employed status would have been sufficient deterrents to stop us from continuing the business. From the teleworkers' point of view, self-employment gives them greater flexibility. We had to argue the point with the local tax office, but a number of points eventually convinced them.'

... *continued*

These points were:

- *The teleworkers provide their own equipment.*

- *The client deals with the teleworker directly.*

- *There is no guarantee about the amount of work which the teleworker might expect to receive.*

- *It is the responsibility of the teleworker to correct poor work at their own cost.*

- *The teleworker's ability to take on other work is not restricted.*

- *Separate invoices are issued from the teleworker to the main 'work getter' (such as Proto-type) and from the 'work getter' to the client company.*

of a specified project by the teleworker for his or her client as a self-employed activity on which no PAYE (or PRSI in Ireland) is levied.

■ Contracts of service are standard employments – a teleworker operating on a payment by the hour for one single client is likely to be considered to have a contract of service, on which PAYE and national insurance (PRSI in Ireland) are payable, regardless of the location of the teleworker in relation to the client/employer.

The IR35 ruling

One way of avoiding the employed/self-employed dilemma, particularly popular with contract computer programmers who tend to find their work through employment agencies, has been the limited company route. Here the teleworker sets up a limited company, which is contracted to do the work by the client. The limited company pays a salary to the teleworker, which of course is subject to income tax and national insurance contributions. Unfortunately a number of contractors took to paying themselves low salaries but high dividends from their limited companies, which effectively reduced their tax and national insurance contributions.

The response of the Inland Revenue was to issue a regulation known as IR35 in 1999, which it says: 'is aimed at engagements with the essential characteristics of employment where these characteristics are disguised through the use of an intermediary such as a service company or partnership. There is no intention to redefine the existing boundary between employment and self-employment'. The changes have caused controversy in the engineering and computer contracting sectors . The Telework Association's financial advisers comment: 'Payments of dividends out of the income in such cases have become ineffective – company expenditure outside permitted expenses will be taxable under PAYE for a relevant engagement, which is one where the income would have been taxed as employment income if the worker had contracted directly with the client organisation under the same terms. The rules for detemining whether the engagement is relevant are the same as the rules for establishing whether an individual is employed or self-employed.'

EMPLOYMENT LAW

Rights to flexible working arrangements

A clause in the Employment Act 2002 due to come into force in April 2003 allows anyone with six months' service and a child under the age of six to request to work a flexible pattern, such as jobsharing, term-time working or working from home. The employer must arrange to meet the employee within 28 days, and write within 14 days of the meeting to either agree to a new work pattern and start date, or to provide clear business grounds as to why the application cannot be accepted – including specific reasons why the grounds apply in the particular circumstances. The grounds for rejection are listed:

- The burden of additional costs.
- Detrimental effect on ability to meet customer demand.
- Inability to re-organise work among existing staff.
- Inability to recruit additional staff.
- Detrimental impact on quality.
- Detrimental impact on performance.
- Insufficiency of work during the periods the employee proposes to work.
- Planned structural changes.
- Other grounds that the Secretary of State for Employment may specify by regulations.

If the employee believes that there has been either a breach of procedure or provision of incorrect facts (such as false information presented as one of the business grounds), they can take their case to an Employment Tribunal or to binding arbitration. *See* **http://www.dti.gov.uk/er/individual/workparents_features.htm**

The European framework agreement

A Europe-wide agreement between the employer's organisation UNICE and the European trade union confederation ETUC on teleworking was signed in 2002. Details of the agreement, which has yet to be implemented, are given on p. 65.

Employment agencies

Although it is no longer necessary to obtain a licence if you are getting work for other people, a number of legal strictures apply regardless of whether you are a commercial concern or a non-profit-making body (but charities are exempt).

EVEN TAX INSPECTORS TELEWORK...

The Inland Revenue has its own well-established teleworking scheme which has some interesting features. Many of its teleworkers have to work around a major security issue. No remote access whatsoever to the country's sensitive tax and national insurance databases is allowed.

In practical terms, if a member of staff is teleworking and needs information from either of these databases, they must phone a designated 'buddy' in the office, who has previously agreed to take on the role, and who is authorised to pass on information from the system.

Because of this restriction, there are many jobs within the service which are not suitable for teleworking. Additionally, consultation with colleagues at an early stage of any proposed move to teleworking is vital. The initial telework trial in the Revenue used staff welfare officers, who have to travel a great deal in their job anyway, and do not normally require access to the sensitive databases.

Another interesting feature of the Inland Revenue scheme is the use it makes of its national network of offices. Sometimes allowing a staff member to work from an office which happens to be closer to their home than the office they are normally assigned to provides a solution both to travelling time problems and to security issues. Some larger offices have dedicated hotdesks for mobile or homeworkers attending the office, and network docking stations for laptops. All staff are encouraged to leave desks tidy and ready to be used by a colleague if required.

The Inland Revenue operates an interesting policy of non-insurance against losses of equipment provided for people working at home, although no figures on whether this has proved less costly than insurance have been released.

Communication with colleagues in relation to the teleworking arrangements is specified in detail in the Revenue's guidance. Homeworkers must let their immediate colleagues know their planned pattern of work, how they can be contacted, what hours they will be taking calls, what callers who cannot reach the homeworker should be told if they call the office, and how post is to be received and sent. (Teleworking, IDS Personnel policy and practice study no. 729, May 2002)

Full information is available from the Department of Trade and Industry's Employment Agency Standards Office (Tel: 0845 955 5105). Anyone thinking of providing employment services is also recommended to discuss the matter with professional advisers and to contact REC, the Recruitment and Employment Confederation, which is the main professional body (Tel: 020 7323 4399, Web: **http://www.rec.uk.com**). The situation in Ireland is complex – contact the Department of Enterprise, Trade and Employment for guidance. (**http://www.irlgov.ie/entemp**).

What are the main issues?

(This list is not comprehensive – use the contacts above for full information.)

- You may not charge fees to workers for seeking to find them jobs, nor offer any financial benefit or benefit-in-kind to persuade workers to use your services (there are a few exemptions, e.g. theatre and modelling).
- You must obtain adequate information from employer and worker clients for the purpose of selecting a suitable worker.
- You must not disclose information about employers and workers other than for the purpose of finding or supplying workers.
- You must ensure that workers possess any necessary qualifications required by law (such as HGV licences for lorry drivers).
- You must ensure that the worker and employer are aware of any legal conditions such as work permits for certain non-EU nationals.
- You must provide employer clients with clearly legible, written terms of business on receipt of an application.
- You must, if you receive money on behalf of a worker client, pay it to the worker within ten days of receipt.
- You must not prohibit or restrict workers from entering the direct employment of a hirer, or replace workers on industrial dispute, or supply workers previously employed directly by the hirer within the previous six months.

Non-compete clauses

Employees are often asked to sign agreements that they will not compete with their employer if the employment is terminated, either within a specified period, or within a specified location. This can affect teleworkers who decide to set up independently and become self-employed, working in the same field in which they had previously carried out work for an employer. Often there are more specific activity-based references to prevent, for example, the use of customer contacts gained through employment by the employee in a competing business.

However, many of these agreements make no sense if the service is delivered through teleworking, where there are no geographical barriers. There have been some cases in the US in relation to non-compete clauses which have shown that courts will not generally support 'blanket clauses' banning competition worldwide, or in very broad circumstances, as these would restrict the employee's ability to earn a living in future.

Companies may be advised to check their non-compete clauses with legal advisers to ensure that they are in keeping with the reality of modern business. The US cases suggest that activity-based clauses must be restricted to those customers with whom the employee actually had contact during their employment, and not broadened to include all past customers of the employer.

Suggestions for self-employment contracts

Teleworking consultancy Cornix prepared the following recommendations for a minimum teleworking contract:

1. Include identities and contact addresses of both purchaser and supplier, and if either is a corporate body, the names of the individuals concerned.
2. Describe, in general terms, the work to be carried out, its purpose and scope.
3. Specify the payment for the work, and whether VAT will be applicable.
4. Specify a timetable both for the work, and for payment for the work.
5. Describe clearly the proposals for confidentiality and security of the work and its Data Protection Act status.
6. Define the ownership of any resulting copyright and intellectual property rights, if appropriate.
7. Where applicable, arrangements for loan or supply of equipment, including insurance arrangements, should be listed.
8. Specify arrangements in the event of illness, incapacity, holidays, etc. and for any consequent subcontracting, if permitted.
9. If the workload exceeds 21 hours per week, and is an exclusive use of the teleworker full-time, then arrangements for PAYE and NI deductions should be made, as in these circumstances the teleworker may be classified as an employee for the duration of the work.
10. Refer to the quality assurance system to be used, if any.
11. Where group working is involved, the identity of the individual responsible for quality within the group should be specified.

PHYSICAL SECURITY

Data security issues are dealt with in the previous chapter; this section considers issues of physical security.

Be wary of working in shared areas if the material you are handling is sensitive. Typical workarounds for increased security in such areas include software that freezes workstations after a period of inactivity and will not allow the screen to be viewed until a user password is given, and secure printing facilities (here the printer will not begin the job until a security code has been entered into its keypad, confirming that the person for whom the job is being printed is ready to collect the pages).

In many ways a burglary has a much more drastic effect on a home office than on a conventional office. In an office, the employer takes responsibility for equipment, and can afford security measures such as closed circuit TV. At home, you will be dealing with all the consequences of any burglary. Telecentres that allow public access to premises should consider the problems of supervision of visitors and casual users.

Computers have a high resale value and are likely to be the main target for a break-in. However, the advantage of most home offices is that they do not advertise 'expensive kit in here'. To all intents and purposes the risks of burglary are actually lower than for an ordinary house, because working from home means there is someone on the premises most of the time. You might want to look at installing blinds if your office is on the ground floor so that the computers are not visible to passers-by. In general it is wise not to allow visitors into your home office unless necessary – the fewer people who know about your equipment, the better. Check the credentials of utility company and local authority officials who call at the house.

Specific deterrence devices for computers include alarms, labelling, etching ID numbers into casings, cables to lock equipment to fixed items like tables, and lockable workstation cabinets.

The Suzy Lamplugh Trust warns that women working from home should ensure they are not running security risks if clients visit them. A survey by Barclays Bank in 1998 found that two-thirds of home-based businesswomen have client visits, but 40% of these women take no steps to ensure their physical safety such as ensuring that another person is present. One-fifth feel the presence of their dog is a help. The Suzy Lamplugh Trust encourages use of the mnemonic acronym PLAN. **Plan** to meet the first time in a busy place rather than at your home. **Log** your visitors with a buddy by phone and phone to check in after the meeting. **Avoid** situations which could be difficult. **Never** assume it won't happen to you.

Telephone and electricity supplies are rarely considered when analyses of security risks are being made, but problems in these areas can effectively stop a business from trading. For most people the cost of providing an uninterruptable power supply (UPS) or generator backup for a whole office will be prohibitive, but systems are available which at least give you sufficient breathing space to close down the computer after a power cut without losing work in progress. Try the RS Components Ltd catalogue at **http://rswww.com** which lists various devices to keep one computer powered for about 15 minutes costing around £80 to £210 (try UPS, uninterruptible power supplies and offline as keyword searches). It may be worthwhile to pre-arrange for the use of workspace elsewhere in the area should you suffer a loss of power for more than a day. The arrangement could be with a neighbouring teleworker or office-services company, or with a telecentre.

Association member Stephen Thomas found that BT will arrange for an alternative number while your own is out of service, so that clients hear a message and can leave voicemail or speak to you, rather than getting a frustrating engaged tone or, more commonly, the phone appearing to ring as though you were out. Dial 154 to ask for this service – but as it operates through call diversion, you need to have another, functioning number to which the calls can be diverted.

FIRE SAFETY

Many home offices do not have fire extinguishers, smoke alarms, first-aid kits or clear evacuation routes. If you are worried that an official safety inspection by the fire brigade might lead to your office being 'banned' on fire-safety grounds, ask advice from a supplier of firefighting equipment on suitable measures.

Fire officers advise that all home offices should be fitted with smoke detectors. Costs are in the range of £4–14 each – those which are interlinked by cable so that all go off if one goes off are better, and mains-driven systems are preferable to battery-operated ones. Bryan Bates of Gloucestershire Fire and Rescue Service said: 'The main thing that we suggest is for people to get interlinked smoke detectors fitted. One in the hall, one in the landing, and one in the home office, particularly if it is a converted loft space. All new properties have to have them by law, but when people convert lofts they often forget to do it. It is the biggest life-saver because a smoke detector goes off at the first whiff of smoke, giving people time to walk out of the house, shut the doors and call the fire brigade. But systems must be maintained properly. Once a week – perhaps first thing on a Monday morning – it is important that they press the test button and get into a routine. Local fire brigades can supply a free brochure, *Fire Safety in the Home*, to give further advice.'

Around 500 people a year die in home fires in Britain. Ted Savill of ES Safety Supplies points out that many insurance policies are invalid if you don't have fire extinguishers. The most suitable type of extinguisher for a home office is a CO_2 (carbon dioxide) extinguisher. Ted explains: 'Dry powder can be used on anything, but it's very messy and will get into the works of your computer. CO_2 extinguishers are more expensive but better suited to electrical fires. A typical 5 kg model retails for around £65 plus delivery, while a 9 kg dry-powder model costs around £48.' Whichever model you choose, check that it is British Standard approved, and ensure that it is maintained according to the manufacturer's instructions (usually it will need servicing every 6–12 months).

Try **http://www.firesave.co.uk** or **http://www.spectrumfireprotection.com** for more recent prices.

For those with upstairs home offices, check escape routes if a fire were to make the stairs impassable. The most important point is that windows should be easy to open and large enough to climb out through. Steel ladders or stairs fixed to the outside of the house may be a possibility, but could be expensive, a security risk or unsightly. They may require planning permission. In some circumstances 'rope ladders' which are bolted firmly inside the house and can be thrown down from a large window to provide an escape route may be an option. The ladder should have metal chains, and metal steps which hold the chains away from the wall in use so you do not scrape your knuckles. These ladders are not recommended by some fire-safety experts because they require agility and familiarity for use. However, if you feel confident using such an escape route, and you alone are the usual occupant of the home office, it might be worth looking into.

INSURANCE

The first point to remember is that, whether you are employed or self-employed, if you are working from home, you need to inform your home-contents and buildings insurers of this fact in writing. Many employers provide a draft standard letter for doing this (*see* below). Employers also need to ensure that their employer liability policies are extended to cover the home office (*see* below).

Beyond this, there are three other bases to cover. You need to be insured against public liability by your employer, or through your home-contents policy if you are self-employed. If you will be meeting people at home in the course of your work, check that this is covered. Your equipment also needs to be insured (again, this is normally done by the employer if they own the equipment, or through a home-office policy if it is your own equipment). Finally, there needs to be insurance in place to cover people and equipment in transit.

Dear Sir/Madam

Working from Home

I am about to begin working from home, initially for Y days per week, in connection with my employment for X organisation. There will be no structural alterations to the property, and no marked increase in the number of people calling to the property.
[If relevant: The equipment provided by the employer (*see* attached list) is insured by the employer.]

Can you please advise if this is acceptable or whether it would affect my existing policy [give policy number if you can] in any way?

Yours faithfully
Etc.

Employer-liability insurance

The usual arrangement is to extend the company's insurance to cover the home workplace, although in many cases companies find that employees are already covered for working offsite. The employer will need to consider including public liability for visitors to the home workplace in some situations. Some employers offset the additional home-office risk by requiring a health and safety risk assessment of the home workplace. Normally there is no great increase in the employer's premiums as liability premiums are based on wages and salaries plus previous claims experience. Because of a potential clash with domestic policies, teleworking employees must also inform their home insurers that they will be working from home as noted above – most home insurers then reply 'thanks for informing us, it's not a problem'.

If, alternatively, an employer asks an employee to take out a home-office policy to cover the equipment belonging to the employer used at home, they should also sign an agreement that transfers the insurable interest in the equipment to the employee.

An interesting case in the US involved someone who slipped and fell on a sidewalk (pavement) outside a house. Usually residential property owners are immune from this kind of liability, but owners and tenants of commercial property abutting the sidewalk can sometimes be liable. A 'creative plaintiff', as the legal jargon goes, attempted to expand the definition of commercial premises to include the residence of a telecommuter, based on his business card which gave his home address. The court upheld the employee's home as residential but noted that giving the home address on the business card would change the status of individuals visiting the property from social guests to business invitees.[61]

In relation to insuring mobile workers, because of the high rate of claims, insurers will often impose conditions (e.g. that laptops and mobiles must not be left unattended in cars or hotel rooms). Your standard car policy will normally cover a teleworker travelling from home to work.

Home-office policies

A standard home-contents policy may already cover a small amount of home-office equipment (do check your policy), but there may be a number of other reasons to go for a home-office policy – such as a domestic policy single-item claim, limit or wishing to cover other business items such as public liability or business interruption.

Home-office policies generally cover equipment valued in the range of £5000 to £20,000 and tend to cost about 60% of the cost of an equivalent office policy. The higher the value of the equipment, the higher the premium. Whether your office is part of the house or a separate outbuilding may also affect the premium (in the house is considered more secure because it is constantly occupied). When adding up the cost of your equipment, don't forget extras and small items such as mice and tape drives which can easily turn a £1000 basic PC into a £2000 replacement cost. Be sure to base your calculations on replacement value, not current value, since computers depreciate in value so quickly.

Also remember to inform your insurers about any changes, such as purchase of new computers, or a change in the number of visitors or employees, which affects the risk insured. Failure to inform can cause problems if you have to claim.

If you use an insurance broker who, on your behalf, moves your policy around different insurers to get the best deal, check that the material details (such as serial numbers of equipment) are properly recorded every time the policy is renewed, and that any unusual items, like garden offices, are still covered. Other items which affect the premium vary from insurer to insurer and include:

- Client visits to your premises.
- Employees.
- Window locks.
- Mortice locks on doors.
- Presence of burglar alarm.
- Membership of neighbourhood watch (Community Alert in Ireland).
- Age of policy-holder.

TELEWORKING TALES FROM THE TOLSON FILES

The Telework Association has had a long-term relationship with insurance brokers Tolson Messenger, who specialise in the home-office market. Tolson opened their files to reveal some of the stranger claims they have received.

'My mobile phone came loose from its mounting on the car dash while going round a corner. It slid along the dash and flew out of the open window, landing terminally on the road.'

'I was using the PC outside in the garden. A dog chased a cat towards me. I moved to get out of the way and in doing so knocked over the table. The PC fell into the carp pond, which is deep. No loss of data as full backup disks maintained. But I have not yet been able to retrieve the computer, though will be part-draining the pond in order to do so very soon.'

'The train stopped suddenly, pitching another commuter forwards and trapping my fingers in the laptop. Unfortunately the screen suffered irreparable damage.'

'We had set up the PC in an alcove which was a large, disused, walk-in fireplace. A freak storm deposited gallons of water down the chimney and into the PC.'

'I was working in the garden with my laptop on a sunny day and my daughter was also playing in the garden. I heard the phone ring in the house and went off to answer it. When I came back both my daughter and my laptop were in the paddling pool.'

'I fell asleep with my notebook computer on my lap. It fell off my lap, waking me up. I stood up and stepped right through the screen of the laptop.'

'I was carrying my laptop upstairs to my home office. I opened the door and a trapped cat ran out, startling me. The laptop fell onto the landing below.'

Mobile phones, eminently portable and stealable, are usually excluded from home-office policies. Another area often omitted is stock held for resale such as paper, disks or publications. Other areas to consider (which are usually available at the cost of extra premium) are:

- Loss of data (e.g. through virus or malicious attack).
- Public liability or employer's liability insurance, if people visit or work at your home office (this is imperative for anyone operating in the Republic of Ireland). It is also important for employers to ensure that employees other than the teleworker visiting the home office are covered (e.g. managers or those involved in health and safety checks).

- Business interruption insurance, which compensates you for time spent putting your business back together, and for other costs incurred after an incident.
- Computer breakdown insurance – this has become very expensive in recent years, so compare costs for taking out a maintenance contract as well.
- Cover off the premises (e.g. portable computers on business trips).

Health insurance

In Britain, everyone has access to the National Health Service for free medical care. However, you may need to think about extra health insurance if you are opting for self-employment. You will also need access to welfare benefits or insurance payouts to replace your income should you become unable to work. Typical categories of insurance policy are:

- Access to fast, private healthcare to reduce time out of work (private medical insurance).
- Insurance against certain illnesses preventing you from working and earning that provides a lump sum (critical illness insurance).
- Income protection insurance to provide a regular income if you are unable to work due to a serious injury or illness (permanent health insurance or PHI – *see* below).
- Insurance against the consequences of accidents (personal accident insurance).

Private healthcare policies are available from a range of suppliers in the UK, such as BUPA and PPP. These regular-payment policies are not the same as the critical-illness insurance policies currently being marketed and which need very careful assessment. Although many cover the basic unhappy events such as heart attack, stroke or cancer, they do not cover chronic conditions such as arthritis or endometriosis which can prevent you from working just as effectively. The small print is well worth reading!

Self-employed people do pay national insurance, but it only entitles them to the health service, disability benefits and the old-age pension – not to unemployment benefit if their business goes under (although depending on circumstances, other means-tested benefits may be available). The benefits system has become increasingly complex in the past few years, and it is worth consulting your local library or Citizens' Advice Bureau on your entitlements.

Any teleworker becoming self-employed should think seriously about taking out PHI to secure their income level should they become unable to work through ill-health. PHI does not pay your medical bills – instead, it replaces your lost income. Normally the policy provides around 75% of your usual salary (to give you an incentive to go back to work). Premium levels depend on your medical history when you take out the policy, your deferral period, and any exemptions you select. The deferral period is normally around 13 weeks, and is a time delay between the onset of illness and the date when the policy begins to pay out. The longer the deferral, the lower the premium.

Exemptions are usually created where you have a pre-existing problem (such as back trouble) which makes your premiums very high, although some may still find they are effectively uninsurable due to their medical condition. With an exemption, if you agree not to claim with regard to, say, back problems, you can get insurance for other conditions at more reasonable premiums. It is extremely important that you ensure that your medical conditions are fully disclosed when taking out a permanent health-insurance policy (check your doctor's report and make sure that you let the insurer know if you think anything has been omitted). Otherwise, if you need to claim and have to undergo an independent examination, your claim may be denied. Permanent health insurance isn't a particularly remunerative sector for insurance companies, and many will only offer these policies if they are taken out in tandem with personal pensions. Small businesses with employees or partners can also consider buying 'key person' insurance for owner-managers so that the business receives a payout if the key person dies or becomes incapacitated.

In Ireland, membership of VHI or BUPA is to be recommended to ensure swift treatment of health problems for the self-employed. Premiums can be partially claimed against tax.

Professional indemnity

Companies that give advice or provide services owe their clients a duty of care. Professional indemnity insurance covers problems such as negligent acts, errors or omissions; unintentional breaches of statutory terms or warranties; unintentional infringement of intellectual property rights; dishonesty of subcontractors or employees, etc.

http://clickforcover.com also have policies to cover damage to the company through viruses, hackers, employee fraud, etc.

Other forms of insurance

Depending on the nature of your business, you may also want to think about other forms of insurance. The website **http://www.clickforcover.com** gives information about various 'E-sure' policies it provides which may be relevant for people who do business on the Internet, including third-party liabilities. These could include libel or slander due to email or website content; breaches of intellectual property rights; breaches of confidentiality, privacy or data-protection legislation; damage to computer systems belonging to others (e.g. through forwarding a computer virus); and website mispricing issues.

DATA PROTECTION ACT

The Data Protection Registrar has a comprehensive website at
http://www.dpr.gov.uk which includes a useful online questionnaire to help
you decide whether or not you need to register. As a general guide, a large
number of teleworkers are defined as 'data controllers' who process 'personal
data', but as much of this data is exempt, only a small percentage will need to
register. The main exemptions are data held for:

- Staff administration, including payroll.
- Advertising, marketing and public relations for your own business (but not
  if you carry out these activities for other businesses).
- Accounts and records.

However, there are a number of purposes which are not exempt that may affect
teleworkers. Data held for research, provision of financial services, education,
health admnistration, etc. are not exempt and you will be required to register.
You can also use the website to fill in an online notification form, which you
then print out, sign and send to the Data Protection Registrar along with a fee
of £35 on which no VAT is payable.

If your information-handling practices are found to be negligent, you can be
liable for civil action due to damage caused by inaccurate data, unauthorised
data, loss of data, or destruction of personal records, including liability for
related distress caused. Data subjects can request access to their personal data,
and where appropriate, demand correction or deletion of a record. In return,
data users can charge up to £10 for a copy of the data.

In general, if you are processing information on behalf of an employer, it is
the employer's duty to register, not the employee's. If you are transferring any
personal data outside the European Economic Area then you will also need to
ensure that there is adequate protection for the data subject in the country that
you are exporting to. Everyone is required to comply with the Act, even if they
don't actually need to register.

A code of practice on employment relations – including a section on
monitoring which is likely to be relevant to some teleworkers, such as
call-centre 'agents at home' – is currently being drafted. If you think you might
be affected by this issue, check the Data Protection Commissioner's website.

In July 2002 the EU passed a directive on the processing of personal data
and protection of privacy relating to electronic communications. This directive
has been transposed into national law and describes rights for inviduals not to
have to receive unsolicited forwarded calls, SMS messages, faxes and emails.
However, there is no clear understanding of how the legislation can actually be
enforced as yet.

On a practical basis, data protection legislation also affects you in relation to
email marketing. If you send out marketing material by email you must be able to
show that you obtained the email address fairly – usually by asking permission

DATA PROTECTION PRINCIPLES AND DEFINITIONS
Personal data that you process must be

● *fairly and lawfully processed;*

● *processed for limited purposes;*

● *adequate, relevant and not excessive;*

● *accurate;*

● *not kept longer than necessary;*

● *processed in accordance with the data subject's rights;*

● *secure;*

● *not transferred to countries without adequate protection.*

Personal data covers both facts and opinions about living, identifiable individuals. It includes information regarding the intentions of the data controller towards the individual, though some limited exemptions apply. Data processing includes obtaining, holding and disclosing data. Data subjects are those to whom personal data relates.

directly or because they have volunteered their email address for your website enquiry form. If someone requests to be removed from your email list you must comply with their request. It is illegal to sell personal data without the permission of the person involved. You should also ensure that you advertise and comply with a privacy policy in any Internet business dealings – do not share personal data with any third parties without permission from the person involved.

In the UK it is already illegal to fax or phone individuals (including sole-trader businesses) who have previously registered their desire not to receive unsolicited communications under the Telecommunications (Data Protection and Privacy) Regulations 1999 (*see* p. 140). Penalties include fines of up to £5000. A service to check numbers against the databases of people who do not wish to be called is offered by OSL. The service costs around 6p per number, reducing according to the volume of numbers checked. OSL give a reference number for each number checked, and the service is backed by professional indemnity insurance (**http://www.osl2000.com**).

The data protection laws in the Republic of Ireland are less restrictive than those in the UK and substantially simpler for laypeople to understand. A comprehensive website is available at **http://www.dataprivacy.ie**

INTELLECTUAL PROPERTY AND COPYRIGHT

Although prosecutions for infringements of copyright and intellectual property rights (IPR) are rare, it is important to have a basic grasp of your rights and responsibilities, especially with regard to online material. In practical terms, most people don't necessarily want to be paid if you re-use something of theirs in your work. However, they almost certainly do want to be asked, and to have their IPR acknowledged in your document. These days, many authors and agents distinguish rights for paper publication from those for online distribution.

Most countries in the world operate to the Berne Convention, which means that even if a document does not have a copyright notice or use the © symbol, the work is copyright, even if it's merely a shopping list. Pictures are covered as well as text, and it is irrelevant whether or not you charge for your publication – even if you give it away free, if you include someone else's copyrighted material without permission it's an infringement of their IPR.

If you want to assert your own copyright on a document, add:

Copyright © [date] by [author].

In professional publications there is often a more detailed copyright statement such as: 'No part of this publication may be reproduced or used in any form by any means – graphic, electronic or mechanical including photocopying, taping or information storage or retrieval systems – without prior permission in writing from [the publishers].'

With regard to information on the Internet, including newsgroups and listservs, nothing is 'in the public domain' and therefore free to use unless it has an explicit statement granting it to the public domain attached. This particularly applies to material from online news services; you may be able to extract information, rephrase it and sell it on in some circumstances, where it could be regarded as 'fair use', but in general beware of all but the most minimal quotation.

An excellent guide to copyright and IPR by Brad Templeton is available at **http://www.clari.net** and includes this summary of 'fair use':

'The "fair use" exemption to copyright law was created to allow things such as commentary, parody, news reporting, research and education about copyrighted works without the permission of the author. Intent, and damage to the commercial value of the work are important considerations. Are you reproducing an article from the *New York Times* because you needed to in order to criticise the quality of the *New York Times,* or because you couldn't find time to write your own story, or didn't want your readers to have to pay to log onto the online services with the story or buy a copy of the paper? The first is probably fair use, the others probably aren't.

'Fair use is almost always a short excerpt and almost always attributed. (Do not use more of the work than is necessary to make the commentary.) It should not harm the commercial value of the work – in the sense of people no longer needing to buy it (which is another reason why reproduction of the entire work is generally forbidden).'

Training materials do not normally fall into the fair-use category. Also bear in mind that uploading and downloading software or graphics on the Internet may cause an infringement of someone's copyright or IPR and could lead to financial liabilities.

David Flint, a partner in MacRoberts, Solicitors, is a specialist in intellectual property and gave this summary of IP to *Teleworker Magazine*: 'The general rule for most types of IP is that it is owned by its creator unless created by employees acting within the scope of their employment, in which case it is owned by the employer. It's important that employment contracts address this issue. In the IT industry the use of contractors is common. Where the work involves design, the IP produced belongs to the contractor unless you have a written contract which assigns the IP rights. This is also true for graphic design such as logos. Computer software is also considered to be a literary work and so can benefit from copyright protection.

'In relation to copyright it's important to remember that it is a right to stop someone from copying, not a monopoly right. If someone can show they independently developed something without copying your work then they will not have infringed your copyright.'

David Flint can be contacted at **http://www.macroberts.co.uk**

CONSUMER PROTECTION AND DIRECT SELLING RULES

Consumer protection directives issued by the EU also apply to electronic commerce, and to any interchange via an electronic medium such as telemarketing, or kiosk-based services. The 1997 EU directive on distance contracts affects telephone, mail-order and Internet-based sales. In summary, it provides that:

- The consumer is entitled to the name and address of the company selling the goods, to details of the goods and a clear price.
- On receipt of goods, whatever the quality of the goods, the consumer has seven days in which to return them.
- All goods must be delivered within 30 days (except perishable goods, and allowing for public holidays, etc).

The EU's consumer protection law also applies to electronic commerce requiring that you must:

- Provide goods that are of merchantable quality and fit for their purpose.
- Own or have title to what you are selling.
- Provide samples that are similar to any bulk sales.

LEGAL EAGLE FLIES SOLO

Virtual law firm Davis & Co specialises in international transactions such as mergers and acquisitions, as well as in intellectual property law. For large projects, which can involve up to 300 people in different countries, sharing and synchronising documents by traditional means is 'a complete nightmare', according to Christopher Davis.

Over the years Davis has built up expertise in how to manage these projects, which he now plans to develop as a saleable product through subsidiary company Gobalhelm. Gobalhelm sets up secure extranets which all parties to the transaction can use to access the relevant documentation. A data manager is brought it to act as co-ordinator, ensuring that all the documents are collected, scanned and updated.

Using the Gobalhelm portal, clients, lawyers, accountants and other advisers such as banks can access everything they need. Christopher is now working on an extension to the system which refers beyond the case-specific documents to relevant legal guidance or business practice relating to the topic in hand. 'Instead of just delivering legal advice we will now be providing ways of delivering that advice,' comments Davis.
http://www.davisco.net

- Provide services with the necessary skill and diligence that would normally be expected.
- Avoid advertising which is misleading or likely to deceive.

The EU's Unfair Terms in Consumer Contracts law applies to any contract which is not individually negotiated, such as websites which provide 'click here to see terms and conditions' pages.

THE INTERNET

Defamation

In general you should resist putting anything which could be considered defamatory in an email message, even one that is sent on a one-to-one basis. In ordinary written correspondence, a letter from one person to another in a closed envelope is considered to be 'privileged' correspondence and it is unlikely that a defamation lawsuit could be made to stick in such circumstances. Email is not the same at all – it is not assumed to be private unless previously agreed between the parties. It's also very easy for a slip of the finger to send an email to entirely the wrong person. If in doubt, leave it out, particularly on public forums or newsgroups.

Metatags and linking

David Flint, a partner in MacRoberts, Solicitors comments: 'Another point which may seem a little obscure concerns the use of metatags on web pages. These are HTML tags used by search engines to index pages. A cookery page might be indexed using a metatag including words like food, baking and cakes, which is fine. However, if the metatags contained a reference to a real person such as Jamie Oliver or Delia Smith, it could infringe their rights or trademarks even though metatags cannot be seen on the web page unless the user looks under the "Source" function of the browser.'

In relation to copyright and links to other website URLs, the common-sense position seems to be that listing a website URL as a source of information is not regarded as infringing the website owner's copyright, in the same way as mentioning a book title. However, the link should normally be to the home page of the website rather than a direct link deep into the website, as the case law in this area is currently unclear. Do not use icons or logos as link buttons if there is any possibility that they could be trademarks of another company. Note that there is a slim possibility that if defamatory material were found on the website you have linked to, you could be held responsible.

Digital signatures

Both the UK and Ireland have implemented Directive 1999/93/EC providing for electronic (digital) signature of documents. In practical terms the directive covers supervision of certification service providers (also known as 'trusted third parties'). In the UK the admissibility of electronic signatures as evidence in legal proceedings was implemented in the Electronic Communications Act 2000. The Irish act is 'future proofed' to allow for the addition of new identification technologies which may become widespread.

Internet misuse

A survey of human resources managers for 500 large UK companies in 2002 found that one-quarter have dismissed employees for Internet misconduct – and over two-thirds of sackings involved online porn. The companies, which employed an average of 2500 people, reported that on average the acceptable time for personal Internet surfing each day was regarded as 20 minutes, but that they believed their colleagues were actually spending about 30 minutes a day on their own Internet interests. (Survey results issued by Websense International and *Personnel Today* magazine.)

This is clearly a slightly more sensitive issue where people are working from their own homes, but should be covered by usual company rules on Internet use, especially where the equipment used by the teleworker has been provided by the company.

Cybersquatters

Cybersquatters are people who register Internet domain names that they think other people want, and may be prepared to pay over the odds for. It doesn't just happen to famous people or companies – there are now organisations which scoop up unused names, or those whose registration has not been kept up to date, and resell them. Morag Macdonald of Bird and Bird, a London firm which specialises in retrieving domain names, gives the following advice on what to do if this happens to you.

- Write to the squatter stating your case and asking that they hand over the domain name in return for administration fees.
- For top-level domain names (.org, .com, .net), there is an agreed procedure administered by ICANN (Internet Corporation for Assigned Names and Numbers) which costs about $1000 but produces a resolution in about nine weeks (**http://www.icann.org**).
- For regional domain names (.co.uk, .ie, etc.) approach the domain registrars and ask about their procedures.
- The last resort should be the courts – and only for valuable domain names.

But it's much simpler not to get into a cybersquatting problem in the first place, so register your domain name and make sure you keep up the annual payments to ensure continued registration.

MISCELLANEOUS

If a customer won't pay

The maximum amount that you can recover through the Small Claims Court is £5000. The Small Claims Court offers a court procedure that is simpler, swifter, less formal, less expensive and less intimidating than traditional legal proceedings. The case is heard by a judge in chambers with evidence given around a table. The judge makes an immediate decision but there is no appeal procedure – the decision is binding on both sides.

You begin by completing a standard form explaining the problem, and stating who the claimant and defendant are. A summons is then sent by post to the defendant who can:

- Admit the claim and pay you in full (payment can be in instalments).
- Admit part of the claim and pay you in part (payment can be in instalments).
- Dispute the claim in its entirety, in which case a date is set for the hearing.

There is a ClaimsLink support service which can advise you in relation to your problem and help you complete documents. More information is available at **http://www.small-claims.co.uk**

Pensions

If you are entering self-employment for the first time, and consequently losing the security of a former occupational pension, it must be replaced by a personal pension. It can still be hard to get clear, unbiased advice because most pension advisers receive commissions on the pensions they sell. The best option is to look for an independent financial adviser (who should be approved by the Personal Investment Authority) whom you can pay on an hourly rate (generally from £30 to £100) to look at your situation and advise you. That way, the adviser is paid by you to look after your interests, and not by the pension company to sell their policies. Contributors to personal pension schemes are entitled to tax breaks which increase as you get older.

VAT (4th schedule)

Where a teleworker is registered for VAT and performs data processing tasks which add value for a VAT-registered business located in another EU member state, no VAT is chargeable despite the transaction being for a service rather than for goods. The existence of this rule is particularly important for Irish teleworkers, because if they were forced to charge their export clients the high Irish VAT rate of 21%, and to oblige their clients to go through the cumbersome process of reclaiming the difference between this rate and that pertaining in their own country, they would be at a competitive disadvantage compared to teleworkers in other EU member states with lower VAT rates.

Sundry scams

The new technologies which provide possibilities for teleworking also provide possibilities for you to be taken in. Here are a few:
- You get a text message on your mobile requesting you call a number urgently. You just get an engaged tone. It's actually a premium service charged at £5 per minute playing a recording of an engaged tone.
- You receive an email from your Internet service provider requesting your credit-card details in order to pay your subscription. Generally, ISPs take such payments either over secured websites or by phone. Suspect a scam – check the email return address and you will probably find it is not in fact from your ISP, despite initial appearances.

The Human Rights Act 1998

The Human Rights Act 1998 states: 'An employer does not have the right to demand an employee's telephone number unless it is specified in the contract that the employee has a duty to be available outside normal working hours [...] Even when an employee has indicated a willingness to be called at home, managers should respect privacy and not make unnecessary or inappropriate calls [...] Everyone has the right to respect for their private and family life, their home and correspondence.'

Teleworking has the potential to offer new employment opportunities to some disabled people. People with mobility, visual or hearing impairments can work from their own homes, or from a centre. This can be of particular benefit to people whose disability causes them fatigue or difficulty in travelling to work or in moving around while at work. In addition to mobility issues, it can also be argued that teleworking reduces the level of prejudice that occurs against some disabled people due to their appearance.

However, home-based working may or may not be the best option for an individual compared to flexible hours, or adaptation to the workplace. Making teleworking the only option can be as bad as denying it entirely – and employers preparing teleworking policies need to be aware that where they offer a teleworking option to those with disabilities, they must ensure that they do not discriminate against the able-bodied by restricting teleworking only to those with disabilities or health problems.

In 1999, according to British Labour Force Survey figures, around 78,000 disabled people in Britain were teleworking, amounting to about 5% of teleworkers (similar to the percentage of disabled people employed overall). A further 198,000 were unemployed. For some disabilities such as visual impairment, the unemployment rate is as much as 75–80%. The charity AbilityNet states that around 75% of disabled employees were able-bodied when first employed, and one in 14 people will be eligible to be registered disabled before reaching retirement age.

The Telework Association/IES/Mitel 1999 survey found that 10% of prospective teleworkers value the anonymity afforded by working from home, and a further 17% were attracted by the idea of not having to dress up or worry about their appearance in order to work.

THE BENEFITS SITUATION

In April 2002 the old therapeutic earnings rules were replaced by new, permitted work rules. These allow people on incapacity benefit, severe disablement allowance or income support to do a limited amount of paid work while still being accepted as incapable of work. There is no longer any need to show that the work will be therapeutic and your doctor is not consulted.

Your earnings from permitted work won't affect your incapacity benefit or severe disablement allowance. However, your earnings will affect your income support. If you are getting a disability premium with your income support, the first £20 a week you earn will be ignored, but everything above this will be taken off pound for pound. If you don't get the disability premium, the first £5 a week is ignored for single people and the first £10 if you are a member of a couple. If you don't receive income support your earnings will also be taken

> ## MILESTONE CASES IN THE US AND UK
>
> In 1997 a US citizen was awarded $90,000 damages in compensation for not being allowed to telework – with implications for future cases in Britain. Jack Nilles, the US telework guru, was called as an expert witness for the plaintiff, Michael Faircloth, in his court case against his employer, the Bay Area Rapid Transit District (BART).
>
> BART operates the light rail transit system for the San Francisco region. Michael Faircloth was a labour relations arbitrator employed by BART who is partially disabled by a neck injury which predated his employment with BART. The injury causes pain when sitting or standing for long periods. Faircloth was commuting 100 miles five days per week, causing him severe pain. He had been telecommuting informally for a number of weeks when he was refused the right to telecommute one day a week. Faircloth sued under the Americans with Disabilities Act.
>
> Nilles reviewed the records relating to the case and administered a teleworking screening questionnaire as well as interviewing Faircloth and concluded that he could easily telecommute at least one day per week.
>
> A 1998 Employment Appeal Tribunal decision (London Borough of Hillingdon v Morgan) established that in Britain, the employer does have an obligation to consider temporary teleworking to assist an employee with a physical problem. Ms Morgan, who suffered from ME, asked if she could work from home temporarily. Hillingdon council refused and attempted to redeploy her instead. The tribunal found that a large employer should have been able to facilitate a staged return to work.

into account for housing benefit and council tax benefit. There are three sorts of permitted work.

Lower-limit permitted work

You can work for less than 16 hours a week and earn not more than £20 a week (at October 2002) for as long as you are on the benefits above. You can do lower-limit work even between periods when you are on the other forms of permitted work described below. The rules say that you don't have to tell the Department of Work and Pensions (DWP) before you start this sort of permitted work, as long as you tell them in writing before you stop. But it's sensible to tell them before you begin. There is a very short form (PW1) which you can fill in and the DWP will then write back and tell you if the work has been accepted as permitted work.

Supported permitted work

This can be work as part of a treatment programme, done under medical supervision while you are an inpatient or outpatient at a hospital or similar institution. You may also undertake work supervised by a public body, local authority or voluntary organisation which provides or arranges work opportunities for people with disabilities. You can work for less than 16 hours a week and earn not more than £67.50 a week (as at October 2002) for an indefinite period. The rules for informing the DWP are the same as for lower-limit work above.

Higher-limit permitted work

You can work for less than 16 hours a week and earn not more than £67.50 a week (at October 2002) for a period of 26 weeks. This can be extended for another 26 weeks if you can show that by carrying on working, you are likely to improve your chances of working full-time. Once you have worked for either the 26 or 52 weeks you have to have a gap of 52 weeks before you can do higher-limit work again. You must inform the DWP in writing not later than 42 days from the day you start work. If you don't do so, the work cannot ever be classed as permitted work; you will be treated as capable of work and your benefits will be stopped. So, as with lower-limit above, we strongly recommend that you tell the DWP about your plans before you start work, or as soon after as possible.

For more information about permitted work, try Barton Hill Advice Service (**http://www.bhas.org.uk**). BHAS provide free downloadable guides to permitted work, disability living allowance and many other benefits topics.

Before undertaking any work, it's vital that you get advice about how this may affect your benefits. In theory, doing permitted work should not result in the DWP looking again at whether you are incapable of work, or at your award of disability living allowance (DLA) if you receive one. However, the next time you have a personal capability assessment (the test to decide if you are capable of work) or your DLA comes up for renewal, the decision-maker is entitled to take into account any activities you undertake as part of your work. So if, for example, your work involves a certain amount of standing or walking, and your award of DLA, or the finding that you're incapable of work, is partly based on difficulties you have with these activities, then what you do at work will be taken into account when making a decision about your benefits.

You should also get a better-off calculation done before starting work, preferably by an advice agency (although many Jobcentre staff and New Deal agencies also do them). This will tell you whether you will actually be better-off if you work, how many hours it would be best to work, what grants and benefits run-ons may be available, and what additional or different benefits you may be able to claim. For example, if you work 16 hours or more you may lose some benefits, such as income support, but you may become entitled to others, such as tax credits, instead. Whether you will be better-off working under or over 16 hours will depend on your personal circumstances. Always insist on being given

A PERSONAL VIEW ON THE TELEWORKING OPTION

Mary Duffy is a journalist and artist who lives in rural Wicklow, Ireland. These are excerpts from her talk to a 1998 conference on teleworking and disability held in Dublin.

'Teleworking is isolated work and it suits some of the people some of the time, often for a variety of reasons. It suits certain disabled people but it's not a panacea for the 70% or 80% of disabled people who are unemployed, underutilised, who feel disregarded and are feeling dumped in the society we live in. Teleworking doesn't eliminate discrimination but it does reduce a major element of it which is prejudice. People can't prejudge you if they don't know that you're disabled because they can't see you.

'I'm convinced that if it were not for my disability, I would not have become the technobabe that I am. Nothing fazes me very much in the electronic world. I have a deep faith in the power of technology to level that playing field. Computers have made the world accessible and friendly and at my toetips. That's fine until something goes wrong. One of the problems I've had as a teleworker has been a paper jam in the printer. That leaves me nearly hysterical. Dealing with suppliers and so-called support from computer sales companies, they assume that you can just bounce around and pull out cables and stick them back in again when you get them on the phone.

'To enjoy teleworking you need to be able to enjoy your morning coffee on your own. You won't have to miss the office gossip. More importantly, you have to be able to deal with the disadvantage of not being there. Not being on the spot, and not being in the right place at the right time. It's also about getting the hang of virtual reality. In my experience I feel isolated about one in every four days and feel like climbing the walls once a week.'

a written copy of any better-off calculation, because if you lose out financially because an agency got it wrong you may be able to get compensation. (All reputable advice agencies have insurance to cover them for this, and government departments should also pay compensation.) Be particularly cautious and get very detailed advice before starting self-employed work. The benefits system has great difficulty coping with the variable income which is typical of self-employed teleworking.

Finally, before starting work, get advice about what your options will be if health problems mean you have to stop again. There are various linking rules, such as 'welfare to work', which may allow you to go back onto your former benefits at the same rate if you stop work on health grounds within a year of starting. But there are various qualifying conditions which you need to know about before you start.

For advice about benefits you can contact:

- National Association of Citizens' Advice Bureaux. Visit **http://www.nacab.org.uk** or call 0207 833 2181 for details of your nearest CAB in England or Wales.
- Citizens Advice Scotland. Visit **http://www.cas.org.uk** or call 0131 667 0156 for details of your nearest CAB in Scotland.
- Disability Information Advice Line (DIAL). There are over 140 local DIALs, all staffed by disabled people and all offering telephone advice. Visit **http://www.dialuk.org.uk** or call 01302 310 123 for details of your nearest DIAL.
- Federation of Independent Advice Agencies (FIAC). FIAC is the umbrella body for independent advice centres in England, Scotland and Wales. Visit **http://www.fiac.org.uk** or call 0207 489 1800 for details of your nearest agency.
- Association of Independent Advice Centres (Northern Ireland). AIAC is the umbrella body for independent advice centres in Northern Ireland. Visit **http://www.aiac.net** or call 028 9064 5919 for details of your nearest agency.
- Law Centres Federation. For contact details of your nearest law centre in England and Wales, where you may be able to get free advice and representation at appeals, visit **http;//www.lawcentres.org.uk** or call 0207 387 8570.
- For details of advice centres and solicitors in your area who are funded under the Community Legal Services (CLS) scheme, call the CLS helpline on 0845 608 1122 or visit **http://www.justask.org.uk** But beware, depending on your financial position solicitors may charge for their services – so ask first.
- For information about benefits from the Department for Work and Pensions visit **http://www.dwp.gov.uk** or call the Benefits Enquiry Line on 0800 882200 (Northern Ireland 0800 220674). But beware, information from the DWP is not impartial and it's not always correct.
- For information about the Working Tax Credit and Child Tax Credit (which replaced Working Families' Tax Credit and Disabled Person's Tax Credit from April 2003), visit **http://www.inlandrevenue.gov.uk/taxcredits** or call 0845 300 3900 (Northern Ireland 0845 603 2000).
- For welfare benefits discussion forums, try visiting **http://www.youreable.com** where, at the time of writing, a CAB adviser and a Disability Appeal tribunal member are among those answering benefits queries.
- For welfare benefits links in general, visit **http://www.benefitsandwork.co.uk**

ASSISTIVE TECHNOLOGY

Any disabled computer-user needs the best access possible to technology if they want to telework. AbilityNet (formerly the Computability Centre), based in

Warwick, is a nationwide charity that offers professional computer expertise to people with all kinds of disabilities, including advice on assistive technology. AbilityNet runs an advice and information service including a phone helpline which received 17,000 enquiries in 2001, as well as giving technical awareness sessions (3000 people attended these in 1999) and providing assessment services (2000 carried out in 2001), as well as training courses and consultancy. There is now a network of 10 AbilityNet centres around the country (more information from **http://www.abilitynet.org.uk**).

In addition to helping those who are already disabled to get better access to computers, AbilityNet helps those who already use computers but suffer from progressive problems of disability. In the case of British Gas payroll supervisor Eileen Knowles, who has Parkinson's Disease, AbilityNet 'saved her job'. Eileen's hand tremors were affecting her keyboarding accuracy and she was having difficulty holding a pen. AbilityNet provided Eileen with a keyguard (a template with holes for each key) and recommended moving the keyboard down to a tray below her desk. Eileen was amazed at the effectiveness of these simple adaptations.

For Jane Thurlow, a biologist at the Imperial Cancer Research Fund, severe back injury meant she could not sit down at all, and could stand for only 20 minutes in an hour. Writing and typing were causing her considerable pain. AbilityNet helped Jane to experiment with different techniques for using the computer while lying down. Jane now has a computer with voice input, and the screen is tilted through 90 degrees so that she can read it lying down.

Improvements in voice dictation software have opened up many new options for some conditions. AbilityNet saw a young woman with RSI affecting her back and preventing her from carrying on her work in data input. A voice dictation solution solved the problem and proved as productive as keyboarding. In another case an inexpensive equipment solution did the trick. An executive suffering increasing discomfort in the right hand and arm swapped his standard keyboard and mouse for a small keyboard with static trackerball at a cost of £150. The change allowed him to use the mouse without the grip action which had become so painful.

AbilityNet points out that the Disability Discrimination Act now forces employers to make 'reasonable adjustment' for employees with either permanent or temporary disability. In Ireland the Central Remedial Clinic carries out similar functions to AbilityNet (*see* **http://www.crc.ie**), while the National Disability Authority website **http://www.nda.ie** has information on standards for creating designs accessible by people with disabilities.

Technical tools

Ger Craddock of the Central Remedial Clinic summarises the recent technology developments as follows:

'The main change in the past few years is the much greater processing power of PCs, which has allowed voice recognition technology to advance in great leaps. Although there was a period of instability after a number of software providers collapsed into one company, the result has been a much more effective product which is widely available. Also, SMS technology combined with phones which can vibrate as well as ring, is now widely used by most younger deaf people as a method of communication. The move to more and more wireless technology will probably make all ICT products more accessible to people with disabilities, but this is not a foregone conclusion. Europe is trying to jumpstart the process through the creation of "Design for All" centres in each country to assist in ensuring that all types of design – products and buildings as well as websites – are accessible and make use of assistive technology. However, there is no clear method for enforcing accessibility in Europe as yet, in contrast to the US, where the 502 telecoms legislation is forcing all federal purchases to be restricted to equipment that is accessible.'

Some typical uses of assistive technology include:

- Latch keys allow users who can press only one key at once, or those who use a stick on the keyboard, to use modifier keys such as shift, alt and control on PCs.
- For users with visual disabilities, brightly coloured keytops, or those with big or bold characters can help.
- Keyguards are rigid plates above keyboard keys that can take the weight of hands or arms, and have holes above each key for accurate key depression.

- Personalised keyboards can be very effective for people with hand/arm difficulties (e.g. smaller sized keyboards, programmable keypads, switches that can be used with keyboard emulation software, and keyboards for those who have the use of only one hand).
- For anyone who has difficulty with data entry, word-processing software can predict word endings, and most likely next words (keystroke savers).
- Computer mice alternatives include tracker balls, which are fixed in position but you roll a ball to move the pointer, touch-sensitive pads and joy sticks. Alternative shapes and sizes are available. Highly specialised devices such as the 'twiddler' operate on delicate tilting movements of the hand, while others can be operated by the head, or can be operated by biometrics from vestigial movements.
- Help for the visually impaired ranges from replacing old-fashioned, poor-quality screens to altering colour combinations and installing larger screens. Another approach is to enlarge the image, but when this is done the whole screen contents cannot be viewed at once. In some systems an enlarged image from part of the computer's main screen is displayed on a second screen (usually a closed circuit TV system that can also be used to enlarge printed material for reading).
- Voice recognition software for blind and physically disabled users can act as a keyboard replacement and is available from a limited 'command level' to 'free text'. The development of laptop computers in conjunction with speech synthesisers and voice recognition can now provide some disabled people with an easily portable communications tool. Another alternative is 'screen reading' using braille output, where whole or half lines from the screen are produced on an electro-mechanical strip close to the keyboard.
- For those who use voice recognition software and a phone, it is now possible to get a combination wireless USB headset which can be used for both functions, such as the ArialPhone. The phone can be switched into dictation mode by giving the command 'Open Mic', and switched back to phone mode to answer or make a call by pressing a button on the earpiece (**http://www.arialphone.com**).
- OCR (optical character reading) text scanning can be used to 'read' text into a computer, producing text on the computer screen, or a synthesised voice, or both.
- Text telephones can help those with hearing disabilities to communicate by displaying conversations on a small screen connected to a normal telephone line. The most commonly used system is the Minicom. Text telephones are great for communications between the hearing-impaired, but need an interpretation service to aid communication with other telephone users. The RNID offers a 'TypeTalk' service where an interpreter 'translates' between the spoken word and the Minicom messages, and BT is equipping 2000 text payphones with its similar TextDirect service.

THE TRAINING AND SUPPORT GAP

A conference on disability and teleworking held in Dublin in 1998 as part of the European Telework Development project looked at the problems disabled people face in obtaining telework opportunities:

- *Teleworking can provide employment options for disabled people, but in the main these options are suitable for those with acquired disabilities who have previous work experience, or those with third-level education. It must not be used to replace the need to make conventional workplaces accessible.*

- *Current IT training programmes for disabled people mostly provide basic IT skills which are insufficient for teleworking, yet most job opportunities are at a professional level requiring third-level education and high-level IT skills.*

- *There is a danger in creating skills registers exclusively for disabled teleworkers, as these may encounter prejudice. Registers have to be actively marketed to companies or they languish unused. Registers should focus on core skills like languages rather than IT skills – though these should also be recorded.*

- *Disabled teleworkers report major problems obtaining technical support and repairs to equipment.*

- *Because many disabled people are unable to work full-time, it is particularly important to encourage the formation of support networks for collaboration, technical and social support and marketing.*

For more information see **http://www.cork-teleworking.com/distele.pdf**

■ Many items not related to computers can help disabled teleworkers, such as page turners for books and journals, lights to indicate ringing telephones, talking calculators and specially adapted work furniture.

Certain items of equipment for disabled people are exempt from VAT, but rules vary according to local VAT offices.

WEBSITE ACCESS

There are a number of campaigns in place to assist people with disabilities to access websites, as errors or omissions in HTML programming can prevent 'reading' software used by the visually impaired from functioning correctly. Julie Howell, campaigns officer of the RNIB, comments: 'At the moment it is not clear whether the Disability Discrimination Act (DDA) does require websites to be fully accessible, but the RNIB believes this is a civil rights issue.'

Guidelines are available from the world-wide web consortium on how to ensure that your website is accessible – *see* **http://www.wc3.org/wai**   The best-known software for checking website accessibility is probably Bobby, available at **http://bobby.watchfire.com/bobby/html/en/index.jsp**

In the UK, JustVanilla is a scheme aimed at providing web access to people with disabilities, especially visual impairment. The website includes over 30 web accessibility features and an Access Gateway which converts most web pages to forms that can be used by those with accessibility aids for visual impairment. The website includes inexpensive talking browser software VanillaTalk, available on free trial (*see* **http://www.justvanilla.com**).

ACCESS TO WORK

The Disability Discrimination Act has the following effects:
- It is against the law for an employer to treat a disabled person less favourably, without good reason, because of their disability. It is also against the law to refuse to serve someone who is disabled.
- It is against the law to run a service or provide goods or facilities in such a way that it is impossible or unreasonably difficult for a disabled person to use the service or goods.

At the moment, one of the main planks of the government's services for disabled people seeking work is in some disarray. This is the New Deal for Disabled People, a voluntary scheme for people receiving health-related benefits from the state which involves partnerships between employers and training organisations, and the apointment of 'job brokers' to those seeking work. However, the scheme has unfortunately underachieved on its targets, and some of the job-broker organisations, such as the long-established training charity Outset, have actually got into considerable financial difficulty as a result of participation in the scheme.

Job Centres now have Disability Employment Advisers (DEAs), who can provide help with a number of government-funded schemes such as the following:

Access to Work
This can help pay for a variety of different technical aids to assist a disabled person to work (sometimes in conjunction with AbilityNet). Support can be provided for an assistant, alterations to work areas, or assistance with transport. To qualify, you must 'have, or have had, a physical or mental impairment which has a substantial and long-term adverse effect on your ability to carry out normal day-to-day activities'. Medical evidence is usually required. The amount available varies and your employer may be asked to contribute. This scheme is also open to the self-employed. Examples of acceptable uses for Access to Work

DICTATING TO THE DRAGON

Rosalind Lawless, a customer care/procurement manager, took to voice dictation after developing RSI (repetitive strain injury) and finding herself unemployed as a result.

Rosalind learned to use the Dragon Dictate™ and Dragon NaturallySpeaking® speech recognition software. Using these products, she went on to get a number of qualifications in IT and training skills, and managed to get back into employment. In 1999 Rosalind designed an award-winning scheme for adult learners which provides disabled people with speech recognition skills, jobsearch and careers advice, and provides funding for a number of trainers.

Rosalind's company 1st Voice Solutions also provides seminars, workshops and one-to-one training sessions in the use of speech recognition software to businesses, as a time-saving alternative to conventional PC use, which can provide dictation speeds of 100–150 words per minute. She can provide an all-in-one service including equipment, software, training and advice on speech recognition and the prevention of RSI.

http://1stvoicesolutions.com

funding include:
- A communicator for the hearing-impaired.
- A part-time reader or assistance at work for someone who is blind.
- Equipment or adaptations to provide help at work.
- Transport or assistance with adaptations to cars.
- Alterations to premises.

http://www.employmentservice.gov.uk/english/employers/access_to_work.asp

Permitted Work
See pages 334–335. Individuals can be allowed to work for up to 16 hours a week and be paid without any threat to social security benefits.

Job Introduction Scheme
Disabled people can be paid a sum (currently £75 for six weeks) while they are bedding into a new job. This is an individually tailored programme designed to help people with specific disability or health problems to return to work after a long period of absence or unemployment. It can also help people who are at risk of losing their job due to difficulties caused by a disability.

Workstep
This is a new name for the former Supported Employment Programme. The programme can provide practical support to employers and employees, including job coaching and financial assistance.

GLITTERING SUCCESS WITH JEWELLERY SERVICE

Mark Francis-Jones operates a service selling quality, British-made wedding rings over the Internet. No stranger to self-employment, Mark had previously operated 60 vending machines around Shropshire and the surrounding counties, despite the limitations of his wheelchair.

Mark regards his wheelchair as the least of the disabilities imposed upon him by a road accident – other problems include pressure sores, dilation of the kidneys and migraines which can cause disturbed vision and vomiting.

Some years ago, Mark was one of the original teleworkers involved in Antur Tanat Cain telecottage's contract to transcribe Weights and Measures documents for ICL. After completion of the project, he was at a loose end. He opted for an Open University course, but found that studying from home as a distance-learning student left him disillusioned and isolated, so he dropped out after completing one module. The vending-machine venture was highly successful but the physical commitment was huge and hard to handle. 'Then I met an old school friend now employed in the jewellery trade, and identified the potential to marry his knowledge of the business with my knowledge of IT.'

Mark found he was a little ahead of the game when he tried selling jewellery over the Internet: 'It's a tactile product. People want to see and feel before they buy,' he reports. However, the Internet proved a great way to get people to visit the wedding rings workshop and business is now steady and rewarding – check out the customer satisfaction comments at **http://www.theringworkshopltd.co.uk**

There is an excellent explanation of the different schemes on the RADAR website **http://www.radar.org.uk/information/faq/employ.html**

For those already in work, but coping with a new or increasing disability, the Employers' Forum on Disability is the national employers' organisation dealing with disability and employment. It is non profit-making, and funded by members. It provides good publications, a regular journal, and a range of introductory literature to support employers in assisting their disabled employees. *See* **http://www.employers-forum.co.uk/**

The Disability Information and Advice Line (DIAL) is another good starting-point for information about a range of services – *see* **http://www.dialuk.org.uk** If you are having trouble tracking down information on a topic, there is also the Disability Information Database DissBASE, which is used by about 170 providers of disability information in the UK. You can telephone DissBASE and ask them to make an enquiry free of charge. The database contains information on over 5500 national and regional organisations and services related to disability.

It is also often useful to consult specialist groups who deal in particular disabilities, such as MS, as they may well have disability-specific relevant

"Horizontal Paul", as Paul Grey describes himself, featured in Teleworker Magazine *in his bedroom-office with his 16-track digital recording equipment*

information. The RNIB's website has a good list of links and URLs for disability organisations at **http://www.rnib.org.uk/linksite/disabili.htm**, as does RADAR at **http://www.radar.org.uk/Links/Linksgraphics.asp**

Employment Opportunities is a leading national charity with 15 regional centres working to place disabled people in employment, and staffed by secondees from commerce and industry. Jobseekers get help in identifying and developing skills, preparing CVs and interview techniques on a one-to-one basis (**http://www.opportunities.org.uk**).

The Prince's Youth Business Trust (PYBT) assists unemployed people, including the disabled aged 18–30, to start their own business. The support comes in the form of low-interest loans of up to £5000, grants of £50 to £500 and test-marketing grants of up to £250. Additional support is given through the services of a Business Adviser. To qualify for PYBT funding, you must have failed to achieve funding through other sources. Examples of disabled people helped through the PYBT include graphic designers and disability access consultants (**http://www.princes-trust.org.uk**).

The Association of Disabled Professionals (ADP) focuses on employment, education and training issues relating to disabled people and actively encourages the principle of teleworking. ADP calls on the experience and connections of its members to help other disabled people to meet their employment potential. *See* **http://www.adp.org.uk**

MS HELPLINE USES TELEWORKING COUNSELLORS

The Multiple Sclerosis Society is using 35 home-based counsellors to staff its helpline. All but one of the counsellors have MS themselves, and volunteer to work on the helpline. The call volume is around 17,000 a year, but prior to the homeworking option, opening hours were limited and around one-third of calls were lost.

Jim Glennon, the helpline manager, explains that many people with MS wanted to be involved but could not get into the office because of mobility difficulties, or problems with intermittent relapses, or with fatigue.

Training of the counsellors including role-playing exercises takes place by phone over a period of 12 weeks, and trainees receive tapes of their sessions. A comprehensive training programme is vital because the work is sensitive and stressful.

Tel: 0171 610 7171 Web: http://www.mssociety.org.uk/about_us/national_centre/helpline/helpline_recruit.html

In Ireland, the state employment and training agency FÁS administers the Workplace Equipment Adaptation Grant (WEAG) scheme through local employment services offices. It is possible to get up to €6350 to provide adaptations to premises or equipment in order to make a workplace more accessible or work equipment easier to use. These grants can be used in certain situations to equip home offices, and are open to registered disabled people who wish to be self-employed. There is also an Employment Support Scheme which provides a wage subsidy to employers for employees whose productivity is severely affected by a disability. A recent development is the employment retraining grant aimed at existing employees who acquire a disability. Finally, there is a scheme to exempt employers from paying PRSI (national insurance) for certain disabled employees for the first two years of employment. *See* **http://www.fas.ie/services_to_jobseekers/employment_supports _disabilities.html**

TRAINING SCHEMES

The main route for provision of training to adult disabled students is now the LearnDirect e-learning programme (*see* p. 353). Courses can be delivered online or through local colleges, or through UKOnline centres which provide high-street access to ICTs. There is a special disability access project attached to LearnDirect but unfortunately its website page is currently 'under construction'. The main LearnDirect website at **http://www.learndirect-advice.co.uk** has detailed lists of courses available, and a page of advice for

THE ROCKY ROAD TO REHABILITATION

Cathy Cumberbeach suffered a car accident, and was left with little use of one hand and arm as well as problems with concentration. Previously Cathy had worked as a bilingual executive secretary and personal assistant, and ran her own business supplying word-processing services and temporary secretaries. One of her customers, a pharmaceutical company, was extremely supportive and continued to send her secretarial work when she was well enough to start working from home, including correspondence, telephone dictation and production of bulk mailings. Cathy also got help from the Irish organisation Ability, which keeps a register of disabled people who have teleworking skills. Cathy took on several typing jobs for United Biscuits through Ability, but found that she could not get help with equipment or software from any organisation.

Cathy is critical of state rehabilitation services, which she feels did not assess her properly and sent her on an inappropriate high-level German course intended to train her as a translator. Another training course which she was offered would have involved spending six weeks at the other end of the country, which was impractical given her disability and personal situation. Instead, Cathy borrowed money from her family to update her computer equipment and buy new software and a laser printer, which she has now paid off. She received some work for a Dublin insurance company through the EU HYPIT project, but technical difficulties with the remote access systems caused frustrating delays. However, the new equipment has also given her the opportunity to take an Open University course in technology.

people with special needs. This advises that in addition to the usual disability access checks, you should:

- Check whether the college you would like to attend has a support or disability co-ordinator who can carry out an assessment with you to make sure that you get the support you need.
- If you feel you need to attend a college with special facilities for students with disabilities, NATSPEC has a directory of contacts and courses – *see* **http://www.natspec.org.uk**
- Check whether the course you want to do is available through distance-learning or flexible-learning methods.

Another organisation you may like to contact is SKILL (the national bureau for students with disabilities), which has a wide range of useful leaflets and guides on issues like funding, exam arrangements for people with disabilities and the realities of distance learning. *See* **http://www.skill.org.uk**

http://jobability.com is the website of the Workability project, where disabled people can peruse jobs from employers who are committed to interview every applicant who fulfills the person specification. Workability is a joint venture between the Leonard Cheshire Foundation, Microsoft and the recruitment website **http://www.totaljobs.com** The project is for unemployed disabled people 'who have been hindered in their search for work'. Applicants must have basic literacy and numeracy, be willing to study at home for a computing qualification through e-learning, and have access to a telephone line for Internet access. A letter of reference from (for example) a Disability Employment Adviser is required. Participants get free computer equipment and Microsoft software (unfortunately MS-Works, not MS-Office) as well as free Internet access. Training is provided to CLAIT stage 1 and a personal tutor is assigned to each student. Workability has links with employment consultancies who assist course graduates in their search for work. Over 3000 people have been trained through Workability.

The Ian Karten Charitable Trust was founded in 1980 as a grant-making trust. Until 1996 it based its activities upon awarding scholarships to allow people to access higher education. In 1997 this activity widened to different kinds of IT training and the first Karten Centre was opened; there are now 48 centres in the UK and five in Israel. It is anticipated that the number of centres will rise to 70 by 2005. The Karten Centres are varied in their specialisms and serve a wide range of disabilities. *See* **http://www.ctec.org.uk/edservs/default.htm** to find out if there is a centre near you.

There have been several schemes for training disabled people in their own homes, but they have tended to be replaced by online learning or centre-based learning for cost and social isolation reasons.

11 Training for teleworkers

This chapter is aimed at everyone who is involved in teleworking. It attempts to help you identify what you need to learn (a 'training needs analysis') and when you need to learn it, as well as what you can delegate to others. It also provides information to help you find out where the training might be available, and how much it might cost.

TRAINING NEEDS ANALYSIS

Teleworkers naturally need to be proficient in the use of IT and telecommunications; but they also need to be able to work as part of a dispersed team, and to have skills in project management and self-motivation. Managers of teleworkers may need training to alter their management style for dealing with virtual or dispersed teams. Unfortunately the need for telework training is often ignored or underestimated.

Plan to evaluate any training which you undertake – did the training suit you, was the money invested well-spent, was the content appropriate? This will help you to make better-informed decisions on training in future. Learning is worthwhile if it helps your business or your employability. Choose your learning experiences based on their quality (fitness for your purposes) rather than on the availability of qualifications or grants. Recruitment agencies can sometimes provide very useful assessments of the value of some qualifications – is it what your future employer or client is going to be looking for?

Who are you?

Your role is going to affect what you need to learn, how you access training, whether you need certification of your learning and how you fund and organise your learning. There are four main roles which require different skills:

- Trainee in a telecottage, telecentre, college or at home.
- Employed telecommuter.
- Self-employed service provider.
- Manager or employer of others who telework.

If you are currently out of work or thinking of going into self-employment, remember that teleworking is a way of work, not a job in itself. The Teleworking NVQ won't necessarily get you a job because it only shows that you know about the way of working called teleworking and all the related IT skills. In addition you will need a core skill which employers or clients want – such as translation or web design.

There's no point in confining your attention to formal training and education in a fast-moving area like teleworking – or in getting hung up on formal definitions. For teleworkers, training means learning stuff, irrespective of how you learn it.

What do you need to know?

There are four sectors into which your training requirements are likely to fall:

- Your own specialism (accountancy, design, sales consultancy or whatever it is) – this kind of training is not covered here.
- Entrepreneurship, business and management skills required to run a business.
- IT skills (hardware, software and Internet).
- Management of virtual organisations (including self-management, managing teleworkers, working with others, project teams, etc.).

Take a moment to write down anything in which you feel you need training. The list will probably be quite long. You might also want to review Chapter 5, *For teleworkers and wannabees* to help you think through some items, as well as reading the outlines of the Teleworking NVQ Level 2, the European Computer Driving Licence (ECDL) and the Irish teleworking qualifications (*see* **http://www.telework.org.uk/curricula.htm**) to give you some ideas. ECDL is widely accepted by employers, and many have found that staff with ECDL make substantially fewer technical support calls.

Think about any gaps that there may be in your communications skills, and about how you will adapt to teleworking as a new way of working. Reading this book should plug many of these gaps but may point up other areas in which you feel you need training.

Next, transfer to a separate list anything that you can get other people to know for you. For instance, how much do you really need to know about taxation? It's important, but (unless you're offering tax-related services to your customers) you can get by with:

- A system for ensuring that you obey the law; and/or
- Expert advice on call whenever you need it.

If you are self-employed and short of time, try to delegate some of the subjects to professional advisers and consultants where this is financially possible. Stick to your core work rather than spending unpaid hours researching points yourself – let the professionals quickly answer queries in their area, because it will save you money in the long run – presuming that you are confident in your professional advisers. If not, why not? Change them. There may also be items on your list which you could find out by being a member of a professional association, or by asking colleagues, customers or clients, rather than by spending time on training yourself.

When do you need to know it?

Now that you're dealing with a shorter list, you can do some more categorisation. This time, prioritise the training subjects based on when you think you will need to know about them. For example, you might need to know how to fill in a VAT return next month, how to export text from a .pdf file today, and how to code XML in six months' time.

The prerequisites – IT skills you must have

If you are lacking in the skills listed below, then it is suggested that you put on ice your plans for teleworking until you have attained them. Companies will find that teleworkers with better IT skills make fewer technical support calls.

- Keyboarding – minimum 25 words per minute touch-typing plus ability to use a mouse.
- Use of Windows (95/98/2000/XP) – particularly for file management.
- Basic PC troubleshooting and maintenance – do you have a plan for diagnosing the problem if your printer stops working?
- How to store and back up files.
- Word processing.
- Spreadsheets.
- Sending and receiving email and attaching files to emails.
- Browsing the web and using search engines to find information.
- Basic PC security – how do you plan to prevent children from accidentally erasing files if they gain access to the PC?

The following skills are also important for many teleworkers:
- Databases.
- Health and safety aspects of computers.

Most computer-literacy courses will cover many of the topics above, but check that the detailed course syllabus includes what you want to learn. Courses described as 'introduction to computers' probably won't cover all these items. Managers of teleworkers should not assume that their staff know these basics – they often know enough to get by and will ask a colleague when stuck, something they can't do when teleworking out of the office. Check competences or look for IT literacy qualifications such as RSA, CLAIT, City and Guilds or ECDL. Self-employed teleworkers will also need to know how to load software packages and do basic hardware installation (such as adding new printers or scanners).

To be really employable, you need more than just basic computer literacy – ideally you should have one of the Microsoft qualifications. These are available as traditional courses through Microsoft Certified Training and Examination Centres (CTECs). There are also online e-learning materials and self-paced open learning materials you can use to teach yourself before taking an online exam through a centre. More information is available at **http://www.microsoft.com/traincert/default.asp**, including web pages that help you find your nearest CTEC, but be warned – the navigation can be a bit confusing.

Microsoft Office User Specialist is usually the first step after a basic computer-literacy qualification. It is suitable for secretaries/PAs, office administrators, first-level trainers and the like (**http://www.microsoft.com/TrainCert/mcp/mous/mous_locator.asp**).

There are also a wide range of more complex Microsoft certifications covering systems engineers and administrators, database administration, application development and training, most of which require 6–18 months hands-on experience plus study.

LEARNING OPPORTUNITIES

The phrase 'learning opportunities' is used here because it encourages you to think of a wide range of ways of learning. Learning opportunities include the following:

Traditional face-to-face courses (full-time)

Face-to-face courses are vital for some subjects which require group work, but they are time-consuming. In making your choices, consider course content and teaching quality, as well as how the course will equip you for subsequent work. One of the best ways to find out about a course is to talk to former trainees. Save full-time courses for topics that really require it.

Company telework training

Irish airports authority Aer Rianta provided an initial day-long orientation

THE LEARNDIRECT SCHEME

LearnDirect is a collection of online training courses which are intended to be used either from a local centre or on a home PC. Some courses are free, and the scheme is aimed at people who would not normally attend a college. According to Gerry Spencer from parent body Ufi Ltd: 'We don't give out qualifications, so you can't fail. It will get you up to a level that you can progress from. We believe we are extending the market – a quarter of our learners say that they wouldn't have done anything if it hadn't been done this way.' See **http://www.learndirect.co.uk**

Tutors for LearnDirect are freelancers who can be based anywhere in the country. The aim of the online tutoring scheme is to support the UKOnline centres and those who study from home. The project, entitled the National Tutor Service, has a national database of tutors who can be called on to support up to 20 learners. The scheme pays around £18 per hour, and tutors use email and message boards for their support with minimal telephone contact. Tutors have to commit to a minimum of three hours' support per week, self-logged onto timesheets. They are contracted locally by each UK Online centre and paid at the completion of the course. See **http://www.ufi.com** for more information on this scheme or call 08000 150750.

There has been something of a hiccup in the funding for LearnDirect courses, which was administered through individual learning accounts (ILAs). Due to problems with fraud, the funding scheme has been suspended and no details of when and how it will be resumed are currently available. The problem does not affect course availability.

session for its staff who were interested in volunteering for a pilot telework programme. The session covered:

- Background to growth in telework, types of telework.
- Benefits for employers and employees.
- Drawbacks for employers and employees.
- Suitable qualities for teleworkers and managers of teleworkers.
- Home office setup.
- Health and safety implications, insurance, company policy.
- Technology issues.
- Common reasons for success and failure of telework pilots.

Those who joined the pilot as teleworkers received a further day's training in these areas before the start of the programme, plus:

- Procedures for technical support, equipment maintenance, data backup, virus protection.
- Remote access to the corporate network – dialling-in from home.

FINDING TRAINING AND HELP ON THE INTERNET

Two e-learning courses on teleworking which work perfectly over a standard 56k dial-up and contain excellent content are the 'Telecommuting' courses for employees and managers produced jointly by US expert Gil Gordon and the Work Family consultancy – see **http://telecom.workfamily.com** Unfortunately the pricing structure is currently aimed at large companies and may prove too high for small companies or individuals – also they are US-oriented although there may be a UK version in the near future. These are the best short courses that we have seen to-date, both in terms of delivery, interaction with the trainee, and content. For more information, or to arrange a free trial if you are thinking of purchasing the courses for delivery by a company, email training@workfamily.com.

The BBC website has a number of examples of online learning which provide an excellent 'taster' to help you decide whether the new techniques are for you, at **http://www.bbc.co.uk/education/languages**

http://www.telecommute.org – free set of training workshops aimed at managers who are implementing a corporate teleworking programme.

http://www.learndirect.co.uk – government website encouraging training outside conventional full-time training courses. Identifies online centres offering both centre-based and online learning courses.

http://www.ilearn.to – access to some 700 IT courses for £175 per year, of which up to £150 could be provided through an ILA (individual learning account).

http://www.tft.co.uk – Technologies for Training resource site listing centres providing training around the country, their courses and facilities.

http://www.trainingzone.co.uk – resource site aimed at HR staff and trainers.

http://www.smartforce.com – one of the world's largest commercial providers of training courses, recently renamed Skillforce.

http://www.wbtsystems.com – company which authors many sector-specific courses.

http://www.click2learn.com – wide range of commercial courses on a fast and easy-to-navigate website.

http://www.edsurf.net – computer courses with free demos, ten free trial courses and a guide to online learning.

http://www.tutorials.com – wide range of courses, including computer courses.

- Interface between work and family when teleworking.
- Time management and motivation.
- Communications skills (effective use of email, handling misunderstandings, telephone skills).

- Administration – expenses, recording time spent, absences.
- Sources of support – what to do if something goes wrong.

Their managers received a half-day session including:
- Guide to selecting and recruiting teleworkers.
- IT issues that may be encountered.
- Managing by results – similarities to and differences from 'eyeball management', communications agreements.
- Monitoring productivity – setting objectives, schedules and deadlines.
- Motivating teleworkers, keeping up the teamwork with in-office staff.
- Legal, health and safety, HR, data security, expenses issues.
- Assessing further training-needs for teleworkers.

The trainer comments: 'I would halve the time-lengths of the courses in future, and try to ensure that the training happened closer to the start date, especially the technical stuff – but sometimes it's hard to predict the rollout dates. Emphasis on the IT training is important – if people can't connect back to base easily then their telework effectiveness is minimal.'

Traditional face-to-face courses (part-time)

Have you checked out evening courses in your local area? You may be surprised by how many now relate to IT skills.

Short commercial face-to-face courses

While these may cost more, they can be the fastest and most effective way to gain a skill. Use the Yellow Pages to find your local training providers and check out their offerings. Also look at Microsoft CTEC centres and UKOnline centres.

Flexible learning, open learning, distance learning

Distance-learning courses which aren't also open learning (you do the modules as you can find time) can be very hard to complete if you are also working. Keeping up motivation when you are learning alone is also an issue for all these types of course, but they are often the only option for teleworkers.

A good Internet-based forum for collaborating and communicating with fellow students is essential, as are proper resources for the extra tutorial support that is needed for distance learning students. US studies have shown that it takes at least one-and-a-half times more tutorial support to successfully provide distance learning over the Internet compared to conventional, publications-based distance learning, so look for courses that offer good backup and support if you choose an Internet-based distance-learning course.

BT OPENS TRAINING TO ALL

The BT Workstyle Consultancy Group, a specialist team that assists companies who are introducing flexible working, is now selling an e-learning product called the Home-based Working Education Package.

The product is available on CD-ROM and is intended for delivery over corporate intranets. Topics include:

- *handling the transition;*
- *mastering working from home;*
- *creating your ideal home office;*
- *staying in touch with HQ;*
- *staying motivated;*
- *managing home-based workers.*

The product is based around BT's experience of training more than 4500 home-based workers of its own. *See* **http://www.wfh.co.uk**

Planned experience

Typically this involves shadowing somebody from whom you need to learn. Two companies in the financial-services industry, Merrill Lynch and Lloyds of London, use a very specific form of planned experience in their teleworker training. Both companies have set up offices which have no physical contact with the rest of the building. Prospective teleworkers have to work in these offices, using electronic means of communication only, as a precursor to working from home or on the road. The intention is to help people understand the feelings of isolation they experience. Although reports from the two companies do not mention this, presumably the cut-off offices also allow the employers to identify those employees for whom teleworking is not going to work, without the capital investment of providing them with home-office equipment.

Internet-based tutorials and learning materials

Many commercial Internet-based courses are moving towards small 'bites' of knowledge that people fit in between other aspects of their work, or else access when they need to know about a particular topic. The Internet can also be used to 'webcast' lectures, presentations or demonstrations. Students log in and watch, using software such as RealPlayer, though the quality is not wonderful. Internet-based tutorials are particularly good for learning new features of a software upgrade.

There are a number of sites on the Internet which sell guides to software

packages aimed at those who find that conventional computer manuals drive them to distraction. A typical example is MousePointer Manuals based in Wiltshire. Managing director Jonathan Gale explains: 'Many computer manuals are very daunting and very expensive. We have made ours user-friendly. They are written in an easy-to-understand, chatty style, with colour screen shots. They have been roadtested and developed with the feedback we have received.'

The manuals can be bought online inexpensively (currently £5.99 per manual) and downloaded as Acrobat .pdf files that can be printed out or read onscreen. Current offerings include Word 2000, Excel 2000, Powerpoint, Access, Outlook, Publisher and Sage Line 50 (**http://www.mousepointers.co.uk**).

Books, magazines, videos and CD-ROMs

Books are among the cheapest learning resources available, covering practically any subject which you care to mention, to any depth. They're much easier to read than anything comparably detailed on the web. Many people automatically buy a 'how-to' guide when they purchase a new piece of software. Computer magazines often contain useful tips and tricks as well as information on new products and trends. Make time for this reading – train journeys may fit the bill for short 'self-training' sessions through reading magazines. Training videos and CD-ROMs are to some extent being superseded by Internet-based materials, but training materials on many specialist subjects are held by college libraries in these formats. They are usually quite expensive to buy but available on loan through libraries and colleges.

LEARN WHILE YOU SHOP AT GATESHEAD'S LEARNING WORLD

Learning World is a computer training centre located at Gateshead's Metro shopping park which is open for six days a week, allowing students to combine shopping and learning. The project is a joint venture between the University of Sunderland and Gateshead College dating from 1996. Courses offered range from introductory to degree level.

Chief Executive Sally Coady explains: 'We appreciate that modern life is often hectic, leaving little time for commitments outside of work, friends and family. That's why we've designed courses to fit around even the busiest lifestyles. You can learn as quickly – or slowly – as you like, wherever you happen to be – at home, at work, online or out shopping. We're so flexible, you don't even have to come to the centre – we have hundreds of courses available online. What's more, many of the courses are free if you are on benefit. Free travel and childcare is also available to many students. Come in for a coffee and see for yourself!'

Feedback from the students has been excellent, borne out by a 90% retention rate for courses and a total intake over six years of 10,000 adult learners. Most students go on to take at least three courses.

http://www.learning-world.ac.uk Tel: 0191 440 7777

Conferences, Internet discussion lists and online tutorials

These learning opportunities are about sharing experience with other people. Although conference presentations are often interesting and provide new information, most people will agree that it is the questions that are asked afterwards, or the conversations and contacts that happen over the coffee break, that are the really valuable part of attending many conferences. It's vital to swap experiences and insights with other people working in the same area, so make the effort to attend conferences – good ones will reinvigorate you, teach you new things and increase your network of useful contacts, as well as helping you keep up to date on terminology and technology. The Internet has many specialist websites and forums that can also provide contacts whom you can ask for help or advice. Remember that many sites have archives of frequently asked questions (FAQs) which may answer your question straight away.

Your own experience/a knowledgebase

Knowledge management, and the idea of creating knowledgebases – databases of experience and information – are currently trendy topics in management studies. The idea is to provide all the information normally locked up in people's heads to everyone who needs it within an organisation, usually through the company intranet. The excellent *Financial Times Knowledge Management Fieldbook* gives this definition of knowledge management: 'the process by which the organisation generates wealth from its intellectual or knowledge-based assets'. The result is more efficient and effective processes that lower costs, reduce cycle times and improve cashflow. However, many companies have found that it is not easy to get people to volunteer their intellectual assets – either because knowledge is power, or because it is time-consuming, or because the person does not realise that the piece of knowledge could be valuable to the organisation.

But you can create your own very basic knowledgebase which will help you to learn from your own experience as you go along! It might just be a hardback notebook where you write down how you fixed software problems step-by-step, so that someone else can check the book and find the solution straightaway instead of repeating your research. It might be a spreadsheet or database where you record information about problem customers, or keep contact details for computer technical-support services.

However you decide to organise your knowledgebase, make an effort to record information in a format that others can easily access and understand.

CERTIFICATION

In considering which learning opportunities to pursue, you will also need to think about whether you need certification at the end of the course. In general, the more full-time and traditional, the more likely that the course will carry a certificate, but this is not always true – for example, both the ECDL computer literacy course and the Microsoft Computer Professional qualifications can be learned using online flexible learning materials, and the exams can also be taken online. Both training providers supply certificates which are widely accepted in industry. Reading a magazine may provide the answer to your problem, but definitely won't give you a certificate.

FUNDING THE TRAINING

First, you need to know what the course is going to cost. Typical expenses will include:

- Registration fees – usually a small sum to cover administration unless you intend to do a higher education qualification.
- Tuition fees.
- Books or other equipment.
- Transport to the course (unless it's distance learning).
- Internet subscription and Internet calls (if it's distance learning).
- Childcare (if you have young children).

CERTIFIED COURSES

Certified courses are those which provide you with a certificate at their conclusion. They are not always the most appropriate for the fast-changing world of the teleworker, but it is always worth considering what is on offer.

RSA, City & Guilds

These bodies award certification for further education vocational courses. RSA has a largely secretarial bias and is well-respected by employers for its insistence on high levels of accuracy. City & Guilds has a wider remit, covering subjects from photography to IT.

NVQs

NVQs are are vocational training courses which emphasise on-the-job training, taking into account existing skills plus some classroom and private study. NVQ students normally build up a portfolio of documentary evidence of their skills in order to achieve certification. There is a teleworking NVQ – see **http://www.telework.org.uk/curricula.htm** for more details.

Degree courses and extramural studies

Degrees in themselves may or may not be useful to a teleworker – it depends on the individual's skills and profession. Many universities and colleges also offer shorter, non-degree courses. On these extramural courses, students do not become full members of the institution and therefore may not have to meet normally stringent entrance requirements. Extramural courses, like NVQs, often award credits for existing skills. They are also modularised, like NVQs, with modules building towards the final certificate, and can often be 'moved' from one college to another if the student needs to move.

A certified online e-working course is due to be launched shortly by Irish state training agency FÁS – check out **http://www.fas-netcollege.com**

- Examination fees.
- Lost earning hours (for self-employed).

If you are on benefit, generally any money you receive to cover course fees, books or other equipment and transport to the course will not affect your benefit – but check with your local Benefits Agency office.

The Department of Education and Science has a comprehensive website on sources of funding for training at **http://www.lifelonglearning.dfes.gov.uk/moneytolearn/index.htm** which gives information on:

- Childcare support fund – some colleges offer free or subsidised childcare places if you have children under 15.
- Access or hardship funds – run by colleges to help students in need. These usually cover course and exam fees, books or other equipment, and

transport, but are allocated on a 'greatest hardship' basis to students who are already enrolled. They do not normally cover living expenses.

- Grants and bursaries – try the Educational Grants Advisory Service on 0207 249 6636 (Mondays, Wednesdays, Fridays 10–12 a.m. and 2–4 p.m.).
- Career Development Loans – commercial bank loans with a deferred repayment period. These are operated by the Department of Education and Science in conjunction with four banks: Barclays, the Co-op, Clydesdale and Royal Bank of Scotland. Career Development Loans can cover 80% of your course fees, or 100% if you have been out of work for over three months. Money for living expenses can only be claimed if the course is full-time.
- New Deal training funding – available for those who are under 25 and long-term unemployed, the disabled and lone parents. Your Personal Adviser under the New Deal scheme must recommend training or education as the best option for you.
- Small Firm Training Loans – available to all existing trading businesses with fewer than 50 employees, regardless of their legal structure (i.e. they are available to sole traders, but not to subsidiary companies where the holding company has over 50 employees in total). You can borrow from £500 to £125,000. Training for any one individual cannot exceed £10,000, and where several trainees are involved, the maximum average amount should be less than £5000. More information is available at **http://www.lifelonglearning.co.uk/sftl/**

The Department of Education and Science intends to provide funding and subsidies for training through 'individual learning accounts'. Information on its website states that 'The Individual Learning Account programme was launched nationally in September 2000. By October 2001 it had 2.5 million members registered with the Learning Account Centre as eligible to undertake subsidised learning. Some 9000 organisations were registered as learning providers.' Unfortunately, due to some problems with fraud the scheme is currently suspended and no information is available on when and how it may resume.

For self-employed teleworkers, fees paid on training courses can be claimed as a business expense. The situation for employed workers is slightly more complex. According to Mark Dyer of Netaccountants, the cost of a 'qualifying course of vocational training' can be set against taxable income (assuming that you, not your employer, paid for the course). Such courses include those which count towards National or Scottish Vocational Qualifications, and it may be possible to obtain basic-rate tax relief 'at source' by paying a lower amount to the training provider. Higher-rate tax relief has to be reclaimed through your tax return.

The expenses must be incurred 'wholly, exclusively and necessarily' in conjunction with your employment. Generally it is difficult to convince the

IT training at the Ross-on-Wye telecentre

Inland Revenue that the costs were 'necessarily' incurred, unless there is a clause in your contract of employment or other contractual arrangement for you to undertake the specified training.

In Ireland, only courses run by certain approved, publicly funded colleges with a duration of over two years can be claimed by employed teleworkers. The situation for the self-employed is the same as for Britain – training courses can be claimed as a business expense. The state training agency, FÁS, provides a number of free training courses for the registered unemployed. There is also a subsidised e-learning course on e-working, developed with support from the Irish government's e-work action forum and certfied by the state certification agency FETAC in conjunction with City and Guilds. *See* **http://www.fas.ie**

VIRTUAL TEAMS

Although this chapter is really about finding and funding training, there is one area that we felt was very lacking in good, publicly available courses or training materials – so here are some tips, based on our experiences over the years, in relation to virtual teams (these tips could be adapted into a short training module).

A team is a group of people working on tasks towards a shared objective. Where the team does not work at the same place, at the same time, the term 'virtual team' is often used. There is a great deal written about the need for trust between virtual team-members. Bear in mind, as Dr George Metes pointed out, that the word 'trust' is usually used in this context to indicate that we believe people will act in a predictably good or positive manner.

A lot of team-building or trust-building exercises are actually about allowing people to work out whether they can predict someone's behaviour – be that good or bad behaviour. Most people find that a face-to-face meeting, or a previous relationship or track record of behaviour, is the best way of discovering whether they 'trust' another team member. This is why they tend to be uncomfortable or reluctant to work on a virtual team with someone they have not met or worked with before. Few teams are truly 100% virtual, with no face-to-face interaction at all.

So where possible, if the team-members don't know each other, hold a face-to-face kickoff meeting in relaxed surroundings so everyone can get a handle on who's who, their characters and attitudes. If there is negotiation to be done about responsibilities, deadlines and budgets, this face-to-face meeting is the time to get it sorted out – it may well be the only time you all meet during the lifetime of the project. Make it clear from the start that each team-member is responsible for understanding what is required of them, and for querying the project manager if they have any doubts or confusions about what they are being asked to do.

Collect current contact details and working-hours information for all team-members; and make sure that everyone on the team gets a copy and knows it is their responsibility to notify people of any changes. Establish the rules of communication for the team in writing at an early stage, so everyone knows the expectations for returning calls and emails, and the situations in which other forms of communication, such as audio conferences, will be used.

If appropriate, state what hours people are expected to be available (e.g. many companies encourage availability during certain core hours to facilitate virtual meetings, while allowing flexibility on schedules outside those hours). To quote Dr John Gundry: 'Confusion is poison to virtual teams.' Here's an example of part of a policy from Good Enough Information Consultants (**http://www.goodenough.ca**), which specialises in helping not-for-profit companies to work effectively as virtual teams.

'We need a quick turnaround on emails between team-members, with a maximum of one business day unless you have already told the team you will be unavailable. Your response can be very short, for example, "I'm interested in the project but too busy to look at it now; will respond with an estimate on Friday before 5 p.m.," or even an automatic response such as, "I will be on holiday from 14–21 May".'

If necessary, create a quality-control document on communications methods and ask everyone to agree and sign it. This document can also specify document formats (e.g. if you have one member working from Eastern Europe on an older computer, you might want to specify that everyone is to use Word

364 THE TELEWORKING HANDBOOK

6.0/95 and not Word 2000 because of compatibility issues). Specify that all documents must be page-numbered – it makes it a lot easier to find the page everyone else is on during those audio conferences.

Make sure that version control is addressed in your procedures where a document is likely to be edited by a number of team-members – either use an intelligent naming and numbering system for files, or have a 'sign out, sign in' process where only one team-member at a time can work on the document (or both).

Create a clear description of the project with plenty of interim milestones, deadlines, progress reports and responsibilities. If the project is complex, break it down into different workpackages, and divide up responsibility and lead authority for each workpackage among the team according to skills and workload. Get positive agreement on this document from everyone, ensuring that the deadlines are feasible.

Create spaces for team brainstorming, questions, arguments and so on. Ideally these sessions should be face to face, but often other methods have to be used (e.g. through a project forum or email list, or via audio conferences, perhaps held in combination with the use of datasharing software such as Netmeeting).

Always be clear who is responsible for delivering on time and within the allocated resources. Where there has been a brainstorming session, make sure the project manager knows the results. Suggestions, revisions and changes to the project should normally be negotiated with the project manager, and not with other team-members or with clients directly.

Address the administration function. Who is acting as team 'librarian', ensuring that all documents are available in the project's web-space? Who deals with expense claims? Who provides the information about where or when the next face-to-face meeting or audio conference is taking place? Technical information on some software tools that help provide electronic assistance with these tasks is given on pages 116–121.

Where the virtual team-members are likely to change over time, it's particularly important to keep good documentary records on decisions by using tools like shared databases of emails, FAQs or web-based forums for discussions, in order that new team-members can use these resources to familiarise themselves with prior discussions and decisions.

Have a clear feedback mechanism with performance metrics, and keep using it – people tend to lose track of where their pieces fit into the whole puzzle. When someone delivers their piece of work, let all the other relevant team-members know it's been done; and if it's been done well, say so. But be sensitive that not everyone likes publicly broadcast 'online recognition' – some people find it false and prefer their plaudits to be delivered in an individual meeting, or where this isn't possible, in a private email or phone call. For serious negative feedback, try to make sure it's done face-to-face and always privately.

Because virtual teams have more limited communications resources available to them, some frustration and conflict between team-members must be expected and anticipated. You need a method for resolving conflicts – first of all, a method of feedback for problems or suggestions (normally through the project manager). Secondly, a voting procedure if this is appropriate for the team. Thirdly, some sort of external person to whom team-members can resort if their problem is a direct conflict with the project manager. And of course you can always arrange a face-to-face meeting if needed.

Simple ways of improving team identity include:

- Web page with team logo, list of members with pictures and biographies, summary of objectives.
- Team identity gifts – mugs, badges, pens, T-shirts, baseball caps, etc.
- When face-to-face meetings take place, get a picture of the team and put it on the website.
- Schedule social time into your face-to-face meetings – a pleasant meal, an activity trip.
- Articles in corporate newsletters explaining the work and membership of the team.

KEEPING THE FOCUS

If you're choosing a long course, look for one that provides significant support, in many different ways, to help the learners. That applies as much to classroom-based courses (are there tutorials? study-group sessions? individual discussions with lecturers?) as it does to distance-learning courses.

If you decide to plan some learning from materials like books, videos, magazines or computer-based packages, you should try to provide yourself with structure and support. Just as you plan your work, so you should plan your learning. Set goals, monitor progress, assess performance. Build in some supports. One of the best forms of support is to work with someone else, in your own organisation or elsewhere. Discuss what you've learned. Share your insights. Question each other – and encourage each other too.

By all means find out what grants and other support you can get. But don't sign on for an unsuitable course just because it's cheap or it's grant-supported. Instead, get your customers to pay for your training. Every time you bid for a contract, include an element to cover anything new you'll have to learn for that contract — and some extra learning as well. Put that money aside; don't spend it on anything but learning.

Focus on what you need. Nobody knows your business as well as you do. Keep managing the learning. Note new needs as you come across them; check and revise your lists of needs. Work out how best to meet each need, then arrange to do it. And remember to learn from experience; record what went wrong and how you fixed it. Don't try to learn everything yourself, by yourself.

Delegate some learning to professionals and more to your colleagues and your staff. Network with others; learn from them and let them learn from you. Make arrangements so that you can call on them in time of need, but make that sure you reciprocate.

References and contacts

This chapter has three sections. *Quoted references* gives details of literature quoted in the chapters. *Bibliography* lists other useful literature. *Contacts and URLs* provides some extra contact information. There is also an index on page 385.

QUOTED REFERENCES

Overview

[1] Corder N, *Escape from the Rat Race*, Elliot Right Way Books **http://www.right-way.co.uk**

[2] Pratt JH, *Telework America National Telework Survey*, International Telework Association and Council **http://www.telecommute.org** 2000

[3] Frank M, North-Smith L, Meredith S, *Human Resources considerations for mobilising your workforce*, IBM Global Services, March 2002

[4] *Psychological Aspects of Teleworking in Rural Areas*, **http://www.swan.ac.uk/psychology/patra/patra.htm** 1993

[5] Citigate Technology, *Flexible working – business benefit or personal perk?*, sponsored by Nextra, **http://www.nextra.co.uk** April 2002

[6] *Work at Home 2001*, United States Department of Labor, **http://www.bls.gov.news.release/homeynr0.htm**, 2001

[7] Citigate Technology, *Flexible working – business benefit or personal perk?*, sponsored by Nextra, **http://www.nextra.co.uk** April 2002

For researchers

[8] Hotopp U, Teleworking in the UK, *Labour Market Trends*, **http://www.nationalstatistics.gov.uk/downloads/theme_labour/LMT_June02.pdf** June 2002

[9] Citigate Technology, *Flexible working – business benefit or personal perk?*, sponsored by Nextra, **http://www.nextra.co.uk** April 2002

[10] *Business use of the Internet*, Oftel small and medium business survey Q9 **http://www.oftel.gov.uk/publications/research/2002/q9intb0702.pdf** May 2002

[11] Huws U, Podro S, Gunnarsson E, Wijers T, Arvanitaki K, Trova V, *Teleworking and Gender*, Institute of Employment Studies report 317, **http://www.employment-studies.co.uk** 1996

[12] Hotopp U, Teleworking in the UK, *Labour Market Trends*, **http://www.nationalstatistics.gov.uk/downloads/theme_labour/LMT_June02.pdf** June 2002

[13] Institute for Employment Studies **http://www.employment-studies.co.uk**

[14] de Martino V, *The High Road to Teleworking*, ILO, 2001 **http://www.ilo.org/public/english/protection/safework/telework/hrdptl.pdf**

[15] *Work at Home 2001*, United States Department of Labor **http://www.bls.gov.news.release/homeynr0.htm**, 2001

[16] de Martino V, *The High Road to Teleworking*, ILO, 2001 **http://www.ilo.org/public/english/protection/safework/telework/hrdptl.pdf**

[17] Bates P, Huws U, *Modelling eWork in Europe: Estimates, models and forecasts from the EMERGENCE project*, IES Report 388, **http://www.employment-studies.co.uk** 2002

[18] Huws H, Jagger N, and Bates P, *Where the Butterfly Alights, The Global Location of eWork*, Institute of Employment Studies Report 378, **http://www.employment-studies.co.uk**

2001 and Huws U, Jagger N and O'Regan S, *Teleworking and Globalisation*, Institute of Employment Studies, **http://www.employment-studies.co.uk** 1999

[19] Hotopp U, Teleworking in the UK, *Labour Market Trends*; **http://www.nationalstatistics.gov.uk/downloads/theme_labour/LMT_June02.pdf** June 2002

[20] Felstead A, Jewson N, Phizacklea A, Walters S, *A statistical portrait of working at home in the UK: evidence from the Labour Force Survey*, ESRC Future of Work Programme Working paper no. 4 **http://www.esrc.ac.uk**, March 2000

[21] *Disconnected: Social Housing Tenants and the Home Working Revolution*, Joseph Rowntree Foundation/Housing Corporation Available from 01904 430033, 2002

[22,23] Kodz J, Harper H, Dench S, *Work Life Balance: Beyond the Rhetoric*, Institute of Employment Studies Report 384, **http://www.employment-studies.co.uk** 2002

[24] Lewis S, Smithson J, Cooper C, Dyer J, *Flexible futures: Flexible Working and Work-Life Integration – summary of findings from stage 1*, Work Life Research Centre, 2001

[25] Booz Allen Hamilton, *Analysis of Home-Based Telework Technology Barriers Final Report on Technology Barriers to Home-Based Telework*, US Government General Services Agency, 2002

[26] Alcatel, *Broadband Teleworking: Making DSL More Profitable*, **http://www.alcatel.com**, 2002

[27] *Business use of the Internet*, Oftel small and medium business survey Q9 **http://www.oftel.gov.uk/publications/research/2002/q9intb0702.pdf** May 2002

International perspective

[28] Roitz J, Allenby B, Atkyns R, *2001/2002 Employee Survey Results: Telework, Business Benefit and the Decentralized Enterprise*, AT&T 2002

[29] *Telecommuting – overview of potential barriers facing employers*, United States General Accounting Office, 2001

[30] FAMILIES Project, *Results of family survey*, **http://www.families-project.com** February 2002

[31] E-living project, *D7.5 Homeworking and teleworking*, **http://www.eurescom.de/e-living/index.htm** 2002

[32] Bates P, Huws U, *Modelling eWork in Europe: Estimates, models and forecasts from the EMERGENCE project*, IES Report 388, **http://www.employment-studies.co.uk** 2002

[33] de Martino V, *The High Road to Teleworking*, ILO, 2001 **http://www.ilo.org/public/english/protection/safework/telework/hrdptl.pdf**

[34] Fine-Davis M, Fagnani J, Giovannini D, Hojgaard J and Clarke H, *Fathers and Mothers: Dilemmas of the Work-Life Balance – A Comparative Study in Four European Countries*, Final Report to the European Commission and the Irish Department of Justice, Equality and Law Reform, July 2002

[35] The Home Front by Marianne Kolbasuk McGee, *Information Week*, **http://www.iinformationweek.com** 22 October 2001

[36] New telemanagers better learn fast by Jeff Zbar, *Net.Worker*, **http://www.nwfusion.com/net.worker** 12 November 2001

[37] Clark MA, *Teleworking in the Countryside*, Ashgate Publishing Ltd, **http://www.ashgate.com** 2000

[38] Grimes S, *Information and Communications Technologies and Peripheral Rural Areas*, AsPIRE project, 2002

[39] Home Office Partnership, *Telecommuting 2000 – the future of transport in the information age*, **http://www.flexibility.co.uk** 2000

[40] NERA/RAC, *Motors or Modems? Virtual travel becomes a reality*, 1997 (and updated 2000)

[41] Mohktarian PL, Handy SL, Salomon I, Methodological issues in the estimation of the

travel, energy and air quality impacts of telecommuting, *Transportation Research* 29A(4) pp 283–302, 1995

[42] Choo S, Mokhtarian PL, Salomon I, *Impacts of Telecommuting on Vehicle Miles Travelled: A Nationwide Time Series Analysis*, California Energy Commission, 2001

[43] Eircom, Dublin Transportation Office, Amárach, *The shortest route to work*, 1998

[44] Hamer R, Kroes E, van Oostrom H, Teleworking in the Netherlands: an evaluation of changes in travel behaviour, *Transportation* 18(4), pp 365–382, 1991

Alternative workplaces

[45] Alcott JT, Washington Metropolitan Telework Centres, Powerpoint presentation, **http://www.opm.gov.wrkfam/seminart/wmtcppt.htm**

[46] International Facility Management Association, *Alternative Workplace Study*, 1998

For teleworkers and wannabees

[47] Froggatt C, *Work Naked – Eight Essential Principles for Peak Performance in the Virtual Workplace*, 2001

Implementation in organisations

[48] Curran K, Williams G, *Manual of Remote Working*, Gower Publishing Ltd, 1997

[49] Wustemann L, *IRS Handbook of Flexible Working law and practice*, IRS 2001

[50] *Teleworking*, IDS Personnel policy and practice study no. 729, May 2002

[51] Wustemann L, *IRS Handbook of Flexible Working law and practice*, IRS 2001

[53] *Teleworking*, IDS Personnel policy and practice study no. 729, May 2002

[53] *Teleworking*, IDS Personnel policy and practice study no. 729, May 2002

[54] Wustemann L, *IRS Handbook of Flexible Working law and practice*, IRS 2001

[55, 56, 57] Frank M, North-Smith L, Meredith S, *Human Resources considerations for mobilising your workforce*, IBM Global Services, 2002

[58] Huws U, *Teleworking and local government: What are the costs and benefits?*, Local Government Management Board, 1999

[59] de Martino V, *The High Road to Teleworking*, ILO, **http://www.ilo.org/public/english/protection/safework/telework/hrdptl.pdf** 2001

Staying safe and legal

[60] *Corporate Solutions study*, Health and Safety Executive, 1999

[61] Head C Andrew, *Telecommuting: Panacea or Pandora's Box*, Holland & Knight LLP **http://www.hklaw.com**

BIBLIOGRAPHY

Periodicals

European Journal of Teleworking
Source: Addico Cornix Publications, 64 Morrab Road, Penzance, TR18 2QT Tel and fax: 01736 334702 Web: **http://www.cornix.co.uk**

Flexibility
Editor: Andy Lake *Source:* Home Office Partnership (HOP), Jeffreys Building, St John's Innovation Park, Cambridge *Comment:* Periodical available at **http://www.hop.co.uk**

Internet Magazine
Publishers: emap Business Communications *Source:* Subscriptions Hotline (+44) (0) 181 956 3015 Email: custserv@readerlink.emap.co.uk Web: **http://www.emap.com/internet**

Telecommuting Review
Editor: Gil Gordon *Source:* Gil Gordon Associates, 11 Donner Crt, Monmouth Jn, New Jersey, USA Tel: +001 8852 732 329 2266 *Comment:* US periodical publication available at **http://www.gilgordon.com**

Teleworker Magazine
Editor: Alan Denbigh Tel: 01453 834874 Fax: 01453 836174 Email: info@telework.org.uk *Source:* Telework Association Tel: 0800 616008 or 01203 696986 Fax: 01203 696538 Web: **http://www.telework.org.uk** *Comment:* Bi-monthly magazine for Telework Association members

Telewerken
Source: Overkleeft Uitgeverij BV, Brinkpoortstraat 38, 7411 HS Deventer, Netherlands Tel: +31 570 611044 Fax: +31 570 612042 Email: kene@wxs.nl *Comment:* Dutch teleworking magazine

Publications

1999 Telework America National Telework Survey   *Date: 2000*
Author: Joanne H Pratt *Source:* International Telework Association and Council Web: **http://www.telecommute.org**

30 Minutes to write a Business Plan   *Date: 1997*
Author: Brian Finch *Source:* Kogan Page, 120 Pentonville Rd, London N1 9JN ISBN 0-7494-2364-1

30 Minutes to write a Marketing Plan   *Date: 1997*
Author: John Westwood *Source:* Kogan Page, 120 Pentonville Rd, London N1 9JN ISBN 0-7494-2363-3

A Guide to Help for Small Businesses   *Date: 1998*
Source: Tel: 0870 1502 500 Email: dtipubs@echristian.co.uk Ref: 98/942
Comment: Department of Trade and Industry free booklet of practical information, support and advice for new and existing small businesses

A Manager's Guide to Teleworking   *Date: 1995*
Author: Ursula Huws on behalf of Department of Employment *Source:* Dept of Employment, Cambertown Ltd., Unit 8 Goldthorpe Ind. Estate, Rotherham, S. Yorks Tel: 020 7273 6969

Analysis of a Major (UK) Teleworking Survey   *Date: 1992*
Author: W Murray *Source:* The National Computing Centre, Oxford Road, Manchester M1 7ED

An evaluation of homeworking in ACAS   *Date: 2000*
Author: Ursula Huws *Source:* ACAS Tel: 020 7396 5100 Web: **http://www.acas.org.uk**

An Organizational Guide to Telecommuting   *Date: 1998*
Author: George M Piskurich *Source:* American Society for Training and Development ISBN 1-56286-086-0

Business 2010   *Date: 2000*
Authors: Amarach Consultants for Allied Irish Bank *Source:* Web: **http://www.aib.ie/roi/business/businessbanking.asp**

Business guide to e-work *Date: 2000*
Authors: Imogen Bertin, Brian Goggin and Brian O'Kane *Source:* Enterprise Ireland
Web: **http://www.e-work.ie**

Changing Places – A Manager's Guide to Working from Home *Date: 1996*
Source: New Ways to Work, 309 Upper Street, London N1 2TY Tel: 020 7226 4026

Code of Practice: E-working *Date: 2000*
Source: Department of Enterprise, Trade and Employment, Ireland
Web: **http://www.irlgov.ie/entemp/telework/tele-cop.pdf**

Corporate Telework Survey *Date: 1997*
Authors: Small World Connections *Source:* PO Box 162, South District Office, Manchester
M20 3BB Tel: 0161 445 0630 Fax: 0161 445 1403 Email: small_world@compuserve.com
Web: **http://www.smallworldconnections.com**

Daily Telegraph How to Set Up and Run Your Own Business *Date: 1996*
Source: Kogan Page, 120 Pentonville Road, London N1 9JN 12th edn
ISBN 0–7494–1969–5

Directions for Teleworking *Date: 1998*
Stoke City Council Tel: 01782 232889 Email: dennis.a.marsh@stkoe01.stoke-cc.gov.uk

Disability and Teleworking *Date: 1998*
Author: Imogen Bertin for ETD project and the Aphrodite assistive technology project
Source: Available in .pdf format at Web: **http://www.cork-teleworking.com/distele.htm**

DTI Teleworking Study 1992–1993 *Date: 1993*
Author: Horace Mitchell *Source:* Brameur Ltd, 237 High Street, Aldershot, Hants GU11
1TJ

Employed or Self-Employed?
Source: Inland Revenue Ref: Booklet no. IR56, free of charge
Web: **http://www.inlandrevenue.gov.uk/pdfs/ir56.htm**

Europe's Growing IT Skills Crisis *Date: 2000*
Authors: Andrew Milroy and Puni Rajah of IDC for Microsoft *Source:* Microsoft or IDC
websites

E-work in Ireland *Date 2002*
Authors Bates P, Bertin I, Huws U, available at the Emergence project website
http://www.emergence.nu/pubs/form394.html

Flexible Working *Date: 1996*
Author: Steve Simmons *Source:* Kogan Page, 120 Pentonville Road, London N1 9JN
ISBN 0–7494–1713–7 *Comment:* practical guide to flexible working including tick-box
express implementation guide for the project manager in a hurry

Flexiplace Scheme *Date: 1994*
Author: Oxfordshire County Council *Source:* Commercial Services Print Unit,
Oxfordshire County Council Tel: 01865 815672 Ref: C21-17

Guide to Teleworking *Date: 1996*
Source: Surrey County Council, County Hall, Penrhyn Road, Kingston-upon-Thames,
Surrey KT1 2DN

Homeworking: Guidance for employers and employees on health and safety   *Date: 1996*
Author: Health and Safety Executive *Source:* HSE Books, PO Box 199, Sudbury, Suffolk CO10 6FS Tel: 01787 881165 Fax: 01787 313995. Web:
http://www.hse.gov.uk/hsehome.htm/pubns/homeindx.htm

How to Change Your Life with Technology   *Date: 1998*
Author: Anthony B Capstick *Source:* Management Books 2000 Web:
http://www.mb2000.com ISBN 1–85252–239–9 Tel: 01285 760722 *Comment:* Practical and realistic guide to using technology to streamline working life

How Vehicle Pollution Affects our Health   *Date: 1995*
Source: Ashden Trust, 9 Red Lion Court, London EC4A 3EB

ISO9000 Standard
Copies are available from BSI Standards, Chiswick High Road, London W4 4AL Tel: 020 8996 9001 Fax: 020 8996 7001 Web: **http://www.bsi.org.uk** A list of quality certification bodies can be obtained from the United Kingdom Accreditation Service (UKAS) at **http://www.ukas.com** or from the QA Register, published by The Stationery Office, PO Box 276, London SW8 5DT or at **http://www.quality-register.co.uk**

Keep IT Safe and Secure (Security and Telecentres)   *Date: 1995*
Author: Bill Murray, Small World Connections *Source:* Send SAE with 47p stamp to KISS Booklets, WREN Telecottage, Stoneleigh Park, Warwickshire CV8 2LZ *Comment:* Part of 1994 security survey analysis, free of charge to Telework Association members, subject to availability

Managing Telework: strategies for managing the virtual workforce   *Date: 1998*
Author: Jack M Nilles Web: **http://www.jala.com** *Source:* John Wiley and Sons, Inc. ISBN 0–471–29316–4

Manual of Remote Working   *Date: 1997*
Authors: Kevin Curran and Geoff Williams *Source:* Gower Publishing Ltd, Gower House, Croft Road, Aldershot, Hampshire GU11 3HR

Marketing Telecottages and Teleworking   *Date: 1992*
Author: Various *Source:* TCA/ACRE, Somerford Court, Somerford Road, Cirencester, Glos GL7 1TW

Moral dilemmas and issues of providing telework for disabled people
Source: **http://www.ccsr.cms.dmu.ac.uk/pubs/papers/distwpa1.html** *Comment:* a paper by the Ben Fairweather Research Fellow at the Centre for Computing and Social Responsibility, De Montfort University

Motors or modems? *Date: 1997*
Authors: National Economic Research Association *Source:* RAC Web:
http://www.rac.co.uk

New Information and Communications Technologies at Work   *Date: 1997*
Source: Trade Union Congress Publications, Congress House, Great Russell St, London WC1B 3LS

Planning Policy Guideline 13   *Date: 2000*
Author: Department of the Environment *Source:* The Stationery Office Ltd, National Publishing, 2nd Floor, St Crispins, Duke Street, Norwich NR3 1PD

Prepared for the future? The British and Technology   *Date: 1996*
Author: Motorola *Source:* Tel: 01753 575555 Web:
http://www.mot.com/General/Reports/British-Tech/future.html

Psychological Aspects of Teleworking in Rural Areas   *Date: 1993*
Author: PATRA deliverable report *Source:* Available from Professor David Oborne,
Psychology Department, University of Swansea *Comment:* This report is a literature
review; other reports from the PATRA project may also be available from Professor
Oborne

Safe Homeworking   *Date: 2000*
Authors: Royal Sun Alliance and Merline Marketing *Comment:* A video used by Royal Sun
Alliance complete with a homeworkers' and managers' guide and sample self-assessment
checklist which was developed for RSA's 1500-odd field-based staff. Price £499 or £299
for the CD version – free five-day trial available Email:
orders@merlincommunications.co.uk Tel: 01285 641851

Self-Employment and Labour Market Restructuring   *Date: 1993*
The Case of Freelance Teleworkers in Book Publishing
Authors: Celia Stanworth, John Stanworth, David Purdy *Source:* Future of Work Research
Group, University of Westminster, 35 Marylebone Road, London NW1 5LS Tel: 0171
911 5000

Setting up an IT Centre in a Village Hall   *Date: 2000*
Source: ACRE Tel: 01285 653477

Starting your own business in Ireland   *Date: 2000*
Source: Oaktree Press Web: **http://www.oaktreepress.com** ISBN 1-86076-091-0

Survey of Telecottage Activity and Finance   *Date: 1995*
Authors: Small World Connections with support from the Telecottage Association
Source: Bill Murray, Small World Connections, Tel: 0161 4456 0630

Sussex Telecentre Network   *Date: 1995*
Authors: Sussex Rural Community Council *Source:* Sussex Rural Community Council, 212
High Street, Lewes, East Sussex BN7 2NH Tel: 01273 473422 ISBN 1 873850 13 1

Telecommuting Centers and Related Concepts: A Review of Practice   *Date: 1994*
Authors: Michael Bagley, Jill Mannering, Patricia Mokhtarian *Source:* Institute of
Transportation Studies, University of California, Davis, California 95616
ISBN UCD-ITS-RR-94-4

**Telecottages: How the Usage of Information Technology can counter Rural
Disadvantages**   *Date: 1995*
Author: Tatjana Gosau, MA in European Business Administration
Source: University of Northumbria

Telecottages: the UK Experience   *Date: 1992*
Author: Various *Source:* Telework Association/ACRE, Somerford Court, Somerford Road,
Cirencester Glos GL7 1TW

TeleFutures – a study on teleworking in Ireland   *Date: 1996*
Authors: Imogen Bertin and Gerard O'Neill *Source:* International Services, Forbairt,
Wilton Park House, Wilton Place, Dublin 2 Tel: +353 1 660 2244 Contact: International
Services – Declan Murphy Web: **http://www.cork-teleworking.com/telefutu**

Teleworking – A Director's Guide   *Date: 1996*
Authors: Various *Source:* BT, IoD, Tel: Director Publications, 020 7730 6060

Teleworking and Gender   *Date: 1996*
Author: Ursula Huws Web: **http://dialspace.dial.pipex.com/town/parade/hg54**
Source: Institute for Employment Studies, Mantell Building, University of Sussex,
Brighton BN1 9RF Tel: 01273 686751 Fax: 01273 690430

Teleworking and Globalisation   *Date: 1999*
Authors: Ursula Huws, Nick Jagger and Siobhan O'Regan *Source:* Institute of Employment
Studies, Mantell Building, Falmer, Brighton BN1 9RF Tel: 01273 686751 Web:
http://www.employment-studies.co.uk

Teleworking and Local Government – assessing the costs and benefits   *Date: 1999*
Author: Ursula Huws *Source:* Local Government Management Board Tel: 020 7296 6756
Email: david.maycock@lgmb.gov.uk

Teleworking: an overview of the research   *Date: 1996*
Author: Ursula Huws *Source:* Analytica, 46 Ferntower Road, London N5 2JH
Tel: 020 7226 8411 Fax: 020 7226 0813

Teleworking and Potential Reduction in Work Travel   *Date: 1997*
Authors: Institute for Transport Economics, Norway Tel: +47 22 573800

Teleworking and Rural Development (report 27)   *Date: 1996*
Author: Rural Development Commission *Source:* RDC, 141 Castle Street, Salisbury, Wilts
SP1 3TP Fax: 01722 432773 ISBN 1 869964 53 5

Teleworking Britain   *Date: 1998*
Authors: Mitel/MORI Tel: 0870 909 888 or 020 7381 4505 Web: **http://www.mitel.com**
or **http://www.firefly.co.uk**

Teleworking – BT's Inverness Experience   *Date: 1993*
Author: BT *Source:* BT Tel: 0800 800 060 *Comment:* Much of the information from all
pre-1994 BT booklets is summarised in *Teleworking Explained*, listed below

Teleworking Explained   *Date: 1993*
Authors: Mike Gray, Noel Hodson, Gil Gordon *Source:* John Wiley & Sons, Baffins Lane,
Chichester ISBN 0 471 93975 7 *Comment:* Extremely comprehensive though dated
teleworking guide

Teleworking: Guidelines for Good Practice   *Date: 1997*
Author: Ursula Huws *Source:* Institute for Employment Studies, Mantell Building,
University of Sussex, Brighton BN1 9RF Tel: 01273 686751 Fax: 01273 690430
Web: **http://www.employment-studies.co.uk**

Teleworking in Britain – A report to the Employment Dept   *Date: 1993*
Author: Ursula Huws *Source:* Research Strategy Branch, Employment Dept, Moorfoot,
Sheffield, S1 4PQ, Tel: 020 7273 6969 ISBN PP51 16304 494 52 *Comment:* Thorough
national survey Ref: Research Series No. 18

Teleworking Survey   *Date: 1999*
Authors: Small World Connections for Gee Publishing Customer Services, 100 Avenue
Road, Swiss Cottage, London NW3 3PG Tel: 020 7393 7666

Teleworking – the Shortest Route to Work?   *Date 1998*
Amárach consultants for Dublin Transportation Office, Telecom Éireann and Telework
Ireland is available at **www.amarach.com/future/telew.htm** This site also holds links to
Business 2010 which includes AIB's survey of teleworking in SMEs (2000)

Teleworking: Thirteen Journeys to the Future of Work   *Date: 1996*
Author: Andrew Bibby Contact: Turnaround Distribution, 27 Horsell Road, London N5
1X2 Tel: 020 8829 3000

Telework – The Human Resource Implications   *Date: 1992*
Authors: John and Celia Stanworth *Source:* Institute of Personnel Management, IPM
House, Camp Rd, Wimbledon, London, SW19 4UX ISBN 085292 465 8 *Comment:* Very
clear and comprehensive guide to issues affecting employed teleworkers and personnel
management

The Business Traveler's Survival Guide   *Date 1997*
Author: June Langhoff Web: **http://www.aegisbooks.com/btsg.html** ISBN 1-890154-03-2

The Economics of Teleworking   *Date: 1992*
Author: Noel Hodson, SW 2000, for BT *Source:* BT Tel: 0800 800 600 *Comment:* A shorter
version of this report was available free as part of the BT Teleworking Programme

The Future of Work-Life Balance   *Date: 2002*
Author: Robert Taylor for Economic and Social Research Council
Web: **http://www.esrc.ac.uk**

The Knowledge Management Fieldbook   *Date: 1999*
Authors: Wendi R Bukovitz, Ruth L Williams *Source: Financial Times/*Prentice Hall
ISBN 0–273–63882–3 Web: **www.ftmanagement.com**

The Social Implications of Hypermobility   *Date: 2000*
Author: Professor John Adams, University College London *Source:* Prospect Magazine
http://www.prospect-magazine.co.uk/highlights/hypermobility/index.html – or full
research at **http://www.oecd.org/env/docs/epocppct993.pdf**

The Social Implications of Teleworking   *Date: 1996*
Source: The European Foundation for the Improvement of Living and Working
Conditions, Loughlinstown House, Shankill, Co. Dublin Tel: +353 1 282 6888
Web: **http://www.eurofound.ie** *Comment:* A series of three informative papers covering
the legal situation in a number of European countries: 1) The legal and contractual
situation of teleworkers 2) The social security position of teleworkers 3) Teleworking
health and safety issues

The Wired Habitat   *Date: 1999*
Authors: Jan Simmons and Dot Gavin *Source:* Morrison House Inc. Old Hereford Road,
Mt Evelyn 3796, Australia Email: mhouse@eisa.net.au
Web: **http://www.vicnet.net.au/~morrison**

The Work-Life Manual   *Date: 2000*
Authors: Lucy Daniels and Lucy McCarraher *Source:* Industrial Society
ISBN 1-85835-875-2 Web: **http://www.indsoc.co.uk**

Trade Unions and Telework   *Date: 1996*
Author: Andrew Bibby *Source:* Fiet, Avenue de Balexert 15, CH-1219 Chatelaine-Geneva,
Switzerland Web: **http://www.eclipse.co.uk/pens/bibby/fietrpt**

Virtually There: The Evolution of Call Centres   *Date: 1999*
Authors: Institute for Employment Studies and the TCA for Mitel *Source:* Firefly
Communications Ltd, 25/4 The Coda Centre, 189 Munster Road, London SW6 6AW

Working Anywhere – exploring telework for individuals and organisations   *Date: 1998*
Authors: Department of Trade and Industry Web: **http://www.dti.gov.uk** and
Department of Environment, Transport and the Regions

Working at a Distance – UK Teleworking and its Implications *Date: 1995*
Source: Parliamentary Office of Science & Technology, Houses of Parliament, Millbank, London ISBN 1 897941 85 4

Working at Home – A Study of Homeworking and Teleworking *Date: 1996*
Author: Celia Stanworth *Source:* Institute of Employment Rights Tel: 020 7738 9511 Fax: 020 7738 9577

Work for Yourself – A Guide to Self-Employment and Setting up a Small Business/ Earning Money at Home (two publications)
Source: Consumers' Association, Castlemead, Gascoyne Way, Hertford

Working from home – balancing the issues *Date: 1998*
Babergh District Council Tel: 01473 822801 Fax: 01473 825708

CONTACTS AND URLS

Action for Blind People (two reports on teleworking opportunities for the visually impaired) 14–16 Verney Road, London SE16 3DEZ Tel: 020 7732 8771 Fax: 020 7639 0948 Web: **http://www.afbp.org**

Ability Enterprises, Ballindine, Co. Mayo, Ireland Contact: Derek Farrell Tel: +353 94 65054 Email: ability@iol.ie

AbilityNet (formerly Computability), PO Box 94, Warwick, Warwickshire CV34 5WS Tel: 01926 312847 Fax: 01926 311345 Web: **http://www.abilitynet.co.uk**

ACRE – Action With Communities in Rural England. ACRE can put you in touch with your local rural community council who may know of other schemes or funding awards in the area. Tel: 01285 653477 Email: acre@acre.org.uk Web: **http://www.acre.org.uk**

Adaptors and kits for linking up to collect your email or browse the web anywhere in the world Web: **http://www.teleadapt.com**

Andrew Bibby's home pages which contain a number of articles on telework at **http://www.eclipse.co.uk/pens/bibby/telework.html**

ASLIB, the Association for Information Management, offers a number of Internet-related courses from a library/information management perspective Tel: 0171 903 0000 Fax: 0171 703 0011 Email: aslib@aslib.co.uk Web: **http://www.aslib.co.uk**

Association for Disabled Professionals, PO Box BCN ABP, London WC1N 3XX Tel and fax: 01924 283253 or Minicom: 01924 270335 Email: assdisprof@aol.com Web: **http://www.adp.org.uk** Contact: Sue Maynard Croft

Association for the Advancement of Assistive Technology (US) Web: **http://www.resna.org**

Australian Rural Telecentres Network. Has produced a best-practice guide released in 1997 Web: **http://www.telecentres.wa.gov.au**

British Computer Society Disability Group focuses on the role of IT in providing disabled people with a better quality of life. Tel: 01245 242924 Email: geoffrey.busby@gecm.com Web: **http://www.bcs.org/sig/**

Broadband – regional development agencies responsible for encouraging broadband connections:
Scottish Enterprise **http://www.scottish-enterprise.com** 0845 607 8787
Highland and Islands Enterprise Board **http://www.hie.co.uk** 01463 234171
North East **http://www.onenortheast.co.uk** 0191 261 2000
North West **http://www.nwda.co.uk** 01925 400100
Yorkshire Forward **http://www.yorkshire-forward.com** 0113 243 9222
East of England **http://www.eeda.org.uk** 01223 713900
East Midlands Development Agency **http://www.emda.org.uk** 0115 988 8300
South West of England **http://www.southwestrda.org.uk** 01392 214 747
South East of England **http://www.seeda.co.uk** 01483 484 226
Welsh Development Agency **http://www.wda.co.uk**
Northern Ireland **http://www.broadbandforbusiness.com** 02890 529900
Also **http://www.ukonlineforbusiness.gov.uk**

BT Featureline 0800 400 400. BT telephone sales and services information 152 (Tollfree UK only)

BT Homehighway ISDN Web: **http://www.homehighway.bt.com**

BT's Working from Home site has information provided by its Workstyles consultancy Web: **http://www.wfh.co.uk**

BTEC: Central House, Upper Woburn Place, London WC1H 0HH Tel: 0171 413 8400 Web: **http://www.edexcel.org.uk/btec**

Business Bureau small business information resource Web: **http://www.businessbureau-uk.co.uk**

Center on Disabilities, California State University (a partner in the Aphrodite Assistive Technology project) Web: **http://www.csun.edu/cod**

Central Remedial Clinic, Penny Ansley Building, Vernon Avenue, Clontarf, Dublin 3 Tel: +353 1 805 7560 Fax: +353 1 833 5496 Contact: Ger Craddock Web: **http://www.crc.ie**

City and Guilds of London Institute, 1 Giltspur Street, London EC1A 9DD

Cornix Teleworking Consultancy, 64 Morrab Road, Penzance, Cornwall TR18 2QT Tel: 01736 369477 Fax: 01736 369477 Email: 100021.2563@compuserve.com or srs@cornix.co.uk Web: **http://www.cornix.co.uk** Contact: Stephen Simmons

Communications Workers' Union of Ireland, 575 North Circular Road, Dublin 1 Tel: +353 1 836 6388 Fax: +353 1 836 5582 Contact: Chris Hudson Email: chris@cwu.ie Web: **http://www.cwu.ie**

Community Investment Fund (created by English Partnerships)is for projects from priority areas such as rural development blackspots, former coalfield areas, city challenge areas and so on. Grants of between £10,000 and £100,000 in value are possible and can be for capital works to buildings or for revenue projects that are expected to produce social and economic benefits. Contact 020 7976 7070.

Compression utilities: PKZIP **http://.www.pkware.com/shareware/pkzip_win.html** or Aladdin Dropzip and Stuffit Expander **http://www.aladdinsys.com**

Cygnet Solutions, Swan House, Darvel, Ayrshire KA17 0LP Tel: 01560 323444 Fax: 01560 323432 Email: sgf@cygnets.co.uk Web: **http://www.cygnets.co.uk** Contact: Suzanne Flynn. Helps companies to achieve ISO9001, ISO9002 and TickIT registration

Data Protection Registrar Tel: 01625 545745 Web: **http://www.dataprotection.gov.uk**

DIAL – Disability Information and Advice Line Tel: 01302 310123 Fax: 01302 310404 Email: dialuk@aol.com Web: **http://www.dialuk.org.uk**

Disability Discrimination Act Tel: 0345 622633 for a copy or Web: **http://www.disability.gov.uk**

DissBASE – the Disability Information Database Tel: 01306 742282 Web: **http://www.diss.org.uk/dissbase.html**

EA Technology (EU SAVE programme) Contact Andrew Wright Tel: 0151 347 2364 Web: **http://www.eatechnology.com**

ECATT project tracking telework and e-commerce changes through surveys Web: **http://www.ecatt.com**

Effective Quality Management (EQM), Lake House, Wythop Mill, Cockermouth, Cumbria CA13 9YP Tel: 01768 776687 Fax: 01768 77629 Email: malcolm.lake@btinternet.com Contact: Malcolm Lake

Emergence EU project tracking movement of work, and trends in telework and mobile work in 22 countries Web: **http://www.emergence.nu**

Employers for Work Life Balance Web: **http://www.employersforworklifebalance.org.uk**

Enterprise Ireland, the Irish business development agency, has a comprehensive website including a business guide to telework and video clips Web: **http://www.e-work.ie**

European Foundation for the Improvement of Living and Working Conditions, Wyattville Road, Loughlinstown, Dublin, Ireland Tel: +353 1 204 3100 Fax: +353 1 282 6456 Web: **http://www.eurofound.ie**

European Telework Development project maintains the European Telework Online (ETO) pages Web: **http://www.eto.org.uk**

Fax Preference Service – to register your wish not to be faxed by direct selling organisations Tel: 0845 070 0702 Web: **http:// www.fpsonline.org.uk**

Freeagentnation ezine – Dan Pink's throughts on the change to increased self-employment over the Net Web: **http://www.freeagentnation.com/newsletter.cfm**

Future Work Forum at Henley Management College Web: **http://www.henleymc.ac.uk/fwf**

Gil Gordon's website is a mine of useful information – probably the best telework website in the world – **http://www.gilgordon.com**

Glossary of computer terms: **http://www.webopedia.com**

Greenet (Internet access specialising in community groups) 74–77 White Lion St, London N1 9PF Tel: 020 7713 1941 Fax: 020 7837 5551 Email: support@gn.apc.org Web: **http://www.gn.apc.org**

Headset manufacturer Danacom UK office at 25 Broadway, Maidenhead, Berkshire SL6 1LZ Tel: 01628 676768 Fax: 01628 773806 Web: **http://www.danacom.com**

Headset manufacturer, Plantronics Ltd, Interface Business Park, Bincknoll Lane, Wootton Basset, Wiltshire SN4 8QQ Sales Enquiries: 0800 410014 Fax: 01793 848853 Web: **http://www.plantronics.com**

Health and Safety Executive, HSE Tel. 01422 892 345 Web: **http://www.hse.gov.uk**

Health and Safety issues: Éilis Duggan, Ergonomics consultant Tel: +353 45 861148

Heriott Watt University's Computer Based Learning centre Web: **http://www.icbl.hw.ac.uk**.

History of computing and the Internet: Computerscope Online article The Digital Century December 1999 in the Computerscope archives at **http://www.techcentral.ie** or Smithsonian Online **http://smithsonian.yahoo.com/index.html**

Information Society Commission of Ireland (which has included questions on teleworking in some of its survey work) Web: **http://www.isc.ie**

Inland Revenue self-assessment enquiry line: Tel: 0345 161514 Web: **http://www.inlandrevenue.gov.uk**

Intermec Ireland, 19/20 York Road, Dun Laoghaire, Co. Dublin, Ireland Tel: +353 1 280 0899 Email: simon@intermec.ie Web: **http://www.intermec.ie**

Internet service providers listings, rates, contact numbers: **http://www.internet-magazine.com/resource/isp/isp_list.html**

Institute of Employment Studies website has a number of reports relating to teleworking including several by Ursula Huws – **http://www.employment-studies.co.uk**

Institute of Occupational Safety and Health – datasheet on teleworking health and safety issues and form for telework premises assessment. Web: **http://www.iosh.co.uk/files/technical/teleworking.pdf**

Irish Internet service providers listings: **http://www.techcentral.ie**

ITAC, the main American teleworking association **http://www.telecommute.org**

Jack Nilles website with information on selecting and managing teleworkers: **http://www.jala.com**

Jim Lubin's disability resources – a cornucopia of disability and assistive technology information Web: **http://www.makoa.org/index.html**

Kendlebell personal call-handling service for people who don't like to use voicemail when they are out Web: **http://www.kendlebell.co.uk**

Labour Market enquiries, ONS, 1 Drummond Gate, London SW1V 2QQ Tel: 020 7533 6176 Web: **http://www.statistics.gov.uk/themes/labour_market/default.asp**

Labour Telematics Centre, GMB National College, College Road, Whalley Range, Manchester M16 8PB Tel: 0161 860 4364 Fax: 0161 881 1853 Email: labourteladmin@mcr1.poptel.org.uk Web: **http:// www.labourtel.org.uk/**

Law Centres Federation Tel: 020 7387 8570 or 0161 236 3365 Email: info@lawcentres.org.uk Web: **http://www.lawcentres.org.uk**

Learning World, Units 9–11, Allison Court, MetroCentre Retail park, Gateshead NE11 9YS
Tel: 0191 488 3232 Fax: 0191 488 3111 Web: **http://www.learningworld.ac.uk**

Madentec Internet Accessibility Center Web: **http://www.madentec.com/**

Manchester Women's Electronic Village Hall – has an open learning course on teleworking issues on its website. The course is intended to be used in conjunction with face-to-face learning at the WEVH but you could use it as distance learning on your own Web: **http://www.wevh.org.uk**

Microsoft Netmeeting PC conferencing software Web: **http://www.microsoft.com**

MSF Union. Contact Peter Skyte at MSF, 40 Bermondsey Street, London SE1 3UD Tel: 020 7939 7086 Fax: 020 7403 2964 Email: skytep@msf.org.uk Web: **http://www.msf.org.uk**

National Council for Vocational Qualifications: 222 Euston Road, London NW1 2BZ Tel: 0171 387 9898

National Lottery website with information on obtaining funding: **http://www.nlcb.org.uk**

National Work-Life Balance Challenge fund: **http://www.dti.gov.uk /work-lifebalance**

Netaccountants: **http://www.netaccountants.com**

Networking sales and information sites **http://www.3com.co.uk**, **http://www.techworks.co.uk, http://www.smc.com**

ODTR Irish telecommunications regulator: **http://www.odtr.ie**

Oftel UK telecommunications regulator: **http://www.oftel.co.uk**

Oldham MBC has revised its planning guidelines to take account of teleworkers. Its guidelines are available to other planning authorities. Contact Dave Hashdi, Oldham Metropolitan Borough Council Tel: 01619 114 156 Email: dhashdi@gmnresearch.u-net.com

Opportunities for People with Disabilities, 1 Bank Buildings, Prices Street, London EC2R 8EU Tel: 020 7580 7545 Email: edwa36@ibm.net Web: **http://www.opportunities.org.uk**

Oregon Office of Energy website has information on telecommuting at **http://www.energy.state.or.us/telework/telehm.htm**

Parents at Work 43 Beech Street, London EC2P 2LX Employment rights advice: Tel: 020 7628 212. Information for employers: Tel: 020 7628 3565 Email: parents-at-work@gn.apc.org

Peter Fowler is a solicitor with a niche practice in businesss-related legal matters and commercial property Tel: 01202 849 242 Email p_fowler@lds.co.uk Web: **http://www.peterjfowler.co.uk**

Posturite – ergonomic office furniture including chairs, desks, wrist supports, ergonomic mice, document holders, back supports. PO Box 468, Hailsham, East Sussex BN27 4LZ Tel: 01323 833353 Fax: 01323 833999 Email: support@posturite.co.uk Web: **http://www.posturite.co.uk**

Princess Royal Trust for Carers, 16 Byward Street, London EC3R 5BA Tel: 020 7480 7788

Royal Mail – details of postal services and conditions, a two-way postcode lookup table, tariff calculators, track-and-trace facilities **http://www.royalmail.co.uk**

RNIB, 224 Great Portland Street, London W1N 6AA Tel: 020 7388 1266. Specialist benefits advisers can be contacted on 020 7388 1266. There is a guide called *Access*

Technology detailing available equipment for blind people and covering braille, large print and speech technology, available from 020 8968 8600. Web: **http://www.rnib.org.uk**

RNID, 105 Gower Street, London WC1E 6AH Tel: 0208 740 9531 Web: **http://www.rnid.org.uk**

RSA Examinations Board (IT courses and exams including word processing and DTP, held in high regard by employers because of the level of accuracy required to achieve the qualification) has been taken over by the Oxford and Cambridge Board – *see* **http://www.ocr.org.uk**

Shaw Trust – champions the abilities of disabled people through providing rehabilitation, training, work tasters, employment support and occupation Tel: 01225 716300 Web: **http://www.shaw-trust.org.uk**

Small World Connections Tel: 0161 445 0603 Web: **http://www.smallworldconnections.com**

Sulzer Infra CBX – web-based survey on teleworking infrastructure including health and safety information: **http://www.sulza-infra.com**

Technology news services: **http://www.theregister.co.uk**, **http://www.zdnet.co.uk**, **http://www.electricnews.net**

Telework Association web pages are at **http://www.telework.org.uk**

Telecoms infrastructure figures and research reports can be found at **http://www.analysys.com**

Telephone Preference Service – to register your wish not to be contacted by direct selling organisations Tel: 0845 070 0707 Web: **http://www.tpsonline.org.uk**

Tolson Messenger – specialists in home-office insurance Tel: 0800 374 246 Web: **http://www.tolsonmessenger.co.uk**

Uninterruptible power supplies – try the RS Components Ltd catalogue **http://www.rswww.com** or http://www.upspower.co.uk

Ursula Huws website: **http://dialspace.dial.pipex.com/town/parade/hg54** – full of fascinating research

US National Institute of Disability and Rehabilitation Research Web: **http://www.abledata.com/**

Video conferencing – Picturephone direct: **http://www.picturephone.com** A cheap and cheerful video-conferencing system is Connectix QuickCam for about £150 **http://www.logitech.com** Sony's Polycom system is often used for high-quality video conferences such as conference presentations **http://www.polycom.com**

Voluntary action councils
WCVA – Wales Council for Voluntary Action Tel: 029 2085 5100 Email: enquiries@wcva.org.uk Web: **http://www.wcva.org.uk**
SCVO – Scottish Council for Voluntary Organisations Tel: 0131 556 3882 Email: enquiries@scvo.org.uk Web: **http://www.scvo.org.uk**
NCVO – National Council for Voluntary Organisations (UK-wide) Tel: 020 7713 6161 Web: **http://www.ncvo-vol.org.uk**
NIAA – Northern Informatics Application Agency – aims to improve communications

and information access in the Northern area including Northumberland, Tyne & Wear, Cumbria, County Durham and Cleveland Tel: 0191 528 0039 Web: **http://www.niaa.org.uk**

Webmail (free email) sites: **http://www.hotmail.com**, **http://www.yahoo.co.uk**, **http://www.web2mail.com**

Western Provident Association. Health insurance plans aimed at the self-employed Tel: 0800 783 0784

Wilson Insurers – specialists in non-standard home insurance such as people who work from home, problems with subsidence, adverse claims, etc. Tel: 0990 239 607 Web: **http://www.quotelinedirect.co.uk**

Workability c/o Leonard Cheshire Foundation Tel: 020 7802 8200 Email: a.anderson@london.leonard-cheshire.org.uk Web: **http://www.jobability.com**

Work-life balance case study publications can be ordered from **http://www.dti.gov.uk/publications**

Reduced cost & improved service – now

ON LINE WITH
consorte

Consorte Group AS is a developer of advanced inbound voice routing systems. About five years ago Telenor, the national telecommunications carrier in Norway, started investigating more advanced IN (intelligent network) solutions to deliver higher levels of customer service. They commissioned their own Research and Development team to devise a new platform for delivery of advanced services. The prototype was duly delivered by the R&D team only to be quashed for fear of canabalising existing revenue streams. Subsequently the R&D team left the company to form Consorte; the rest they say is history.

The fundamental design philosophy of Consorte was to develop a flexible, location-independent, virtual-call-centre solution that could deliver all the current features of IN technology and more without the need for customer premises equipment. The system had to be easy to administer and in addition, any statistical information to assist in managing the service was to be available to managers on demand.

The PULSE solution as delivered is PBX and ACD independent, allowing any operator with a direct dial-in (DDI) number, mobile or home phone to participate as a full member of the virtual-call-centre team. Our solutions do not require a PBX at the customer premises but can work with all current PBXs. Being technology independent we are able to deliver full functionality to any location, using analog phones, ISDN, GSM or IP.

The challenge facing most companies today is about retaining customer loyalty, and one way of improving your chances is to provide higher levels of customer service. In order to provide high levels of customer satisfaction many organisations scale to deliver a good service at peak load.

By choosing a virtual solution our customers are provided with greater flexibility to deal with operational peaks. Imagine the typical situation of the 10.00 to 11.00 a.m. peak; now any company is able to provide flexible working to home agents to help deal with peaks without the need and expense of having its agents travel to the call centre. Full comparitive agent statistics are available on demand using SONAR, our Web-based statistical tool, to enable the call-centre manager to assess the effectiveness of home-based agents. Where CTI integration is required, the home agent need only have an Internet link with VPN to operate the same systems from home.

Consorte solutions are provided on a pay-as-you-go basis, so no large capital investments are required to turn your current call centre into a virtual call centre, deliver the benefits of lower line charges, eliminate call forwarding costs, and provide better customer service.

For further information please visit our website
http://www.consorte.co.uk

Index

3Com 37, 79–80, 186
AA (Automobile Association) 6–7, 45
Abbey National 188
Ability (Ireland) 347
AbilityNet 333, 337–339
absenteeism 8
abstracting 211
ACAS 34, 182
access (for disabled) 339–348
accountancy services 212
ACT NOW scheme 78
Adams-Spinks, Geoff 197
Adobe software 267
ADSL 42, 77–79, 268
advantages of teleworking 8–13
advertising (see also publicity) 228–232
Aer Rianta 167, 352–355
affiliate web marketing 242, 245
age of teleworkers 30–31
agreements and contracts 181, 183–184, 247–248
Allenby, Dr Brad 88
Alliance and Leicester 44
Amárach consultants 87
American Express 70
Americans with Disabilities Act 334
Amicus-MSF 45, 90, 153, 184, 188
anti-virus software 268, 275, 291
Antur Tanat Cain telecottage 344
appointment-fixing services 221
Arizona State University 13
ARO call center 10
assistive technology 337–341
asynchrous digital subscriber line (ADSL) 42, 77–79
AT&T 9, 19, 21–22, 88, 174
    telework surveys 56–57
audio bridge 103
audio typing 211–212
audio conferencing 16, 101–103
Australian Bureau of Statistics 65
authentication systems 272
Automobile Association (AA) 6–7

Babergh District Council 304
BackCare charity 302
background and history of teleworking 23–45
backing up 232, 290–291
Baisley, Laura 125–126
balancing home/family and work 143–148
Barclays Bank silver surfer survey 31
Bay Area Rapid Transit (BART) case 334
BBC 197, 354
BEEP project 118
benchmarking 165, 192–193
benefit-in-kind (BIK) 180–181

benefits of teleworking 8–13
Bennett, Paul 243
Berne Convention 326
BIK (benefit-in-kind) 180–181
bills (invoices) 143
bookkeeping services 212
Booz Allen Hamilton 19, 41, 164
Boston Consulting Group 40–41
Boyle, Jennifer 214
Bradford University – BT research 4, 20, 31, 86
Britannia Building Society 178
British Gas 6, 186, 338
broadband 19, 41–42, 47–49, 77–79, 280–282
BT (British Telecom) 4, 125, 188, 193, 205
    Cellnet (now mm0$_2$) 4, 118
    Products 76, 98, 99–102, 110, 131, 284, 309
    Research 4, 14–15, 20, 32, 86, 108, 147–148, 356
building regulations 88, 303–305, 311–313
business
    charges by public utilities 309
    ideas 209–220
    networking 231–232
    objectives 209–210
    planning 220, 222, 253
    rates 306–308
    start-up checklist 253–254
Business Link advice centres 152, 208, 220, 229

cable broadband 41, 281
California Energy Commission 86
call centres 84, 123
Cambridge 87
Cambridgeshire County Council 198, 203–204
capital gains tax (CGT) 308
Capital Modernisation Fund 76, 126
Capstick, Anthony 209, 228–229, 233
career development 20–21, 38–39, 57, 149–150, 177, 361
cashflow 223, 227
Cashion, Deirdre 37
CD-ROM drive 263, 357
Central Remedial Clinic 339
Central Statistics Office (Ireland) 28
Centrica 6
certification of training 359–360
charities 74
Chiat Day 119
childcare 35, 145–146, 174
Cisco 9, 162
Citrix 190
Clapperton, Guy 245
Clark, Michael 45–54, 72–73, 75
class 28–29

Clifford, Ian 126
code of practice 34, 67, 170, 184, 247, 299
Collins, Ann 310
communication agreement 97–105, 176–177
Communications Workers' Union (CWU) 91, 153, 184
Community Network audio conferences 102
community resource centres 122, 127
commuting 5, 10–11
companies (table of), teleworking 158–159
Compaq 170
Computability Centre – see AbilityNet
computer
  conferencing 285–286
  laptop (portables, notebooks) 107–108, 261, 300
  literacy levels needed 352
  networks 264–265
  programming 213–215
  purchasing 260–265
  reconditioned 129, 260
  security 268–276
  software 266
  viruses 232, 268–270, 274–275, 291
CompuTrace 186
Comunicado translators 131–132
concerns about teleworking 13–21
conferencing 102, 123, 285–286
confidentiality 233
consumer protection and direct-selling rules 327
contracts and agreements 183–184, 247–248, 311, 315
contractors, self-employed 181
copyright 326
Corel Draw, Corel WordPerfect 267
Cornell University empty desk research 88
Cornix 45, 315
corporate amnesia 165
costs/benefits of teleworking 135–137, 162–164
Countryside Agency 75–76, 78, 129
County Enterprise Boards (Ireland) 208
couriers 104
covenants (freehold, leasehold, restrictive) 307
Cox, Denise 242–243
Craddock, Ger 339
Creedon, Tadgh 80
CTI (computer telephony integration) 100
Cumberbeach, Cathy 347
customer care and retention 248, 251
CWU – see Communication Workers' Union
cybercafés and web kiosks 113, 114–115, 117
cybersquatters 330

Daily Information 121
data
  backup 142–143, 186, 290–291
  entry, input, processing 124, 214

  protection 213, 247, 314–315, 323–325, 332–335
  security 186, 233, 268–274
  sharing 285–286
  synchronisation 275–276
database-cleaning services 221
Datamonitor 139
Davis, Christopher, & Co 131, 328
deadlines 140–142
de Bruin, Kitty 45–54
defamation 328–329
deliveries 110–111
Dell 129, 256–257, 261
Department of Defense (US) 12, 70
Dept. for Education and Employment 130
  of Education and Science 360–361
  of Enterprise, Trade and Employment 312–313
  of Environment (Ireland) 304
  of the Environment 304
  of Environment, Transport and the Regions 10, 84, 129, 304
  Labor (US) 55
  of Trade and Industry (DTI) 34, 67, 128–129, 252, 256, 303, 312–313
  of Work and Pensions (DWP) 334–335
Design for All centres 339
desksharing 117
desktop publishing (DTP) 217–218, 267
digital
  cameras 266
  signatures 329
  subscriber line (DSL) 41, 77–78, 268
Digital Peninsula 78
di Nicola, Patrizio 89
direct-selling rules and consumer protection 327
directories as a marketing tool 231–232
directory enquiries 14, 15, 89
disability 35, 333–348
disasters and teleworking 69–71
discussion forums 243–244
distance-learning 355
Downs, Anthony 87
DSL (digital subscriber line) 41, 77–78, 268
DTO (Dublin Transportation Office) 87
DTP (desktop publishing) 217–218, 267
Dublin Transportation Office (DTO) 87
Duffy, Mary 336
Duggan, Éilis 301
Durham County Council 164, 173, 178, 185, 299
DVD-ROM drive 263
DWP (Department of Work and Pensions) 334–335
Dyer, Mark 308, 361

EA Technology 88
Eagle, John 215
Eaglestone, Bernadette 221
East Clare Telecottage (ECT) 125

East Riding of Yorkshire County Council 9, 205
easyEverything cybercafés 117, 276
Easyoffices 115
ECDL (European Computer Driving Licence) 125, 350, 352
e-commerce (electronic commerce) 242, 327
Economic and Social Research Council 34
editing 211
e-enabled self-employed 30–31
e-lancers 10, 31, 62, 64, 199, 238
e-learning 177, 356–357
electronic workspace 116–117
e-living project 62
e-London and the London Plan 79
email 103, 278, 325
  junk (spam) 287–288
  marketing 242–243, 324
  viruses 269
EMERGENCE project 28, 31–33, 46, 62–64
Emergency Recovery Disk 291
Empirica 72
employed or self-employed 309–311
employees 10–13, 19–21
employers 8–10, 13–19, 135–137
employment
  agencies 312–313
  for disabled persons using IT 342–346
  law 312–315
Employment Act 2002 36, 135, 312
Employment Appeal Tribunal 35, 312, 334
encryption 109, 272–273
energy saving 88
Enfield, London Borough of 198
enhanced corporate portal solutions 273
enquiries, responding to 232–233
Enterprise Ireland (EI) 164, 208
environmental impacts 4, 84–88
e-outsourcing 31
Epsom neighbourhood telecentre 202
equipment
  costs 17, 41, 93, 255–258
  provided for staff 26, 66
  rental 124, 257
  security 113, 268–299
ergonomics 93–94, 118, 300–302
Eurobarometer surveys 40, 59
European
  Commission 61, 118
  ECATT survey 61–62
  TOSCA project 45, 84
  Computer Driving Licence (ECDL) 125, 350, 352
  directives and laws 67, 148, 189, 296–297, 324, 327, 329
  directorates 29, 61–62
  employers' organisation (UNICE) 312

projects and programmes 45, 61, 76, 88, 125, 170, 199, 201, 204, 341, 347
  Survey of Working Conditions 59
  Trade Union Confederation (ETUC) 312
  Framework Agreement on teleworking 65–66, 90, 93, 184, 194, 295, 312
  Teleworking Award 153
Eurostat 24
Evergreen Business Support 208, 213
e-work 1, 63–64
expenses, allowances 178, 180–181
e-zines 63, 153, 237, 243

facilities, shared 276
fair use and copyright 326–327
FAMILIES project 61
family life 12, 19–20, 30, 144–147
FÁS 208, 346, 362
Fast Company magazine 116
fax 103, 109–110, 112, 124, 265
Fax Preference Service 140
feasibility studies 156–165
FI group 195
file stuffing or zipping 278
finance 226–228
Finance Act 2000 180, 309
fire safety 93, 317–318
firewalls 268–271, 274
first-aid kit 93
Fletcher-Price, Ian 93–94, 302
flexible working 1, 27–28, 36, 38, 156, 312
Flexible Working magazine 13, 15, 46, 167, 170
flexiplace working 1, 117, 179
Ford UK 192
Fotheringham v. Wood 306
Francis-Jones, Mark 344
Frazier International 129
freelancers 10, 29, 31, 62, 238–240
funding 227–228, 359–361
furniture 93–94, 116, 173

gadget wish-list 39–40
garden offices 94, 95–97
Gartner/Dataquest surveys 19, 71, 164, 284
Gateshead Learning World 358
Gee Publications 14, 27–28
gender and teleworking 28–30, 47–48
GlaxoWellcome 173, 176, 178
globalisation and teleworking 31–32
Gloucestershire Fire and Rescue Service 317
Gobalhelm 328
Golden Pages 231
Goldman Sachs 39
Goldstein, Arnold S 228
Good Enough Information Consultants 363
Gordon, Gil 39, 45–54, 68, 71, 87, 119, 149, 161, 237–238, 354
Government Services Agency (GSA) (USA) 69

Govindasamy, Kamini 160
GPRS services 39, 105
GPS (2.5G) networks 39
Grampian Regional Council 199
graphics software 266
Grey, Paul 345
Grimes, Seamus 76
groupware 267
growth of teleworking 22, 46–47
GSM service 79
Gundry, Dr John 363

hacking 17, 269–270
hard disks 262–263
Hart, Phil 251
Harvey, Marcus 217
Hawkins, Pete 152
HCSCD service 105
Headway 74
health and safety 34, 66, 175–176, 295–303
health insurance 322–323
Helpline Computer 269, 290
Henderson, Pauline 303
Hereford and Worcestershire Community
  Council 127
Hertfordshire County Council 85, 119
Hewitt, Patricia 77
Hewlett Packard (HP) 261
Highlands and Islands Enterprise (HIE) 91, 125
HK Union (Denmark) 91
home-office equipment 93–98, 99, 101–113,
  145, 172–175, 296–298, 320–321
homeworkers 35, 45, 139, 141, 145, 216
HOP (Home Office Partnership) 85
hotdesking 117, 202, 261, 301, 313
hotel connectivity, international 112
hotelling 117
housekeeping tasks 143–147, 292
housework 146
HSBC Asset Finance 297
HSE (Health and Safety Executive) 34, 175,
  295–296, 301
HTML 239, 241, 243, 329
human resource (HR) issues 170–174
Human Rights Act 1998 189, 332
Hunter, Andrew 83
Hunter, Ian 6–7
Huws, Ursula 29, 45–54, 62, 195–196

IBM 9, 12, 165, 175, 193–194, 196, 261
ICANN 330
ICSA Labs 274
ICT access centres 73–74
IDC survey 58
IDP (International Data Processing) 214
IES (Institute of Employment
  Studies) 30, 33, 36, 38, 45

ILO (International Labour
  Organisation) 30, 32, 65, 90
IM (instant messaging) 284–285
I'm in touch 109–110
Imperial Cancer Research Fund 338
implementation of teleworking 155–206
income tax 309–311
indexing 211
Infogenie 218
information broking services 214–215, 218
Information Society Commission (Ireland) 28
Inland Revenue, teleworking in the 313
instant messaging (IM) 284–285
Instant Search 209, 228–230, 233
Institute of Employment Studies
  (IES) 30, 33, 36, 38, 45, 182, 333
Institute of Management 189
Institute of Occupational Health and Safety 296
insurance 172, 174–175, 318–323
integrated services digital network (ISDN) 42,
  101
intellectual property and copyright 326–327
Intermec Ireland 252
International Data Processing (IDP) 214
International Labour Organisation 30, 32, 65, 90
International Telecommunications Union 71
International Telework Association
  and Council (ITAC) 56, 90
international travellers 111–112
Internet
  services 27, 73, 79, 83, 112, 100–101,
    106–112, 215, 238–239, 242–243, 276,
    277–287, 327, 329–330
  learning 354, 356–357, 359
  marketing 100, 235–237, 337–338
Internet Magazine 114, 277
interpreting services 132
Iouannou, Stelios Haji 117
Irish Government Code of Practice 170, 247
Irish Times, The 68, 288
IRS 167, 173, 192
ISDN 42, 101, 104, 106
Isles telecroft 125–126, 128–129
ISO9000 standards 250–252
isolation 15–20, 66, 89, 151–152
ISPs (Internet service providers) 111, 239,
  277–279
IT centres 122
IT departments 53–54
IT for All initiative 128
IT requirements and support 185–191
ITAC 56, 90
ITU 71

job satisfaction 10, 57, 61, 89
job-hunting sites 240
jobs suitable for teleworking 5

junk email (spam) 287–288
JustVanilla 342

Karten Charitable Trust 348
Kendlebell Take-a-Message service 143, 215
Kinko's 114–115
Kirklees Council 204
knowlege base 359–360
Korte, Werner 72
Kropla, Steve 112

labour rights 90–92
Labour Force Survey (UK) 23–28, 30–31, 33, 45, 333
Lake, Andy 85–86
LAN (local area network) 265
laptop computers, 106–109, 261, 301
Lasair and Western Isles Project 72, 81
LEADER scheme 208
LearnDirect scheme 73, 126, 129–130, 346, 353
learning 355–356, 358–359
Learning World (Gateshead) 358
legal clerking 220
Leonard Cheshire Foundation 348
LFS 23–28, 30–31, 33, 46
Lillington, Karlin 288
limited liability structures 224–225, 309
Lloyds of London 356
Lloyds TSB 129, 191
local government employers' organisation 34
Local Government Management Board 195
loft conversions 304–305
London Borough of Enfield 198
London Borough of Hillingdon v. Morgan 334
Lotus software 137, 267, 276

MacRoberts, Solicitors 327, 329
Macromedia software 267
mail-order purchasing 256, 327
mailing lists 246–247
Mailing Preference Service 140
Mailwasher 288
management 13–14, 38–39, 51, 166, 173, 199
marketing 143, 208, 219, 228–247
McPherson, Steve 45–54
media relations 230–231, 236
mediauk.com 234
Merrill Lynch 356
messaging 258–259
metatags and linking 329
Microsoft 17, 129, 272, 284
  Netmeeting 285–286
  network (MSN) 97, 272
  Office 191, 267, 271
  Outlook 137–138, 257, 269, 276
  qualifications 352
  Windows 252, 257, 275–276, 284, 290
  Works 267

middle-management syndrome 165
Mitel 5, 18, 29, 45, 333
mm0$_2$ 173
McMillan, Josie 125–126
mobile
  messaging 112–113
  PCs (laptops) 106–109, 300
  phones and PDAs 105–107, 258–260
  teleworking 1, 9, 55, 60–61, 104–113, 298, 300–301
modems 265
Mohktarian, Patricia 86
monitoring progress 194–195, 197
monitors, computer 263–264
Moorlands telecottage 121
MORI 5, 18, 77, 108
Morrison, Donnie 72, 81
mortgages 305–306
motorway touchdown centres 110, 203
MRBI survey (Ireland) 28
MS (Multiple Sclerosis) Society 346
MSF union see Amicus-MSF
Murray, Bill and Cathy 71–73, 122, 170

National Lottery 126, 129
National Rural Environment Centre (RuralNet) 74, 128
National Telework and Air Quality pilot project (US) 69
National Union of Journalists (NUJ) 153, 184
National Vocational Qualifications (NVQs) 349–350, 360
Nationwide Building Society 160, 303
NERA 11, 85–86
neighbourhood offices 113–114
Netaccountants 361
netiquette (online etiquette) 243, 283–284
networks,
  business 231, 264–265
  computer 264
  informal 231–232
newsgroups 243–244
Nextra 14
Nilles, Jack 23, 161–162, 334
non-compete clauses 314–315
Nortel Networks 16, 164
NUJ (National Union of Journalists) 153, 184
NVQs 349–350, 360

objectives, establishing 209–210
occasional teleworkers 24, 60
occupations of teleworkers 29
Occupational Safety and Health Administration (US) 303
OCR (optical character recognition) 266, 340
office
  services 124, 215
  software suites 267

Office Ghosts 209
Office for National Statistics (ONS) 23, 26, 29
Oftel 308
O'Kane, Brian 210
Oldham Borough Council 304
online park bench, the 97, 277
optical character recognition (OCR) 266, 340
ORBIT project 127
organisations using teleworkers 158–159
OSL number checking service 325
overwork 148–149, 171
Oxfordshire County Council 173–174, 175, 178–179
parents rights re working arrangements 135
Parents at Work 146
park bench, the online 97, 277
partnership, business 225
Partnership Act 225
Partnerships Online 74
passwords 270–273
Patent Office (US) 91
PATRA report 10
PC Anywhere 109, 273
PCs (personal computers) 107–109, 129, 201, 257, 259
PDAs (personal digital assistants) 107, 258–259, 276
pensions 331
Pentax Pocketjet 110
performance appraisal 21
permanent health insurance 322
Personal Investment Authority 331
Phillips, Sue 269, 290
physical security 113, 315–316
pilot project for teleworking 165–169
Pink, Dan 31, 115
planning and building regulations 88–89, 303–305
planning, business 220, 222, 223, 253
points of presence (POPs) 273
policies 18, 172–181
Positively Broadband alliance 41
post-office computer access 111
postal equipment and services 104
posture and telephonitis 301
power supply problems 317
Powergen 161
PPP healthcare 322
practical necessities for start-up 253–254
Pratt, Joanne 45–54, 55, 215
press cuttings service 211
press relations 233–237
press review services 213
Price, Gill 208, 213, 232
pricing work 223–224
Prince's Youth Business Trust (PYBT) 229, 345
printers 109–110, 264
private healthcare 322–323

privacy 173
productivity 8, 11, 57
programming 213–216
Project Cosmic 126–127
Projectplace 118
proofreading 211
property costs 9
Proto-type 310
Prudential Insurance 7, 160, 193
public relations (PR) and advertising 228–231
public sector teleworking 57
publishing services 124, 211–212, 215–218
purchasing computers 260–261
screen (monitor) 263–264

quality control 249–253
Quark Xpress 267
quoting 223–224
Qwest Communications 70

RAC Foundation 11, 95–96
radio interviews 236
RAM or memory 262–263
Rank Xerox 195
Raven, Denise 6
RDC (Rural Development Commission) 76, 84
reasons for implementing teleworking 3–4
recovery CD 294
recruitment and retention 205
Recruitment and Employment Confederation (RECI) 313
Regus 114–115, 131–132
relocation and teleworking 10, 12
responding to enquiries 232–233
Revenue Commissioners (Ireland) 67
RNIB 74, 341–342, 345
RNID 340
Royal Mail 111, 143
RoSPA 106
Rowntree Foundation, Joseph 34, 149
RSA examinations 352, 360
RSA Security Inc 272
RSI (repetitive strain injury) 302
rural issues 49, 71–85, 129–130
Rural Telecentre Association (Australia) 83
RuralNet 74, 128

safety,
  fire 93, 317–318
  health and 66, 175–176, 295–302
sales 327–328
SANS Institute 274
SAVE project 88
satellite broadband connection 281–282
satellite technology 79, 280
scams 216, 331–332
scanners 266
screens (monitors) 263–264